# NINE TO FIVE

*Nine to Five* provides a lively and accessible introduction to the laws and policies regulating sex, sexuality, and gender identity in the American workplace. Contemporary cases and events reveal the breadth and persistence of sexism and gender stereotyping. Through a series of essays organized around sex discrimination, sexual harassment, pregnancy discrimination, and pay equity, the book highlights legal rules and doctrines that privilege men over women and masculinity over femininity. In understanding the law – what it forbids, what it allows, and to what it turns a blind eye – we see why it is far too soon to declare the triumph of working women's equality. Despite significant gains for women, gender continues to define the work experience in both predictable and surprising ways. A witty and engaging guide to the legal terrain, *Nine to Five* also proposes solutions to the many obstacles that remain on the path to equality.

Joanna L. Grossman is the Sidney and Walter Siben Distinguished Professor of Family Law at the Maurice A. Deane School of Law at Hofstra University. An expert in sex discrimination law, she has coauthored numerous books, including *Inside the Castle: Law and the Family in 20th Century America*, winner of the David J. Langum, Sr. Prize in American Legal History, and *Gender Equality: Dimensions of Women's Equal Citizenship*.

# Nine to Five

## HOW GENDER, SEX, AND SEXUALITY CONTINUE TO DEFINE THE AMERICAN WORKPLACE

### JOANNA L. GROSSMAN

CAMBRIDGE
UNIVERSITY PRESS

# CAMBRIDGE
## UNIVERSITY PRESS

32 Avenue of the Americas, New York NY 10013-2473, USA

Cambridge University Press is part of the University of Cambridge.

It furthers the University's mission by disseminating knowledge in the pursuit of education, learning, and research at the highest international levels of excellence.

www.cambridge.org
Information on this title: www.cambridge.org/9781107589827

First published 2016

Printed in the United States of America by Sheridan Books, Inc.

A catalog record for this publication is available from the British Library.

Library of Congress Cataloging in Publication Data
Grossman, Joanna L., author.
Nine to five : how gender, sex, and sexuality continue to define the American workplace / Joanna L. Grossman, Maurice A. Deane School of Law, Hofstra University.
New York NY : Cambridge University Press, 2016.
Includes bibliographical references and index.
LCCN 2015039156    ISBN 9781107133365
LCSH: Sex discrimination in employment – United States.   Sex role in the work environment – United States.   Labor laws and legislation – United States.
Sex discrimination against women – Law and legislation – United States.
LCC KF3467.G76 2016    DDC 344.7301/4133–dc23
LC record available at http://lccn.loc.gov/2015039156

ISBN 978-1-107-13336-5 Hardback
ISBN 978-1-107-58982-7 Paperback

*For my parents, Mary Hengstenberg Grossman and Joel Grossman,*
*who started me on this path by sending me to*
*elementary school with a T-shirt that read:*
*"A woman's place is in the house . . . and in the Senate."*
*– J. L. G.*

# Contents

# Foreword

Joanna Grossman wrote the essays collected in this book during fifteen years as a biweekly columnist for the online legal publications Justia's *Verdict* and FindLaw's *Writ*. Of the 350 columns she produced during those years, she has selected 57 dealing with the law of women in the workplace. Each one combines a lively presentation of the facts of an actual legal case decided by an American court with an exemplary analysis of its implications for the law of sex discrimination in employment.

Because the chapters were written under deadline and in the moment, they have the immediacy of the best journalism. Yet taken together, they could well serve as part of a scholarly history of the legal women's movement in the opening years of the twenty-first century. The reader can follow the law's development from earlier cases that raise questions about the fundamental nature of sex discrimination to later ones that wrestle with conflicting sophisticated theories about the functioning of workplaces and markets.

Perhaps the most interesting part is the one on sexual harassment, a form of discrimination first recognized in modern times, though a feature of women's experience from the earliest days of their regular employment outside the home. Many of the cases combine dramas arising in the increasingly gender-integrated workplace with the repeated challenge of resolving competing claims of "That's sexism!" and "No, it is just life!"

For instance, a stenographer in the writers' room of the wildly successful and mildly raunchy sitcom *Friends* complained that the flood of sexual allusions and crude language that saturated her workaday world made it inhospitable to her as a woman. The employer responded that such loose talk was inevitable among comedy writers and indeed a "creative necessity" if they were to do their work successfully. The plaintiff lost, but the court left open the possibility that such a barrage of sex talk, if aimed at a particular woman, could indeed be a basis of a sex discrimination claim. Hovering over the case, but barely to be found in the lawyers' arguments or the judges' opinion, was the real-life fact that comedy writing was at the time (as it may be still) mostly a man's game, and a lucrative one, too.

Producing these regular topical columns requires special knowledge and skill wedded to authorial commitments to inform more than to impress, to simplify more than to complicate. It also means staying on track and signaling the reader about the next turn. Professor Grossman is a respected legal scholar with plenty of traditional law review articles and books to her credit; in this work she stakes her claim to pioneering a new form of legal scholarship for the digital age.

I read it with special pleasure because Professor Grossman began her legal career as a favorite student and research assistant of mine. Knowing as I do that her decade and a half's worth of column essays include many on other subjects, such as sex discrimination and family law, I am looking forward to more books like this one by her hand.

Barbara Babcock
*Stanford Law School*
*July 2015*

# Acknowledgments

As this project has spanned several years, it has benefited from a long line of wonderful research assistants, who are now blazing trails as part of a new generation of women lawyers: Brianne Richards, Jacqueline Smith, Caitlyn Steinke, Jaclyn Waters, and Katie Weitzman. I also owe a debt of gratitude to Patricia Kasting, a reference librarian at Hofstra Law School, who never shies away from a wild goose chase for a key source. This book would not exist without FindLaw, the website that provided my fellow columnists and me the forum for online commentary for more than a decade, nor without Justia, the terrific website that gave our commentary a new and wonderful home beginning in 2011. Julie Hilden, a longtime friend and brilliant writer, edited hundreds of my columns from 2000 to 2014, and David Kemp has seamlessly taken up where she left off. In turning these essays into a book, I have been grateful for feedback from Deborah Brake, a dear friend and fellow traveler in gender law, and Grant Hayden, my loving husband, co-equal parent to our amazing three sons (Luke, Ben and Milo), and most ardent supporter. Linda McClain, a former colleague and mentor, and Deborah Brake have graciously permitted me to reprint columns they coauthored in this collection. And for piquing my interest in gender issues, I gratefully credit Barbara Babcock, who was kind enough to write a preface for this book. She suggested during my second year of law school that I write my law review note on the history of women's jury service. At the time, I couldn't imagine why this would be of any interest to anyone. But it was, most definitely to me, and the eye-opening research launched me on a decades-long (and continuing) excursion into the world of gender law and policy. Finally, I greatly appreciate the support of my editors at Cambridge, John Berger and Stephen Acerra, and the anonymous reviewers who helped the manuscript come together more fluidly.

# Introduction

INTRODUCTION

In the 1980 movie *Nine to Five*, Dabney Coleman plays the perfect feminist foil. He's *that* boss. The one who propositions his secretary, takes credit for the work of his female subordinates, and never met a sex-based stereotype he didn't pick over the truth staring him in the face. Coleman's character, Mr. Hart, unleashes his sexism most intensely on three women at the office – Lily Tomlin (Violet), a long-suffering widow who has inched up the ladder while raising four kids on her own; Jane Fonda (Judy), a middle-aged divorcée returning to work after years as a housewife; and Dolly Parton (Doralee), the buxom secretary whose southern mix of sweetness and sass forces Mr. Hart to work for his gropes and advances. And he relies on the most unwomanly of women – Roz – to be his eyes and ears, especially in the ladies' room where the others might meet and complain.

Fast-paced dialogue and short cuts of the physical and hierarchical layout of Consolidated, a business of an unspecified nature, make clear in just a few minutes that this is a man's world. No "personal items left in view" on the cubicle desks, Roz chastises, because Mr. Hart says an "office that looks efficient is efficient." When showing Judy around on her first day, Violet tells her that she has "never seen anyone leapfrog so fast to the top," and that she has "the bad back to prove it." He is now Violet's boss, but he was once her trainee.

Showing off his managerial skills to the very green Judy, Mr. Hart describes his "philosophy of business" as "teamwork." But it is not a concept he thinks they'll ever fully understand. "You girls, of course, never got a chance to play football or baseball . . . and I've always felt that's unfortunate, because I think it is the best place to learn what teamwork is about." He promises not to bore them with a "long harangue," but just asks for their faith in his philosophy and leadership. "If we all work together, we can cut the balls off the competition and be sitting pretty." Judy politely says she's happy to be working there, and he compliments her on being "a welcome addition, and a damn pretty one, too." Then he turns to Violet, one of two managers who reports directly to him, and asks her to buy a present for his wife – how about "a nice scarf," he suggests. She starts to say that it is not her place to run personal errands, but he interrupts her gruffly: "Violet, goddamn it. I've been here talking about teamwork, and you're not there for the handoff." She talks about her job description; he says he likes people who are "flexible," especially when they want to be "promoted." From those employees, he expects "cooperation. Savvy?" Flash to the dead deer head hanging on his wall, and a wistful look on Mr. Hart's face as he recalls the "lucky shot" that brought them together.

As Judy and Violet turn to leave, Mr. Hart asks if Doralee is back yet. When told no, he directs Violet, a manager, to get him some coffee. Luckily, she runs into Doralee as she is leaving the office and tells her "your boss wants coffee." "I was just gassing up his car," she says. "If I'm not filling one tank, I'm filling another." Violet fills Judy in on the office gossip as they return to their desks. "Rumor has it that [Doralee] has been banging the boss." This hits a sharp chord for Judy, who was herself left by a husband who ran off with his secretary. Meanwhile, back at Mr. Hart's office, he asks Doralee to "bring your pretty face in here," asks her to turn around so he can check out her backside, and then purposely knocks something on the floor so he can ogle her more invasively when she bends over to pick it up. He feigns regret over an advance he made earlier and apologizes; he "got a little carried away." She tells him not to worry – she's "been chased by swifter men" and "ain't been caught yet." She tells him not to worry about what he describes as his "mistake about the convention in San Francisco"; she'll "just make sure that the next time I'm asked to a convention that there is a convention." But his apology is short-lived, and he returns to his quest for sex. He tries flattery: "You know, you mean so much more to me than just a dumb secretary." He tries kindness and gives her the scarf that Violet has picked out for his wife. He tries a quid pro quo: "I'm a rich man. I've got a checkbook on that desk. You just say the word, and you can write your own figure." (She's not impressed, promising him that she can sign his name better than he can.) He tries pragmatism, telling her that it is perfect that she's married, because he is, too. He begs, he lunges, and then he ultimately ends up on the floor after she successfully fights him off. His wife shows up unexpectedly, and Doralee is spared the next escalation.

The plot thickens as Violet suffers ever more indignant slights at the hands of her sexist boss. She asks him if he has had a chance to read her report outlining a way to improve efficiency by 20 percent; he demurs and says he "looked into it, but it needs work." He changes the subject by asking if she has read his memo and then reminds her to "clamp down hard on any signs of unionization." But Mr. Hart secretly had passed Violet's proposal off to the higher-ups as his own. Violet learns this when the head of the company walks by and tells Mr. Hart that they will be implementing *his* proposal for color-coded accounts forthwith. The boss praises Mr. Hart as a "fine piece of manpower," while Violet turns to her female coworkers and bemoans his complete lack of shame. She explains that she didn't call him on his deceit because he will decide the fate of her long-awaited promotion. She soon finds out, though, that she has been passed over for the promotion; he has given it to Bob Enright instead, who is lower down the ladder than Violet. However, Mr. Hart explains to the single mother of four, Bob has "a family to support." He also concedes that the "company needs a man . . . Clients would rather deal with men when it comes to figures." An exasperated Violet complains that she has lost "a promotion because of some idiot prejudice," but Mr. Hart interrupts and warns her to "spare me the women's lib crap." She warns him never to call her "girl" again. "I'm no girl. I'm a woman. Do you hear? I'm not your wife or your mother or even your mistress."

Hearing talk of a mistress, and understanding the accusing looks being shot in her direction, Doralee finally figures out why her coworkers have ostracized her. Or, in her southern slang, have treated her "like some dime-store floozy." She confronts Mr. Hart and says she's had it. She has put up with the "pinching and staring and chasing." Despite having a gun in her purse, she's "been forgiving and forgetting." But no more, she promises: "If you ever say another word about me or make another indecent proposal, I'm gonna get that gun and change you from a rooster to a hen with one shot!" Mr. Hart is unfazed, moving quickly to a conversation with Roz, who had overheard a woman violating the company's ban on pay secrecy. Mr. Hart quickly retorts with "get rid of her," and then escalates to "fire the bitch" when Roz doesn't react quickly enough to his order.

At the end of this scene, the three leading women have had it. They storm out, get drunk, light up a joint, and fall quickly into a sisterhood, bound by their hatred of Mr. Hart and their consignment to a "pink-collar ghetto" with economic circumstances that make them need the jobs they have come to loathe. They share their fantasies about how each would torture and murder Mr. Hart. In Judy's fantasy, she tells Mr. Hart she can't save him from a lynch mob because he's a "sexist, egotistical, lying, hypocritical bigot." Doralee fantasizes that she would sexually harass him first – to give him a taste of his own medicine – before turning the gun on him. Violet considers the poetic irony of putting poison in the coffee she is so tired of bringing him.

The next morning, the bond of the new sisterhood is palpable in the office. The sharing of fantasies was cathartic, and the women steel themselves for more rounds with Mr. Hart. The movie plot then shifts quickly, as fantasy becomes reality. Violet goes to the store at her lunch hour to pick up "Skinny and Sweet" for the office coffee station, and a few things for home, including rat poison. But the artificial sweetener and the rat poison are both contained in big yellow boxes, and when Mr. Hart sends Violet to get him coffee, she accidentally sweetens his java with poison. He ends up in the hospital, and a wild plot ride ensues.

At a key point, Mr. Hart tells the women he knows they poisoned him and plans to call the police. They figure out that he might be embezzling, but need time to get paperwork from headquarters to prove it. They hold him prisoner in his own house for weeks (while his wife is on an extended cruise) and do his job so he won't be missed at work. Doralee's penchant for signing Mr. Hart's name comes in handy as they remake the office in a kinder, gentler form. Across the screen flash company memos first allowing personal items and plants back on the desks, then flextime, then job sharing, then on-site child care, then a substance abuse program, and then the pièce de résistance – equal pay for equal work. When Mr. Hart finally escapes his in-home prison and comes back to work, he is greeted by the company president, who compliments him on the new policies and the "very splendid environment" they have helped create. He gives a nod to Violet as his "right arm" but takes full credit for the happier and more productive workplace. (The boss objects to only one component of the new workplace; "the equal pay thing, though, that's got to go.") Violet quietly accepts the quid pro quo – Mr. Hart gets credit, again, for her transformative ideas, but at least he now has an incentive to keep quiet about the false imprisonment and assorted other crimes. But karma haunts Mr. Hart. The president is so impressed with Mr. Hart's decisive yet creative management style that he sends him to Brazil on a two- to three-year assignment to oversee a new office. When Mr. Hart hesitates to embrace the move, he is reminded of the importance of "teamwork" and told to start packing his bags.

To be sure, aspects of this movie can seem dated to a twenty-first-century viewer. The mannish blouses and faux ties worn by the women trying hardest to assimilate into a man's world. The hairstyles (ouch). The polyester. But what of the gender dynamics in the workplace? The openness with which Mr. Hart expresses his "traditional" views about women in the workplace have a passé ring to them. But the issues that drive Violet, Judy, and Doralee into a murderous rage (or at least a fantasy of such a rage) still very much define the American workplace. Unequal pay. Sexual harassment. Sexual favoritism. Inflexible work schedules. Sex stereotyping. Unfair promotion practices. These problems are, regrettably, not a thing of the past. To the contrary, working women in the United States are likely to face most of these issues, along with some others, at some point during their careers. This is so despite the development over the past fifty years of antidiscrimination laws that purport to make all these things illegal. The Equal Pay Act of 1963 requires that employers pay men and women equally for equal work. Title VII of the Civil Rights Act of 1964 prohibits employers from making employment decisions based on sex, from engaging in sex stereotyping, and from adopting neutral rules that disproportionately disadvantage women. The Pregnancy Discrimination Act of 1978 prohibits employers from discriminating against women on the basis of "pregnancy, childbirth, or related medical conditions." The Family and Medical Leave Act (FMLA) of 1993 requires employers of a certain size to give employees unpaid leave when necessary to care for newborn or newly adopted children, or to tend to their own serious health conditions. In addition, the Equal Protection Clause of the U.S. Constitution has been interpreted to forbid sex-based classifications by public employers in most circumstances. And layered on top of these federal laws are a set of state antidiscrimination laws that are often even more protective of women's rights than federal law is, requiring employers to accommodate pregnancy-related disability or funding paid parental leave through state disability insurance or applying general antidiscrimination norms to even smaller employers.

To hear the story told by some, the fight for gender equality in the workplace has been won. A 2009 headline in the *Economist* announced, "We did it!" The story reported that women were poised, for the first time, to compose more than 50 percent of the American workforce.[1] The article, accompanied by the classic image of Rosie the Riveter, the woman who symbolized women's participation in the industrial labor force during World War II, cited "women's economic empowerment" as "the biggest social change of our times." Women, it claimed, have gone from a world of being "routinely subjected to casual sexism" and "expected to abandon their careers when they married and had children" to "running some of the organizations that once treated them as second-class citizens." And this revolution, the article claimed, was "achieved with only a modicum of friction." Men, for their part, have "by and large, welcomed women's invasion of the workplace." The article noted that women's progress has come with a few minor "stings" – that women lead only 2 percent of the largest companies and are paid "significantly less than men on average." They also have significant difficulties "juggling work and child-rearing" and despite early career successes in their twenties often "drop out in dramatic numbers in their 30s and then find it almost impossible to regain their earlier momentum."

This article is one of many that judges workplace equality by an overly simplistic measure. It is true that women's workforce participation has improved relative to men's and also true that women fared much better in the recession that began in 2008 than men did. But those numbers tell us very little about continuing forms of workplace inequality or the ways in which women still do not have the benefit of a level playing field. One might watch the movie *Nine to Five* and note that many of the employees, including those at the managerial level, were women. But that would of course be a meaningless observation about a film depicting not their numerosity, but the quality (and inequality) of their working conditions.

Other headlines tell a different story – or at least complicate the story of women's workplace equality. "Twenty-seven countries that trump the U.S. when it comes to gender equality: Report shows U.S. moving backwards in closing gender gap."[2] This disturbing headline reports on the 2015 Global Gender Gap report, which ranks countries by gender equality in economy, politics, health, and education. Ranking only twenty-eighth worldwide, the U.S. has never made it into the top 15, and its rank is dropping rather than rising, due in large part to significant gaps in labor force participation and wage equality.[3]

"Among 38 nations, U.S. is the outlier when it comes to paid parental leave," is the lead-in to a story about a 2013 Pew Research Center report concluding that the U.S. ranks dead last in government-supported time off for new parents.[4] This is particularly damaging for women, as another headline reminds us that "Men do more at home, but not as much as they think."[5] "The Gender Pay Gap Widens as Men's Earnings Grow Twice as Fast as Women's," reports a *Wall Street Journal* article, one of many showcasing the many facets of the gender wage gap, all bad for women.[6] "Twenty-one harrowing stories of harassment on the job," is just the most recent of headlines to remind us of the continuing prevalence of workplace harassment.[7] And there are countless headlines to remind us of the entrenched problem occupational segregation, which is at the root of so many aspects of gender inequality. But the clear winner is this one: "Mustaches Outnumber Women Among Medical-School Leaders."[8]

These headlines are not the end of the story, but rather the beginning, a reminder that gender inequality might not be everywhere but can be anywhere. And while a recent poll found that most Americans say they believe in women's equality, it also concluded that they have little understanding of its prevalence or effects and, as the conventional wisdom would tell us, have a negative view of "feminism" as a both a word and a concept. But 79 percent agreed there is "still more work to be done" to achieve "equality for women in work, life, and politics."[9] It is in the spirit of this last sentence that I have undertaken this project.

Federal antidiscrimination laws were central to opening the doors of the American workplace to women and to eradicating the most common and overt forms of sex discrimination that consigned women to traditional female (and lower-paying) jobs or excluded them from work altogether. But real questions remain about what women find once they cross those thresholds and join the ranks of working men. Rather than ask how many women *have* jobs, we should ask how many women are paid less than their male counterparts for doing the same work; how many women work in jobs that are paid less than comparable jobs predominated by men; how many women have faced difficulties when they try to work in traditionally male-dominated fields; how many women are sexually harassed or assaulted by coworkers or bosses; how many women are denied positions or promotions they deserve because of bias against female workers or false assumptions about their economic needs; how many pregnant women are forced out of work despite their ability to do the job, or denied minor accommodations necessitated by short-term disability that would enable them to keep their jobs – and paychecks – when they need them most; how many mothers are stifled by inflexible work schedules that force them to choose between work and motherhood, or work and caring for aging parents; how many mothers are assumed to prioritize child rearing over work or presumed to be less competent than non-mothers; how many workers are treated poorly because of their sexual orientation or gender identity; or how many women are sabotaged or undermined simply because someone resents their presence in the workforce.

In many cases, numbers like these are available, at least in broad brush. The gender wage gap remains stark and stagnant. Women experience sexual harassment at quite alarming rates, especially in certain types of jobs (the military, to take just one example). The glass ceiling is real in virtually every field, leading to a "pyramid" formation for women in many of them. (Women hold 4.6 percent of CEO positions in Fortune 500 companies.[10]) Stereotypes persist. Gay, lesbian, and transgender individuals experience especially high rates of discrimination and harassment, and they benefit from the least robust protections against it. Pregnant women are routinely forced out of jobs because of short-term incapacity, or fired because the leave available to them is not long enough to cover recovery from childbirth.

One indicator of women's lives at work – which are no longer cabined between the hours of nine and five – and the real state of the gender revolution in the American workforce comes from the stories they tell (and prove) to judges and juries when they sue to enforce their rights against workplace discrimination. And in understanding the law – what it forbids, what it allows, and things to which it turns a blind eye – we see why it is far too soon to pronounce the end of the battle of sexes. Or to pretend that the workplace is gender blind so long as we can count an equal number of male and female heads.

This book is a collection of essays about the laws and policies that regulate sex, sexuality, and gender identity at work. For more than fifteen years, I have written an online column that focuses on, among other issues, sex equality in the workplace. These columns were published from 2000 to 2010 by FindLaw's *Writ* and, since 2011, by Justia's *Verdict*, both Internet sources for legal commentary on contemporary issues.[11] Over this period of time, I have written about federal and state law, major and minor cases, proposed and existing legislation, and new data and reports that together represent contemporary controversies over gender in the workplace. For some issues, the columns show the stubbornness of old problems, or the reticence of policy makers to be more aggressive in their efforts to eradicate them. For others, the columns trace the development of new laws, or reformed laws, and the impact of the changes. For still others, we see initial grappling with new problems and frustration with the complexity of finding solutions. The columns have been largely preserved in their original form to show the law's development over time, but they are tied together through introductions to each of the book's four parts and made current with chapter-by-chapter epilogues.

Together, these essays explore the gendered workplace in all its modern glory. Overt sexism may be old-fashioned, but covert sexism is not. Nor is a workplace that is designed in every respect for men – and stubbornly resistant to change. Nor the maternal wall that impedes the ability of women to form labor force attachments that are as strong and long lasting – and as lucrative – as men's. The Dabney Coleman of today might be embarrassed to chase a secretary around a desk, but he might fire her so his wife doesn't get jealous. The range of issues tackled in these essays – all drawn from real and contemporary cases and events – shows the breadth of sexism and stereotyping in the American workplace today and the complex forms it sometimes takes. These more nuanced and complex iterations are no less damaging, and no easier to eliminate, than the 1970s style of yore. The resilience of sexism may even explain the resurgence of interest in *Nine to Five* itself, which was reinvigorated as a Broadway musical in 2009.

The book is divided into four parts. Part I takes up the question, "What is sex discrimination?" This is not a simple question. Is it discrimination when a male boss fires his female employee because she is "too hot" and he fears he might harass her? What about when a transit police department requires its officers to run at a speed that is more commensurate with men's average ability than women's? What if a school refuses to hire a man to coach female athletes? Or if a school punishes a male coach who was not himself discriminated against but spoke up for his female athletes who received far inferior resources than the school's male athletes? What if an employer requires women to wear makeup and tease their hair, but requires men holding the same jobs only to be clean and neat? Or if an employer fires an employee who wears a skirt because he was born a man but lives life as a woman? Is it discrimination to retaliate against someone who complains of discrimination? These are just some of the cases discussed in this first set of essays. And each bears on this basic question of what we mean when we say it is illegal to discriminate on the basis of sex.

Part II considers the law of sex and sexuality in the workplace. Its primary focus is sexual harassment, a problem with a long pedigree that has proved fungal in its resistance to remediation. Essays in this part consider a wide variety of cases that bear on the question of what constitutes unlawful harassment. Is it harassment for a correctional officer to show favoritism toward the subordinates with whom he is having sex? Can a teenage employee consent to sexual conduct at work when the age of consent generally is eighteen? Does a bisexual harasser "discriminate" when he makes sexual advances toward both male and female subordinates? How do we know when same-sex harassment conduct is "because of sex"? Is it sex discrimination when coworkers pepper an effeminate gay waiter with girlie insults? What about a gay dentist who makes sexual advances toward his straight male employee? Does a supervisor sexually harass when he says nothing sexual but bullies only women at work? Is extremely graphic sex talk off-limits for a comedy-writing team of a famous sitcom? This part also takes up the equally important issues surrounding employer liability for sexual harassment. Harassment is like the proverbial tree in the forest – if it happens, but no one is legally responsible, then there is no remedy. Several essays thus focus on the increasingly complicated law of vicarious liability for employers. Should a victim lose her redress if she waits too long to complain? Is it the employer's fault if a supervisor commits a sudden, severe act of harassment without warning? When a supervisor threatens to fire a subordinate if she does not submit to sexual conduct, can she sue if she submits and keeps her job? Do the incentives created by antidiscrimination law reduce the amount or severity of harassment in the workplace? What happens to employers that ignore obvious problems of harassment?

Part III tackles the thorny and very much unresolved issues related to pregnancy and motherhood in the workplace. Eighty-five percent of working women will become pregnant at some point during their careers. Although Congress passed the Pregnancy Discrimination Act of 1978 to end the forced exclusion of pregnant women from many jobs and employment benefits, as well as the rampant stereotyping about their abilities, women continue to struggle with conflicts between pregnancy and work and doctrine that increasingly is not meeting their needs. Likewise, women at other stages of the reproductive process – struggling with infertility, breast-feeding a child, recovering from childbirth – confront workplace structures that are based on male bodies and lifestyles and are often unforgiving. The essays in this part first consider the nature of the protection against pregnancy discrimination. Can employers refuse to grant light-duty assignments to pregnant employees while granting them to some other employees? Can a company pay lower retirement benefits to once-pregnant retirees because they took unprotected leave before the Pregnancy Discrimination Act (PDA) was passed? Why are pregnancy discrimination complaints on the rise thirty-five years after the PDA was passed? What are the effects of refusing to accommodate pregnancy-related disability on women's ability to participate in society as equal citizens? Should Congress amend the PDA to provide a right of reasonable accommodation for pregnancy-related disability? The essays then turn to the question of what it means to discriminate on the basis of pregnancy. Can an employer offer comprehensive health insurance to its employees but exclude coverage for contraception used only by women? Can it refuse to cover the cost of fertility treatments? Can it fire a woman because of absenteeism related to fertility treatments? Is firing a woman for breast-feeding a type of pregnancy discrimination? Finally, the essays in this part consider the FMLA, with a focus on its shortcomings, and the related problem of caregiver discrimination.

Part IV focuses on the female breadwinner and the persistence of the glass ceiling. Recent news reports have focused on the rising number of female breadwinners – in 40 percent of households today, a woman is the primary breadwinner. But less is said about how women are still paid less than their male counterparts, or about how the median income in a household with a female primary earner is less than one with a male one. Or about how many women, especially single mothers, live in poverty despite engaging in paid labor. The central focus of this part is the persistent problem of pay inequity and the failure of current law to provide sufficient remedies. The essays trace the story of Lilly Ledbetter, the sole female manager at a tire and rubber plant in Alabama, who proved to a jury that she was the victim of egregious pay discrimination. Her legal story had many chapters – through every level of federal court culminating in a loss at the U.S. Supreme Court and a new federal law in her name to overturn the Court's ruling, followed by a new life as a civil rights folk hero who stood up for her rights and brought national attention to the problem of pay inequity. This part concludes with an eclectic selection of essays that consider, with a broader brush, the continuing challenges for gender equality in the workplace and beyond.

# What Is Sex Discrimination?

*"No, Mr. Kurlander, I don't have, nor have I ever had, a recipe for cranberry muffins."*

ART 1 © Robert Weber / The *New Yorker* Collection / The Cartoon Bank. Used by permission.

*Can you believe that? A female linesman. Women don't know the offside rule.*

(Andy Gray, Sky Sports Presenter)

*[Elena Kagan] put on rouge and lipstick for the formal White House announcement of her nomination, but mostly she embraced dowdy as a mark of brainpower.*

(Robin Givhan, *Washington Post* staff writer)

At the heart of this collection is a basic question: What is sex discrimination? The answer may seem obvious, but, in truth, it is complicated. Are *all* classifications on the basis of gender discriminatory, or are there times or places when sex differentiation, or even sex segregation, are permissible or desirable? Should seemingly benign classifications be prohibited because they might perpetuate damaging stereotypes and gender subordination? If so, when? Is there anything wrong with Mr. Kurlander's assumption that the one woman in the boardroom would have a recipe for cranberry muffins at the ready?

Consider a simple example: "ladies' night." A New Jersey bar had a typical promotion – it admitted women one night each week without a cover charge and sold them drinks at discounted prices. A male customer filed a complaint, alleging that the practice violated the New Jersey Law Against Discrimination (LAD) because it discriminated on the basis of sex.[1] The director for civil rights issued a ruling, in *Gillespie v. Coastline Restaurant*,[2] agreeing with the plaintiff and ordering Coastline to charge men and women the same prices. The public reaction to the decision was curiously strong. The state's then-governor, James McGreevey, later driven from office by a sexual harassment scandal,[3] issued a written statement denouncing it as "bureaucratic nonsense" and an "overreaction that reflects a complete lack of common sense and good judgment."[4] One television commentator began coverage of the story by asking, "Is nothing sacred?"[5] The complainant's own mother, age 82, told him "there were bigger fish to fry than this."[6]

Is this a form of sex discrimination the law should address? One question raised here is whether sex discrimination laws have built-in "de minimis" exceptions – for practices that, while they differentiate based on gender, seem to do so in relatively innocuous ways. (The expression "de minimis" comes from the saying "De minimis non curat lex" – Latin for "The law does not bother with trifles.") But the applicable statute – like most antidiscrimination statutes – makes no mention of such an exception. The LAD broadly bans discrimination by places of public accommodation on the basis of sex.[7] And prior cases established that this extends not only to equal access or service but also to the furnishing of "accommodations, advantages, facilities or privileges."[8]

Might this type of seemingly benign discrimination mask harmful stereotypes? Coastline argued that its policy did not reflect any animus against men and was justified by its legitimate, nondiscriminatory goal of increasing patronage and revenue. The conventional "theory" of a ladies' night discount is that more women will come because of the reduced prices, and more men will come because more women will be there. (Although oddly enough, in this case, the owner admitted that 70 percent of the patrons on an average ladies' night were still male, and that men were the main users of the discount, giving women money to buy their drinks.)

It may well be that Coastline bore no ill will toward men, nor embraced negative stereotypes about them – and that, indeed, it did want to attract them, indirectly, with "ladies' night." But might it nonetheless have harmed men with price gouging – and harmed women by setting the stage for them to drink too much and potentially be victimized by the men for whom they had been used as bait? And might harmful stereotypes be embedded in something as simple as a ladies' night discount? Maybe a drink discount perpetuates views about women's purported economic dependence – that they could only afford to go out drinking if someone gives them a discount. Or maybe the discount perpetuates male sexual dominance – by luring men to a bar because of an expectation that they will find a bar full of women who might be drinking more than usual because of the cheaper prices. Maybe, as the complainant also argued, the promotion degrades men as "irresistibly driven" to places where women gather. Or maybe, because it is too hard to know when harmful stereotypes are being perpetuated, it is just easier to prohibit sex-based classifications altogether. The Washington Supreme Court, in a glaring embrace of gender stereotypes, upheld the Seattle Supersonics ladies' night on grounds that lower ticket prices were reasonable given that women "do not manifest the same interest in basketball as men do," and thus might miss out on the attractions they might enjoy like halftime fashion shows and gifts and souvenirs.[9]

Whether or not the New Jersey bar's owners intended, or even were cognizant, of any potential adverse effects is, under standard antidiscrimination doctrine, irrelevant. A formal policy like the rule behind "ladies' night" need not be born of animosity against the disadvantaged group to be illegal.[10] The New Jersey DCR was not persuaded by any of Coastline's arguments.[11] Places of public accommodation, under New Jersey law, cannot vary the price for a good or service based on nothing more than a patron's gender. A sign that had advertised this promotion every Wednesday for twenty-six years came down.[12]

The legality of sex-specific discounts is hardly the most pressing issue of our times, yet it provides a window into important and often unique features of sex discrimination law. After all, no court would countenance a bar's offering of "whites' night" as a legitimate means to entice white customers, nor would any court think that the offering of "blacks' night" on another day of the week would cure its discriminatory impact. Yet courts have entertained both these possibilities for sex-specific discounts.[13] What, if anything, is different about sex discrimination?

Do the questions or answers change when we shift the setting from bars to the workplace? Certainly the questions become both more numerous and more complex – and the answers more important. For rather than resolving the price of a drink, or the terms on which single people in bars negotiate the social landscape,

we are determining people's livelihood and their access to economic security. The
chapters in this part explore how legislatures and courts ferret out the types of gender
discrimination that impede equal access to the workplace – and where they fall short.
The answers may be varied, but the question is clear: What is sex discrimination?

Part I of the book explores this question primarily in the context of Title VII of
the Civil Rights Act of 1964, the centerpiece of federal antidiscrimination law, and
its state analogs. At the core of Title VII is a prohibition on employment actions
based on an individual's "race, color, religion, sex, or national origin."[14] And, as
explained in detail in Part III, the ban on sex discrimination was expanded in
1978 to include discrimination on the basis of "pregnancy, childbirth, and related
medical conditions."[15] Reciting the statutory language is easy, but figuring out which
decisions and actions constitute an unlawful employment practice and how one
proves that a decision was based on a protected characteristic in a particular case is
hard. More so in the context of sex discrimination because, as already discussed, not
all instances of sex-based classification or even segregation are objectionable. The
focus of the chapters in this first part is on drawing that line, a process that entails
probing beneath the status quo and questioning our common intuitions.

The first three chapters consider cases where there is little or no dispute about
what happened, but the parties disagree about whether a decision in which gender
clearly played a role constitutes a form of illegal discrimination. Chapters 1 and 2
take up a thorny, but surprisingly common, issue: whether it is unlawful for a man to
fire a female subordinate because his wife is jealous. Title VII prohibits employment
decisions made "because of" or "on the basis of" sex. But for the sex of the subordinate
employees in these cases, the wives would not have been jealous. And if the wives
had not been jealous, the female employees would not have been fired. Does that
mean they were fired, for Title VII purposes, because of sex? Chapter 3 continues
exploring the definition of sex discrimination through a case in which a prominent
university admitted it did not hire a male coach for its women's crew team because
it preferred a woman for that position. Are there legitimate reasons to prefer a coach
of the same sex as the athletes, and should a man be able to sue even though the
bulk of the discrimination in coaching falls on women?

Chapter 4 turns to the problem of unadmitted discrimination – when an employer
denies, sex was the reason for the adverse employment action. A case in which a
woman was seemingly fired both because she had a history of disciplinary problems
and because the employer harbored some gender bias provides the perfect occasion to introduce Title VII's proof structures, which guide factfinders (sometimes
confusingly) in the determination of whether a prohibited characteristic played an
impermissible role in the employer's decision.

Chapters 5 and 6 explore the role of sex stereotyping in discrimination law. The
Supreme Court has embraced the idea that the application of sex stereotypes by
an employer is a form of unlawful discrimination under Title VII.[16] But, as these
chapters show, courts have been at times hesitant to preclude all stereotyping,

particularly as applied to sex-specific dress and grooming codes. They have been more willing, as recent cases illustrate, to recognize the sex stereotyping inherent in transgender discrimination.

Chapter 7 takes up yet another type of discrimination claim, in which a plaintiff argues that an admittedly neutral employment practice violates Title VII because it has a disparate impact on a protected group such as women. This cause of action is explored here in a case brought by a group of women who had sought unsuccessfully to become transit officers in Philadelphia but were thwarted by a requirement that they run 1.5 miles in less than twelve minutes.

Chapter 8 considers the important question of *who* is protected by Title VII. The statute protects employees from discrimination by employers, but in the modern workplace, the line between these two groups is not always clearly demarcated. Are law firm partners "employers"? Or might some, because of a lack of power and control over firm management and profits, be deemed employees? This chapter discusses a case that tries to draw the line and considers the implications for workplace equality of taking too formalistic an approach.

Part I concludes with Chapters 9, 10, and 11, which explore the law's protection against retaliation. Courts have begun to recognize that protecting against retaliation is as important as protecting against discrimination in the first instance, given how common it is for discrimination complainants to be penalized for challenging their employers and what a deterrent the anticipation of those penalties can be. These chapters, respectively, consider whether a coach who complains about discrimination against his female athletes should be protected from retaliation; whether a woman's reassignment to a less desirable position and suspension without pay were sufficiently adverse to be actionable; and, finally, whether a witness who cooperates in an internal harassment investigation is protected from retaliation, or whether such protection is limited to the complainant.

# 1

# Sexual Jealousy

If a man fires his pregnant secretary to appease his jealous wife, can the secretary sue him for discrimination? In the case of *Mittl v. New York State Division of Human Rights*, an appellate court in New York said no.[1] But isn't this a classic case of sex discrimination?

The plaintiff in the New York case worked as a secretary for a physician at Columbia Presbyterian Hospital. About a year after starting work, she announced that she was pregnant. Her boss initially greeted her announcement "in good spirit" and gave her advice about seeking disability benefits during maternity leave.[2] But, as the date grew closer, the tone of his reaction changed. The reason for the change, it turned out, was that his wife was angry because she believed that her husband might have fathered the child.

There was no apparent evidence that the wife's belief was correct; indeed, the appellate court described it as "irrational."[3] Nor was there even any evidence that the doctor-secretary relationship was anything other than professional. Nevertheless, the doctor's wife clung to her belief. She made hostile phone calls to the plaintiff and, at some point, even threatened to fire her, although she had no authority to carry out such a threat. The doctor at first found his wife's reaction humorous, but his efforts to calm her down were ultimately unsuccessful. He thus fired his secretary to placate his wife.

## THE LAWSUIT AND THE DECISIONS OF THE AGENCY AND THE APPEALS COURT

The secretary then filed a lawsuit alleging that she had been subjected to pregnancy discrimination, in violation of New York's antidiscrimination law.[4] (That law is roughly coextensive with the federal ban on sex and pregnancy discrimination, embodied in Title VII of the Civil Rights Act of 1964, as amended by the Pregnancy Discrimination Act of 1978.[5])

Her boss was found liable by the agency charged with implementing this law and ordered to pay nearly $200,000 in damages.[6] However, with little or no analysis, the appellate court reversed the agency's decision. The only facts the court seemed to find relevant were that the doctor had not initially reacted negatively to the secretary's announcement, nor had he given her any initial indication that her condition would jeopardize her employment. Without evidence of animosity toward the pregnancy by itself, the court refused to call the doctor's actions pregnancy discrimination. Rather, the firing was, according to the court, "at worst, disloyalty to a valued secretary."[7]

The court described the husband's decision between firing the secretary and potentially losing his wife as a "Hobson's choice."[8] According to the court's logic, then, the husband had essentially been compelled to fire his secretary and should not be faulted for doing so. Even on its own terms, the court's logic was faulty. It is also contrary to law. A firing may still constitute pregnancy discrimination even if the pregnancy was not the sole factor in the firing.

## FIRINGS DUE TO "RATIONAL JEALOUSY"

The New York court that ruled against the secretary also noted that, at least in New York, "[h]usbands presented with just this Hobson's choice have found support in the courts in the face of charges of sex discrimination law."[9] These cases were different, however, for most of them involved an employer who was indeed romantically involved with an employee, whom he then fired to avoid further marital conflict.[10] In *Mittl*, in contrast, the doctor apparently was never involved with the secretary despite his wife's suspicions.

This is a distinction with a difference. It is more convincing to suggest that husbands who truly do have affairs, as compared with those whose wives simply imagine or fear affairs, are put to a true Hobson's choice: fire the employee or lose your wife. Of course, that still leaves the question of why the employee should suffer because of a predicament that the husband, who, after all, is the one who has cheated, largely created for himself.

There is also another problem with citing the "rational jealousy" cases, in which an affair did occur, to support the holding in *Mittl*. To the extent that these cases suggest that a firing due to "rational jealousy" does not constitute sex discrimination, they are themselves poorly reasoned and contrary to controlling discrimination law principles.

Consider, for example, the case of *Kahn v. Objective Solutions, Int'l*, decided in 2000 by a federal district judge in the Southern District of New York. There, the plaintiff alleged that a company president had an affair with her while she was on his staff, broke off the relationship because "his family disapproved," and then fired her.[11] She sued for sex discrimination, but the court rejected her claim on the ground that the termination was based on a sexual relationship but not on sex itself.

This distinction cannot hold water. Granted, a scenario like the one in *Kahn* does not squarely present a problem of sexual harassment. As long as the intimate relationship was truly welcome and voluntary (i.e., not submitted to because of an implicit or explicit threat of consequences), the relationship itself is not harassment. And as long as the termination was *not* an act of retaliation based on the employee's refusal to continue to submit to sexual conduct, the termination is not harassment either.

But expressly applying different rules to men and women is an obvious example of sex discrimination. And contrary to the suggestion of the *Mittl* court, animosity toward one sex or toward pregnancy is not legally required. It is not the *motivation* for the action but the mere *fact* of disparate treatment that makes these actions illegal. Thus, a "well-meaning" employer who seeks to "protect" women from physically hard work by refusing to hire them or limiting their assignments is just as liable as an employer who refuses to hire women simply because he hates them or believes them incompetent. Similarly, an employer who refuses to hire men because he thinks they are too good for "women's work" is just as liable to discrimination suits by the men as an employer who refuses to hire men because she bears animosity toward them.

Put simply, if a woman is fired when a man in her situation would not have been, that is illegal sex discrimination. Similarly, if a pregnant woman is fired, and a nonpregnant person in an analogous situation would not have been, then that is pregnancy discrimination.

## IN *MITTL*, WOULD A MAN, OR A NONPREGNANT WOMAN, ALSO HAVE BEEN FIRED?

Thus, the real question in the "rational jealousy" cases is whether husband-employers who fire their female ex-paramours would have taken a similar action against their male employees. The answer is almost certainly no, save for the rare bisexual employer who has relationships with both men and women and then fires both when he tires of them.[12]

The reason female employees are vulnerable to the jealous insistence of their bosses' wives is precisely, as Title VII prohibits, "because of . . . sex."[13] It is their sex that made them a desirable paramour for the boss in the first instance; their sex that created the predicate for jealousy; and their sex that got them fired.

Similarly, the real question in "irrational jealousy" cases such as *Mittl* is whether husband-employers who fire female employees whom their wives imagine to be sexual competitors would have taken a similar action against their male employees. Again, the answer is almost certainly no.

To see why, imagine that instead of telling his wife his secretary was pregnant, the doctor in *Mittl* instead had told her one of his male employees had contracted a sexually transmitted disease, one from which the doctor himself also, hypothetically, happened to suffer. Solely because the employee was male, the wife's jealousy and suspicions would not have been triggered, and the firing would not have occurred.

## COURTS HAVE EFFECTIVELY, AND WRONGLY, GIVEN JEALOUS WIVES HIRE/FIRE AUTHORITY

The consequence of allowing an employer's wife to dictate who gets hired and fired is that women are deprived of equal opportunity to work. This seems almost too obvious to mention. Wifely jealousy, if controlling, may keep women from being hired in the first place. It may also, as the plaintiff in *Mittl* learned, get them fired – and even get them fired at the worst possible moment, when they need health and pregnancy benefits the most.

More subtly, effectively giving wives power to choose and control their husband's female coworkers can also prevent the female coworkers from advancing and enjoying equal work opportunities. For example, the "wife's veto" may deprive female workers of assignments that require travel or close working conditions with male bosses, or even with more senior male coworkers who also have jealous wives. Wives who refuse to have their husbands work with women, and husbands who decline to work with women "so as not to upset my wife," are carrying out sex discrimination. Rather than nodding sympathetically at their domestic woes, we should fault them for putting their relationship troubles above workplace equality and creating limitations on female employees' opportunities that do not apply to men.

No one would think a husband should be able to maintain an all-white workforce because his wife is a bigot. Nor would anyone nod sympathetically if an employer explained that it would just be "easier" for him at home if he declined to hire African Americans. Nor would a husband be taken seriously if he claimed in court that he was put to an impossible Hobson's choice because his racist wife would leave him if he did not fire his black secretary, so the secretary simply had to be fired. Yet courts have no trouble validating parallel situations when sex or pregnancy rather than race is the deciding factor.

In the end, there is no federal law saying husbands need to make their wives happy, while there is one saying they can't unfairly discriminate against their female employees. Perhaps the court in *Mittl*, interpreting New York's analogous law, should have preferred disloyalty to an irrational wife than disloyalty to a secretary at the very point when she needed loyalty – and benefits – most.

A version of this chapter appeared on April 23, 2002, at writ.findlaw.com.

*Update: The* Mittl *case was later reversed by New York's highest court.*[14] *The lower court had failed to apply the proper standard of review to the agency determination and disregarded substantial evidence that the discharge was in fact discriminatory. The defendant's explanation that his wife – who did not work for him – had fired the plaintiff was "incredible and unsubstantiated." Moreover, the court explained, the lower court should not have relied on the line of cases in which the parties had engaged in a consensual sexual relationship because there was no such relationship here.*

**2**

# Too Hot to Be a Dental Hygienist?

In 2009, the Iowa Supreme Court made national news for its surprising and unanimous decision in *Varnum v. Brien*, in which it held that the state's ban on same-sex marriage violated the state constitution's guarantee of equal protection.[1] Iowa was not the first state to legalize same-sex marriage – Massachusetts came first in 2004,[2] followed by a handful of others in 2008 – but it was the first to do so outside the liberal confines of the Northeast.

Iowa's high court made headlines again in 2010, when three of the justices who joined the Varnum opinion were recalled from the bench because of the decision.[3] The three included the court's only woman, and all three vacancies were filled by men.

Now the court is back in the news, this time for an illogical decision that misinterprets governing civil rights statutes and reaches a preposterous result.[4] In this ruling, *Nelson v. Knight*, the court held that a male dentist did not violate a law banning sex discrimination when he fired his very competent female dental assistant because he found her to be an "irresistible attraction" whose very presence might incite him to commit sexual harassment and, perhaps ultimately, cost him his marriage.[5]

This ruling hearkens back to mistakes of the 1970s, when courts, including the U.S. Supreme Court, struggled to figure out just exactly what "sex discrimination" is. But forty years of antidiscrimination law later, we know it when we see it. And this is definitely it. The Iowa court has done women's workplace equality a colossal injustice by allowing men's inability to control themselves to define women's employment rights.

## A DAY IN THE LIFE OF DR. KNIGHT'S DENTAL OFFICE

In 1999, dentist James Knight hired Melissa Nelson to be a dental assistant in his office. She was twenty years old and had just received a two-year college degree. She worked in that position for more than ten years and was, according to Dr. Knight, a "good assistant." She, in turn, said he was a person of "high integrity" and that he generally treated her in a respectful manner. Both Knight and Nelson were married with children.

The tenor in the office seemed to change in the last year and a half of Nelson's employment. (The opinion does not reveal Knight's age, but a midlife crisis jumps out as one possible explanation.) Knight began to comment to Nelson that her clothing was "distracting," too tight, or too revealing. Nelson denied that her clothing was inappropriate, but she did put on a lab coat whenever he complained.[6] At some point, Knight and Nelson began texting each other about both work and personal matters. Some of these matters were innocuous – such as updates on their respective children's activities – and others were more intimate. According to the available evidence, the in-person comments and texts of a sexual nature seemed to emanate exclusively from Knight. Knight admits that he once told Nelson if she saw his pants "bulging," then she would know she was dressed in too sexy a manner.[7] He texted her once to complain that the shirt she wore that day was too tight. Nelson replied that she thought his complaint was unfair. His surreply? He told her it was a good thing she did not wear tight pants, too, because then he would get it coming and going.

A comment by Nelson about infrequency in her sex life met with this retort from Knight: "That's like having a Lamborghini in the garage and never driving it."[8] And Knight admits that once he texted Nelson to ask how often she experienced orgasms. Nelson did not complain about such comments, nor did she ask Knight to stop making them, but neither did she reciprocate with sexual innuendo of her own.

If this had been the end of the story, one might assume that Nelson had brought this case in order to complain about persistent sexual harassment by her supervisor, who was also the head of the office. She might not have won her case – either because a jury might have found that Knight's conduct was not unwelcome or was not sufficiently severe or pervasive to be actionable. But it would not have been a frivolous case.

## ENTER MRS. KNIGHT AND THE FAMILY PASTOR

In 2009, Knight took his children to Colorado for a vacation. His wife, Jeanne, who also worked in his dental office, stayed behind. While home, Jeanne discovered that her husband had been texting with Nelson. She was upset about the texting, but also about Nelson's clothing and Nelson's alleged flirting with Knight. Jeanne also testified in court that Nelson would hang out at the office after work hours, which Jeanne characterized as "strange" – she questioned why Nelson "after being at work all day and away from her kids and husband . . . would not be anxious to get home like the other [women] in the office."[9]

Jeanne viewed Nelson as "a big threat to our marriage" and demanded that her husband fire her. Thus, in January 2010, Knight called Nelson to his office in order to terminate her employment. He brought a pastor with him as a witness, and he read Nelson a prepared statement, which said Nelson had become a detriment to his marriage and that it was in the best interests of the Knight and Nelson families for the two not to work together. Nelson cried upon learning that she had been let go, because she loved her job.

That night, Nelson's husband, Steve, called Knight to ask why his wife had been fired. They met in person – again, with the pastor as a witness – to discuss the situation. Knight told Steve Nelson was the best dental assistant he had ever had, and that she had done nothing wrong or inappropriate. But Knight told Steve *he* was getting too attached to *her* and, in the court's words, "feared he would try to have an affair with her down the road if he did not fire her."[10]

Knight replaced Nelson with another female dental assistant. He had never, in his practice, had a male assistant.

## IS THIS SEX DISCRIMINATION? THE RIGHT ANSWER IS YES, BUT THE COURT FAILS TO SEE IT

Nelson filed suit under the Iowa Civil Rights Act, a statute analogous to Title VII, the main federal antidiscrimination law. (Iowa courts have held repeatedly that the Iowa act is coextensive with Title VII and should be interpreted the same way.[11]) She sued for sex discrimination, arguing that she was terminated because of her gender.

The Iowa Supreme Court held, by a vote of 7–0, that Nelson's firing did not constitute sex discrimination. The court's reasoning reveals an almost comical misunderstanding of the concept of sex discrimination. The question under Title VII – and the analogous Iowa statute under which this claim was brought – is whether Nelson was fired "because of sex."[12] Under the statutes the question is this: Would Nelson have been fired if she were a man? The answer is clearly no. In reaching the opposite conclusion, the court made a series of logical and doctrinal missteps.

## WHEN IS DISCRIMINATION "BECAUSE OF SEX"?

Under Title VII, an employment action is unlawful if sex is a motivating factor, even if other factors were relevant. In many employment discrimination cases, the employer's true reasons behind an adverse employment action are unknown – or at least unadmitted. The plaintiff-employee thus has to rely on a procedure established by the U.S. Supreme Court called "pretext analysis." This procedure is designed to smoke out the employer's true motivations for taking the adverse employment action in question.

To utilize this approach in a wrongful termination case, the plaintiff must make out a prima facie case by showing that she was subject to an adverse employment action, that she was qualified for the job, and that a person of the opposite sex was not fired or was hired to replace her. The burden of producing evidence then shifts to the employer, who must articulate a legitimate, nondiscriminatory reason for her termination. The plaintiff then bears the ultimate burden of proving that the employer's reason is unworthy of credence, or that discrimination is the real reason for the firing.[13]

Here, however, the employer admitted his reasons. (Although this case was decided on summary judgment, which means that a full airing of the facts never occurred, most of the key facts appear to be undisputed.) Knight concedes that he fired Nelson, in the court's words "because of the nature of their relationship and the perceived threat to Dr. Knight's marriage."[14] Is that unlawful discrimination?

Knight argues that this had nothing to do with Nelson's sex. Nelson, on the other hand, contends that "neither the relationship nor the alleged threat would have existed if the employee had been male."[15] The Iowa court erroneously resolved this dispute in favor of Knight by making three basic mistakes.

## WHY THIS IS NOT ANALOGOUS TO A CASE OF SEXUAL FAVORITISM

First, the Iowa court looked to "sexual favoritism" precedents to say that actions based on sexual *relationships* in the workplace are not "based on sex."[16] Sexual favoritism occurs when a supervisor is engaged in a consensual, romantic relationship with a subordinate and provides her with benefits, or protects her from employment detriments, because of the relationship. Although this seems unfair, especially to other subordinate employees who are losing out on the perks of sleeping with the boss, courts have struggled to figure out how this conduct can be deemed "because of sex" vis-à-vis the adversely affected employees. In most cases, the subordinate will have been chosen for the relationship because of sex, but the coworkers who suffer its effects will typically be of both sexes. Thus the discrimination – being treated less favorably than a coworker – does not really occur because of sex.

The Equal Employment Opportunity Commission (EEOC) issued a policy guidance on sexual favoritism that has been largely followed by courts.[17] According to the guidance, isolated incidents of sexual favoritism are not actionable. Sexual favoritism that is rampant or widespread, however, can violate Title VII by creating a sort of implicit quid pro quo – giving other female employees the impression that they must sleep with the boss to get ahead – or creating a hostile environment for all members of one sex.[18]

The Iowa court makes two mistakes with this body of law. First, it reasons that if it is not actionable to treat an employee favorably because of a consensual sexual relationship, then it is also not actionable to treat an employee *unfavorably* because of a consensual relationship that may have triggered personal jealousy or created other complications at work. The two situations, however, are not analogous.

In the former case, as explained above, the discrimination complaint comes from third parties who have been adversely affected by the favoritism. The "because of sex" problem relates to their claim, not to a claim by the subordinate in the relationship who presumably was chosen "because of sex."

In the latter case – the employee suing for discrimination is the one chosen by the boss for a personal relationship – a selection that very much turned on gender. Moreover, and perhaps even more importantly in the *Knight* case, the subordinate employee who is treated unfavorably was *not* involved in a consensual sexual relationship with her supervisor. Knight and Nelson were not sexually or romantically involved, and, to the extent that their relationship involved sexual innuendo or explicit sexual conversation, it was both initiated and carried out by Knight. Nelson was thus not fired because of her relationship with her boss. As she correctly argued to the Iowa Supreme Court, she "did not do anything to get herself fired except exist as a female."[19]

## WHY THIS CASE IS MORE AKIN TO A SEXUAL HARASSMENT CASE THAN A SEX DISCRIMINATION CASE

When the head of a company sexually harasses a subordinate employee, the company is automatically liable (there are no affirmative defenses) based on an alter ego theory of liability – he *is* the company.[20] And if that same man engaged in a series of unwelcome sexual advances against that same female subordinate, we would have no trouble concluding that his actions were "because of sex." The law is clear that if a man is motivated to harass a woman because of heterosexual desire, then he is discriminating against her on the basis of sex.

Dr. Knight's actions fit neatly into this conception of sex discrimination. He found Nelson "irresistibly attractive" because she was a woman. He feared he might try to have an affair with her (as he allegedly told her husband) because she was a woman. And his wife was jealous of Nelson's presence in the office because Nelson was a woman.

If a supervisor's sexually harassing an employee constitutes sex discrimination, why doesn't his firing her to stop himself from sexually harassing her constitute discrimination, as well? In either case, a similarly situated male dental assistant would not find himself subjected to such consequences. (I can't help but recall here being told once by a male lawyer he doesn't work with women because if they are attractive, he's too tempted to come on to them, and if they're not attractive, what's the point?) If the Iowa court has this right, then could a man with a very jealous wife be excused for having a "no women in the office" policy? The Iowa court claims it would be a different case if Knight had fired more than one woman because of alleged personal relationship issues. But why?

## SEX-PLUS DISCRIMINATION IS STILL UNLAWFUL DISCRIMINATION

The Iowa court seems impressed by the fact that after Nelson was fired, Knight hired another woman as a dental assistant. And, in fact, Knight had only ever employed women in that position. Thus, the court inquired, how could Nelson's firing be "because of sex"? The answer is that whether Nelson was preceded or succeeded by another woman is irrelevant. Such evidence can be relevant to a prima facie case that relies on pretext analysis, because it helps support an inference that the adverse action was taken "because of sex." Here, as discussed above, pretext analysis was unnecessary, because Knight freely admitted his reasons for firing Nelson.

Moreover, an employer who discriminates against a subset of one gender – for example, women with small children – violates antidiscrimination law just as clearly as if it had discriminated against all members of that gender. This type of discrimination, termed "sex-plus discrimination," has been clearly held to violate Title VII and analogous state antidiscrimination laws.[21] Thus, even if Knight fired Nelson not merely because she is a woman but also because she is an attractive, sexy woman, his conduct is still actionable.

## WITH THE IOWA SUPREME COURT'S RULING IN KNIGHT'S FAVOR, AND NO TITLE VII CLAIM AT ISSUE, NELSON HAS NO FURTHER LEGAL RECOURSE, THOUGH SHE OUGHT TO

When the first cases alleging sexual harassment as a violation of Title VII were brought in the 1970s, courts did not know what to make of them. The question that troubled them was whether unwelcome sexual advances were a form of "discrimination." A few early opinions from federal courts said things like this: (1) sexual harassment is a necessary consequence of letting women into the workforce unless men are to suddenly become asexual; and (2) rape isn't a form of employment discrimination just because it happens to occur in an office rather than a back alley.[22]

We look on those cases now with horror, or at least with an understanding that they were reflective of courts' fumbling their ways through uncertain legal terrain. But those days are gone. When women are treated worse than men are because they are women, as was the case for Nelson, then discrimination law must come to the rescue. Because this suit was brought only under the Iowa antidiscrimination law, without a parallel claim under Title VII, it cannot be appealed any further. The Iowa Supreme Court is the final arbiter of the meaning of Iowa statutes, even if they are interpreted by analogy to Title VII and interpreted bizarrely. Thus, Ms. Nelson has no further avenues to complain about being fired for being, in her employer's eyes, too sexy for this job.

A version of this chapter appeared on January 8, 2013, at verdict.justia.com.

*Update: The Iowa Supreme Court, perhaps responding to criticism like this, vacated the opinion and reissued a new opinion several months later.*[23] *In the new opinion, however, the court reached the same conclusion, but with a more bare-bones opinion that left the court less vulnerable to criticism. In the end, it stuck to its guns, holding, in essence, that being "irresistibly attractive" is a fireable offense. In her own defense, Nelson told one reporter she wore nothing but T-shirts and medical scrubs to work.*[24]

# 3

# A Twist on the Problem of Sex Inequality in Coaching

Andrew Medcalf, an assistant coach for the men's crew team at the University of Pennsylvania ("Penn"), with British National Championships to his name as both a rower and a coach, applied to be head coach for the school's women's crew team. He did not get the job, and a woman was hired instead. Medcalf then sued Penn, claiming the decision constituted sex discrimination in violation of Title VII of the Civil Rights Act of 1964. A federal jury found for Medcalf, awarding him $115,000 in damages.[1]

Medcalf's claim of reverse discrimination is unusual, given that equality for *female* coaches in collegiate athletics has long been elusive. Given the evidence, the verdict for Medcalf may well have been the right one. But Medcalf's individual situation should not cause us to lose sight of the heart of inequality in coaching: discrimination against female coaches.

## THE EVIDENCE AGAINST – AND FOR – PENN

According to the evidence introduced at trial, Medcalf was told by Penn's rowing director he was not hired – or even interviewed – because Penn wanted to hire a woman for the position. He charged that an assistant director of athletics told him, "We're going to get a woman at least as good as you, if not better."[2] There was some evidence that Penn preferred a woman because it was looking for a female role model for the female athletes. And the woman Penn did hire was by no means unqualified. Indeed, she came with substantial head coaching experience, both for Dartmouth College and the U.S. junior women's national team.

Nevertheless, the jury was instructed to return a verdict for Medcalf if they believed sex was a "determinative factor" in Penn's decision not to hire him. To understand why this instruction was given, some background in discrimination law is necessary.

## THE TWO DEFENSES AGAINST CLAIMS OF SEX DISCRIMINATION IN HIRING

Title VII generally precludes employers from taking sex into account when making employment decisions, including decisions about hiring. There are only two exceptions to this rule. The first is for hiring decisions based on a bona fide occupational qualification (BFOQ).[3] The second is for hiring decisions made pursuant to a valid affirmative action plan.[4]

The BFOQ exception permits employers to make sex-based hiring decisions when only employees of one sex are qualified do the job. Thus, a sperm bank can legitimately refuse to hire women as donors, and men may be excluded from jobs as wet nurses.

Even beyond those obvious examples, however, the BFOQ defense may be used to justify sex-based hiring in other cases. A few courts have permitted the BFOQ defense to be raised on a role model theory – which might have worked here – but most courts have rejected that approach.[5]

Why wasn't Penn able to successfully mount a BFOQ defense? For one thing, the BFOQ defense is generally raised by an employer trying to explain a formal policy of sex discrimination – and Penn never admitted it passed Medcalf over because of his sex in the first place.

What about an affirmative action defense for Penn? Under the Supreme Court's jurisprudence, affirmative action can only be a defense when the employer has a valid affirmative action plan in place – and there was no evidence Penn had such a plan. (To be valid, an affirmative action plan must be enacted to combat a real problem of past discrimination and must be narrowly tailored to avoid any unnecessary trammeling of the rights of the majority.[6])

In short, because neither of the two defenses Penn might have raised could work, this case essentially came down to the single factual issue of whether Title VII's "because of sex" requirement was fulfilled. The issue boiled down to this: Did Penn in fact decide not to interview or hire Medcalf because of his sex? If so, it probably violated Title VII, and the jury's verdict was correct.

## SEX SEGREGATION IN COACHING JOBS

The Medcalf verdict should not be taken to suggest that the problem of inequality in athletics' coaching is primarily one of reverse discrimination. For even if male coaches like Medcalf occasionally face sex discrimination, which is unfair and wrong, sex discrimination against female coaches is far more prevalent and widespread.

Female coaches face two significant forms of inequality in collegiate athletics: unequal job opportunity and compensation discrimination. The first is a problem of occupational segregation. The term "occupational segregation" describes a situation where some jobs are largely "women's jobs" (for example, being a nurse) and others largely "men's jobs" (for example, being a plumber). For the most part, jobs coaching male athletes are seen as "men's jobs."

Women hold fewer than 3.5 percent of the coaching jobs in men's sports in all divisions, and the coaches for men's teams are paid more than twice the amount paid to coaches for women's teams.[7] The percentage of head coaching jobs for women's teams held by female coaches has declined from 90 percent to 42 percent since enactment of Title IX, largely owing to the increase in resources and status of women's sports.[8] As the jobs get more desirable, men are more interested in pursuing them. Moreover, female coaches tend to be clustered in lower-paid sports like swimming, diving, or track. From this overall pattern, one might conclude that women are effectively foreclosed from the more lucrative coaching jobs.

There is no single explanation for why women so seldom coach men's teams. Many factors may contribute. An old boys' network may lead athletic directors to recruit people they know, who just "happen" to be men. There may also be resistance by some male athletes to being coached by women. In addition, in coaching decisions, credit may be given for the applicant's experience playing the sport, or playing it at a professional level. That effectively takes women out of the running for football coaching jobs and puts them at a significant disadvantage in other sports, as well. (It may also favor male ex-athletes over women as coaches for women's teams in sports where women are just starting to play.) Finally, female coaches may be reluctant to apply because they assume they won't get the job – or might face hostility if they do.

## UNEQUAL PAY FOR FEMALE COACHES: THE STATUTES AND THE EEOC POLICY GUIDANCE

The problem of job segregation is exacerbated by differences in pay. In general, coaches of male athletes are paid more – often vastly more – than are coaches of female athletes. Because women infrequently coach male athletes, this pay differential means in effect that male coaches are often paid more than female coaches.

Litigation over unequal coaches' pay has been a hot area of the law in the past ten years. There are three federal statutes potentially implicated in coaches' pay litigation. First, there is Title IX, which prohibits sex discrimination by educational institutions.[9] Second, there is Title VII, which prohibits sex discrimination in employment.[10] Third, and finally, there is the Equal Pay Act, which guarantees women equal pay for equal work.[11]

Although there are slight differences among the three statutes, the Equal Employment Opportunity Commission (EEOC) has issued a policy guidance establishing a single method of analysis to be used in coaches' pay litigation.[12] According to the guidance, the following is how a case claiming sex-based pay disparities in coaching should proceed.

First, the female plaintiff selects a male comparator – a man employed by the same school with a substantially equal position. (The comparator need not be in the same sport, but he must be a real person, actually coaching another team for more money.) The plaintiff has the burden of proving the two positions are equal in skill, effort, responsibility, and working conditions. Then it is the employer's turn. The employer has the opportunity to prove, as an affirmative defense, that the pay differential is based on a factor other than sex.

## IMPROPERLY INCORPORATING PAST DISCRIMINATION INTO PRESENT PRACTICES

Most coaches' pay litigation revolves around this second step – and different arguments by schools as to why they pay similarly situated male coaches more. Schools claim, for example, that male coaches have greater responsibility for revenue production – and must, for example, make media appearances on the team's behalf.

Schools also argue that men have to be paid more to induce them to come coach at the school, and that men's prior salaries, which serve as a benchmark for their current salaries, are higher than women's. Finally, schools argue that men have more experience in both coaching and playing the sport.

On their face, all of these factors are unrelated to sex. But they are also built on past discrimination against female coaches. If they are allowed to explain pay differentials, they only perpetuate that past discrimination. For example, different responsibilities for coaches are often the result of different opportunities. Men's coaches (who are usually men) sometimes have to make television and radio appearances because the school has actively sought those opportunities for them – but not for their counterparts coaching women's teams.

Likewise, relying on prior salaries – as well as the need to induce the coach to switch schools – in order to set coaches' salaries will certainly have the effect of building in wage discrimination from other schools. Once one school discriminates in favor of men, every other school has an excuse to do so; conversely, if no school can discriminate, the rationale of having to compete in salaries falls apart.

Favoring men because they had more opportunities to play and coach in the past is perhaps the most blatant example of using past discrimination to ensure discrimination in the present. Women face the classic catch-22: you can't get a job unless you have experience, and you can't get experience unless you have a job. The fact that jobs were once denied based on sex makes the catch-22 not just frustrating but discriminatory, too.

The EEOC's approach is designed to strictly enforce federal guarantees against sex discrimination. Nevertheless, the problem of inequality in terms of both pay and job opportunities for female coaches persists. Greater attention needs to be paid to the role that schools play in allowing this discrimination to continue.

While what happened to Andrew Medcalf was unfair, at least it was not epidemic. Female coaches face similar discrimination every day.

A version of this chapter appeared on November 6, 2001, at writ.findlaw.com.

*Update: After being passed over for the job, Medcalf combined his love of rowing and Ph.D in science to study and train athletes.*[13] *For a powerful look at the impact of Title IX on the sport of women's rowing, watch* A Hero for Daisy (50 Eggs Productions 1999), *which profiles the efforts of future Olympic rower Chris Ernst to obtain equal university resources for women's rowing at Yale in the 1970s.*

# 4

# Mixed Motives

The federal courts of appeals have long disagreed about what to do in "mixed-motive" discrimination cases – that is, cases in which an adverse employment action (such as a firing, demotion, or failure to hire) occurs for both legitimate and illegitimate reasons. In its decision in *Desert Palace, Inc. v. Costa*,[1] the Supreme Court provided some much needed clarity on this issue.

The bottom line of the Court's decision is this: plaintiffs do not need a "smoking gun" to bring a mixed-motive discrimination case. Instead, less obvious evidence of discrimination can also suffice. That's welcome news for discrimination victims. Employment decisions are rarely made for a single reason. If discrimination enters into the mix, plaintiffs should have the opportunity to sue without facing any special, higher standards for the proof they must use. The Court rightly recognized Congress's intent on this point.

## THE FACTS OF THE *DESERT PALACE* CASE

The case was brought by Catherina Costa, who was fired from her job as a warehouse worker and heavy equipment operator, the only woman in that job. She sued under Title VII of the Civil Rights Act of 1964.[2] Costa alleged that her firing was an act of sex discrimination. After a physical altercation with a male coworker, she was fired. He, in contrast, received only a short suspension. On the basis of this disparity in discipline, other alleged acts of discrimination, and claims of sexual harassment, Costa sued.

Her employer, however, points to Costa's documented history of disciplinary problems. It says the firing was its response to this history; she was a "problem" employee, it argues. Both Costa and her employer may be telling the truth – both Costa's history on the job (legitimate consideration) and her gender (illegitimate consideration) may have played a role in her firing.

Should the jury get to decide this case? If a jury believes both sides, what should it do? How good does Costa's evidence of sex discrimination have to be for her to prevail on a theory of mixed-motive discrimination? These are important legal questions on which the judge must instruct the jury. Unsurprisingly, the related question of exactly what form the jury instruction in a mixed-motive case should take has been intensely controversial.

## THE BASIC BURDEN-SHIFTING FRAMEWORK IN DISCRIMINATION CASES

In 1973, in *McDonnell Douglas Corp. v. Green*, the Supreme Court made clear how burdens of proof and production work in a discrimination case.[3] (A "burden of proof" is the standard for how persuasive the proof of a claim must be. In contrast, a "burden of production" is not a burden to persuade; rather, it is a burden to come forward with at least some evidence.)

First, the plaintiff must make out a "prima facie" case, proving some very basic facts necessary to support an inference of discrimination. For instance, suppose that a woman says she was not hired for a particular job because of sex discrimination. To make out her prima facie case, she must prove that she is, indeed, a woman; that she was qualified for and applied for the job; and that she was rejected. She also must prove either that a man was hired for the job or that the employer continued to seek other applicants after rejecting her.

The employer then has a burden of production. It must articulate a legitimate, nondiscriminatory reason for the challenged employment action. For instance, in our hypothetical woman's case, it might say that its interviewer was unimpressed with her educational background. It does not, however, have to persuade anyone that this was the real reason.

Finally, the plaintiff has the opportunity to disprove the employer's articulated reason. For instance, she might show that the company hired men with very similar educational backgrounds. Alternatively, she can offer other evidence to show that the offered reason is a pretext for discrimination. For instance, she might show the jury the interviewer's notes on her and point out a little doodle of her in a short skirt under the heading "personality."

At the end of the case, the jury is instructed that it *may* find for the plaintiff if she has either disproved the employer's articulated reason *or* offered other evidence that the reason given is pretextual. The plaintiff retains the burden of proof, but the jury is instructed that acceptable proof to satisfy that burden can take one of several forms.

This proof structure is useful in the typical employment discrimination case in which there is no "smoking gun." (After all, most people who discriminate do not announce, or leave evidence, that they are doing so.) The *McDonnell Douglas* model gets around that problem by forcing the employer to explain its actions. In this way, it narrows the litigation so it revolves around an actual reason offered by the employer, rather than forcing the plaintiff to disprove all conceivable, legitimate justifications for the employment action. It also gives the plaintiff a chance to take issue with a decision-making process to which she otherwise might have little, if any, access.

## BURDEN SHIFTING IN MIXED-MOTIVE CASES: *PRICE WATERHOUSE* AND THE 1991 ACT

The *McDonnell Douglas* model has inherent limits, and a mixed-motive case soon arose to test them. The case, *Price Waterhouse v. Hopkins*, led to a 1991 Supreme Court decision that significantly altered Title VII litigation.[4] In *Price Waterhouse*, a firm denied partnership to a female candidate. There was some evidence that the decision was made *both* on the basis of her sex (an obviously illegitimate motive) *and* on the basis of her behavior at work (a legitimate motive).

Here is where *McDonnell Douglas* breaks down. The employer would satisfy its burden of production, coming forth with its legitimate reason for not making Hopkins partner: her behavior. Then the burden would be on Hopkins to disprove that reason or show it was a pretext. If she couldn't, she would lose, even if she could show that there were other, illegitimate reasons for the denial.

In sum, then, it seemed under *McDonnell Douglas* that Hopkins might lose even if the firm took her gender into account when making an employment decision, a clear Title VII violation. Unless the Court took action, Hopkins would thus have a right not to be discriminated against under Title VII, but no remedy for its violation. And her employer would be given a free pass despite having committed an act of discrimination.

That anomaly inspired the Supreme Court, in *Price Waterhouse*, to devise an alternative proof structure for mixed-motive cases. The proof structure the Court set forth in *Price Waterhouse* was superseded by Congress's amendments to Title VII in the Civil Rights Act of 1991.[5] Those amendments made clear that discrimination with mixed motives is still discrimination: it occurs whenever a prohibited characteristic was "a motivating factor for any employment practice, even though other factors also motivated the practice."[6] The amendments also made clear that if an employer can show that it would have taken the same action even without the discriminatory motive, the plaintiff cannot collect damages. But the employer is not completely off the hook. If that defense is proven, the plaintiff can still hold the defendant liable and obtain injunctive relief and attorneys' fees, both potentially valuable remedies.

## THE LINGERING "DIRECT EVIDENCE" ISSUE

As noted above, the 1991 amendments largely superseded *Price Waterhouse*. Yet one aspect of the decision remained relevant even after 1991. This is the issue that *Desert Palace* finally resolved.[7] The Court's *Price Waterhouse* decision had been splintered, with the main opinion garnering only a plurality of four, not a majority of five. (Justices White and O'Connor each concurred in the judgment but did not completely agree with its reasoning.) Justice O'Connor wrote that the burden should not shift to the employer unless and until the plaintiff could "show by *direct evidence* that decision-makers placed substantial negative reliance on an illegitimate criterion in reaching their decision."[8]

Justice O'Connor's was the only opinion to mention the "direct evidence" requirement, which led to a variety of ambiguities. First, was the mention of "direct evidence" in her concurrence sufficient to make it part of the holding? Had the other justices agreed with her, or did standard rules of vote counting make it the "narrowest ground" and therefore the holding? Second, had the 1991 amendments, which neither adopted nor rejected the "direct evidence" requirement, rendered her concurrence, if it had been binding on lower courts, irrelevant?

To add even more confusion, courts also disagreed as to what "direct evidence" meant. Literally, "direct evidence" means evidence that is sufficient to prove a fact without the need to draw any inferences. In contrast, "circumstantial evidence" gives the factfinder related facts from which it might conclude the existence of a particular, central fact.

The testimony of a witness who saw a suspect commit murder is direct evidence. Evidence that a hair from the suspect's head was found in the victim's apartment near the body is circumstantial evidence from which a jury may draw an inference of guilt. In a murder case, that's relatively straightforward. But what about in a discrimination case? A few courts took "direct evidence" literally, dismissing the claims of plaintiffs who couldn't come up with evidence of a virtual confession (written or oral) by their employers.[9]

Other courts, instead, said "direct evidence" of discrimination might simply be evidence that shows animosity toward the protected class (for instance, women). In contrast, "indirect" evidence would show only that the employer's proffered reason was false. In both cases, a jury would need to draw inferences to decide the ultimate fact: whether the act was motivated by an illicit consideration of a protected characteristic.[10]

Some courts also said that the evidence, whether technically direct or circumstantial, needed to bear directly on the decision-making context in particular – it needed to be direct in the sense that it was immediate. Thus, if a boss commented at a company picnic that women should be barefoot and pregnant in the kitchen, but not in his interview notes, he might be off the hook for later failing to hire a pregnant woman.[11]

## THE COURT'S DECISION IN *DESERT PALACE*

In *Desert Palace*, the Supreme Court achieved a simple, neat resolution of the "direct evidence" issue. It approved a jury instruction, in a mixed-motive case, that did not even mention what kind of evidence plaintiffs must offer to carry their burden.

Its reasoning was simple, too. The 1991 amendments had codified their own proof structure – one substantially different from that of *Price Waterhouse*. The amendments never mentioned any "direct evidence" requirement. Nor did the original statute. Therefore, there was none.

Justice Thomas, a former EEOC head with experience interpreting Title VII and a conservative justice with a preference for narrow interpretation of statutes, wrote the opinion. He reasoned that the amended statute plainly says that a plaintiff "need only 'demonstrate' that an employer used a forbidden consideration with respect to 'any employment practice.'"[12] It also goes on to define "demonstrate" to mean "meet[ing] the burdens of production and persuasion."[13] Nowhere, he pointed out, does it impose a requirement that direct evidence be offered to prove the "forbidden consideration."

## THE DIFFERENCE THIS DECISION MAKES

The Court's decision in this case opens doors for more plaintiffs to get their cases to a jury. After *Desert Palace*, a plaintiff who has faced mixed-motive discrimination, and who can offer some proof of animus or hostility to his or her group status, may be able to win – or at least get before the jury. Prior to *Desert Palace*, in contrast, many courts would have required that proof to not only be convincing but also "direct" in order for a plaintiff's claim to survive summary judgment.

The change is obviously a good one: if a plaintiff can persuade a jury that there was discrimination, she should not also have to rely on a special kind of evidence to do so. Prior lower court cases on this issue – now overruled – unfairly hamstrung plaintiffs as to what kind of evidence they could present.

These decisions required "smoking guns" even at a time when, as employers become more and more wary of litigation, such evidence is less and less likely to appear. Any modern employer who fails to put together employment files with an eye toward possible litigation is a fool.

Unfortunately, however, much discrimination in the workplace continues. For instance, Costa's isolation as the only woman doing her job should itself be troubling, though it was not directly at issue in her case. Doubtless, it affected her working conditions. Why, nearly four decades after Title VII was enacted, was Catherina Costa – a *female* heavy equipment operator – such an anomaly? One answer is that Title VII has been ineffective in addressing occupational segregation – the channeling of men and women into separate careers and jobs. That is doubly a problem. Not only is such segregation itself a system of discrimination but it also closely linked to higher levels of sexual harassment and other forms of discrimination. Ending sexual segregation in employment would be a true victory.

A version of this chapter appeared on June 17, 2003, at writ.findlaw.com.

*Update: In a 2009 case,* Gross v. FBL Financial Services, Inc., *the Supreme Court refused to apply this provision of the Civil Rights Act of 1991 to the Age Discrimination in Employment Act (ADEA), and rejected use of the mixed-motive proof structure altogether, somewhat inexplicably, for claims brought under the ADEA.*[14] *In a powerful dissent, Justice Stevens criticizes the majority's rejection of the "most natural reading" of the statute, which "proscribes adverse employment actions motivated in whole or in part by the age of the employee."*[15]

# 5

## Sex Stereotyping and Dress Codes

In 1989, the U.S. Supreme Court held in *Price Waterhouse v. Hopkins* that Title VII prohibits employers from penalizing employees for failing to conform to the gender stereotypes associated with their sex.[1] Two decades later, courts continue to show ambivalence in sex-stereotyping cases.

More specifically, courts continue to uphold employers' dress and grooming policies that differentiate by sex and, in the course of doing so, demand that their employees adhere to the stereotypical appearance standards assigned to their sex. A federal court ruling, in *Creed v. Family Express Corporation*, involving a transgender employee, illustrates, and repeats, the mistake of many other courts that have refused to see these policies as a form of illegal sex stereotyping.

### PRICE WATERHOUSE'S REACH

In *Price Waterhouse*, the plaintiff was denied partnership in an accounting firm, at least in part because she was too aggressive, cursed like a truck driver, and did not walk, talk, or dress in a feminine manner. In short, she was a woman who acted like a man, and for that she was dealt a career-stunting blow. The Court held in *Price Waterhouse* that Title VII forbids employers from discriminating against an employee for failing to live up to gender role expectations. You can't, in other words, punish a female employee for not being feminine enough, nor a man for being insufficiently masculine. (As discussed in Chapter 4, *Price Waterhouse* is also significant for having established the mixed-motive proof structure.)

How far has the reasoning in *Price Waterhouse* reached? Ideally, it would reach as far as necessary to serve one of the central aims of antidiscrimination law: to promote equal employment opportunity through the eradication of sex-stereotyped decision making. The reach of *Price Waterhouse* has been tested primarily in three types of cases: (i) cases of gay men or lesbians challenging harassment or other discriminatory behavior; (ii) cases of women challenging sex-differentiated dress or grooming codes; and (iii) cases of transgender persons challenging all varieties of employment policies and decisions. Cases in each category, as well as cases that involve intersecting categories, reveal both the limits and the untested waters of the law's protection against sex stereotyping.

## DRESS CODES AND TITLE VII: HOW COURTS HAVE IGNORED THE STATUTE'S MANDATE

To begin, Title VII plainly prohibits employers from discriminating on the basis of sex. Other than for a very small subset of hiring decisions, the statute contains no defenses to a claim of facial discrimination – that is, discrimination that is pursuant to a policy that expressly differentiates persons based on sex. And it contains *no* exception for dress codes.

Yet courts have upheld the right of employers to maintain sex-specific dress and grooming codes.[2] Decisions upholding these kinds of rules are anomalous because they seemingly permit precisely what Title VII clearly forbids: treating employees differently on the basis of sex. Not surprisingly, the reasoning of these decisions is unconvincing. To justify the dress and grooming codes at issue, courts have at times resorted to platitudes about employers having the prerogative to run their businesses the way they see fit. But, of course, there are lots of ways employers might see fit to run their businesses that we do not allow. For example, we neither allow employers to hire only white employees nor to fire older workers and replace them with "new blood." Yet dress code cases in effect allow employers to insist on Archie Bunker's world, where "girls were girls, and men were men."

Other courts have attempted to claim that dress and grooming codes are not really discriminatory but are actually gender-neutral, because they require that men and women alike adhere to generally accepted community standards. That these standards are different for men and women, and themselves the product of sex stereotypes, is conveniently ignored. After all, it is not as if, for example, men traditionally happen to wear beige, while women happen to wear navy. Rather, high heels, long hair, and dresses connote particular "female" traits – suggesting the wearer is pretty, sexy, demure, fashionable, or what have you. Conversely, short hair and business suits connote the "male" traits of being no nonsense, all business, and in control.

Moreover, the extra time needed to take care of long hair and the impediments to movement that high heels and dresses can impose suggest that they embody not just a style but a concept of how women should spend their days, and how they should move and behave. The sheer time investment in dressing "like a woman" can be daunting. Just ask any businesswoman running, in high heels, to make her plane after blow-drying her hair and putting on makeup for an hour. Or better yet, ask her male colleague, already calmly seated on the plane and reading the newspaper.

## THE *JESPERSEN* CASE: THE NINTH CIRCUIT RULES ON A DRESS CODE REQUIRING WOMEN TO MAINTAIN A HIGHLY SEXUALIZED APPEARANCE

Perhaps the most surprising case in this area is *Jespersen v. Harrah's*,[3] a 2006 case in which an en banc panel of the Ninth Circuit upheld by a vote of 7–4 the casino's sex-differentiated grooming policy under Title VII. The policy was startling in the degree to which it required female bartenders to maintain a highly sexualized feminine appearance.

Employees at Harrah's were required to wear the same uniform, and all were required to be "well groomed, appealing to the eye, be firm and body toned, and be comfortable with maintaining this look while wearing the specified uniform."[4] In addition, men and women had sex-specific grooming requirements. Male employees had to wear their hair short, trim their fingernails, and refrain from wearing makeup or nail polish. Female employees had to wear their hair "teased, curled, or styled," as well as wear stockings, colored nail polish, and specific types of facial makeup outlined by an "image consultant." Employees were made up by the image consultant, photographed, and held to the "personal best" image standard each day at work.[5]

Darlene Jespersen, a longtime, well-regarded bartender at the casino, objected to the requirements for female employees. She was not in the habit of teasing her hair or wearing makeup and claimed that being forced to do so interfered with her chosen identity and constituted sex discrimination. Jespersen's claim seemed promising, because the Ninth Circuit had applied *Price Waterhouse* broadly in two prior cases brought by gay men claiming they were harassed for being too effeminate.[6] In those cases, the court correctly treated gender policing, punishing gay men for failing to act according to expectations of masculinity, as a form of unlawful sex discrimination. But Jespersen was foiled in her attempt to take a similar stand against forced femininity. The court sidestepped *Price Waterhouse* by simply noting that any stereotype being applied did not inhibit Jespersen's ability to do the job. "The only evidence in the record to support the stereotyping claim is Jespersen's own subjective reaction to the makeup requirement," the court claimed.[7] The court ruled, in effect, that sex-differentiated grooming and dress codes are permissible under Title VII as long as they do not impose unequal *burdens* on men and women.

But even under that standard, it seems puzzling why Jespersen did not prevail. It was obvious that women, even apart from any identity or stereotyping objection, bore more of a burden in complying with Harrah's "personal best" policy. It is neither expensive nor time-consuming for men to keep their hair and nails short and to *not* apply makeup or nail polish. Women, on the other hand, were burdened with the expense and time involved with hair teasing, nail polishing, and the application of heavy facial makeup every single day. The court refused to take judicial notice of this difference, however, and claimed, unpersuasively, that the record did not support a claim of unequal burden.

The court in *Jespersen* did a tremendous disservice to the cause of sex equality. Dress and grooming codes may seem insignificant, but they are not established in a vacuum. They reflect, instead, societal stereotypes and prejudices about what men and women should look like. These stereotypes punish both men and women who do not happen to fit traditional expectations of masculinity and femininity.

Meanwhile, dress and grooming codes also reinforce a gender hierarchy, in which a working woman is evaluated on both appearance and job performance. The requirement that women must wear leg-revealing business dresses or skirts, for instance, is not innocuous. (Nor is the burden of a working woman's need for a costly, varied wardrobe when a man can get away with a few nearly identical business suits.) Dress codes serve to emphasize gender differences, rather than to highlight similarities of skill, credentials, or effort. The refusal of courts to confront these cases head-on, including the refusal to apply precedent that is obviously applicable, has only served to perpetuate existing gender hierarchies.

## THE RECENT RULING IN *CREED V. FAMILY EXPRESS CORPORATION*

This history brings us directly to the recent case with which I began this chapter: *Creed v. Family Express Corporation.*[8] The post–*Price Waterhouse* case law is inconsistent – upholding dress and grooming codes that transform employees into walking stereotypes, while at the same time taking a nuanced and often correct view of the same stereotyping problem in other contexts, such as in cases involving transgender discrimination (discussed at length in Chapter 6). *Creed* presents both issues together, a juxtaposition that reveals the incoherence of prior case law even more clearly.

Amber Creed was born a male but suffers from gender identity disorder, a condition in which her gender identity does not correspond to her birth sex. She was hired by Family Express to work as a sales associate. When she interviewed, she had a masculine demeanor and appearance, but after beginning work, she began to assume a more feminine look. Over time, she began to wear her hair longer and in a more feminine style and to wear nail polish and facial makeup. Like other employees, she wore the required unisex uniform, a polo shirt and slacks.

Creed received positive performance evaluations and had been selected as "Greeter of the Month" on several occasions. Ultimately, however, Creed's employment was terminated. She was told all employees were required to follow the company's dress and grooming code, both the general portions and the sex-specific ones. At Family Express, men were required to maintain "neat and conservative hair that is kept above the collar" and forbidden from wearing makeup or jewelry.[9]

Employees were told this code was a "nonnegotiable part of employment," with no exceptions.[10]

As part of her preparation for sexual reassignment surgery, Creed assumed a traditionally feminine appearance. But a manager informed her that she could no longer present herself in a feminine manner at work. She was given twenty-four hours to conform her appearance. Instead, she terminated her employment because of the ultimatum. She then filed a lawsuit alleging that she lost her job because the company perceived her "to be a man who did not conform with gender stereotypes associated with men in our society."[11]

Is it unlawful sex stereotyping to punish an anatomical male for assuming a feminine appearance? Oddly, the federal district court in Indiana that ruled on Creed's claim said it certainly could be, but not if the discrimination is embodied in a formal dress and grooming code, with sex-specific requirements that do not impose unequal burdens on men and women. The court refused, unlike some courts, to exclude transgender individuals altogether from protection under Title VII. But it effectively accomplished the same exclusion by allowing Family Express to hide behind its dress and grooming policy.

The *Creed* court articulated the correct standard under Title VII: employment actions taken "because of sex" are unlawful. It also correctly cited *Price Waterhouse* for the proposition that "Title VII doesn't allow an employer to treat employees adversely because their appearance or conduct doesn't conform to stereotypical gender roles."[12] Then, it appropriately cited a case from the U.S. Court of Appeals for the Seventh Circuit, *Doe v. City of Belleville*, for the proposition that a man cannot lawfully be harassed because "his voice is soft, his physique is slight, his hair long, or because in some other respect he exhibits masculinity in a way that does not meet his coworkers' idea of how men are to appear and behave."[13]

Yet, despite citing these precedents with approval, the *Creed* court ultimately rejected the claim of unlawful sex stereotyping. It held that penalizing Creed for failing "to embody sexual stereotypes" is a prohibited purpose, but that penalizing her for "breach of the grooming policy" is a legitimate one. It held, ultimately, that no reasonable jury could find that she was the victim of illegal stereotyping, because, apart from her noncompliance with the grooming policy, there was no proof that the employer acted "because of sex."

## CASE LAW SHOULD EVOLVE TO RECOGNIZE THAT DRESS CODES, TOO, CAN CONSTITUTE ILLEGAL SEX STEREOTYPING

The *Creed* court is not the first to misunderstand the nature of a sex-stereotyping claim after *Price Waterhouse*. (*Jespersen* stands out in this category, but its convoluted reasoning in a case that involves both a transgender employee and a sex-specific grooming code shows the true incoherence of cases in this area.

Courts ought to take *Price Waterhouse* on its face, which means refusing to allow employers to rely on sex stereotypes when crafting policies or making employment-related decisions – whether or not those policies are deemed "dress codes" or are applied case by case without formal company recognition or based on the biases of individual managers. Isn't codifying bias in a policy as bad or worse, from a sex discrimination perspective, as applying it case by case?

Transgendered employees would certainly benefit from a more honest and fair assessment by courts of these dress-code claims. So would women like Darlene Jespersen who simply wish to be assessed on the basis of the work they do, not on their hair and makeup.

A version of this chapter appeared on March 3, 2009, at writ.findlaw.com.

# 6

## A Victory for Transgender Employees

In a thoughtful, well-reasoned opinion, a federal district judge handed transgender individuals a significant victory against employment discrimination.[1] The case was *Schroer v. Billington*,[2] and the court was the federal district court for the District of Columbia.

### THE CASE AGAINST THE LIBRARY OF CONGRESS

The facts of the case are these: Diane Schroer applied for a position as a terrorism specialist with the Congressional Research Service (CRS) at the Library of Congress. The job, which requires a security clearance, entails providing expert policy analysis to congressional committees, as well as members of Congress and their staffs.

No one disputes that Schroer possessed excellent qualifications for the job, which included an impressive set of relevant academic credentials and twenty-five years of service in the military, including time in combat as part of a Special Forces unit. The dispute arose, instead, because of Schroer's male-to-female transgender status. (A transgender person is someone whose gender identity diverges from his or her anatomical sex at birth.)

At the time she interviewed for the position, she had been diagnosed with gender identity disorder and had been working with a social worker to develop a plan to transition to a completely female identity. When she had interviewed at CRS, however, she used what was then her legal name, David Schroer, and presented herself to the interviewer with a male appearance. After the interview, on which she scored higher than any other applicant, CRS offered her the position.

After receiving the offer, Schroer called Charlotte Preece, the staff member with whom she had interviewed, and asked her to lunch. At lunch, Diane disclosed her transgender status and explained that, by the time she reported for work, she would have had feminizing facial surgery and would have assumed a permanent, full-time female appearance, to be followed by sexual-reassignment surgery at a later date.

After an initial response of "Why in the world would you want to do that?," Preece told Schroer, "Well, you've given me a lot to think about. I'll be in touch."[3] When Preece did get back in touch, it was to rescind the job offer. She explained over the phone: "Well, after a long and sleepless night, based on our conversation yesterday, I've determined that you are not a good fit, not what we want."[4] The job was then offered to and accepted by the next-highest-scoring candidate on the list.

## TRANSGENDER INDIVIDUALS AND EMPLOYMENT DISCRIMINATION: THE UNFRIENDLY LEGAL LANDSCAPE PRIOR TO THIS RULING

Transgender individuals have generally been unsuccessful in establishing direct rights under federal antidiscrimination laws. Most courts have held that neither transgender individuals nor gays and lesbians are a protected class under Title VII, which means that employers can base employment decisions on those characteristics without running afoul of federal law.

Efforts to enact federal legislation to protect transgender persons against both these forms of discrimination have been sustained, but thus far, unsuccessful. The House of Representatives has more than once passed the Employment Non-Discrimination Act, which would extend Title VII protection to gays and lesbians but not transgender employees. An earlier bill had included both categories, but "gender identity" discrimination was dropped in a last-minute political compromise.

Although state antidiscrimination laws often operate as a supplement to Title VII, transgender persons do not find much protection at that level either. Although about a third of the states have now adopted laws banning sexual-orientation discrimination, only a handful of those extend the protection to discrimination on the basis of transgender status or gender identity.[5]

## AN AVENUE FOR LEGAL PROTECTION FOR TRANSGENDER EMPLOYEES: USING THE SEX DISCRIMINATION RUBRIC

With such a dearth of formal protection, transgender employees have had to draw on other theories to challenge the discrimination they suffer. (And studies suggest that at least half of transgender do experience some form of discrimination at work.[6]) Title VII doctrine presents two possibilities for transgender to claim they have suffered illegal sex discrimination. First, transgender individuals might argue that an employer has acted "because of sex" – and thus committed sex discrimination – when it discriminates against an employee who converts from one sex to the other.[7] Second, transgender individuals might argue that the discrimination they suffer constitutes sex stereotyping (and thus sex discrimination) to the extent that employers discriminate because transgender individuals take on a gender that differs from their biological sex.

The court in *Schroer* examined (and ultimately validated) both of these theories. But let's first consider the prior rulings in transgender discrimination cases.

## EARLY RULINGS REFUSED TO RECOGNIZE TRANSGENDER RIGHTS, BUT A WATERSHED SUPREME COURT DECISION SHOULD HAVE CHANGED THAT

In the early cases, courts routinely rejected the argument that discrimination against transgender employees is a form of sex discrimination prohibited by Title VII, just as they had rejected the notion of transgenderism as a protected class under the statute.[8] The U.S. Court of Appeals for the Seventh Circuit's 1984 ruling in *Ulane v. Eastern Airlines*[9] was among the first such rulings, and set the tone for a pattern of exclusion of all transgender claims under Title VII.[10]

However, the Supreme Court's 1989 decision in *Price Waterhouse v. Hopkins* should have been a watershed case for transgender workers.[11] After all, gender non-conformity is *the* essential trait of transgenderism. Accordingly, refusing to allow employers to discriminate against transgender persons who dress and maintain an outward appearance that is inconsistent with their anatomical sex would seem to be a logical consequence of the Court's decision. If a female employee cannot be punished by an employer for not being "feminine enough," then certainly a man cannot be punished by an employer for not being "masculine enough." And perhaps the most dramatic way not to be "masculine enough" in an employer's eyes is to assume a female identity.

Despite the clarity of this argument, however, the post–*Price Waterhouse* results in transgender discrimination cases have been mixed. Several courts have simply refused to apply the sex-stereotyping theory to transgender plaintiffs, suggesting rather absurdly that their transgender status deprives them of a "sex" altogether, and thus dispenses with the usual protections against sex discrimination.[12]

The tides have begun to turn, however, in favor of transgender plaintiffs. A handful of state courts have interpreted state antidiscrimination laws to protect transgender individuals against sex discrimination, most by using a Price Waterhouse–type theory.[13] At the federal level, meanwhile, the U.S. Court of Appeals for the Sixth Circuit set the stage for a new era with its 2004 ruling in *Smith v. City of East Salem*.[14]

In that case, a transgender firefighter argued that he had suffered adverse employment actions and retaliation because of his gender identity disorder. Disagreeing with several other federal appellate courts that had faced the same question, the Sixth Court ruled that the plaintiff *was* discriminated against on the basis of his sex. The court in *Smith* relied on *Price Waterhouse* to hold that the plaintiff was protected by Title VII. Discriminating against a male who assumes a female identity, the court reasoned, is a form of gender policing, as well: a "real" man wouldn't do this, so a man who does is singled out for maltreatment.

## THE RULING IN *SCHROER V. BILLINGTON* AND
## THE REASONING BEHIND IT

That brings us up to the point of the case with which I began this chapter, *Schroer v. Billington*. There, CRS tried first to argue that it had a number of reasons for refusing to hire Schroer that were *related* to her transgender status, but nonetheless *nondiscriminatory*. They ostensibly had concerns about her ability to receive a timely security clearance, her trustworthiness, her ability to focus on work while undergoing such a significant life change, and, finally, a concern that she would be unlikely to benefit from the military contacts in her past after assuming a female identity.

Judge Robertson, who presided over Schroer's case, rejected all these explanations as either pretextual – believing that CRS actually made its decision because of her newly disclosed transgender status, and not these other concerns – or themselves discriminatory. But did basing an employment decision on an applicant's transgender status violate Title VII? CRS argued no, but the court ruled against it on two separate theories.

First, the court ruled that Schroer was a victim of illegal sex stereotyping, though not in the usual way transgender employees might experience.[15] Preece, Schroer's interviewer who first selected, then rejected her, did not seem to care that Schroer was a man taking on the appearance of a woman, something a "real" man would not do. Rather, when Preece saw pictures of Schroer with a female appearance, she admitted that her concern was that Schroer did not look feminine enough – that she instead looked like a man dressed as a woman. Preece thus seemed to accept the notion that Schroer had changed her sex, but believed that Schroer, as a woman, was not living up to the expectations for *her* gender.

The court took the view that transgender individuals are protected against sex stereotyping, regardless of which way it runs ("too much" or "not enough"), just as other plaintiffs are. It cited both *Price Waterhouse* and the Sixth Circuit's ruling in *Smith* for the proposition that punishing gender nonconformity in the workplace violates Title VII.[16] The court acknowledged that because gender nonconformity is the defining aspect of transgenderism, it may be that the anti-sex-stereotyping rule is the same as banning discrimination against transgender individuals outright, but still adopted the rule.

Second, the court ruled that Schroer was a victim of sex discrimination, even apart from the stereotyping and gender policing. It took the position that CRS discriminated against Schroer because she was converting from one sex to the other, and that such a decision falls within Title VII's prohibition on employment decisions made "because of sex."[17]

Here, the court paved genuine new ground. No federal court has ruled similarly on this issue. Yet this court seems to have the better of the argument. Judge Robertson drew an analogy to religion: the court reasoned that if an employer discriminated against an employee because she converted from Christianity to Islam, and harbored bias only against "converts," "that would be a clear case of discrimination 'because of religion.'" So, too, the court concluded, should it be a clear case of discrimination when an employer singles out for adverse treatment an individual who converts from male to female. The court thus read Title VII literally to ban discrimination "because of sex" and swept this act of discrimination within its reach.[18]

## IN THIS LANDMARK RULING, JUDGE ROBERTSON
## CHOSE THE RIGHT PATH

The ruling in *Schroer* is a landmark one, both for the inclusive protection it offers transgender individuals who experience employment discrimination and for the careful way in which the court grappled with a tough legal and social issue. In doing so, the court honored the *Price Waterhouse* precedent in a way that other federal courts have not been willing to do, and struck a blow at the entrenched sex stereotyping that harms not only transgender individuals or gays and lesbians but also all women. The law must be a tool to breakdown gender stereotypes – and Judge Robertson has moved it in the right direction.

A version of this chapter appeared on September 30, 2008, at writ.findlaw.com.

*Update: In April 2012, the EEOC issued a ruling in an agency proceeding,* Macy v. Holder, *in which it concluded that gender identity discrimination against a transgender employee is a form of sex discrimination because the social and cultural expectations of gender are as much an aspect of sex as biological and anatomical differences.[19] Thus, the EEOC reasoned, transgender discrimination is always "related to the sex of the victim." This is so "whether an employer discriminates against an employee because the individual has expressed his or her gender in a non-stereotypical fashion, because the employer is uncomfortable with the fact that the person has transitioned or is in the process of transitioning from one gender to another, or because the employer simply does not like that the person is identifying as a transgender person." In each case, the employer is "making a gender-based evaluation," and "violating the Supreme Court's admonition" in* Price Waterhouse *that "an employer may not take gender into account in making an employment decision."*

# 7

# How Fast Must Female Transit Officers Run?

How fast should an applicant be able to run 1.5 miles if she wants to be a transit police officer in Philadelphia? That is the question at the heart of an opinion by the Third Circuit Court of Appeals, in the case of *Lanning v. Southeastern Pennsylvania Transit Authority (SEPTA)*.[1]

The plaintiffs are five unsuccessful female applicants, who, according to SEPTA, could not run fast enough to become transit officers. They have sued under Title VII, the main federal antidiscrimination statute.[2] In their complaint, the five women allege that the transit authority's fitness requirements constitute "disparate impact discrimination" – that is, they discriminate against women candidates because they result in very few women being hired as officers.

*Lanning* provides a lesson on how to analyze cases of "disparate impact" discrimination. ("Disparate impact" discrimination occurs when a facially neutral employment practice has a disproportionately adverse effect on a protected group, such as women or African Americans.) *Lanning* also provides a cautionary tale about the way in which an appropriate legal standard – here, the standard for disparate impact discrimination – can be undermined if courts misapply it.

## HOW THE RUNNING TEST WAS DEVISED

The test the women are challenging was developed by an exercise physiologist, Dr. Paul Davis. In 1991, SEPTA hired Dr. Davis to develop a fitness test for its police officers. To do so, Dr. Davis accompanied existing transit officers on the job for two days to gain an understanding of their day-to-day job tasks. He also conducted a study with twenty experienced officers to determine what physical abilities and what level of fitness were required for adequate performance of their jobs. He concluded that applicants must run, jog, and walk on the job.

The officers in the study suggested that an applicant should be able to run a mile in 11.78 minutes, while wearing full gear. But Dr. Davis rejected that standard as too low, based on his assessment that any individual could do that. He also considered heightening the standard to force applicants to demonstrate an aerobic capacity of 50 mL/kg/min, but he dismissed that option because of the "draconian effect" it would have on women.[3]

Finally, Dr. Davis decided that something in between would be just right and recommended that SEPTA insist on an aerobic capacity of 42.5 mL/kg/min. To prove they had this capacity, applicants would have to run 1.5 miles in twelve minutes.

That was the standard ultimately adopted by SEPTA. Transit officers rarely if ever have to actually run 1.5 miles on the job. However, the test was used as a proxy for measuring the aerobic capacity Dr. Davis felt the applicants would need to perform actual job functions successfully. It turned out that only a very small percentage of female applicants, between 6 percent and 12 percent, could pass this test. In contrast, a majority of male applicants could. That difference resulted in a hiring pattern that significantly favored men over women.

## DISPARATE IMPACT ANALYSIS: WHAT THE SUPREME COURT REQUIRES

The Supreme Court first recognized that Title VII outlaws "disparate impact" discrimination in the 1971 case of *Griggs v. Duke Power Co.*[4] In *Griggs*, the employer had added a high school diploma requirement for certain jobs that had traditionally been reserved for whites only. The new requirement took effect the day after Title VII did. The Court did not accept the employer's argument that a race-neutral process was insulated from Title VII claims. Rather, it reasoned, the statute was intended to eliminate not only overt discrimination but also "practices that are fair in form, but discriminatory in operation."[5]

That ruling gave birth to disparate impact claims under Title VII. Then, in 1991, Congress amended the statute to expressly recognize that Title VII prohibits disparate impact discrimination.[6] According to the amended statute, disparate impact analysis involves a three-step inquiry by the court.

First, the court asks whether the plaintiff-employee made out her prima facie (that is, threshold) case, by showing that the application of a facially neutral standard has resulted in a discriminatory hiring pattern. If so, the court asks whether the employer, who now bears the burden, proven that the particular standard or practice is justified by "business necessity."

That leads to another important question, though: What constitutes "business necessity"? After *Griggs*, an increasingly conservative Supreme Court weakened the standard so that almost any job requirement could be justified as a business necessity.

But then, in the Civil Rights Act of 1991, Congress overruled the Supreme Court and went back to the initial, stringent standard, under which "necessity" truly means necessity – not, say, convenience.[7] After that, appellate courts had to reinterpret the standard consistent with Congress's direction. This type of back-and-forth between Congress and the Supreme Court is not unique to employment discrimination law, but it is certainly an important feature of it.

If the employer has not borne its burden to show "business necessity," the plaintiff wins. If it has, the court goes on to yet another question: Has the plaintiff proved that the employer rejected an alternative employment practice that would both have a less disparate impact and satisfy its legitimate business interest? If so, the plaintiff still wins.

Disparate impact litigation revolves around experts. Each side typically calls its own expert: the plaintiff's expert is used to make the initial statistical showing of disparate impact, and the employer's expert is used to validate the practice – that is, to show that it is indeed necessary. Experts are particularly central to cases that, like *Lanning*, involve a strength or fitness requirement. In such a case, they must analyze the nature of a particular job and then translate it into concrete fitness requirements: For instance, how many push-ups should a firefighter be able to do in order to show her ability to fight fires effectively?

## THE FIRST APPELLATE DECISION: *LANNING I* INTERPRETS "BUSINESS NECESSITY"

The *Lanning* case actually went to the appeals court twice – first in 1999,[8] and then again in 2002, as discussed above. SEPTA conceded from the start that its fitness requirement had a disparate impact on women. Also, it seemed relatively clear (though this was the subject of fact-finding) that the test was, at least, job related: transit officers did have to have some aerobic capacity; the question was, how much?

As a result, the first appellate decision, *Lanning I*, revolved only around the following question: Did SEPTA prove that the fitness requirement was "consistent with business necessity"? Answering the question was complicated by the fact that *Lanning I* was the case in which the U.S. Court of Appeals for the Third Circuit first responded to the 1991 Civil Rights Act's command to reinterpret, and heighten, the "business necessity" standard. Thus, the Third Circuit there considered two possible interpretations of "business necessity."

SEPTA argued for what was roughly a "more is better" standard: transit officers need to be able to apprehend perpetrators and make arrests, and better fitness levels will make them better at those jobs. More fitness is always better, so a demanding test is necessary. But under this approach, an employer could set a standard so high that virtually all women would be excluded. Surely that could not be right.

The appellate court concluded instead that businesses must prove that the standard enforces a "minimum qualification necessary for successful performance of the job in question."[9] The court was particularly concerned about "excessive cutoff scores that have a disparate impact on minorities."[10] If the employee could perform the job's requirements, the court decided, "business necessity" could not be used to justify further qualifications.

The court thus remanded the case to the district court with instructions to determine, among other things, whether having the particular aerobic capacity Dr. Davis's standard required (42.5 mL/kg/min) was a "minimum qualification." Could someone with a lesser aerobic capacity successfully perform the tasks required of a transit officer? If so, the fitness requirement would be invalid.

On remand, the district court made new factual findings. But it reached the same conclusion it had reached the first time: the fitness requirement was consistent with business necessity. The plaintiffs then appealed to the Third Circuit again – leading to the 2002 decision discussed at the start of the chapter, *Lanning II*.[11]

### *LANNING II*: MISAPPLYING THE STANDARD AND THWARTING CONGRESS'S INTENT

Before a new panel of Third Circuit judges, the plaintiffs lost, 2–1, with one judge dissenting. Although the panel paid lip service (as it had to) to the earlier panel's articulation of the legal standard, it did little to see that the standard had been implemented correctly by the lower court. With only a cursory review of the evidence, the majority upheld the district court's conclusion that applicants who fail the fitness test would be much less likely to "successfully execute critical policing tasks."[12]

Shooting fish in a barrel, the dissenting judge pointed out the myriad flaws in the evidence put forth by SEPTA to defend its fitness requirement as a "minimum" qualification. (SEPTA's own expert, Dr. Davis, admitted he had used "intellectual creativity" to come up with the requirement, suggesting it was hardly written in stone.[13])

If the appellate court had looked at the evidence more carefully, it would have been obvious that, as the dissenting judge concluded, the fitness requirement was no minimum qualification. Several points make this very clear.

### WHY THE FITNESS REQUIREMENT WAS NOT A "MINIMUM" QUALIFICATION

First, the fitness requirement was not used to disqualify existing transit officers, many of whom could not satisfy it. Incumbent officers were given incentives to meet the goal, but there were no consequences for failing. Obviously, unless SEPTA viewed all those who failed as unqualified, the test was not in fact a "minimum qualification" necessary for performance of the job. Indeed, many officers who failed the test satisfactorily performed their jobs nonetheless. (One female officer who had failed the fitness test, but been hired by mistake, was even repeatedly commended for her work.)

Second, the fitness test is given only upon application, not upon beginning work two or two and a half years later. Fitness at the time of application is certainly not a job qualification, even if fitness as an officer might be (though not at this level). Evidence in the record suggests that, with moderate training over the interim period, a significantly greater number of female applicants could meet the standard by the time they begin work. But SEPTA did not offer this training, or even give the applicants an opportunity to improve their running times on their own and then be retested. Meanwhile, there is no test to ensure that candidates can still meet the fitness goal when they actually begin work. As the dissent mused, what about "the possible intervening intake of pizzas, burgers, and that extra helping of dessert every now and then?"[14] In sum, if SEPTA truly believed the fitness test were a minimum job qualification, it would administer it just before employees started and periodically thereafter, and fire everyone, incumbent or not, who failed. It did not take this approach.

Third, while the "1.5 miles in twelve minutes" standard SEPTA settled on may not sound harsh to runners (indeed, I successfully completed it myself before writing this), it is stricter than the standard imposed by many branches of the U.S. military, the FBI, and the New York City transit authority. It is not clear why being a transit officer in Philadelphia would be so much more demanding than these other positions.

Fourth, the studies used to defend the necessity of the fitness requirement were vulnerable to serious criticism. For example, one study purported to measure the speed of an "average perpetrator" as a basis for determining how fast officers would need to run to apprehend them. That's fine in theory, but in practice, as the dissent pointed out, the average perpetrator's speed was measured based on one group of individuals, two-thirds of whom were high school or college track stars – and thus probably much, much more fit than the average turnstile jumper in Philly.

## THE LESSONS OF *LANNING*

The *Lanning* case is important on a number of levels. First, it is distressing because it allows SEPTA to employ a standard that will result in significantly fewer women being hired for the job of transit police officer – perpetuating the unfortunate reality that most law enforcement jobs are held by men.[15] And it does so for no good reason: this standard is not really a minimum qualification for the job, and female officers (as the accidental hiring of one showed) can succeed well without meeting it.

The *Lanning* case also tells a cautionary tale about the limited power of law to change culture. Here, the first appellate panel, in *Lanning I*, established a strict legal standard designed to eliminate discriminatory hiring practices and to ensure that greater numbers of women were given the opportunity to obtain the job of transit officer. Yet the district court repeated its initial conclusion despite the new, stricter standard, and then, in *Lanning II*, the next appellate panel rubber-stamped the district court's decision. The solution to hiring practices that create discriminatory gender patterns may thus have to come from outside the legal system.

A version of this chapter appeared on November 19, 2002, at writ.findlaw.com.

# 8

# Who Is Protected by Antidiscrimination Laws?

The U.S. Court of Appeals for the Seventh Circuit has suggested that some law firm partners may qualify as "employees" for purposes of federal antidiscrimination law. The colorful opinion, written by Judge Richard Posner, was issued in the case of *EEOC v. Sidley Austin Brown & Wood*.[1]

The decision is certain to inspire fear in law firms across the country. If partners indeed qualify as firm "employees," that means they can sue their firms under laws such as the Age Discrimination in Employment Act (ADEA); Title VII, the major federal antidiscrimination statute; and other federal laws that only "employees" can invoke. Historically, firms have been virtually immune from lawsuits based on decisions relating to their own partners. That immunity would be gone. And although obvious beneficiaries of the recent ruling are older lawyers, who may be able to challenge a variety of practices common to law firm partnerships, women and minorities who are likely to be at lower rungs of the partnership ladder may benefit, as well.

## THE FACTS OF THE SIDLEY CASE

The case arose when the law firm of Sidley Austin Brown & Wood decided to demote thirty-two equity partners (most of whom were over age fifty) to "counsel" or "senior counsel."

The EEOC subsequently began an investigation. It issued a subpoena to Sidley, seeking information relating to two issues: First, did the demoted partners qualify as employees under the ADEA? Second, were the demotions undertaken on the basis of age? The EEOC sought information relating not only to the demotions but also to the firm's mandatory retirement policy, as well.

With respect to the first issue the subpoena addressed, Sidley complied only in part. It argued that the EEOC had sufficient information to determine that the

45

partners were "true partners," and, therefore, were not protected as employees under the ADEA.[2] With regard to the second issue, Sidley provided no information, on the theory that because the partners were not "employees," the EEOC had no jurisdiction to conduct the investigation, because none of the statutes the agency enforced could apply.[3]

The EEOC then applied for an order to enforce the subpoena, and the district court ordered the firm to comply in full.[4] The firm appealed the order, and the dispute – which at base raised the issue of who constitutes an employee under the ADEA – thus came to the Seventh Circuit under the guise of a technical question about the EEOC's subpoena authority.

## WHO IS AN "EMPLOYEE" UNDER FEDERAL ANTIDISCRIMINATION LAWS

The EEOC's subpoena was not enforceable unless Sidley's demoted partners could be considered "employees" for purposes of the ADEA. Could they?

The answer is not crystal clear. And antidiscrimination statutes typically offer little to define the two terms beyond circular definitions of "employee" as "an individual employed by an employer." Fortunately, though, in most cases it is obvious whether an individual is an "employee" who is protected by the law, or, alternatively, an "employer" who is liable under it. But at the margins, certain types of workers are hard to classify.

For example, at a law firm, support staff – such as secretaries, copy room workers, and paralegals – are clearly "employees" for purposes of discrimination laws. They are hired by the firm, are paid a set salary regardless of whether the firm prospers, and can be fired at will unless their contracts provide otherwise. Law firm associates occupy a similar status.

## ARE PARTNERS "EMPLOYEES"? IN MODERN LAW FIRMS, PERHAPS

But what about law firm partners? Do they, by virtue of being "members" of a firm, occupy a different status? The conventional wisdom has been that they do. Courts have traditionally assumed that partners are employers because, unlike support staff and associates, they own a share of the firm, participate in major firm decisions, and share in the firm's profits and losses.

The structure of the modern law firm, however, necessitates that this assumption be revisited. Law firms have grown in size, and with that, many have centralized power and decision-making authority, devolving it on only a small executive or management committee, or even a single managing partner.

Many have also created multiple tiers of partnership, including nonequity partners who are salaried and own no share of the firm. Those changes make it far less clear whether some partners – those who are not full equity partners, or who do not belong to the committee that, in practice, runs the firm – should be considered "employees."

Sidley's firm structure is a good example of such a modern firm. The firm has more than 500 partners, of whom only a select few sit on the self-perpetuating executive committee. Arguably only these powerful few are truly "employers" and not "employees." The executive committee at Sidley delegates authority to other partners to hire, fire, promote, and determine compensation for their subordinates. But the other partners themselves work at the mercy of the executive committee: on the basis of the unappealable decision of the executive committee, partners can be fired, demoted (as it did in this case), or have their pay lowered.

At Sidley, important decisions all come from the executive committee. The firm has taken only one firm-wide vote in the past twenty-five years. That vote – on whether to merge with another firm – took place after the EEOC filed this case. Otherwise, the executive committee has exercised full control.[5]

Sidley's partnership presents a good case for reexamining the general rule that equity partners cannot be employees. The demoted partners in the Sidley case had many of the incidents of partnership – such as ownership of a share of the firm, profit sharing, and liability in proportion to capital contribution. But they lacked other important ones, such as coequal control and power over the firm.

## A SUPREME COURT CONCURRENCE SUGGESTS PARTNERS MAY NOT BE EMPLOYEES

In the 1984 case of *Hishon v. King and Spalding*,[6] the Supreme Court addressed the question whether an associate being considered for partnership still qualified as an "employee" for Title VII purposes. The Court said yes.

Justice Powell concurred, writing separately to suggest that decisions regarding partners made *after* they had joined the partnership would not be constrained by Title VII. Thus, according to Justice Powell, a law firm could not be taken to task for deciding to unfairly compensate, demote, or mandatorily retire an employee, even if that decision was clearly based on age, sex, race, or some other characteristic protected by Title VII. (Partners discriminated against on the basis of race may independently have a claim under section 1981, a federal statute prohibiting race discrimination in employment contracts, among other things.[7])

*Hishon*, however, did not resolve the issue of whether partners may under some circumstances be protected by federal antidiscrimination laws. For one thing, it is not clear how many, if any, other Justices shared Justice Powell's view. For another thing, the issue was not squarely presented in the case, which involved a firm's decision as to who would be a partner, not its decision about a current partner's fate.

## LOWER COURTS HAVE FOUND THAT PARTNERS CAN FUNCTION AS "EMPLOYEES" AT TIMES

Since *Hishon*, courts have struggled with the boundary between "employer" and "employee" with respect to partners (in law firms as well as other types of partnerships). Many have adopted a general rule that partners are not employees. But many also recognize that exceptions might be made on the basis of a functional analysis of the partner's role in the firm or the firm's structure. Under such exceptions, a partner may indeed be deemed an "employee" under certain circumstances.[8]

Some courts have drawn bright lines: partners in firms that have incorporated are employees, while those in unincorporated partnerships are not. Likewise, many courts distinguish between equity partners, who profit share, and nonequity partners, who are paid a fixed salary, and treat only the latter, as "employees." Other courts have adopted a more fact-intensive approach, such as the "economic realities" test. That test asks whether a person who is formally labeled a "partner" in fact bears the incidents of partnership: the ability to participate in the control and operation of the business, compensation based on profits, and long-term job security.

## THE APPELLATE DECISION IN THE *SIDLEY* CASE: SUGGESTING PARTNERS ARE EMPLOYEES

The Seventh Circuit did not resolve whether equity partners can ever be employees. Nor did it resolve whether the demoted Sidley partners should be considered employees for purposes of the ADEA. But it did strongly suggest that the district court, on remand, should treat them as employees – for several reasons.

First, the majority was swayed by the fact that virtually all the power in the firm was concentrated in a relatively small (thirty-six-partner), unelected, self-perpetuating committee. Judge Posner rejected Sidley's argument that because the partners delegated their authority to this unelected committee, they, rather than just the small committee, were managing the firm: "That would be like saying that if the people elect a person to be dictator for life, the government is a democracy rather than a dictatorship," he explained.[9]

Second, one of the justifications for excluding partners from the protection of federal discrimination laws is that they have other mechanisms under partnership law to protect themselves. Here, however, the partners who were not on the executive committee had essentially no voting power. Thus, they could not, for example, vote to expel partners who were engendering unnecessary liability for them.

Third, Sidley partners do not appear to share what Justice Powell found significant in a traditional law partnership – an understanding that decisions affecting the firm will be made by agreement or consent among *all* the partners. And a firm that lacks this type of coequal decision making does not necessarily deserve the immunities granted to traditional partnerships.[10]

For these reasons, the majority ordered Sidley to fully comply with the subpoena, to the extent it sought evidence of the partners' functional status, by producing responsive documents. Moreover, the majority held that if the documents produced were to show a truly unequal partnership – in which some partners clearly "employ" others – then the EEOC would be entitled to get a response to that part of its subpoena relating to the merits of the age discrimination claim, as well.[11]

Judge Easterbrook, who concurred in the result, wrote separately. While he believed that the thirty-two demoted partners, who maintained capital accounts and profit shared, were clearly beyond the reach of the ADEA, he thought the EEOC was entitled to determine whether that was true of every partner in the firm. Because all partners were subject to the firm's mandatory retirement rule, the status of each partner was relevant to the EEOC's investigation.[12]

## WHY THE DECISION MATTERS: NEW RIGHTS FOR WOMEN, MINORITIES, AND OLDER LAWYERS

Granted, the majority did not ultimately hold that these particular thirty-two law firm partners *are* employees for purposes of federal antidiscrimination laws. But it strongly suggested they might be – and even more strongly suggested that some partners, in some circumstances, would be. It decisively rejected any argument that partners are, by their nature, not employees. Instead, it suggested, the nature of partners' status would be determined by the facts.

That idea was previously unthinkable to most law firms. Law firm partnerships have always operated in private, and partners dealt a bad hand have, until now, had relatively little recourse against fellow partners.

This decision may signal a whole new ball game, one that is fairer for women and minorities, who have historically been excluded from the partnership ranks of elite law firms and continue to suffer discrimination. Older partners, who may fear being edged out by the very lawyers they once mentored, may also benefit.

This case is also a reminder of the EEOC's broad power. Here, the EEOC initiated this action without a complaining party; since then, none of the demoted partners has joined the case. The EEOC was able to do so because it has the power to independently enforce the discrimination laws within its jurisdiction, regardless of the interest or cooperation of the alleged victims. That makes sense: victims may be too concerned about retaliation to cooperate, and may tend to settle a case the EEOC would prefer to try, to send a strong antidiscrimination message.

The EEOC even has the right to vindicate the public interest in eradicating employment discrimination when the individual victims have waived their own right to sue in court – as the Supreme Court held in *EEOC v. Waffle House.*[13] Partnerships thus need to be wary not only of their own members but of the EEOC, as well.

A version of this chapter appeared on December 17, 2002, at writ.findlaw.com.

*Update: Litigation in this case continued for another five years and included another appeal to the Seventh Circuit Court of Appeals, this time on the question whether the EEOC could obtain monetary relief on behalf of partners who were barred from suing individually because they failed to timely file administrative charges of their own. The district court said yes, and the Seventh Circuit agreed on appeal.[14] The suit ultimately settled with a consent decree requiring Sidley Austin to pay $27.5 million to the band of 37 partners. The decree also ordered the firm to discontinue its practice of mandating retirement at a certain age.[15]*

# 9

## Punishing the Coach Who Stood Up for His Female Athletes

People don't like "complainers." Or, more accurately, people in power don't like people who complain about wrongdoing within institutions. And that is especially true if the complaint is about alleged discrimination and the complainers are women and/or persons of color.

According to social psychologists, women and racial minorities who complain about discrimination are perceived as irritating, hypersensitive, and all-around troublemakers.[1] And these negative perceptions persist even in the face of persuasive evidence that their complaints of discrimination are entirely justified.

People who experience discrimination know the uphill battle they face. Even if a victim is aware that discrimination has occurred, statistically, he or she is overwhelmingly unlikely to tell anyone in a position of authority. Research shows that victims are acutely aware of the costs of raising concerns of discrimination.

Not surprisingly, the fear of retaliation is the number one reason victims give for their silence: a victim who is not promoted because of discrimination may fear that if she complains, she will find herself out of the running for any future advancement within the company – or, worse, demoted, or fired.

For all of these reasons, the Supreme Court's decision in *Jackson v. Birmingham Board of Education* ranks among the most important of the Court's 2005 Term.[2] There, the Court recognized the right to sue for retaliation under Title IX, the federal law barring sex discrimination in federally funded education programs. (Title IX protects employees of educational institutions as well as students, although sometimes their claims are decided under Title VII instead.)

There is, however, a looming question the decision did not resolve – one that may be as, or even more, important than the basic question of whether a coach's suit for retaliation can succeed. The question is whether a complainer who happens to be legally or factually wrong about his or her claim of discrimination, can *legally* suffer retaliation for that complaint.

## THE FACTS AND CLAIMS IN *JACKSON*

In 1993, Jackson began coaching the girls' basketball team at Ensley High School in Birmingham, Alabama. He alleges that his team was denied equal funding and equal access to sports facilities and equipment, as compared with the boys' teams at the same school. Jackson also alleged that he complained to his supervisors about the discrimination.[3] After complaining, Jackson began receiving negative performance evaluations, and he was finally removed from his coaching position. (Jackson continues to hold a tenured position as a physical education teacher at the school.) He says that his removal from coaching was retaliatory.[4]

The Birmingham School Board has claimed in court that even if Jackson is right, he has no case. It argues that Title IX does not create a "private right of action" for retaliation – that is, even if the school retaliated, the statute does not allow Jackson to sue it for damages, or even prohibit the school from retaliating in this way.[5] The trial court and the U.S. Court of Appeals for the Eleventh Circuit both agreed with the school board.[6]

## THE LEGAL LANDSCAPE BEFORE THE SUPREME COURT'S DECISION IN *JACKSON*

Before Jackson sued, federal courts had uniformly assumed the existence of a right to sue for retaliation under Title IX and its parallel statute, Title VI, which prohibits race discrimination in all federally funded programs.[7] Granted, neither statute expressly creates any private cause of action. But implied rights of action are not uncommon in this context: the U.S. Supreme Court has held, for example, that a right of private individuals to sue for discrimination is implied under both Title IX and Title VI.[8]

The right to sue for retaliation, in the view of most courts, was implied as well in Title IX's broad guarantee against sex discrimination. (Even the U.S. Courts of Appeals for the Fourth and Fifth Circuits, widely thought to be the two most conservative federal appellate courts in the country, had reached this conclusion.[9]) But when Jackson's case went before the U.S. Court of Appeals for the Eleventh Circuit, this universally held, commonsense understanding of Title IX's scope was cast into doubt. The Eleventh Circuit suggested that *no one* was protected from retaliation under Title IX – not even, say, a player who pointed out discrimination and found herself cut from the team she loved. And certainly, the Eleventh Circuit claimed, a male coach was not protected under a statute meant to protect female athletes from discrimination.

The Supreme Court thus stepped into the fray, and sided against the Eleventh Circuit's crabbed reading of the statute. It is fortunate that it did: the Eleventh Circuit's interpretation would have transformed Title IX into a legal train wreck.

After all, who's more likely to point out discrimination to the authorities – a teenage athlete focused on her game, or a seasoned coach, with a long-term perspective, who's familiar with how both genders' teams are treated?

## THE MAJORITY OPINION: A THOUGHTFUL EMBRACE OF TITLE IX'S BROAD PURPOSE

Justice O'Connor's opinion for the five-member majority wisely recognized that failing to provide legal rights against retaliation would make a mockery of Title IX. Discrimination laws are meaningless and a waste of paper if people are forced or pressured to remain silent in the face of perceived discrimination. A lack of protection from retaliation would be particularly unfair under Title IX, which has been held to require individuals to give an institution notice of certain types of discrimination before they can pursue legal remedies against it. (For example, the Supreme Court has interpreted Title IX to mean that school officials have no obligation to respond to sexual harassment, either teacher-student or student-student, until they have *actual* notice it has occurred.[10])

Without protection from retaliation, this notice requirement would create a cruel catch-22 for the victim of harassment: either say nothing, and have no legal recourse against the harassment, or speak up and risk retaliation with no legal recourse to challenge it. The majority of the Court prudently chose to resolve this dilemma by protecting the victim from retaliation if she speaks out. That result comports with common sense and carries out the goals of Title IX, which include *effectively* preventing discrimination in high school and college athletics.

## FOUR JUSTICES JOINED AN UNPERSUASIVE DISSENT

Common sense should never be taken for granted, though, and the five to four split in *Jackson* is a reminder of that. Justice Thomas authored a dissent concluding that courts should never infer *any* protections that Congress has not explicitly spelled out.[11] However, as noted above, this view contradicts the Court's own precedent because the Court has many times inferred private rights of action of different sorts in order to effectuate Congress's goals in passing a given statute. Moreover, in this case, the argument for inferring a private right of action was especially strong. Congress opted for broad statutory language banning sex discrimination, and failing to imply a cause of action for retaliation would, in many cases (including this one), completely undermine the statute.

So Justice Thomas is doing no favors to Congress by declining to go beyond the literal words of its statute here. To the contrary, his view would only have ensured that Congress's objective in passing Title IX was severely undermined, and in many cases, defeated.

## WHO IS PROTECTED FROM RETALIATION?

Crucial to the majority opinion in *Jackson* is its recognition that Title IX must be read to protect *anyone* from retaliation for complaining against discrimination – whether or not the person retaliated against is the same person who was targeted for the underlying discrimination. The lower court in *Jackson* had ruled that a coach could not claim whatever protection Title IX offered against retaliation because the coach was not among the class of persons who experienced the discrimination.

The Court held, instead, that the coach was still, in the legal sense, a victim of sex discrimination. After all, the Court reasoned, the coach was punished because he complained about sex discrimination in particular. The discrimination, then, ended up affecting not only his players but him, as well.

The Court's ruling in this respect is extremely important. People who are not the primary targets of the discrimination are often in the best position to complain about it. Certainly in the school and university settings, teachers and employees are much more likely than students to have the information, courage, and presence of mind necessary to raise concerns about discrimination against students. Their complaints may also have the best chances of success. Again, social psychology research is informative. Studies confirm that the strongest social disapproval is reserved for persons who complain that they *themselves* have been subjected to discrimination. They are the most likely to be perceived negatively, as self-interested and oversensitive.

Granted, Jackson himself complained to a hostile administration, and, thus, his complaint did not, in fact, succeed. But some administrations will listen better than others (and many lawyers will advise them to listen closely) – and a coach may not know if his or her administration is hostile or receptive until he or she complains.

For the complaints to reach the ears of receptive administrators who can correct sex-based disparities, they must also be able to reach the ears of hostile administrators and yet not result in retaliation. Ironically, protecting complainants against retaliation also serves the interests of schools, which can avoid costly lawsuits by taking action to ensure equality. In this case, giving boys and girls equal access to the far superior gym, the expense account, and the team bus (or buying a second bus) would doubtless have been cheaper than defending the lawsuit.

## A QUESTION LEFT OPEN: CAN SCHOOLS BE LIABLE FOR RETALIATING AGAINST ULTIMATELY ERRONEOUS DISCRIMINATION CLAIMS?

Like many of Justice O'Connor's carefully worded opinions, *Jackson* leaves open a number of unanswered questions. Yet these questions ultimately may have a greater real-world impact for discrimination claimants than even the *Jackson* ruling itself. The biggest issue is how broadly Title IX's protection against retaliation extends. How, for example, will courts treat a claimant who honestly, *but erroneously,* believed a Title IX violation had occurred? Is such a person still protected from retaliation?

There's an important ambiguity here. *Jackson* says that retaliation is covered by Title IX because it *is* a form of intentional sex discrimination, by virtue of the fact that the underlying complaint was "about sex discrimination." Does that mean a complaint must be based on *actionable, unlawful* sex discrimination in order to be retaliation-proof? Or does that language simply mean the complaint must literally be "about sex discrimination," meaning that the complaint relates to a concern about *alleged* (but not, in the end, actual) sex discrimination?

Justice O'Connor's opinion does not resolve this important issue. In a footnote, Justice O'Connor notes that "[w]e agree with Justice Thomas that plaintiffs may not assert claims under Title IX for conduct not prohibited by the statute."[12] But that language is insufficient to tell us whether it is enough that the complainant honestly perceived sex discrimination, or whether that perception must be judged "reasonable," with the limits on reasonableness set by courts' own interpretations of the law.

## SEVERAL FEDERAL APPEALS COURTS HAVE DISMISSED RETALIATION CLAIMS BASED ON ULTIMATELY ERRONEOUS DISCRIMINATION CLAIMS

Consider another federal case, *Peters v. Jenney*,[13] which involved Title IX's sister statute, Title VI. There, the plaintiff was hired by a Virginia school district to serve as the director of the gifted program. The school had historically had problems with Title VI and was under investigation by the Office for Civil Rights. She thought she had uncovered a Title VI violation when she realized the program's selection criteria yielded a disproportionately low number of African-American students. She made efforts to correct the problem on the school's behalf, and, for her efforts, she was fired.

The Fourth Circuit allowed her retaliation claim, but said she could only prevail if the conduct she pointed to actually did violate Title VI. Only then, it held, could she have had a "reasonable belief" that there had been a violation. Under the law of Title VI, that meant she had to prove *intentional* discrimination, not simply disparate impact on the protected class (here, the African-American students). Yet intentional discrimination is notoriously hard to prove. No lawyer, much less a layperson, can predict with certainty whether a practice that unnecessarily disadvantages a protected class is based on an intent to discriminate.

That's unfair: it might make sense to require a plaintiff to have a good-faith belief that discrimination occurred. But it is not fair to allow a plaintiff to legally suffer retaliation because, while she pointed to evidence of discrimination (here, the small number of African-Americans in gifted classes), that evidence did not, in the end, turn out to be enough.

## A "REASONABLE BELIEF" OF RETALIATION: A MISGUIDED REQUIREMENT

Unfortunately, courts that interpret Title VII have similarly held that if a plaintiff isn't right on the law, then retaliation against her is perfectly legal. In *Galdieri-Ambrosini v. National Realty & Development Corporation*,[14] for example, a female secretary complained that her employer assigned her duties based on gender stereotyping. For instance, she had to attend to her boss's personal matters during work hours. After complaining to her employer, she said, she suffered retaliation. But the U.S. Court of Appeals for the Second Circuit rejected her retaliation claim because it said she was wrong on the law: Title VII, according to the court, does *not* prohibit supervisors from giving secretaries "female-gendered" work or requiring them to assist them with personal matters. In effect, this secretary was asked to be a lawyer – and a conservative one at that. (Many legal scholars have persuasively argued that Title VII should cover the assignment of gender-stereotyped work to persons in female-dominated jobs, and the devaluation of female-gendered jobs.)

The U.S. Court of Appeals for the Seventh Circuit reached a similar conclusion in *Hamner v. St. Vincent*.[15] There, a male nurse claimed he was terminated for complaining of harassment based on his sexual orientation. But courts have held that Title VII does not prohibit sexual orientation discrimination, as discussed in Chapter 19, so even though the plaintiff thought the law was otherwise, the court rejected his retaliation claim. (Here, too, legal scholars have made persuasive arguments agreeing with the plaintiff and a growing number, albeit a minority, of courts have begun to break down the distinction between sex and sexual orientation as a basis for discrimination.)

## EVEN COMPLAINANTS WHO TURN OUT TO BE WRONG SHOULD BE PROTECTED FROM RETALIATION

No layperson is likely to have a perfect understanding of the contours of discrimination law. After all, even lawyers often disagree in their interpretations of what discrimination law requires. So courts should not punish laypersons who bring good-faith retaliation claims just because they are mistaken about the law's coverage. Ironically, under Rule 11 of the Federal Rules of Civil Procedure, even attorneys can escape sanctions when they argue for a good-faith extension of the law. Certainly, laypersons should, if anything, have more leeway. If they do not, we may see an ugly trend of complainants who lose their cases because they did not have a perfect understanding of the law.

Imagine, for instance, that Coach Jackson had missed an important legal caveat to Title IX – say, the inequities between the girls' and boys' basketball programs were counterbalanced by similar inequalities that favored girls' teams in other sports. In such circumstances, the overall athletic program would not violate Title IX, notwithstanding the coach's good-faith belief otherwise. If the court had applied a reasonable belief standard, the coach's good-faith attempt to protect his team members would have left him out in the cold. Such a result would chill persons from complaining of discrimination, regardless of the merits of the claim, because few people would be willing to bet their careers on their certainty of their knowledge of the law. That can't be the right interpretation of a law that means to protect against discrimination rather than encourage it.

A version of this chapter appeared on April 5, 2005, at writ.findlaw.com, and was coauthored by Deborah L. Brake.

# Broader Protection against Workplace Retaliation

On June 22, 2006, the Supreme Court issued an important decision interpreting Title VII of the Civil Rights Act of 1964. Title VII not only bans discrimination on the basis of protected characteristics like race and sex but also expressly prohibits retaliation against those who assert their rights against discrimination. The two main questions for the Court in *Burlington Northern & Santa Fe Railway Co. v. White* were the following: Must a retaliatory act be work related in order to violate Title VII?[1] And when is retaliation serious enough to be actionable?

The Supreme Court, in a majority opinion authored by Justice Breyer and joined by all but one justice, answered these questions with a new test that has the potential to provide employees with robust protection against retaliation. (Justice Alito concurred in the judgment but refused to join the opinion because he felt the newly adopted test was too broad.) Whether the test's potential is realized, however, will depend on whether lower courts, in applying it, take into account the ways in which employees experience retaliation at work, and the lengths to which employees will go to avoid such consequences.

## SHEILA WHITE: A WOMAN IN A MAN'S WORLD

Here are the facts of the case that came before the Court: Sheila White, a woman with experience operating forklifts, applied for a job in the Maintenance of Way department of Burlington Northern & Santa Fe Railway Company. The roadmaster, Marvin Brown, hired White as a track laborer, a job that included everything from removing litter to replacing track components. Soon after White was hired, a more skilled, more desirable position – operating the forklift – became available. Brown immediately assigned her to it.

White's immediate supervisor, Bill Joiner, however, told her women should not be working in the Maintenance of Way department. She complained, and he was suspended for that, for other insults, and inappropriate remarks directed at White.

The suspension made sense, for his hostile behavior was of the type that can contribute to an unlawful, sex-based hostile environment, which violates Title VII.

According to the jury's findings, White suffered retaliation for complaining about Joiner's behavior: she was removed from forklift duty and restricted to track laborer tasks. When informing her of the reassignment, Brown told her a "more senior man" should have the "less arduous and cleaner job" of forklift operator.[2] Faced with more evidence of sex discrimination, White complained again – this time to the EEOC – alleging that her reassignment was retaliation for her earlier complaint.

Shortly after White filed this second complaint, another supervisor reported that White had been insubordinate during a dispute about the proper location of a truck. White was suspended without pay for thirty-seven days, supposedly because of the insubordination, though she was ultimately reinstated when the company concluded during an internal grievance procedure that she had not in fact been insubordinate. The jury found that White had once again suffered retaliation for complaining about discrimination – hidden by the flimsy pretext of her supposed insubordination.

## WHAT CONSTITUTES UNLAWFUL RETALIATION?
## TWO KEY QUESTIONS

The question in White's case is whether the retaliation she suffered was sufficient to constitute a violation of Title VII. The statute's anti-retaliation provision prohibits employers from taking actions that "discriminate against" an employee or applicant because she has "opposed" a practice made unlawful by Title VII's antidiscrimination provisions.

When does retaliation "discriminate against" an employee? Again, that depends on how one interprets Title VII's anti-retaliation provision with respect to those two crucial issues: (1) whether the retaliatory action has to be workplace related, and (2) how serious the retaliatory action must be in order to be actionable.

## THE FIRST QUESTION: MUST THE RETALIATION BE
## WORK RELATED?

The U.S. Court of Appeals for the Sixth Circuit had ruled in this case that a plaintiff must show an "adverse *employment* action" in order to prove retaliation.[3] In earlier cases, the Fifth and Eighth Circuits had adopted an even stricter version of this standard, requiring that a retaliatory act constitute an "ultimate" employment action – such as demotion, firing, or change in compensation – in order to be actionable.[4]

Under both versions of this standard, only work-related retaliatory acts could be held to run afoul of Title VII. So, for example, if a supervisor phoned in a death threat to an employee at home after she complained about his sexist behavior at work, the employee would not have an actionable claim of retaliation even if the supervisor's underlying conduct violated Title VII, there was clear evidence of a causal relationship between the complaint and the threat, and a similar threat would deter any employee from filing a complaint of retaliation. It is hard to believe Congress would have wanted to leave this kind of retaliation out of Title VII's purview as such behavior could seriously undermine enforcement of the statute's antidiscrimination provisions.

Fortunately, the U.S. Courts of Appeal for the Seventh, Ninth, and D.C. Circuits took a broader view of what kind of retaliation is illegal under Title VII. They all held that retaliation need not be work related as long as it is sufficient to dissuade a reasonable employee from complaining about discrimination.[5]

The Supreme Court in *Burlington Northern* took the broader view, as well, holding that the "scope of the anti-retaliation provision extends beyond workplace-related or employment-related retaliatory acts and harm."[6] This broad protection, the Court explained, would help "ensure the cooperation upon which accomplishment of the Act's primary objective [to prevent employment discrimination] depends."[7]

The Court was right to reach the holding it did. (Note that the question of work relatedness should not have been much of an issue in White's case. The suspension without pay was clearly work-related and any harm resulting from the loss of income was arguably work related, as well.) Employees who fear non-workplace retaliation are just as unlikely to complain or cooperate with an internal investigation as employees who fear workplace retaliation are. The retaliation provision, thus, must be broad enough to provide employees with meaningful protection.

## THE SECOND QUESTION: HOW BAD DOES THE RETALIATION HAVE TO BE

The second question, more relevant for White's suit, relates to the proper legal standard for retaliatory acts: How bad do they have to be before Title VII is violated?

Again, federal appellate courts disagreed with one another; although they all agreed that retaliation must produce some injury or harm in order to come under Title VII, they articulated different standards for harm. The Supreme Court in *Burlington Northern* adopted the formulation set forth by the U.S. Courts of Appeal for the Seventh and D.C. Circuits: "[A] plaintiff must show that a reasonable employee would have found the challenged action *materially adverse*, which in this context means *it might well* have dissuaded a reasonable worker from making or supporting a charge of discrimination."[8]

According to the Supreme Court, this standard, by requiring that the retaliatory act be "materially adverse," will "separate significant from trivial harms."[9] Also, by using a "reasonable employee" as the reference point, it will avoid "the uncertainties and unfair discrepancies that can plague a judicial effort to determine a plaintiff's unusual subjective feelings."[10]

In addition, this standard rightly leaves the way open for claims that coworker harassment that is tolerated, condoned, or encouraged by management is "materially adverse" enough to come under Title VII. Lower courts have split over whether coworker harassment, however egregious and flagrant, can *ever* be considered unlawful retaliation under Title VII. But misbehavior by coworkers can be just as chilling to victimized employees as that of their supervisors, and the law needs to sweep broadly to protect an employee's right against retaliation.

Applying the newly articulated standard to White's case, the Supreme Court upheld the original jury verdict in her favor. On the first question, the company did not appeal the jury's finding that the actions taken against her were in retaliation for her complaints, and the Court made clear it didn't matter whether or not the actions were work related. On the second question, the Supreme Court deemed a suspension without pay for more than a month and reassignment to a less desirable position sufficiently adverse to satisfy its materiality standard.

The Supreme Court's new test for retaliation preserved Sheila White's victory against her employer, vindicating her right to work in a man's world without punishment. But will the test, on balance, be effective in combating retaliation more generally? That depends on whether lower courts take into account the ways in which retaliation occurs in the actual workplace and the impact it has on real victims.

## JUSTICE ALITO'S MISGUIDED DISSENT

In a concurring opinion, Justice Alito refused to endorse the new test, arguing, instead, for a much stricter standard that would likely prove fatal to many claims of retaliation.[11] His approach is a conservative first step for the newly appointed justice, one that does not bode well for future support of workplace equality. Whereas the Court's test deems a "materially adverse" retaliatory action sufficient until Title VII, Justice Alito, in his concurrence, seems to endorse the much-tougher "tangible employment action" standard – which would count only demotions, firings, changes in compensation, and the like as retaliation.[12]

Justice Alito has it precisely wrong: in light of the realities of retaliation, and its power to deter employee complaints, the Court's standard for how serious retaliation must be should not be more strict and, more important, must be implemented in a way that is sensitive to workplace realities.

Unfortunately, when people complain of on-the-job discrimination, retaliation is more the norm than the aberration. Among all the different types of discrimination claims in the employment context, retaliation is the most common. In 2005, nearly 30 percent of charges filed with the EEOC were for retaliation.[13]

Hard data are tough to come by, but studies typically show that between 30 percent and 60 percent of employees who report discrimination experience retaliation.[14] Workers know this reality, and they understand that complaining about discrimination comes with significant risks. Indeed, according to survey data, the fear of retaliation is the single most common reason why people decide not to report discrimination in the first place.

Given the obvious chilling effect of retaliation, the Supreme Court was right on target in holding that Title VII must prohibit *any* employer action – workplace related or not – that would deter a reasonable person from reporting discrimination. But, while the Court adopted a broad legal standard, its explication of it significantly understates the extent to which concerns about retaliation actually chill the reporting of discrimination.

Justice Breyer's opinion suggests that "normally petty slights, minor annoyances, and simple lack of good manners," along with "'snubbing' by supervisors and cowork-ers" are *not* the kinds of actions that would deter a reasonable employee from reporting discrimination.[15] Yet social science data on retaliation suggest that this prediction about the effects of anticipating seemingly "trivial" retaliatory actions (or seeing others endure these actions) on the average employee's likelihood to complain is probably not accurate.[16]

The cold, hard truth is that even apart from retaliation, the social costs of reporting discrimination are extremely high. A woman or person of color who complains of discrimination in the workplace is likely to be perceived as hypersensitive and a trou-blemaker. Perversely, this reaction is all the more likely when discrimination claims are well-founded; apparently, some colleagues and supervisors are especially angered when a complainant voices an ugly truth. Even in the face of solid evidence that a person has indeed experienced discrimination, reporting discrimination triggers strong social penalties.

The social costs of complaining act as a powerful deterrent to reporting discrim-ination. Study after study has shown that employees are very unlikely to report discrimination unless they have reason to believe they will have strong *social* sup-port.[17] Yet the loss of social support is exactly what the Court dismisses as "trivial" and, therefore, not actionable. Trivial or not, the reality is that the fear of an adverse social response is, by itself, enough to deter many victim-employees from reporting discrimination.

The Court's assumptions about what might deter employee complaints are not surprising. The realities of reporting, and of the impact of anticipated retaliation, contrast sharply with how most people *think* they themselves would respond if confronted with discrimination. In studies of college-age women, for example, the subjects typically insist that they would respond quite forcefully if they were sexually harassed. But in reality, when actually faced with such behavior in the workplace, most women respond timidly – by ignoring it, avoiding instead of confronting it, and almost never reporting it.[18]

Given the gap between expectations and reality, the danger is that judges and juries applying the new reasonableness standard will use their own assumptions about how they think they would behave if they experienced discrimination. If so, then this exercise will no doubt lead, as it has in the sexual harassment context, to a legal world in which employees are deemed *unreasonable* for being deterred by seemingly modest adverse actions – even though those supposedly modest actions, in practice, can have a powerful, chilling effect. The danger is that the typical employee, who exhibits the typical response to "trivial" actions, will be deemed unreasonable – and only the rare employee who is "an island unto himself" (or herself) will be deemed reasonable.

Given the realities regarding retaliation, the inquiry whether retaliation in a particular case would likely deter a reasonable person from complaining should be undertaken with great care. Judges and juries must be careful not to add to the disincentives that already operate to suppress discrimination claims, by tolerating retaliatory acts.

Federal courts, of course, must obey the Supreme Court in its choice to rule out teasing and social slights as insufficiently adverse to support a claim of retaliation. But at the same time, they should deem negative treatment that goes beyond mild forms of social disapproval from colleagues and supervisors sufficiently retaliatory.

A version of this chapter appeared on July 7 and 11, 2006, at writ.findlaw.com, and was coauthored by Deborah L. Brake.

*Update: Although the Court in* Burlington Northern *purported to expand protection against retaliation, lower court interpretations have taken a cramped and narrow approach when determining whether an employer action "might have dissuaded a reasonable worker from making or supporting a charge of discrimination." For example, in* Higgins v. Gonzales, *the Eighth Circuit ruled that withholding mentoring or supervision did not meet the standard for "likely to deter" a complaint without proof that it had a tangible impact on the plaintiff's employment situation.[19] Nor would transfer to a lateral position in a different city; the plaintiff's concerns about relocating her family and changing her child's school were dismissed as "the normal inconveniences associated with any transfer" and not likely to impact a discrimination victim's decision whether to file a complaint.[20] Courts seem to have little regard for context or the individual circumstances that might make certain employees especially sensitive to particular adverse actions. As a result, many employers' actions that are quite likely to deter reporting of discrimination are left undisturbed and unregulated.[21] The law protects only those complainants who fit a mythical ideal–highly vigilant, fully informed, and not easily deterred. In later Title VII cases, Justice Alito continued on this trajectory–rejecting considerations of context in favor of clear, bright-line rules that often do not comport with the practical realities of discrimination in the workplace (see Chapter 47). This focus may explain why some boys who had once played on his little league team told me he was their favorite coach: "He never yells and frankly doesn't care whether we win; it was all about keeping the stats book accurately."*

11

## The Supreme Court Protects Retaliation Victims but Still Leaves Gaps in the Law

The Supreme Court voted unanimously in *Crawford v. Metropolitan Government of Nashville and Davidson County* to reverse a federal appellate ruling that had denied protection from retaliation to employees who participate as witnesses in an employer's internal investigation of sexual harassment charges brought by other employees.[1] This was a clear win for victims of discrimination, but the ruling stops short of a slam dunk for employees who risk retaliation for participating in an employer investigation into discrimination charges.

The Court's ruling in *Crawford* was *essential* to keeping the entire liability scheme under Title VII from becoming a charade – one in which employers avoid liability by conducting internal investigations but render such procedures useless by deterring employees from coming forward with information. The appellate decision in *Crawford* was an obvious obstacle to the integrity of Title VII's enforcement scheme and needed to be reversed. Even so, however, further development of the law is needed to ensure the adequate protection of employees from retaliation, and to fully enforce Title VII's core promise of nondiscrimination.

### THE CLAIM OF RETALIATION IN *CRAWFORD*

Here are the facts in *Crawford* itself: Vicky Crawford had worked for city government for thirty years when she was called in by a human resources officer to answer questions about allegations by other employees of "inappropriate behavior" by the city school district's director of employee relations, Gene Hughes. Although Crawford herself had been sexually harassed by Hughes, she never filed a complaint because, as she explained, Hughes was the very person responsible for receiving such complaints. Other employees, however, did come forward with allegations of Hughes's sexually harassing behavior, prompting the employer to investigate. At the time the internal investigation took place, none of the complaining employees had yet filed a charge with the EEOC.

Crawford, along with two other women interviewed in the course of the investigation, expressed the fear that she would be fired if she told the truth about Hughes. As she saw it, Hughes was "very good friends" with the school district director. Nevertheless, Crawford cooperated in the investigation and told investigators Hughes had, in fact, sexually harassed her and other employees, describing his lewd behavior in detail. She told the investigator, among other things, Hughes had "asked to 'see her titties' on numerous occasions," and that she would say "'Hey Dr. Hughes, What's Up?" and he would "grab his crotch" in response and state, "You know what's up." She also mentioned that he "would approach her window and put his crotch up to the window." Finally, she told the investigator, on one occasion, Hughes had come into her office, and, when she asked what she could do for him, "he grabbed her head and pulled it to his crotch."[2]

Although all three women who were interviewed described similar sexually harassing behaviors by Hughes, the city's investigators were unwilling to conclude that Hughes had actually engaged in the behaviors described because each of the women was alone with Hughes at the time of the alleged harassment and because Hughes denied that the behaviors occurred. The investigation did conclude that Hughes had engaged in "inappropriate and unprofessional behavior" in some respects, but the company took no disciplinary action against him. And, just as they had feared, all three of the women who provided information were fired shortly thereafter.

If, as Crawford claims, the employer fired her *because* she corroborated the sexual harassment allegations about Hughes in an internal investigation, is that unlawful retaliation? That was the question for the Supreme Court in *Crawford*, and the Court answered it affirmatively – and, we will argue, rightly so.

## TITLE VII'S PROTECTION AGAINST RETALIATION

The decision turned on the Court's construction of Title VII's anti-retaliation provisions. Title VII from retaliating against employees for enforcing their rights. The specific protection comes in two separate clauses:

First, the "participation" clause makes it unlawful to discriminate against an employee "because...he has made a charge, testified, assisted, or participated in any manner in an investigation, proceeding, or hearing under this subchapter."[3] This clause is most often invoked to protect employees who participate in Title VII's formal enforcement mechanisms, by, for example, filing a charge with the EEOC or a lawsuit. Employee actions that are covered by this clause receive the broadest protection from retaliation, for this clause protects employees from adverse consequences regardless of the merits of the underlying discrimination complaint, as long as the employee acted in good faith.

Second, an alternative source of protection from retaliation makes it unlawful for an employer to discriminate against an employee "because he has opposed any practice made an unlawful employment practice by this subchapter."[4] The "opposition" clause has been applied to protect from retaliation those employees who oppose discrimination outside formal processes – for example, by bringing concerns to the attention of the employer informally, rather than (or prior to) filing an EEOC charge. But the protection for employees under this clause is narrower. Specifically, it is limited to only those acts of "opposition" that rest on an objectively "reasonable" belief, both factually and legally, that the employer actually violated Title VII.

In this case, Crawford argued that both the participation clause and the opposition clause applied, and should have protected her from being fired for providing truthful, good-faith information about Hughes's alleged harassment. Yet the U.S. Court of Appeals for the Sixth Circuit disagreed on both counts, leaving her unprotected under either clause.

## THE ISSUE IN *CRAWFORD*: WHAT IS "OPPOSITION" TO DISCRIMINATION?

In *Crawford*, the Sixth Circuit ruled first that the plaintiff's participation was outside the reach of the participation clause because no formal EEOC charge had yet been filed. It also ruled that she was not protected under the opposition clause because, by merely answering questions, and not bringing a complaint herself about Hughes, she did not "oppose" the discrimination. In support of this conclusion, the appellate court distinguished "active, consistent 'opposing activities'" from mere cooperation in an employer investigation. This cramped interpretation of the opposition clause was at odds with rulings from other federal appellate courts, which had treated an employee who provides corroborating information to support another complaining employee's allegations as "opposing" the discrimination.

Fortunately, the Supreme Court took a more commonsense and reasonable view of "opposition," assigning the term its ordinary meaning: "to resist or antagonize . . . to content against; to confront; resist; withstand."[5] Although "opposition" certainly encompasses the kind of active resistance and instigation contemplated by the Sixth Circuit, the Court reasoned, it includes other forms of opposition, as well. As the Court wrote, "Countless people were known to 'oppose' slavery before Emancipation, or are said to 'oppose' capital punishment today, without writing public letters, taking to the streets, or resisting the government. . . . There is, then, no reason to doubt that a person can 'oppose' by responding to someone else's question just as surely as by provoking the discussion."

For further support, the Court cited the EEOC Compliance Manual, which provides that an employee's description of discriminatory conduct in the workplace virtually always "constitutes the employee's *opposition* to the activity," unless she makes clear that she condones or supports the behavior.[6] Accordingly, the Court concluded that Crawford's statement "is thus covered by the opposition clause, as an ostensibly disapproving account of sexually obnoxious behavior toward her by a fellow employee, an answer she says antagonized her employer to the point of sacking her on a false pretense."[7]

Justice Alito and Thomas concurred in the judgment, but wrote separately to caution that protection under the opposition clause does not extend to "silent opposition" or opposition that is "not active and purposive."[8] Their concern was that extending the protections of the opposition clause to reach, for example, informal chats with coworkers or private expressions of feeling outside the workplace would create practical proof problems and expand the retaliation claim too far. They wrote separately to emphasize that they would not extend the statute's protection to "employees who do not communicate their views to their employers through purposive conduct" – admittedly, not the scenario at issue in the *Crawford* case, in which Vicky Crawford purposefully accused her boss of sexual harassment in an investigation by her employer.[9]

## WHY THE SUPREME COURT GOT IT RIGHT

The Court's definition of "opposition" is far superior to the Sixth Circuit's, for several reasons. It does not, for example, impose a stereotypically male view of opposition that is combative, adversarial, and overtly assertive. Surveys and studies show that most women who experience sexual harassment tend to avoid direct challenges to the behavior or confrontations with the harasser. The clear tendency, instead, is to minimize, excuse, or trivialize it – a rational response to the powerful social and institutional pressures on lower-level employees generally, and women especially, not to complain. And yet women who are courageous enough to tell the truth about a sexual harasser in an employer investigation into harassment – as these three employees were, to their peril – surely "oppose" the discrimination even though they did not initiate the underlying complaint.

In a rebuke to the court below, Justice Souter did not mince words when he observed that "nothing in the statute requires a freakish rule protecting an employee who reports discrimination on her own initiative but not one who reports the same discrimination in the same words when her boss asks her a question."[10] There are many ways of opposing discrimination in the workplace, and the Court appropriately rejected a view that would have protected only one form of opposition, acting as a complainant.

The Court's ruling also takes account of workplace realities, and the very real risk and fear of retaliation that employees face even with "mere cooperation," much less active instigation of a complaint – a risk that allegedly was realized in the *Crawford* case itself, with three firings. As the Court acknowledged, lesser protection for retaliation would mean that "prudent employees would have a good reason to keep quiet about Title VII offenses against themselves or against others."[11] And yet scared employees would find themselves in a real predicament if called to answer questions by their employer or else face punishment for insubordination and obstruction if they refused.

An employee fearing retaliation for telling the truth and punishment for staying silent or appearing uncooperative might be tempted to feign ignorance, memory lapse, or, worse, lie to protect an accused harasser. Such responses would greatly undermine the statutory goal of voluntary compliance, and would leave the complainant out in the cold, with the discrimination unverified and unremedied. Nothing in Title VII requires employees to face such a predicament.

Finally, the Court clearly understood that the Sixth Circuit rule undermined a core piece of the statutory liability scheme: the inducement for employers to establish and follow policies and procedures to investigate, correct, and prevent discrimination. In order to avoid liability in sexual harassment cases, and to minimize the risk of punitive damages in any discrimination case, employers must establish procedures for investigating and responding to allegations of discrimination. The very legitimacy of Title VII would be called into question if the liability rules ensured that employers internally investigated discrimination complaints, but the statute offered no relief if every witness who gave information supporting the complainant in such an investigation was fired for having done so. As the Court forcefully concluded, "Nothing in the statute's text or our precedent supports this Catch-22."[12]

## WHY MORE PROTECTION AGAINST RETALIATION IS STILL NEEDED: COURTS – IDEALLY THE SUPREME COURT – SHOULD ALSO FIND THAT PROTECTION EXISTS UNDER THE PARTICIPATION CLAUSE

Under the Court's interpretation, Crawford's conduct was clearly protected under the opposition clause. As a result, the Court did not need to, and did not, review the lower court's ruling denying Crawford protection under the participation clause. This is understandable in Crawford's case, but it may prove unfortunate for other employees.

Protection from retaliation is substantially greater under the participation clause than it is under the opposition clause. This is because the courts apply an objective "reasonable belief" test to limit protected conduct under the opposition clause. An employee who opposes conduct she perceives as discriminatory is only protected under the opposition clause if the court agrees that her belief that discrimination occurred was objectively reasonable. In a trend that has become increasingly troubling in the lower courts, courts have denied employees protection under this doctrine in myriad cases, including those where the employee's belief was mistaken because it rested on an incorrect understanding of the law, or where it lacked sufficient factual support that discrimination occurred.

As discussed in Chapter 9, some lower courts have applied this doctrine very harshly, cutting far back on the protections employees need to enforce their rights under the law. For example, in one Fourth Circuit case, an employee was denied protection from retaliation under the opposition clause because he did not have a *reasonable* belief that a blatantly racist comment by a coworker rose to the level of creating an unlawful racially hostile environment. In that case, the court ruled that although a pattern of such comments would violate Title VII, that one incident standing alone was not severe enough to support a *reasonable* belief that unlawful harassment had occurred. As a result, any retaliation that the complainant faced for reporting the racially harassing remark through the employer's established procedures was not actionable under Title VII.

As harsh as this doctrine is when it is applied to deny protection from retaliation to employees who complain about perceived discrimination, it is that much worse when applied to employees who provide information in support of a colleague's complaint. An employee who provides information as a witness does not have control over whether someone else files a complaint or whether an employer initiates an investigation. That employee is just told to provide information and respond to questions. Is that employee to be denied protection from retaliation because the complaining party lacked a *reasonable* belief that the employer violated the law?

In the Fourth Circuit case discussed above, for example, if the employer had called in another employee who was present when the alleged offending remark was made, and that employee had verified the complainant's account, could the employer then retaliate against that employee because it turned out that, according to the Fourth Circuit, the belief that unlawful racial harassment occurred was not *reasonable*? Such a result would again make a mockery of internal procedures – the very mockery the Supreme Court was determined to avoid in *Crawford*.

Thankfully, the lower courts need not reach such a result. Although the Supreme Court did not reach the participation clause issue in *Crawford*, this clause can and should be read to cover employee participation in internal employer EEO processes, regardless of whether a formal EEOC charge has yet been filed. Title VII's participation clause is broad enough to encompass participation in internal employer investigations of discrimination, as well as EEOC investigations and lawsuits. Internal employer proceedings have become increasingly commonplace and integral to the liability scheme created by the statute. Employees who cooperate with such investigations should have the same important protection against retaliation whether or not the investigation takes place before or after an EEOC charge has been filed. Participation "in an investigation, proceeding, or hearing under this subchapter" refers to Title VII as a whole, not more narrowly to the specific provision in Section 706(b) that establishes the EEOC enforcement process.

If the choice between the participation clause and opposition clause would make a difference in a future case, courts should pay close attention to the Supreme Court's reasoning in *Crawford* and find protection for those who participate in internal investigations under both the participation clause and the opposition clause.

A version of this chapter appeared on February 3, 2009, at writ.findlaw.com, and was coauthored by Deborah L. Brake.

*Update: The Supreme Court has since heard two additional cases on retaliation, perhaps a record number on a single aspect of discrimination law. In* Thompson v. North American Stainless, *the Court held that retaliating against a complainant by firing her fiancé is actionable retaliation – and the fiancé can proceed as the aggrieved party in an EEOC charge.*[13] *And in* University of Texas Southwestern Medical Center v. Nassar, *a 5-4 majority of the court took a restrictive view of causation in workplace retaliation cases, holding that a plaintiff must prove not simply that the discrimination complaint was a motivating factor for the retaliation, but that it was* the *reason for the action.*[14]

# Sexual Harassment

"He said it's all about holding on to tradition while embracing the future. I told him to keep his hands to himself."

ART 2 © Mike Baldwin / CartoonStock. Used by permission.

*I did a pretty good job of knowing where to draw the line.*
> (Herman Cain, 2012 presidential candidate, accused of sexually harassing several
> female subordinates)

*Most people are robust. If a man puts his hand on a woman's bottom, any woman worth her
salt can deal with it. It is communication. Can't we be friendly?*
> (Jeremy Irons, Actor)


"Sexual harassment" is a familiar term to most people today. We might gossip
about which public figure has recently been accused of it or a salacious detail of
a particular harassment scandal, but we tend not to discuss what harassment is or
whether it is a matter for the law to address. Not so when Jane Corne and Geneva
DeVane filed a complaint in the mid-1970s against their employer, Bausch and
Lomb, in which they complained that a male supervisor had subjected them to
repeated verbal and physical sexual advances at work, escalating to the point that
both women were forced to resign.[1] The complaint in their lawsuit alleged that the
supervisor's behavior violated Title VII of the Civil Rights Act of 1964, which had
been on the books for more than a decade. The imposition of unwanted sexual
advances by a supervisor at work constitutes, they argued, a form of illegal sex discrimination.

The federal trial court judge was incredulous. After all, he pointed out, all previous
cases of actionable sex discrimination "arose out of company policies" and involved
"apparently some advantage to, or gain by, the employer from such discriminatory
practices." But this supervisor's conduct "appears to be nothing more than a personal
proclivity, peculiarity or mannerism. . . . [He] was satisfying a personal urge." How,
then, could "it be construed that the conduct complained of was company-directed
policy which deprived women of employment opportunities?" And how could a
"reasonably intelligent reading of the statute" cover actions, even by a supervisor,
with "no relationship to the nature of employment"? This, the judge concluded,
would be "ludicrous" and would mean "a potential federal lawsuit every time any
employee made amorous or sexually oriented advances toward another." Employers,
he cautioned, would be forced to "have employees who were asexual," the "only sure
way . . . [to] avoid such charges." Were there enough asexual adults in 1975 to make
all those contact lenses? Apparently not. The court dismissed the case, on grounds
that the women had failed to state a claim under Title VII.

The judge in *Corne* was not a rogue caveman. He was the product of an age
when sexual harassment had yet to be labeled, conceptualized, or incorporated into
discrimination law. In a similar case the following year, a federal district judge
dismissed a complaint alleging sexual assault on the theory that Title VII was "not
intended to provide a federal tort remedy for what amounts to a physical attack
motivated by sexual desire on the part of a supervisor and which happened to occur

in a corporate corridor rather than a back alley."[2] While both of these rulings were losses for the plaintiffs, they nonetheless were touchstones in the development of sexual harassment law, signaling emerging awareness that sexual conduct at work, long experienced but seldom discussed, might put women at a disadvantage.

Beginning with a federal appellate ruling in 1977, courts did begin to recognize sexual harassment as a form of discrimination under Title VII. In that case, *Barnes v. Costle*, the court concluded that if a woman proved she was fired for refusing to sleep with her supervisor, she had established actionable discrimination.[3] "It is much too late in the day," the court wrote, "to contend that Title VII does not outlaw terms of employment for women which differ appreciably from those set for men, and which are not genuinely and reasonably related to performance on the job."[4] And "but for her womanhood . . . her participation in sexual activity would never have been solicited. . . . [She] was asked to bow to his demands as the price for holding her job."[5] Moreover, it was no defense for the employer to explain that the conduct violated company policy or that it redressed the misconduct once discovered.

On the heels of this ruling, in 1979, Catharine MacKinnon published her ground-breaking book, *The Sexual Harassment of Working Women: A Case of Sex Discrimination*. The title says it all. MacKinnon set forth a cogent theory that explained why sexual harassment should be treated as actionable discrimination and developed a set of substantive principles about what constitutes harassment and who can be held liable for it. The following year, her principles were adopted more or less wholesale by the EEOC, and the courts came around soon thereafter.[6] The relatively quick acceptance of sexual harassment as an actionable wrong did not occur in a vacuum. Rather, it was a reflection of growing social awareness of the unfair treatment of women in the workplace, depicted so masterfully on the big screen in *Nine to Five*, as discussed in the Preface. But rampant and overt harassment was not the product of an inventive filmmaker's mind. A popular women's magazine, *Redbook*, published results of a survey in 1976, entitled *What Men Do to Women on the Job*, which found sexual comments and advances to be pervasive in the workplace.[7] In 1981, the federal government published a results of a comprehensive survey reporting that four in ten federal employees – the federal government was and is the nation's largest employer – had experienced harassing behaviors in the prior two years.[8] These surveys were part of a growing chorus that led to the collective labeling of certain behaviors as "sexual harassment" and the use of emerging Title VII discrimination doctrine to address them.[9]

The decades that followed would keep courts occupied with lots of questions: What is sexual harassment? What does it have to do with equal employment opportunity? And who can be held liable for it?

The basic contours of harassment doctrine under Title VII were hammered out early on. The EEOC guidelines, discussed above, defined actionable harassment as the following:

Unwelcome sexual advances, requests for sexual favors, and other verbal or physical conduct of a sexual nature . . . when (1) submission to such conduct is made either explicitly or implicitly a term or condition of an individual's employment, (2) submission to or rejection of such conduct by an individual is used as the basis for employment decisions affecting such individual, or (3) such conduct has the purpose or effect of unreasonably interfering with an individual's work performance or creating an intimidating, hostile, or offensive working environment.[10]

In shorthand, the types of harassment described in these guidelines became known as "quid pro quo" and "hostile environment." Those categories stuck, and we still understand claims of harassment to fall into one of the two. Quid pro quo harassment is when the harasser proposes an exchange of sexual consideration for some workplace advantage. In its crudest, iteration: "Sleep with me or you're fired!" Hostile work environment harassment is where the victim is subject to severe or pervasive unwelcome behavior because of her sex. The guidelines also proposed standards for employer liability, providing that employers could be held liable for harassment in some circumstances, depending on "the particular employment relationship and the job functions performed by the individual."[11] The EEOC guidelines flipped the default – from the incredulity of courts to a virtual consensus that harassment struck at the very heart of women's inequality in the workplace.

In 1986, the Supreme Court gave the green light to the approach set out by the EEOC, holding, in *Meritor Savings Bank v. Vinson*, that both types of harassment constitute actionable forms of intentional discrimination.[12] The Court decided two other cases in the formative years of harassment law, in which it spoke to the question of what constitutes harassment. In 1993, in *Harris v. Forklift Systems, Inc.*, the Court considered how badly hostile environment harassment must injure its victims before it becomes actionable (before causing severe psychological injury) and from whose perspective it should be judged (a reasonable person in the victim's shoes).[13] Five years later, it considered whether same-sex harassment could ever constitute unlawful discrimination. In *Oncale v. Sundowner Offshore Services*, the Court concluded that Title VII does not categorically exclude same-sex harassment (as the lower court had curiously held), but that an employee pursuing such a theory must prove that the conduct occurred because of the victim's sex (e.g., the harasser was gay and motivated by sexual desire or he disliked gay men and singled them out for bullying). Harassment need not be sexual in nature, but it must be based on gender to fall within Title VII's scope.[14]

But right from the start there was disagreement, or at least confusion, about whether employers ought to be held responsible for harassment by their employees, even those with supervisory authority, when the harassment itself was so clearly outside the scope of employment in most cases. The Court in *Meritor* perpetuated this confusion by eschewing a clear rule in favor of a vague direction to lower courts to look to "agency principles" in deciding when employers could be held directly or vicariously liable for workplace harassment.[15] The Court rejected a rule of automatic liability, but also rejected a rule requiring actual notice as a prerequisite to liability. For twelve years, lower courts applied wildly different rules of liability in harassment cases, before the Supreme Court weighed in again, this time more definitively. In companion cases, *Faragher v. City of Boca Raton* and *Burlington Industries, Inc., v. Ellerth*, the Court set forth a new standard for employer liability.[16] For harassment by supervisors, employers are automatically liable for harassment culminating in a tangible employment action. These are, in effect, the quid pro quo cases. Even though these supervisors are almost certainly acting in violation of company policy, they are aided by the power the employer has delegated when carrying out the employment action. This, under agency law, is a standard basis for imposing vicarious liability. When supervisory harassment does not result in such a tangible consequence – the traditional hostile environment claim – employers are also liable, but they can raise an affirmative defense to liability or damages if the employer exercised reasonable care to prevent and correct problems of harassment and the employee unreasonably failed to take advantage of corrective opportunities. For harassment by coworkers or third parties, employers are held only to a negligence standard, which means liability is warranted only if the employer knew or should have known of the harassment and failed to take prompt and effective remedial action.

With this array of significant Supreme Court rulings on sexual harassment, one may suspect that there was nothing left for lower courts to do. Not so. In these early cases, the Court had ruled in favor of a broad reading of Title VII and robust substantive law against harassment, but it left many issues for the lower courts to resolve. The chapters in this part consider a wide variety of those open issues, as well as the consequences for women and other vulnerable groups of underenforcing rules against harassment and the consequences for employers of ignoring the problem.

In Chapters 1 and 2, we considered whether male bosses could fire subordinate women to avoid harassing them or to appease their jealous wives. Those questions went to the very heart of understanding what it means to be singled out because of one's sex. But what if the boss, instead, wants to reward a woman at work for being his paramour – to the detriment of her male and female coworkers, as well as, in some circumstances, of her? Should antidiscrimination law recognize a cause of action for sexual favoritism? This is where we begin Part II, with Chapter 12's look at a prison warden who carried on simultaneous affairs with three subordinate female employees, pitting them against each other in a reality-show-style competition for undeserved privileges and promotions, and retaliating against other employees who complained about the work environment. From this cesspool of a workplace, Part II launches into an exploration of sexual harassment law from virtually every angle.

Chapter 13 considers an important, but under-the-radar, problem of sexual harassment of adolescents in the workplace. When a twenty-five-year-old man has sex with a teenage girl working as a scooper in an ice cream shop, does it matter whether she "welcomed" his behavior if she was below the legal age of consent? The scenario illuminates an interesting intersection between discrimination law and criminal law, as well as the needs of an especially vulnerable group of workers.

Through the lens of a lawsuit against the writers of a famous television show, Chapter 14 takes up the important issue of context: Does the line between acceptable behavior and harassment vary based on the type of work environment? Does a woman who works in a traditionally male-dominated job assume the risk of a salty and perhaps hostile environment? Do writers who write jokes about sex and romance have carte blanche to say and do anything that might help them zero in on a guaranteed laugh? This chapter also introduces the overlap between state and federal discrimination law, the distinction between targeted conduct and general sex talk, and the requirement that an environment be both subjectively and objectively hostile to be actionable.

Chapter 15 returns to the prison setting, but this time examining some very unwelcome conduct – the use of a woman's desk at night for sexual liaisons by her coworkers. In addition to being just plain gross, this situation raises the question when sexual conduct constitutes harassment "because of sex"? Did the coworkers choose her office because she was a woman? A sexualized workplace does not necessarily violate Title VII; nor does one that involves bullying, boorish behavior, or incivility. To violate Title VII, the environment must be discriminatory. This is the first of five chapters that focuses on drawing that line.

Chapter 16 visits a supervisor who does not engage in any sexual conduct, but who bullies only women and refers to them using gendered slurs. Chapter 17 considers the so-called equal opportunity harasser who gropes and fondles men and women alike. Chapter 18 looks at a gay periodontist who makes sexual advances toward his male hygienist. Each of these chapters raises the "because of sex" question: Did the unwelcome conduct occur because of the victim's sex?

In Chapter 19, we look at the intersection between harassment and gender stereo-typing, in a case in which an effeminate gay man was taunted by his coworkers for failing to live up to masculine norms. As we saw with Chapters 4–6 in Part I, sex stereotyping is a form of illegal discrimination. And because Title VII does not prohibit sexual orientation discrimination directly, this theory is often the vehicle for protecting some gay and lesbian workers against gender policing.

Scandals involving public figures and celebrities keep sexual harassment in our collective consciousness. They also provide an opportunity to take a broader look at the law and how it does or does not speak to the types of behaviors we may find inappropriate. Chapters 20 and 21 consider harassment complaints against David Letterman, host of the longest-running late night program, and Herman Cain, a presidential candidate in 2012.

After hammering out the contours of actionable harassment, the chapters in this part then turn to employer liability. What must harassment victims do to enforce their rights and under what circumstances are employers responsible for the harassment on their watch? The discussion of liability begins with an important Supreme Court case, discussed in Chapter 22, which considers the statute of limitations for harassment composed of a pattern of similar acts and the proper treatment of constructive discharge (harassment so intolerable that a victim-employee is forced to quit), respectively.

Chapters 23 through 28 take up the *Faragher/Ellerth* affirmative defense and its application to situations like a successful quid pro quo – when the boss coerces sexual submission from a subordinate with the threat of an adverse employment action – and harassment that is instantly severe before the victim has the opportunity to complain. As an overlay, these chapters consider the ostensible purpose of the rules of employer liability and the ways in which they might reward employers for taking cosmetic measures that do little by way of preventing harassment or minimizing the harm to its victims.

Finally, Part II closes with Chapters 29 and 30 on remedies for harassment that violates Title VII – and some cautionary tales, captured in the chapter titles "Costly Mistakes" and "Hands Off the Merchandise," for employers who turn a blind eye to it.

**12**

# Workplace Affairs and Sexual Favoritism

When a married supervisor conducts long-standing, concurrent affairs with three female subordinates at work and grants them professional favors over more deserving employees, does it constitute unlawful sexual harassment?

In *Miller v. Department of Corrections*, the California Supreme Court has held that it does, despite a long-standing reluctance by courts to recognize claims of so-called sexual favoritism.[1]

## THE PLAINTIFFS' ALLEGATIONS ABOUT WORKING CONDITIONS AT THE VALLEY STATE PRISON FOR WOMEN

The case was brought by two former employees at the Valley State Prison for Women (VSPW) – Edna Miller, a correctional officer, and Frances Mackey, a records manager who passed away while the litigation was pending. Miller and Mackey alleged that they were subjected to discrimination and harassment as a result of the chief deputy prison warden's multiple workplace affairs and related conduct.

Although the case involved numerous allegations, the crux of the complaint is its allegation that the deputy warden, Lewis Kuykendall, openly carried on three affairs with female employees at the prison (Bibb, Patrick, and Brown), all subordinate to him, and granted those women undeserved privileges and promotions because of his relationship with them. At the same time, the suit alleges, female employees who complained about these relationships were punished, and retaliated against, for their objections.

Although the facts of the case are too numerous and complicated to recount in detail, a few notable examples will provide a sense of the ways in which, according to the plaintiffs' allegations, these sexual relationships pervaded the workplace and disadvantaged those not involved in them.

When Kuykendall was transferred from another facility to VSPW, the plaintiffs allege that he gradually had all three of his paramours transferred so they would once again be working under him. Once there, the paramours all allegedly benefited in tangible ways from their relationship with Kuykendall.

One paramour, for example, was allegedly granted a promotion over the objection of the committee appointed to make the decision because Kuykendall ordered them to "make it happen." A second paramour was allegedly permitted to report directly to Kuykendall in lieu of her immediate supervisor. A third was allegedly given a series of promotions over more qualified applicants, and, according to plaintiffs, remarked that Kuykendall had no choice but to give them to her lest she "take him down" by revealing "every scar on his body." The culture at the facility, the plaintiffs claim, was such that employees repeatedly questioned whether this was the kind of workplace in which they would have to "'F' my way to the top." There was good reason to think the answer was yes.

The sexual relationships allegedly affected the workplace in other undesirable ways, as well. Kuykendall allegedly engaged in open displays of affection with at least one of the women at work, and the three women allegedly were sometimes heard to be squabbling over their competing affairs in emotional scenes.

Complaints about the sexual relationships, the plaintiffs allege, were met with derision or worse. Allegedly, when plaintiff Miller confronted one of the paramours, Brown, about the relationship and the harm it had caused other employees, Brown physically assaulted her and held her captive in a closed office for two hours.

Then, when Miller complained to Kuykendall and threatened to file a harassment suit, he allegedly said there was nothing he could do to control Brown because of his relationship with her, and told Miller he should have "chosen" her instead. The other plaintiff, Mackey, allegedly had her pay reduced when she complained about the sexual affairs.

## SEXUAL FAVORITISM AS A FORM OF SEX DISCRIMINATION: THE TITLE VII ISSUE

First recognized as a potentially valid claim in the 1980s, sexual favoritism has proved an elusive cause of action for most plaintiffs. Courts have struggled with the question whether the prohibition against sex discrimination in Title VII's prohibition on discrimination in employment is violated when, for example, a supervisor grants preferential employment treatment to a paramour based on their intimate relationship. Does this conduct render other employees victims of sex discrimination?

The struggle comes because Title VII does not apply to all conduct that is immoral, unethical, distasteful, or even demonstrably unfair; it applies only to discrimination. The *New York Times*'s "Ethicist" would surely find it objectionable for a supervisor to hand out promotions only to subordinates he was sleeping with, at the expense of more deserving candidates. But under the law, more analysis is necessary: to prove a violation of Title VII, a plaintiff must show the act was discriminatory – that it was taken because of sex, race, or some other protected characteristic.[2]

When a male supervisor grants favors to his female girlfriend, *all* other employees, both male and female, are disadvantaged. But, arguably, none are disadvantaged *by their gender per se.* So it is not the case that such favoritism is always sex discrimination. However, a variety of theories have developed under which a sexual relationship between two employees might constitute discrimination against other employees.

## CIRCUMSTANCES WHEN A SEXUAL RELATIONSHIP MAY CONSTITUTE DISCRIMINATION

First, if the sexual relationship is coerced, it may constitute implicit "quid pro quo" harassment for other employees. "Quid pro quo" harassment occurs when a supervisor demands sexual favors in exchange for an employee's gaining job benefits or avoiding adverse employment actions, and it is a clear and serious violation of Title VII. An "implicit" quid pro quo might exist if employees understand, after learning of a coerced relationship between their supervisor and another subordinate, that sexual submission is expected of them as a condition of job advancement.

If the sexual relationship is consensual, then other theories might apply instead. Men, for example, might claim that they were discriminated against in that they were deprived of the opportunity to use sex to get ahead, because male supervisors are presumably, at least in most cases, only interested in sexual relationships with female subordinates. The men's lost opportunity could thus be considered discriminatory on the basis of sex. (The same argument could work, of course, for claims by female subordinates deprived of opportunities by female supervisors who have sexual relationships with men, and then favor them in the workplace.)

When a male supervisor favors a particular female employee with whom he has a sexual relationship, do other *female* employees face discrimination? One might contend that they have been denied access to job benefits not because of their sex, but because the boss happened to choose a different woman with whom to have an affair. That, in our conventional understanding of Title VII, does not constitute unlawful discrimination. And a few courts have denied sexual favoritism claims on this reasoning.[3]

But what if favoritism based on sexual favors is so widespread, in a given workplace, that women as a group are demeaned? That, according to a Policy Guidance published by the EEOC in 1990, constitutes a form of illegal gender-based harassment.[4]

The EEOC's Policy Guidance, approved during the period when now Justice Clarence Thomas served as EEOC chairperson, states the agency's position on when sexual favoritism constitutes illegal harassment or discrimination. It recognizes the potential for an implicit quid pro quo claim, discussed above, but it also recognizes the possibility that widespread favoritism can create a hostile environment for both male and female employees.

Isolated incidences of sexual favoritism, while clearly inappropriate, are not considered unlawful by the EEOC. Employers should be careful when it comes to such conduct, though; city or state antidiscrimination provisions could still be interpreted to reach these instances. The safe thing, then, for employers to do is prohibit such favoritism, just as they often have policies banning nepotism.

## THE COURT'S REASONING IN *MILLER V. DEPARTMENT OF CORRECTIONS*

The California Supreme Court followed the EEOC in determining that widespread sexual favoritism can create an actionable hostile work environment. The case was brought under California's Fair Employment and Housing Act (FEHA).[5] And California has always erred on the side of broader protection for victims when construing its antidiscrimination statutes than federal courts tend to grant under Title VII. For example, the California Supreme Court showed greater empathy for victims than federal law when it granted employers a much more limited affirmative defense to liability for supervisory harassment than is available under Title VII.[6]

California law also gives discrimination plaintiffs access to compensatory and punitive damages without caps.[7] In contrast, Title VII caps combined damages at $300,000 for even the largest employer-defendants – meaning that employees who are high salaried, unable to find other work for a long time, and/or treated so horribly that punitive damages are appropriate can be seriously undercompensated.[8]

Considering the validity of a FEHA sexual favoritism claim, the California Supreme Court held that "when such sexual favoritism in a workplace is sufficiently widespread it may create an actionable hostile work environment in which the demeaning message is conveyed to female employees that they are viewed by management as 'sexual playthings' or that the way required for women to get ahead in the workplace is to engage in sexual conduct with their supervisors or the management."[9] Given the facts alleged – many of them uncontested – the court remanded the case for a jury trial to see whether the legal standard could be met.

## THE PLAINTIFFS IN THE MILLER/MACKEY CASE ARE LIKELY TO WIN AT TRIAL

The plaintiffs are likely to meet with success at trial, assuming that they can convince a jury of the truth of the allegations of their complaint. Rightfully so, given that if their allegations are proven, they would establish a rather extreme clash between Kuykendall's personal relationships at the workplace, and workplace conditions for those around him who were not engaged in such relationships.

As the California court noted, according to plaintiffs, "Kuykendall's sexual favoritism not only blocked the way to merit-based advancement for plaintiffs but also caused them to be subjected to harassment at the hands of [his girlfriend], whose behavior Kuykendall refused or failed to control even after it escalated to physical assault."[10]

Sexual favoritism, as a claim, is often met with skepticism because of fear that it might require employers to monitor, or even restrict, consensual office romances. But that is a misunderstanding. Office romances are not, standing alone, problematic – and certainly are not illegal or discriminatory. Indeed, it would be a shame to prevent all such relationships, given the increasing time and importance of work in our daily lives. Sexual relationships, including those begun at work, can be a positive force in women's and men's lives. But such relationships should not go beyond providing personal fulfillment to the participants, to providing a free ticket to career success at the expense of others equally, or more, deserving. In an egalitarian workplace, sex is no way to get ahead – good work is.

Society's interest in preventing exploitation and abuse of subordinates provides an important counterweight to the value of allowing office romances to flourish. Fortunately, given the way both the EEOC's and California's standard is crafted, both interests can be served. Employers need not prohibit office romance. It is only an office romance (or, perhaps, two or three) combined with *repeated* and *widespread* instances of favoritism, to the detriment of other employees, which begins to near the threshold for sex discrimination liability. Commonsense policies by employers designed to guard against abuses of power like those committed by Kuykendall ought to be par for the course – and, as noted above, cautious employers will often have such policies or informal norms in place. As Martha Chamallas has suggested, little sexual liberty is lost when an employer prohibits "amorous relationships in which one party has direct authority to affect the working . . . status of the other."[11]

The dangers of permitting such obvious conflicts of interest to flourish are amply demonstrated by the *Miller* case. An environment like the one alleged to have existed at VSPW not only makes life miserable for women who work there but also reinforces deeply entrenched stereotypes about women who sleep their way to the top.

When sexual favoritism is as pervasive and unfettered as it is alleged to have been at VSPW, no woman can get a fair evaluation on the basis of her abilities and work-related talents. That is the essence of sex discrimination, and the *Miller* court was right to put a stop to it.

A version of this chapter appeared on July 28, 2005, at writ.findlaw.com.

*Update: A former CBS Broadcasting employee who worked on the popular game show* The Price Is Right *cited the* Miller *case in support of her own sexual favoritism lawsuit. She argued, based on alleged relationships involving the CEO and other high-ranking executives, that there was an "unwritten rule" that women must date executives in order to get ahead. But without sufficient evidence to support her claim, she lost on summary judgment. See* Curling v. CBS Broadcasting, Inc., *2012 WL 182112.*

# 13

# Lolita at the Office

Typically, a sexual harassment plaintiff must prove that her supervisor's advances were unwelcome. This is a standard element of the cause of action. But what if the supervisor had sex with the plaintiff when she was below the age of consent? Must his advances still be proven unwelcome? Or in harassment law, as in the criminal law pertaining to statutory rape, is the underage person's attitude toward the sexual conduct irrelevant?

According to the U.S. Court of Appeals for the Seventh Circuit – addressing a claim under Title VII of the Civil Rights Act of 1964 – the answer is that an adult's advances toward an underaged teen need not be unwelcome in order to be actionable.[1]

Under the law of the relevant state, Illinois, the plaintiff in that case was incapable of giving valid consent to sexual intercourse; she was sixteen and Illinois's age of consent is seventeen (or, in special circumstances, eighteen). Thus, the sex she had with her supervisor was a crime on his part: statutory rape. On the basis of this fact, the appeals panel – in an opinion written by noted conservative judge Richard Posner – held that the plaintiff could win her case whether or not she could prove that her supervisor's advances were unwelcome.

This ruling thus creates, in effect, a special doctrine for below-the-age-of-consent teenagers who experience sexual harassment at work – under which these teens can prove their cases even if they welcomed their supervisors' advances.

## THE FACTS AND ALLEGATIONS OF THE CASE
## BEFORE THE COURT

The plaintiff in the case was known only as "Jane Doe" in court papers and the appellate opinion. The sixteen-year-old Jane worked at an ice cream shop, Oberweis Dairy, as a scooper. A twenty-five-year-old man named Matt Nayman was her shift supervisor.

According to Jane, Nayman created a hostile work environment for her and the other female scoopers. For instance, some of the evidence indicated that Nayman regularly hit on the girls he supervised. One witness testified that he would grope and kiss the girls, as well as grab their butts. He also invited them to his apartment, and had sex with two other girls before turning to Jane. While Jane made no claim that Nayman forcibly raped her, Nayman was prosecuted, convicted, and imprisoned for statutory rape.

Subsequently, Jane sued her employer, alleging that Nayman harassed her. She was not able to make a Title VII claim against Nayman directly because Title VII does not hold individuals liable for their harassing behavior – only their employers.[2] The trial court, however, rejected Jane's claim because, in its view, she "welcomed" Nayman's advances. Because the appeals court applied Title VII doctrine differently, Jane can now pursue her case further, to settlement or trial. But there will be some more stumbling blocks, as detailed below.

## THE "AGE OF CONSENT"

Every state sets an "age of consent," at which individuals are deemed legally capable of consenting to sexual intercourse. It was historically a crime – "statutory" rape – for an adult to have sex with a girl below that age, whether or not she in fact gave her consent. Today, all fifty states have gender-neutral laws that prohibit adults from having sexual intercourse with minor boys, as well as girls.

According to a fifty-state survey by Charles Phipps, state laws on the "age of consent" vary with the age of the minor, the nature of the sexual activity, and the presence of any special circumstances, such as the adult's holding a position of trust with respect to the minor.[3] The laws often make exceptions or reduce penalties when both parties are below the age of consent or reasonably close in age. These factors are all used as a proxy for gauging when a minor is least likely to be able to resist the sexual overtures of an adult.

Under Illinois law, here, it is clear that, at sixteen, Jane was under the state's age of consent regardless of the circumstances of the encounter at the time Nayman had sex with her.[4]

## REQUIREMENTS FOR A SEXUAL HARASSMENT CLAIM
## UNDER TITLE VII

It is indisputable that Jane's age alone was sufficient to criminalize Nayman's behavior – because the statutory rape law makes a minor's consent legally irrelevant. But the Seventh Circuit had to answer a different, more difficult question: Of what relevance is her age – and the possibility that she "welcomed" the behavior – under Title VII?

In a landmark 1986 opinion, *Meritor Savings Bank v. Vinson*, the Supreme Court first acknowledged that "hostile environment" harassment is actionable under Title VII.[5] Because the case involved a long-standing sexual relationship between a bank teller and her supervisor, the Court also directly considered the requirement that harassing conduct must be "unwelcome" in order to be actionable.

The sexual relationship in *Meritor* had for the most part been voluntary – that is, it did not involve forcible rape, though the power disparity involved was significant. But while the Supreme Court agreed with the EEOC guidelines that harassment must be "unwelcome" in order to be actionable – and, controversially, that "a complainant's sexually provocative speech or dress" may be relevant and admissible to disprove unwelcomeness – it held that a complainant's participation in "sexual episodes" may be voluntary, but nonetheless "unwelcome."[6] The plaintiff, Mechelle Vinson, proved to the jury that she felt pressured by her supervisor, even in the absence of any direct threat, and engaged in the relationship to keep her job. This was sufficient, the Court held, to show "unwelcomeness," and its ruling made clear that acquiescing to and *welcoming* sexual conduct are not the same thing. Put another way, unhappily submitting to a supervisor's advances to keep one's job is hardly welcoming them.

But suppose Vinson had clearly given her true consent, genuinely welcomed the sexual attention of her supervisor, and had no fear at all of losing her job if she did not comply. In that event, her later claim of harassment would have failed, for she would not have been able to prove unwelcomeness. A power disparity alone, in other words, cannot transform sex into sexual harassment when both partners are above the age of consent and in fact give their consent.

## THE QUESTION FOR THE SEVENTH CIRCUIT: RECONCILING STATE AND FEDERAL LAW

For the court in the *Doe v. Oberweis* case, then, one key question was how to reconcile the doctrinal requirement of unwelcomeness under federal sexual harassment law with the legal incapacity of minors, imposed by the state of Illinois, to consent to sex with adults.

The Seventh Circuit, as noted above, concluded that deferring to state law on the ability of a minor to consent was the better approach. "Federal courts," the court wrote, "rather than deciding whether a particular Title VII minor plaintiff was capable of 'welcoming' the sexual advances of an older man, should defer to the judgment of average maturity in sexual matters that is reflected in the age of consent of the state in which the plaintiff is employed."[7]

One result of this ruling is that teenagers in different states will potentially have different rules applied to their claims of harassment, depending on the law in their workplace's state about the age of consent, and depending on the relevance, under that law, of any other factors, such as age disparity or severity of the sexual conduct.

As noted above, the lowest Illinois's age of consent gets is seventeen, meaning Jane Doe, at sixteen, was plainly under the requisite age. In other cases, the answer to whether the plaintiff was under the relevant state age of consent may be more complicated. While this situation is not ideal, courts do routinely draw on state law to define terms that appear in federal statutes with any accompanying definition.

## WHAT THIS RULING MEANS FOR JANE DOE: INSTRUCTIONS TO THE TRIAL COURT

What will happen to Jane Doe now? She won on one issue: she can still prevail even if she welcomed Nayman's advances. But Judge Posner and the rest of the appellate panel did not hand her a slam dunk: the opinion raised other issues that may undermine her claim.

First, the ruling throws into question whether Nayman qualifies as a "supervisor" for Title VII purposes. The label is doctrinally important, because employers are strictly liable for harassment by supervisors (subject to an affirmative defense), but only liable in negligence for harassment by non-supervisors. In lay terms, what this means is that an employer can only be held liable for harassment by a coworker only if the employer knew or should have known of the conduct and failed to stop it. The requirements for holding an employer liable for a supervisor's harassment are significantly less restrictive.

The opinion queries whether Nayman is really a supervisor, because he did not technically have the power to fire the plaintiff or other workers subordinate to him. Nevertheless, Nayman had real authority over Jane – he directed her work, was authorized to issue disciplinary write-ups, and, often, was the only one on-site with any supervisory power at all. Although the Seventh Circuit panel stated that it would be "inclined" to deem Nayman a supervisor, it left the question open for the factfinder, at the trial court level.[8]

The appeals court did direct, however, that, when it comes to the law the factfinder must follow, Nayman's authority must be used to elevate the standard of care, even under a negligence rule, if he cannot fairly be considered a supervisor. Things do not look promising for Oberweis, if it must try to prove that it met this elevated (or even an ordinary) standard of care. The appeals court remarked, tellingly, "No procedures were in force or utilized for protecting girls like the plaintiff from what happened to her, even though it should have been clear that the situation in the store as a result of Nayman's antics was explosive."

## MORE ON THE IMPACT FOR JANE DOE: CONSENT IS HELD RELEVANT TO DAMAGES

Oddly, though, while taking the employer to task for letting Nayman run amok, Judge Posner at the same time suggested that the victim's consent – even if legally irrelevant to the finding that actionable harassment occurred – might be relevant to the amount of damages the employer has to pay. In a strange reversal of sorts, the opinion, after expressly ruling that Jane's consent to the conduct was irrelevant to *liability*, then invites Oberweis to "put Nayman's conduct in perspective" for the jury choosing how high a damage award to give by showing, for example, whether Jane facilitated his behavior by "sneaking around behind her mother's – and her employer's – back."

Posner suggests that this approach is a "straightforward application" of the avoidable consequences theory – which says, loosely, that plaintiffs should not recover damages for harm they could have avoided. In fact, it is anything but. It is hard to say at the same time that a teenage girl is too young to make good decisions about sex with adults, and yet that her "decision" to sleep with a shift supervisor at work minimizes the harm she suffered.

In addition, the distinction Posner tries to draw – between the relevance of consent to liability, versus it is relevance to damages – is, at the end of the day, meaningless, at least in any practical sense. Nayman, recall, was punished through the criminal law. This suit is to hold the employer liable for it is role in making the harassment of Jane possible. Yet if Jane is able to prove she was the victim of unlawful harassment, but cannot prove that Oberweis should pay damages, then she has little to take home from court other than her pride. Similarly, a verdict of liability with no, or very low, damages hardly provides any incentive for employers to police compliance with the law, and to ensure work environments less "explosive" than the one Judge Posner recognized existed at Oberweis.

In the end, the Seventh Circuit has granted Jane Doe her day in court, though it created some legal obstacles for her to surmount. More important, perhaps, this case has drawn attention to a common but mostly overlooked harassment problem.

Harassment of adolescents is most common in the restaurant and entertainment industries, both of which rely heavily on untrained, part-time, young workers and strive to create a light, friendly atmosphere. Because of their age, inexperience, and expendability, these workers are at once most likely to be preyed on and least likely to know how to protect themselves from unwanted sexual attentions and abuse, or how to seek help once sexual harassment or abuse has occurred.[9]

The ruling in *Oberweis* is thus right, as a matter of policy as well as law, to provide greater protection from harassment to adolescent workers. This vulnerable population deserves at least that much.

A version of this chapter appeared on August 29, 2006, at writ.findlaw.com.

# 14

## Sex Talk in the Writers' Room

The long-running comedy series "Friends" went off the air in 2004, but lived on not only through syndication but also through litigation.

The case, *Lyle v. Warner Brothers Television Productions*, pitted a writer's assistant against the show's writers – who, she claimed, engaged in a course of illegal sexual harassment.[1] The California Supreme Court ruled 7-0 in favor of the sitcom writers. Crucially, however, the court did not insulate "creative workplaces" from harassment claims in general, as the defendants had argued it should.

### THE LAWSUIT: WAS THE WRITERS' ROOM A "HOSTILE ENVIRONMENT"?

Amaani Lyle, an African-American woman, was hired as a "writer's assistant" for "Friends" in 1999. Her primary task in that position was to sit in on creative meetings and take detailed notes for the writers when they were plotting out potential story lines. Being a fast typist was her main qualification for the job.

For four months, Lyle worked primarily for Adam Chase and Gregory Malins, two of the show's writers, and a supervising producer, Andrew Reich. She was then fired, allegedly because she did not type fast enough to keep up with the creative discussions. As a result, the defendants argued, important jokes and dialogue were missing from her notes.

After being fired, Lyle sued in California state court, bringing claims under California's anti-discrimination law. She alleged that she had been subjected to a variety of illegal actions: race discrimination, sexual harassment, retaliation, and wrongful termination. (As we saw in Chapter 12, California's law with respect to these actions is similar, but not identical, to federal anti-discrimination law.)[2]

The trial court granted the defendants summary judgment on all counts, ordered her to pay costs, and, quite surprisingly, ordered her to pay the defendants' whopping legal fees (amounting to $415,800), on the theory that her anti-discrimination claims were frivolous and without foundation. (Civil rights plaintiffs who prevail are often awarded attorneys' fees as part of the judgment; but they are almost *never* required to pay the other side's fees if they lose.)[3]

Lyle appealed both the dismissal of her claims and the award of attorneys' fees. The appellate court reversed the fee award, and resurrected one of her claims for trial: sexual harassment.

## THE SPECIFIC DETAILS OF THE PLAINTIFF'S ALLEGATIONS: A BARRAGE OF SEXUAL BANTER

Lyle's claim of harassment is this: she was subjected to a constant barrage of sexual talk, jokes, drawings, and gestures that demeaned and degraded women by the show's writers during their "creative" meetings. Some of her allegations – even paraphrased, as many of them are here – are striking.

The alleged comments Lyle lists in her complaint revolve around certain themes. One theme is banter about the actresses on "Friends": discussion of which ones the writers would like to have sex with and, if they did, different sexual acts the writers would like to try; speculation about with which "Friends" actresses the writers had missed opportunities to have sex; speculation about the supposed infertility of one of the "Friends" actresses; its supposed cause (her "dried up pussy"); and speculation about the sexual activities of the "Friends" actresses with their partners. She also complained of derogatory words used to describe women.

Another theme of the alleged comments was the personal sexual preferences and experiences of the writers, emphasizing anal sex, oral sex, big breasts, young girls and cheerleaders. Then there were the drawings: cheerleaders with exposed breasts and vaginas; "dirty" coloring books; and penned alterations to ordinary words on the script to make "happiness" say "penis" or to make "persistence" say "pert tits."

Finally, the sexual gestures cited in Lyle's complaint include: pantomiming male masturbation and banging under the desk to make it sound like someone was masturbating in the room.

## THE DEFENDANTS' RESPONSE: JUSTIFIED BY "CREATIVE NECESSITY"

The defendants admitted that many of Lyle's allegations were true. They testified in deposition that they did many of the things she complained of, but argued that the conduct was justified by "creative necessity." The writers' job, defendants argued, was to come up with story lines, dialogue, and jokes for a sitcom with adult sexual themes. To do this, they needed to have "frank sexual discussions and tell colorful jokes and stories (and even make expressive gestures) as part of the creative process."

Could this kind of "creative necessity" defense succeed? Certain, this kind of defense is not well established. But the consideration of "context" has always been permissible in determining the existence of a hostile environment. Here, the writers – and the lawyers who presumably prepped them – seem to be suggesting that in the creative context, anything goes. Thus, they argue, what might count as harassment in, say, a law firm, is just creative, and therefore acceptable, in a TV writing room.

## THE RELEVANCE OF CONTEXT IN EVALUATING HOSTILE ENVIRONMENT CLAIMS

This argument raises an important question: What does context mean, when it comes to sexual harassment claims? And to what extent can "context" provide an excuse for what otherwise would plainly be harassing behavior?

First, what has the Supreme Court said about "context"? In its 1998 decision in *Oncale v. Sundowner Offshore Services, Inc.*, the Supreme Court stated that a court applying Title VII should give "careful consideration of the social context in which particular behavior occurs and is experienced by its target" when determining whether an objectively hostile environment existed.[4] For example, Justice Scalia noted in his majority opinion, context is what differentiates a coach's slapping a football player on the behind after a game from his doing the same thing to his secretary back at the office. Context might justify the former behavior, but not the latter.[5]

But federal courts have struggled with the concept of "context," sometimes running amok with it. The U.S. Court of Appeals for the Tenth Circuit, for example, held in 1995, in *Gross v. Burggraf Construction Co.*, that a female truck driver could not prevail in her hostile environment claim because of context.[6] The court opined that in "the real world of construction work, profanity and vulgarity are not perceived as hostile or abusive. Indelicate forms of expression are accepted or endured as normal human behavior."[7]

Obviously, there is a problem with this logic, however. One might rewrite the court's comment, more accurately, this way: In the real world of construction work, profanity and vulgarity are not perceived as hostile or abusive *by many male, and some female, construction workers.* Indelicate forms of expression are accepted by *many male, and some female, construction workers*, or endured as normal human behavior *by some female construction workers.*

This more accurate rewriting reveals the problem: Does the ability of some women to endure harassment as a cost of working mean that other women cannot sue? And what was the basis for the appeals courts claim that female construction workers endure harassment "as normal human behavior" – rather than enduring it because, though they hate it, they need the paycheck and don't wish to aggravate the hammer-carrying men with whom they work?

Put more formally, it is plain that permitting environments that have traditionally been dominated by men, and hostile to women, to remain so utterly male frustrates the goals of anti-discrimination law – which is to make that very kind of environment less hostile to women, or ideally, equally welcoming of women and men.

Other circuits have rejected the Tenth Circuit's so-called "blue collar" exception and applied the same standards regardless of the workplace context. And history has evolved away from the Tenth Circuit's point of view.[8]

Early on in the history of sexual harassment law, context was routinely urged as a justification for hostile environment harassment in many blue-collar environments. One 1984 case was thrown out because the court concluded that "Title VII was not meant" to change an environment in which "sexual jokes, sexual conversations and girlie magazines may abound."[9]

But most courts today recognize that such a justification cannot fly. Work environments have to be transformed, in some cases, to accommodate gender integration. Traditionally male work environments cannot not be exempted from contemporary standards of equality – indeed, these are the very environments in which such standards must be most rigorously enforced.[10] Unable to count on "strength in numbers" to protect themselves, lone women should be able to rely, at least, on the strength of the law. Persistent occupational segregation by gender continues to be the greatest source of inequality for working women.

## IS "CREATIVE NECESSITY" A DEFENSE TO A CHARGE OF SEXUAL HARASSMENT?

Returning to the "Friends" case, however, it is fair to admit that the argument about context in *Lyle* is more compelling than in the blue-collar cases. Here, the argument is that the work being done actually required sex talk, not simply that it was commonplace. They needed, in other words, to have sexually explicit conversations in order to generate story ideas for the show.[11] The defendants term this claim "creative necessity" and insist that it justifies their behavior. The idea is that it is part of their writing work to talk about sex; in contrast, sex talk plays no part in the actual work of construction: One need not tell a dirty joke to hoist a beam.

The appellate court, though it reversed the defendants' trial court victory, agreed that such an argument could be pursued in the context of a writers' room.[12] The court analogized this "creative necessity" to the "business necessity" defense available in disparate impact cases. In those cases, an employer who relies on some criterion that disadvantages women, for example, can justify the practice by proving business necessity – and that no less disadvantageous method would meet the employer's business needs.[13] So, for example, an employer might be able to use a fitness test that disproportionately eliminates female applicants if it can show that the skill being tested is necessary for the job – a strength test for a job that involved lifting 50-lb bags of cement. (See Chapter 7 on the legality of fitness tests that have a disparate impact on a protected group.) Assuming this defense is viable in the sexual harassment context (which is not at all obvious), the question still remains: Was this conduct truly "necessary" to the writers' job?

## A KEY QUESTION: WAS THE SEXUAL CONDUCT "NECESSARY"?

It is not clear how a judge or jury would make that determination in any meaningful way. On one hand, maybe the episode in which Rachel seduces a slow-to-make-a-pass co-worker by dressing up as a cheerleader arose out of the many lewd drawings of naked cheerleaders and the writers' own fantasies about having sex with them. On the other hand, there is no episode in which any explicit sexual act is shown, and none in which anal sex is even mentioned (though astute viewers will remembers some innuendo along those lines).

On the whole, it is hard to imagine the "necessity" of writers' having detailed conversations about anal sex; talking about which of the "Friends" actresses might have sex with them; or listing the anatomical shapes they find most appealing personally. After all, "Friends" is not a hard-core porn show. To the contrary, the sexual humor relies mostly on innuendo and euphemistic references.

Telling the show's writers that they could not talk about sex would certainly inhibit their ability to invent and draft scripts. Comedy writers say they must go to the edge and then step back to find the right jokes. But giving them carte blanche to say, draw, and do anything – no matter how offensive or degrading to women – runs the risk of creating an environment in which, potentially, no woman would want to work. Interestingly, "Sex and the City" – which has prominent female writers – might not create the same kind of hostile environment. When women are a large part of the discussion and free to speak their minds – not grossly outnumbered, or simply taking down male writers' slurs (as Lyle was) – the context may be very different.

One also wonders about the climate for the "Friends" actresses, especially if any of these comments ever got back to them (which, with public litigation and news coverage, they did). Of course, it is hard to see stars with huge paychecks as victims. But shouldn't a star be able to count on a collegial relationship with the writer – not one in which she is demeaned, objectified, and mocked during writing sessions? Shouldn't she be entitled to enough respect that her infertility isn't mocked in the crudest way?

## THE PLAINTIFF LOSES, BUT NO NEW LEGAL GROUND IS LAID

In the end, the writers won. The California Supreme Court ruled in their favor on the merits. It affirmed the trial court's original grant of summary judgment, and thus, in effect, put an end to the sexual harassment component of the plaintiff's lawsuit.[14]

This case was closely watched by many constituencies. Those in the entertainment world worried that a victory for the plaintiff could cripple the comedy-writing business by forcing writers to censor their thoughts and expressions in order to comply with anti-discrimination mandates. The freedom to say literally anything – including things that might shock outsiders – is, they claim, central to the creative process.[15]

Civil rights advocates and some feminists worried about the opposite problem – they felt that a ruling for defendants might serve as a license to harass women with impunity within the comedy-writing industry. Already numerically dominated by men, and by many accounts hostile to women, the industry would then be permitted to be inhospitable without limit.[16]

Neither of these things happened. The decision in *Lyle* is decidedly middle-of-the-road and amounts to little more than one application of well-established principles of harassment law. This particular plaintiff has lost, but others in similar cases may fare better. This decision is neither a license to harass, nor a requirement to censor.

## THE BASIC PRINCIPLES OF SEXUAL HARASSMENT LAW AND THEIR APPLICATION TO THIS CASE

The crux of this case involved the sexually coarse and vulgar language that all parties admit was used regularly in the writers' room at "Friends." Did it constitute illegal harassment? That depends, under existing harassment law principles, on whether it was "because of sex" and, if it was, whether it was sufficiently severe or pervasive to create an actionable or hostile work environment. In order to run afoul of FEHA (or Title VII, for that matter), conduct must occur "because of sex."[17] That requirement is what separates behavior that is *discriminatory* from behavior that is merely uncivil, unpleasant, or just plain gross.

Although courts sometimes fail to make the distinction, conduct that is sexual in nature is not necessarily "because of sex." To be actionable, the conduct must create an environment that is disadvantageous to members of one sex (read: gender) over the other. That standard can be met when the conduct is motivated by sexual desire and, thus, targeted primarily or exclusively at members of one sex. It can also be met when the conduct is born of animosity or hostility to the presence of one sex in the workplace, or when it obviously targets members of one sex. The use of sex-specific and derogatory epithets can be proof of such hostility or motivation.[18]

According to the court's explication of these principles, a plaintiff must show that the sexual conduct was directed either toward her specifically, or toward women in general. It is not sufficient to simply point to the use of sexually charged or inappropriate language.

## THE PLAINTIFF'S CLAIM: CONDUCT DIRECTED NOT TO HER, BUT TO WOMEN IN GENERAL

The plaintiff conceded in her deposition that she had *not* been subjected to sexual advances, requests for sexual favors, threatening behavior, or sexual touching. Nor had any of the writers made sexually offensive comments directly to her. Thus, the claim turned on her ability to prove that the writers' conduct demonstrated or created hostility to *women in general.*

When conduct is not directed at the plaintiff in particular, the *Lyle* court ruled, it must be severe or pervasive in order to be actionable. It must also take place in the plaintiff's immediate work environment and be witnessed by the plaintiff in order for it to create a hostile environment for her. (Sexual harassment law has long been interpreted to require that an environment be both objectively – to a reasonable person – and subjectively – to the plaintiff specifically – hostile.)[19] Moreover, the court held that undirected conduct must be more severe or more pervasive than directed conduct in order to be actionable. So Lyle not only had to prove that she found the environment to be subjectively hostile but also that it happened with extreme regularity.[20]

Did the writers' conduct create a disadvantageous environment for women in general? The court found it was "neither surprising nor unreasonable from a creative standpoint" that the writers engaged in "discussions of personal sexual experiences and preferences and used physical gesturing while brainstorming and generating script ideas."[21]

The court noted that Lyle herself did not clearly object to the conduct about which she later sued. She described it variously as "silly," "juvenile," and "like being in a junior high locker room."[22] This reaction, the court concluded, was not a clear indication that she subjectively perceived the environment as hostile. Nor was the environment, according to the court, obviously hostile or destructive to female employees in general. To the contrary, the court noted that both sexes contributed to, and were exposed to, the creative process – with all its sexually charged components.

Only one allegation, according to the court, suggested that women might be singled out for derogation or ridicule. Lyle had alleged that the writers made comments about wanting to have sex with some of the female actresses on *Friends,* and about the claimed infertility of one female cast member.

But, the court found, these comments were neither severe nor pervasive. The comments themselves, while offensive, did not involve threats of assault or physical harm and were not made in the presence of the targeted actresses. Nor were they pervasive, apparently, since the plaintiff mentioned only a few occasions on which such statements were made. (Verbal harassment is almost never considered severe and, therefore, must be pervasive in order to be actionable.)

Plaintiff did also allege, in a later pleading, that the writers used gender-related epithets – too indelicate to be repeated here – when referring to or describing women. While such epithets can be sufficient to create a hostile environment, the court found that they were not regular or pervasive enough to do so here. Context was crucial to the court's decision, as it noted that the type of work and the job responsibilities of parties involved were all relevant considerations.

The court thus rejected Lyle's claim, holding that no reasonable trier of fact (the standard on summary judgment) could find that "the conduct of the three male writers was sufficiently severe or pervasive to create a hostile work environment."[23]

## HARASSMENT LAW AFTER LYLE

California sexual harassment law would appear to be essentially the same after *Lyle* as it was before. Thus, the Supreme Court's opinion is perhaps more interesting for what it did *not* do than for what it did.

The court did *not* rule that undirected sexual conduct can, by itself, create a hostile work environment. Such a ruling would have been an extension of existing law in favor of harassment plaintiffs and might have been hard to reconcile with the requirement that conduct must be *discriminatory* in nature. After all, not all sex-related conduct disadvantages female employees. And suppressing sex-related conduct may well have had a chilling effect on the creative process, since the ability to create sexually-themed comedy clearly does require writers to talk about sex.

More generally, the perception that Title VII and its state analogs are simply anti-sex, as opposed to anti-discrimination, has fueled strident critiques in recent years.[24] A ruling that sent every allegation of undirected sexual behavior to a jury would have given those critiques greater traction. (As it is, such critics tend to overstate the law's supposed "anti-sex" stance: Its point is not to make a workplace free of flirting or free of sexual relationships, but rather simply to make it free of the kind of repeated, unwanted, and aggressive sexual advances that few – if any – of us think anyone should have to suffer as a condition of working.)

But the court also did *not* go to the opposite extreme. It did *not* create an exemption for so-called "creative workplaces," something it might have done on a First Amendment theory or a theory of business necessity. That would have been a marked extension of the law that, while letting Hollywood sleep better at night, would have undermined the ability of FEHA to eliminate genuinely discriminatory workplace behavior.

After all, *some* of what is said and done in creative workplaces might well disadvantage women individually or as a group. And the law needs to be flexible enough to permit liability when it happens. And now that comedy writers have been put on clear notice where the line is drawn, they may be more harshly penalized for crossing it.

Portions of this chapter appeared on May 4, 2004 and May 2, 2006, at writ.findlaw.com.

# 15

## Sex Behind Bars

One might watch the Netflix original series *Orange Is the New Black* and think that the rampant sexual encounters in the prison – involving the warden, correctional officers, and inmates in various pairings – are trumped up to appeal to the prurient interests of viewers. But there is no shortage of real cases involving similar behavior, raising complicated questions about harassment or other forms of discrimination.

As discussed in Chapter 12, the case of *Miller v. Department of Correction* showcased the problem of sexual favoritism, arising from a deputy warden carrying on affairs with several subordinate female employees and granting undeserved privileges and promotions to his paramours.[1] Only because his sexual favoritism pervaded the workplace in such a shocking way was it actionable.

In a ruling from the Seventh Circuit Court of Appeals, *Orton-Bell v. Indiana*,[2] the court had to address different questions arising out of sex between prison employees. Among the questions raised is whether using someone's desk for sexual liaisons creates a hostile environment for the office holder and whether differential treatment of two employees disciplined for a forbidden sexual liaison is discrimination. The court's job in this case was to sort through the facts to determine which might give rise to an actionable claim of discrimination and which were merely disgusting.

### WORKPLACE LIFE AT AN INDIANA PRISON

Connie Orton-Bell worked as a substance abuse counselor at a maximum-security prison in Indiana. She had complained at some point about the possibility that someone was using her office computer at night, which raised concerns about a security breach. An investigator looked into her complaint, discovering that her office was being used at night without her knowledge. But it wasn't being invaded by inmates or hackers – it was being used by night-shift employees for sexual liaisons. Specifically, they were having sex on her desk. (This explained why, in the past, she had noticed strange stains on her desk in the morning.) The investigator was apparently relieved by the absence of a security breach and not at all concerned about the sex-on-the-desk problem. Orton-Bell asked the investigator what she should do about the problem, and he replied: "I suggest you wash off your desk every day."[3] When she protested, he insisted that "staff having sex is no concern to us"[4] as long as it does not involve sex between "staff and offender."[5] She also complained to the prison superintendent, and he, like the investigator, said he didn't care as long as offenders were not involved. Orton-Bell learned later that the misuse of her office was widely known and the subject of a long-running office joke.

Sex on the night shift was not the only indicator of a sexualized work environment. Orton-Bell complained of a barrage of sexual comments and incidents that seemed to permeate the environment. (The Seventh Circuit reviewed a grant of summary judgment and thus considered both undisputed facts and disputed facts viewed in the light most favorable to Orton-Bell.) For example, a superintendent who was later fired for an inappropriate sexual relationship with a subordinate had insisted that the subordinate attend department-head meetings, although it was not necessary for her job, just so he could "look down the table at her."[6] The room was apparently filled with attractive women with no job-related reason for attending. And this same superintendent disallowed her, and only her, from taking advantage of a jeans-on-Friday policy because "her ass looked so good that she would cause a riot."[7]

According to Orton-Bell, the sexual comments and innuendo began in the parking lot and extended throughout the workday. In addition to making sexual comments, male employees would "congregate around the pat-down area to watch female employees receive pat-downs on their way into the facility."[8] The onlookers would then comment that they needed a cigarette after watching Orton-Bell get patted down because it was almost like having sex with her. She was asked on one occasion to remove a sweater, leaving her with only a spaghetti-strap camisole underneath. She described the sexualized nature of the work environment as "an onslaught."[9]

Orton-Bell was herself involved in a sexual affair at work. She was involved with Major Joe Ditmer, an officer in charge of custody at the prison and a twenty-five-year veteran of the facility. They were both married but separated from their respective spouses. The affair took place at her home, mostly on lunch breaks, and, on some occasions, in his office. (She disputes this latter fact.) The two also engaged in sexually explicit conversations via work e-mail. The superintendent – the one who told Orton-Bell he did not care whether her coworkers were having sex on her desk – took the position that Orton-Bell and Ditmer's affair was a violation of the State Code of Ethics and the internal standards of conduct. An investigation ensued, which revealed the sexually explicit e-mails and other evidence of the affair, including an admission by Ditmer that they had sex in his office.

Ditmer and Orton-Bell were both suspended for one month and then terminated. Both appealed through a state-employee process. Ditmer's appeal resulted in a settlement that allowed him to resign in good standing, retain his benefits including his pension, and continue to work for the prison as a contractor. Orton-Bell, however, was not able to settle her appeal. It went to a hearing, where the presiding officer determined that she was appropriately terminated. She lost all her employment benefits, was barred from working for the department of corrections in any capacity, and had trouble obtaining unemployment benefits because of the characterization of her termination.

## MAKING SENSE OF THE MESS: ORTON-BELL'S HOSTILE ENVIRONMENT CLAIM

Orton-Bell filed a lawsuit alleging that she had been subjected to a hostile work environment, that she was retaliated against for complaining about the sexual incidents on her desk, and that she was discriminated against by being punished more severely than her male paramour. The trial court ruled against her on all claims and granted summary judgment to the State of Indiana (the defendant in the lawsuit). The Court of Appeals, however, reversed on the hostile environment and discrimination claims, upholding summary judgment only on the retaliation claim.

Orton-Bell's claim of a hostile environment was based on two types of behavior – the constant barrage of sexual comments and conduct (including the unnecessarily public pat-downs of female employees) and the use of her desk for sexual liaisons by night-shift workers. To be actionable, a work environment must be both subjectively and objectively hostile and offensive, severe or pervasive, and based on sex. For an employer to be held liable for an actionable hostile environment, there must also be some basis for direct or vicarious liability.

The constant barrage of sexual comments and manipulations cited by Orton-Bell could meet this standard – a decision for a trier of fact to make on remand. It was inappropriate, in the Seventh Circuit's view, for the district court to preclude a trial by granting summary judgment to the state. The comments were clearly at least as pervasive as those in prior cases in which hostile environments had been deemed actionable. It was also clearly offensive and based on Orton-Bell's sex. She would not have been told to attend meetings unnecessarily just to serve as eye candy for the male supervisor if she were a man; nor would her male coworkers have gawked and made sexual references while she and other women were patted down if they had not been women. And while Orton-Bell did engage in one sexually explicit e-mail exchange with a coworker, the court deemed that an insufficient basis for concluding that the environment was not subjectively offensive to her.

There was also a basis for holding the state liable for this conduct. Much of it was conducted by supervisors, which means the employer is automatically liable unless it can make out the two-pronged affirmative defense based on its efforts to prevent and correct harassment and the employee's failure to take advantage of corrective opportunities. But here, the evidence suggested that Orton-Bell had complained and requested simple changes such as pat-downs in a less public place; her complaints were met with complete indifference.

Sex on the desk raised a different question: Was the use of Orton-Bell's desk and office for sexual liaisons a contributing or independent cause of the hostile environment? It was clearly unwelcome to Orton-Bell, clearly pervasive given its frequency and the widespread knowledge of the practice, and clearly offensive to the objective eye (washing one's desk every morning is hardly a sufficient remedy). Yet, the Seventh Circuit held, this behavior could not create an actionable hostile environment because there was no evidence it occurred because of Orton-Bell's sex. In other words, if the night-shift workers did not choose her office in particular – and the investigator and superintendent did not ignore her complaints – because she is a woman, the environment is not hostile "because of sex" within the meaning of Title VII.

Her retaliation claim lost for the same reason. Although she may well have been retaliated against for complaining about the sex on her desk, her complaint was not about a form of actionable discrimination and, therefore, does not come with protection from retaliation.

## ORTON-BELL'S SEX DISCRIMINATION CLAIM

In addition to her claim of a hostile environment – which is now revived for a trial on remand – Orton-Bell claimed that the state's more favorable treatment of Ditmer's appeal was unlawful sex discrimination. Why would two people being punished for precisely the same conduct end up with such different outcomes? Title VII generally prohibits employers from taking sex into account when setting the terms or conditions of employment – including, of course, termination.

In the Seventh Circuit's view, Orton-Bell made out a prima facie case of discrimination by showing that she suffered an adverse employment action and that a similarly situated employee not in her protected class (i.e., not female) was treated more favorably. The question here is whether Ditmer and Orton-Bell were similarly situated. The burden is on the plaintiff to show that the comparator had the same supervisor, was subject to the same standards, and engaged in similar conduct without mitigating or differentiating circumstances. In this case, the Seventh Circuit concluded that the only differentiating circumstances – Ditmer's twenty-five years of experience and higher position of authority – cut both ways. Perhaps he was treated more leniently because of his long career. But at the same time, one could conclude that he should be judged more harshly for abusing discretion and engaging in behavior that he knew was impermissible. After all, he got his job after his predecessor – the superintendent who made women come to meetings unnecessarily just so he could ogle them – lost his job for exactly the same conduct, engaging in a sexual affair with a subordinate.

It is fair to say, the court concluded, that the two were similarly situated for purposes of being punished for their workplace discretion. Yet they were treated very differently without explanation. More discovery was warranted, the court reasoned, as was a trial on the merits. Thus, it was error for the lower court to grant summary judgment to the state on this claim.

## CONCLUSION

This case does not make one yearn for a job in the Indiana Department of Corrections – perhaps Litchfield Correctional Facility, portrayed in *Orange Is the New Black*, would be less scary – but the Seventh Circuit has done a fair job of matching up the messy allegations with the legal protections against discrimination available under Title VII. Orton-Bell is entitled to her day in court.

A version of this chapter appeared on August 5, 2014, at verdict.justia.com.

# 16

## When the Supervisor Bullies Only Women

Thomas Harvey shouted at his subordinate female employees, and he did so frequently, profanely, and often in public. The shouting had no sexual content and did not involve derogatory language about women. But, the record suggests, only women were subjected to it, at least in its most extreme form.

In its decision in *EEOC v. National Education Association* (NEA), the U.S. Court of Appeals for the Ninth Circuit held that the plaintiffs could proceed to trial on their sexual harassment claim.[1] That decision garnered headlines because neither sexual behavior nor language with sex-specific content was alleged.[2] To those familiar with the law, though, this is not news. Indeed, the fact that the media took note of the case illustrates the wide gap between popular perceptions of sexual harassment law and the actual law of sexual harassment.

In this case, that law was simple and well established: Title VII bans sex discrimination in the workplace. And that ban has long been understood to encompass sex-based harassment – hostile or abusive behavior targeted at employees of one sex, whether or not it is sexual in nature.[3]

Thus, the Ninth Circuit was entirely right to allow this case to go forward.

### THE BOSS'S TREATMENT OF WOMEN AT THE NEA-ALASKA

The alleged harasser, Thomas Harvey, was the executive director of NEA-Alaska, a labor union representing teachers and other public school employees. Plaintiffs Carol Christopher, Julie Bhend, and Carmela Chamara held various positions in the union subordinate to Harvey. According to testimony of plaintiffs and several other witnesses, Harvey routinely yelled at the plaintiffs with "little or no provocation." Worse, his shouting rants were often accompanied by aggressive physical gestures like lunging at, pumping fists at, invading the personal space of, and grabbing plaintiffs while barking commands or complaints at them. Plaintiff Christopher described an incident, for example, where Harvey screamed profanely at her for not reading her work e-mail while away (on an approved day off) visiting her dying sister.

Each plaintiff testified that Harvey's conduct rendered the work environment physically and verbally threatening – so much so that one of them did not seek pay for overtime she had worked because she "was too scared of Mr. Harvey to turn [the records of her overtime hours] in to him."

## DID THESE PLAINTIFFS EXPERIENCE SEXUAL HARASSMENT?

The plaintiffs sued their employer, claiming that Harvey's behavior created a hostile work environment. But the district court granted summary judgment to the employer, concluding that the requirement under Title VII that harassment be "because of sex" had not been met.

After all, the court pointed out, no one alleged that Harvey's behavior was lewd or sexual (either explicitly or through undertones), or that the content of his shouting was gender specific. Nor was there any evidence that Harvey harbored any animus toward women – either generally or just at work – or had some specific motive to make their lives miserable. It is well established that Title VII does not protect against generally brutish or oppressive behavior at work (something lots of employees might experience), but only those behaviors that occur *because of the victim's sex.*

The appellate court, however, found that the "because of sex" requirement was plainly fulfilled by plaintiffs' alleged experiences. Whether or not Harvey derided them because they were women, he – according to the bulk of evidence in the record – only directed his brutish behavior at women and never at men. And that, the Ninth Circuit, held, is sufficient to qualify Harvey's behavior as sex-based, and therefore illegal, harassment. Women were treated differently – and worse – than men were, because they were women, and that, the court held, was the key.

## WHEN IS HARASSMENT "BECAUSE OF SEX"?

When courts first started to recognize sexual harassment as a form of illegal sex discrimination in the late 1970s, they tended not to focus on the "because of sex" requirement found in Title VII. They simply assumed – in many cases, accurately – that male-on-female sexual advances in the workplace were motivated by the man's sexual desire and, therefore, would not likely have occurred *but for* the victim's sex.[4]

That assumption caused problems later, as courts began to confront allegations of same-sex harassment and allegations of harassment that, while directed at women, was not sexual in nature. The usual assumption, that sex harassment always stemmed from men's heterosexual desire, did not work in such cases, and courts and scholars were thus forced to reconsider how the "because of sex" requirement might otherwise be proven.[5]

The answers were, by and large, unsatisfactory. Some courts refused to find illegal harassment without male-on-female sexual behavior.[6] Others looked *only* for proof of sexual desire, whether the harassment was opposite sex or same sex – choosing to ignore even dramatically different gender differences in employment experiences as long as desire was not at issue.[7]

Still other courts – more reasonably – acknowledged that harassment could occur without sexual desire or behavior.[8] But, often, as law professor Vicki Schultz has pointed out, the courts that took this view would evaluate each individual incident separately, and find that none was sufficient to make the harassment actionable.[9] (Harassment, under established Title VII jurisprudence, must either be severe *or* pervasive to be actionable.[10])

## ONCALE V. SUNDOWNER OFFSHORE SERVICES: THE SUPREME COURT WEIGHS IN

Much of the confusion surrounding atypical claims of harassment was resolved by the Supreme Court's 1998 opinion in *Oncale*. There, the court was reviewing a federal appellate opinion that had said same-sex harassment could *never* be actionable under Title VII. Rejecting such an unwarranted and harsh categorical rule, the Court set forth a variety of ways plaintiffs could prove that harassment occurred "because of sex," regardless of whether the conduct was sexual in nature.[11]

According to the unanimous opinion, harassment may be "because of sex" if it is motivated by (opposite-sex or same-sex) sexual desire – motivation the court may infer from the nature of the conduct or find because of direct evidence of the harasser's sexual orientation. But harassment may *also*, according to *Oncale*, be actionable if it is motivated by animus toward one sex or their presence in the workplace, or is simply directed at members of only one sex. Animus might be proven by harassment that uses sex-specific or derogatory terms (e.g., "women have no business working construction"), and differential targeting might be proven by direct comparative evidence about how the alleged harasser treats members of each sex in the workplace.

All of these showings suffice because the guiding principle, which the Court borrowed from an earlier precedent, *Harris v. Forklift Systems*, is "whether members of one sex are exposed to disadvantageous terms or conditions of employment to which members of the other sex are not exposed."[12]

As the Ninth Circuit recognized, the allegations involving Harvey fall squarely into one of the *Oncale* categories: direct comparative evidence about how the alleged harasser treats members of both sexes.[13] The allegations – supported by many of the uncontested pieces of evidence – state that Harvey bullied women almost exclusively. When he did mistreat men, it was less physically threatening, less humiliating, and less severe. This is the kind of comparative evidence *Oncale* suggested would suffice to prove sex-based harassment.

## UNDER TITLE VII, WHAT MATTERS IS TREATMENT, NOT MOTIVE

Does it matter *why* Harvey singled out women for mistreatment? No.

Title VII never looks for specific intent to discriminate or cause harm. Suppose, for instance, a supervisor categorically refuses to hire women for a road crew job, regardless of their capacity, experience, or qualifications. That supervisor is just as guilty of discrimination whether he wants to protect women from an unsavory working environment, wants to exclude them because he feels them to be unqualified for manual labor, or even does not consciously feel any bias against women at all. The point is that the supervisor's hiring practices are biased. Regardless of the supervisor's motive, the sex of the victim is the cause for the imposition of an adverse employment practice. Women are treated worse as a result of their gender: it's as simple as that.

In sexual harassment cases, the specific intent of the harasser is, similarly, not relevant to the viability of a claim. A man may truly believe he is flattering a woman when he makes a sexual advance, and, yet, if she can prove that a reasonable person would perceive the conduct as hostile, offensive, or abusive, she might prevail in a claim of hostile environment sexual harassment. (Social science research suggests that "boundary differentiation" problems – where men and women draw different lines between acceptable and unacceptable social-sexual conduct at work – account for at least some incidents of sexual harassment.[14])

As the Ninth Circuit explained in this case, Title VII focuses on the *effects* of employment practices and harassing conduct rather than their *purpose*. Harvey's conduct had a sex-based effect. And that is true whether he treated women worse because he wanted to drive them from the workplace or because he simply had a bad temper and took it out on those he thought least likely to fight back.

As a result of the Ninth Circuit's decision, the trial court is now directed to make a quantitative comparison of the number of female versus male targets of Harvey's behavior. And because of the focus on effects, the question is not only whether Harvey behaved differently (and worse) toward women. It is also whether his behavior – even if comparable on the surface – had a different *effect* on women. There is evidence in the record, for example, that when men were shouted at, they were able to resume a normal working relationship with Harvey afterward. Women, on the other hand, testified that Harvey's abuse affected all their interactions with him and their comfort at work. The case was rightly sent back to trial to see whether, as the Ninth Circuit put it, "Harvey's behavior affected women more adversely than it affected men."[15]

## A STRAIGHTFORWARD CASE ILLUMINATES
## MISUNDERSTANDING OF SEXUAL HARASSMENT LAW

As noted above, this case was straightforward and correctly decided. Granted, the type of conduct at issue is a bit different than the way one usually pictures sexual or sex-based harassment. Typically, our culture and the media tend to portray sex harassment in the way it was conceived when the law began to be developed, in the late 1970s, as unwanted sexual advances or coerced sexual submission.

But it's worth noting that prohibitions on sex harassment are rooted not in antisex laws, but in antidiscrimination laws. The point of Title VII is workplace equality, not a workplace free of sexual advances. No wonder, then, that the Supreme Court has squarely held that differential bullying on the basis of sex violates federal anti-discrimination law: supervisory bullying that targets women means women have a worse experience at work than men do, simply because they are women.[16] And that is just what the plaintiffs say happened here.

Had Harvey bullied his male and female employees equally – and caused them equally adverse effects – Title VII might not have been implicated. A boss's general workplace bullying does not violate federal law.[17] Perhaps, at least in extreme cases, federal law ought to be amended to reach such bullying: researchers and the media have noted that such bullying is a growing phenomenon, and one should not have to suffer abuse as the price of working. Yet, as it stands, Title VII provides no general protection against abuse at work. Instead, it focuses on protecting employees against group-based, discriminatory harms.

Laws making workplace bullying illegal, regardless of the victim's protected class status, have been introduced in a handful of states in the past few years, but none has yet been enacted into law.[18] However, that does not mean that abusive bosses are immune. In what experts say is the first case of its type, a jury recently held a heart surgeon liable for bullying an employee (screaming and lunging at him in a workplace confrontation) and awarded the victim more than $300,000 in damages for the incident.[19]

Horrible bosses beware: there might be consequences for your actions, particularly if you target one group of employees for abuse.

A version of this chapter appeared on September 20, 2005, at writ.findlaw.com.

# 17

## The Equal Opportunity Harasser

Connecticut fire chief Marquam Johnson may be the man academics like to hypothesize about, a true equal opportunity harasser who is alleged to have harassed both men and women in equally sexual, and equally offensive, ways.[1]

According to complaints from a male deputy, Johnson grabs men by their testicles, gooses them, and puts his hands in their front pockets so he can simulate having anal sex with them. According to complaints from a female secretary, he whacks her on the buttocks and makes comments about the size of her breasts.

Both the male deputy and the female secretary have filed lawsuits against the Torrington, Connecticut, fire department, alleging that Johnson's conduct created a sexually hostile working environment in violation of Title VII, the federal antidiscrimination statute. Both contend, as they must to prevail, that they were harassed because of their sex.

But can it really be the case that both the man and the woman were harassed because of their sex, as Title VII requires? Might it be more accurate to say that if all the allegations against him are true, Johnson harasses regardless of sex, not because of it? Or, put another way, is Johnson's alleged harassment so indiscriminate that while it may constitute a tort, it does not constitute unlawful discrimination in violation of federal civil rights laws?

### THE "BECAUSE OF SEX" REQUIREMENT

As discussed in Chapters 15 and 16, Title VII only prohibits harassment that occurs "because of sex" – it is that hook that distinguishes actionable discrimination from merely bad behavior. The long and hard-fought battle to bring same-sex harassment within the ambit of Title VII was what focused emphasis on the statutory requirement that harassment be "because of sex" in order for suit to be brought.[2]

Title VII's "because of sex" requirement, however, has turned out to be more difficult to interpret than courts initially believed. For instance, the reasoning that says sexual harassment comes from opposite-sex desire, and is thus inherently "because of sex," breaks down when the harassing supervisor is bisexual. If a bisexual supervisor gropes a female subordinate, he or she may well do the same thing to a male subordinate, thus undermining the female victim's claim that she was harassed because of her sex.

This scenario, perhaps discussed more by law professors than courts, has been viewed as an unfortunate, but statutorily required, exception to Title VII. No one harassed by a bisexual supervisor could claim discrimination – so the thinking goes – because male and female victims, while both being demeaned, were being treated equally.[3]

The sexual desire presumption also breaks down when it turns out that harassment is the product of other motivations: the desire to reinforce sex roles, to drive women out of men's jobs, or to exert power over subordinates. In those cases, too, plaintiffs must prove that the harassment occurs because of sex. That leads to another problem: the equal opportunity harasser. He is different from the bisexual harasser in that he is not motivated by sexual attraction to harass both men and women. But he is the same as the bisexual harasser in that he directs his harassing conduct at both men and women. Chief Johnson, if the allegations against him are true, is one of these men.

## A THEORY TO SHOW "EQUAL OPPORTUNITY" HARASSMENT IS STILL "BECAUSE OF SEX"

In an amicus (friend-of-the-court) brief filed in *Oncale*, a group of public interest organizations proposed a theory to make equal opportunity harassment actionable under Title VII.[4]

"Equal opportunity" harassment, they argued, is "because of sex" in that sexual acts are inherently related to the sex of the person subjected to them. Gender affects not only the nature of the sexual acts of harassment (grabbing breasts versus grabbing testicles) but also how the victim will experience the harassment.

If adopted by the courts, this approach would be consistent with the courts' prior treatment of sex-based and race-based harassment. Suppose, for example, that a supervisor uses sex-based stereotypes and slurs against both female employees (e.g., "women are not objective enough to be doctors") and male employees (e.g., "men are not nurturing enough to be nurses"). A female doctor and a male nurse could both sue based on the supervisor's slurs, even though he is an "equal opportunity" user of stereotypes, because each is harassed because of sex. Along the same lines, surely an African-American employee who is the victim of a racial slur would not lose out because the perpetrator directed a different racial slur toward an Asian-American employee. "Equal opportunity" racial discrimination is seen for what it is: racial discrimination.

## WHY EQUAL OPPORTUNITY HARASSERS MAY BE SAFE FROM SUIT

Unfortunately, the public interest organizations' theory that all sexual conduct is because of sex did not persuade the Supreme Court in *Oncale*. And since *Oncale*, only a few courts have revisited the question of the equal opportunity harasser. The Seventh Circuit is one of those courts. In a recent decision, that court refused to allow a married couple to go forward with allegations that the same male supervisor had sexually harassed both of them by soliciting sex from each.[5] Although the Second Circuit, the jurisdiction in which the cases against Chief Johnson have been brought, has not expressly ruled on the viability of a claim against an "equal opportunity" harasser, a federal district court in Connecticut has followed the Seventh Circuit's decision.[6] And given the weight of authority excusing such harassment, the likelihood that such a claim will succeed seems, unfortunately, to be slight.

A version of this chapter appeared on April 10, 2001, at writ.findlaw.com.

*Update: In 2003, the district court ruled that Marquam Johnson's inappropriate conduct did not violate Title VII because it was neither "because of sex" – Johnson was "equally, if not more, sexually offensive to male employees" – nor "severe or pervasive." In 2004, the Second Circuit affirmed,[7] lending some unfortunate reality to the law professors' hypothetical.*

# 18

# Periodontal Perils

Dr. Luis Mota, a periodontist, alleged that he was harassed by his supervisor, Dr. Raul Caffesse, also a periodontist. Accordingly, Mota sued his employer, the University of Texas Houston Health Science Center. A jury ultimately found for Mota, agreeing with him that Caffesse had engaged in a classic pattern of harassment. The Fifth Circuit Court of Appeals upheld the verdict.[1]

The case provides one example of how same-sex harassment cases are being litigated now – in light of the Supreme Court's ruling in 1998, in *Oncale v. Sundowner Offshore Services*. *Oncale* held that same-sex conduct can be the basis for a sexual harassment lawsuit, but only as long as the harassment is "because of sex."[2] The Court observed that this requirement might be met in one of three ways: (i) with evidence of the perpetrator's homosexuality; (ii) with evidence that the perpetrator in fact targeted only members of one sex; *or* (iii) with evidence that the harassment took the form of gender-role policing – that is, it was perpetrated to punish an employee for failing to live up to traditional gender norms. The most obvious type of Title VII claim permitted by the Court in *Oncale* would be one brought based on sexual harassment of a male by a gay male supervisor who was motivated by sexual desire.[3]

## THE FACTS

Caffesse was world-renowned among periodontists. A family friend of Mota's, Caffesse encouraged Mota to apply for a job at the university and, once hired, took him under his wing. After Mota's arrival, Caffesse arranged for them to attend a conference together – and even to share the same room. During the conference, Caffesse sexually propositioned Mota, warning that he had to "get along with him and that people who worked with him had to get along with him and that he only wanted to know [Mota] better."

The unwelcome sexual advances recurred at a series of periodontic conferences across the country over a number of months. When Mota rejected the advances, Caffesse admonished him to keep quiet. He also implicitly threatened to have Mota fired: when Caffesse had grown to dislike people in the past, Caffesse allegedly told Mota Caffesse had "helped them leave" the university.

Mota also alleged (and the jury also agreed) that after he filed a formal complaint, the university retaliated by denying him a stipend he had earned, refusing his request for paid medical leave, and refusing to grant him access to equipment and his office during the unpaid leave he ultimately took.

Mota filed suit initially against the university under Title VII of the Civil Rights Act of 1964, which prohibits sex discrimination in employment, including sexual harassment.[4] Because Mota was an employee of an educational institution that receives federal assistance, he might also have filed his suit against the university under Title IX of the Education Amendments of 1972, which prohibits sex discrimination in education.[5] Plaintiffs sometimes prefer Title IX because it does not have any administrative prerequisites and damages are uncapped. However, many courts have held that discrimination claims brought by employees of educational institutions – as opposed to students – are preempted by Title VII, so Mota may have assumed that, as an employee, he could not bring a Title IX claim. In any event, whatever his reasons, Mota chose to sue under Title VII alone.

After initiating suit against the university, Mota later added claims against Caffesse for defamation and intentional infliction of emotional distress. Because Title VII does not permit individuals (as opposed to employers) to be held liable,[6] those claims were brought under Texas state law. Caffesse and Mota settled out of court for $290,000, but, as noted above, the case against the university went to trial. The verdict against the university came to nearly $900,000 – including compensatory damages, front pay, back pay, and attorneys' fees.

## SAME-SEX HARASSMENT: PART OF THE LEGAL LANDSCAPE NOW?

To prevail against the university, Mota had to prove both that he suffered actionable sexual harassment and that the university should be held liable for that harassment. Hostile environment harassment occurs when an employee is subjected to unwelcome sexual conduct that is severe or pervasive, and which creates a hostile or offensive working environment. Those elements were clearly satisfied by Caffesse's conduct in this case – particularly in light of Caffesse's recurrent advances and his implied threat to retaliate.

So far, what is remarkable about the Mota case is how unremarkable it was. As summarized above, it was litigated more or less just as an opposite-sex harassment case would have been. Did it matter at all that Caffesse was a man harassing a man? The answer is, in theory, yes, but in practice, no.

The Supreme Court confirmed in *Oncale* that same-sex harassment is actionable under Title VII as long as it happens "because of sex." With opposite-sex harassment, courts have often overlooked this requirement, simply assuming that when a man engages in sexual conduct toward a woman, it must be because of sex. But the Court in *Oncale* stressed that courts need proof that this requirement is met before they can conclude that actionable harassment has occurred.[7]

The "because of sex" requirement can be proven in different ways; the easiest is evidence that the harassment is motivated by sexual desire. Where there is no evidence of homosexuality or sexual desire, satisfying the "because of sex" requirement is more difficult. Post-*Oncale* courts have relied on comparative evidence about other victims (does the harasser *in fact* only target victims of one sex?), evidence about the nature of the conduct (did the harasser do something obviously sexual?), and evidence of the harasser's animosity toward his own sex (for example, was the harasser policing gender roles by punishing an effeminate man?).

## CAN FULFILLMENT OF THE "BECAUSE OF SEX" REQUIREMENT BE PRESUMED?

Strikingly, the Fifth Circuit's opinion in this case is devoid of any discussion about whether Caffesse singled out Mota "because of sex." The opinion contains no discussion of whether Caffesse is gay, nor does it note whether his past victims (there allegedly were some) were all male or whether Caffesse bore animosity toward men.

It seems that the conventional presumption in opposite-sex cases – that a harasser engaging in sexual conduct is acting out of sexual desire that is reserved for one sex alone – was indulged here, even though the case involved same-sex harassment. That may be evidence that cases of same-sex harassment cases are becoming a regular part of the legal landscape – a development that is part and parcel of an increased tolerance for, and normalization of, homosexuality.

Nevertheless, even if this presumption is applied in same-sex and opposite-sex case alike, it may be in conflict with *Oncale* – which stressed the need for proof of the "because of sex" requirement in sexual harassment cases in general, and in same-sex harassment cases in particular.

A version of this chapter appeared on August 28, 2001, at writ.findlaw.com.

# 19

# Punishing Effeminacy

The U.S. Court of Appeals for the Ninth Circuit has done it again. It issued an opinion that sounds extreme, may be vulnerable to reversal by the Supreme Court, and, yet, is correct. The case was *Rene v. MGM Grand Hotel*, and the opinion was issued by an en banc panel – that is, a large panel of judges reconsidering an earlier, three-judge panel's decision. (Here, the three-judge panel had dismissed the claim.[1])

In *Rene*, the *en banc* panel held that a man harassed by his coworkers because he was gay could maintain an action for sexual harassment under Title VII.[2] The plaintiff in the suit, Median Rene, is an openly gay man who worked as a butler in a Las Vegas hotel, on a floor reserved for high-profile and wealthy clients. According to his complaint and evidence obtained during discovery, Rene was subjected to a hostile environment by his fellow butlers, all male, over a two-year period.

## THE SEXUAL ORIENTATION CONUNDRUM UNDER TITLE VII

Rene filed suit alleging that this harassing behavior violated his rights under Title VII, which prohibits discrimination (including harassment) on the basis of sex, but not on the basis of sexual orientation. Contrary to the views of former House Speaker John Boehner, whose spokesperson claims that he has "always believed this is covered by existing law,"[3] current federal antidiscrimination law does not prevent employers from taking adverse employment actions against someone because he or she is gay. Every court to address the issue has held that Title VII does not prohibit sexual orientation discrimination,[4] and Congress has failed to amend Title VII to add sexual orientation to its list of prohibited characteristics despite several bills that have been introduced over the years.

The first bill to include protections against sexual-orientation discrimination was introduced by Congresswoman Bella Abzug in 1974. That bill was broader than the current one, proposing broad protection for gays and lesbians against discrimination in employment, housing, and public accommodations. Throughout the 1970s and

1980s, similar bills were introduced, but none became law.[5] In 1994, the first version of ENDA, a bill focused solely on protections against workplace discrimination, was introduced in the Senate by the late Senator Ted Kennedy, which held hearings on the bill. ENDA's express purpose is to fill the existing gap in federal antidiscrimination law for gays, lesbians, and transgender individuals. Under ENDA, employers would cease being able to take these characteristics into account when deciding whether to hire, fire, or promote someone. Neither that bill, nor any versions that succeeded it, made it through the Senate. The House passed a version of ENDA in 2007, by a vote of 235–184, but the Senate never voted on the bill and then-president George Bush issued a veto threat that made any future legislative action futile.[6] In 2013, by a vote of sixty-four to thirty-two, the U.S. Senate passed another version of ENDA, but the Republican-controlled House never brought it to a vote.[7]

The only direct prohibition on sexual orientation discrimination under federal law comes from Executive Order 13087, issued in 1998 by President Bill Clinton, which bans such discrimination in the civilian federal workforce.[8] This order was in response to a long, if little known, history of the federal government's banning gays from federal civil service jobs. It left in place the "Don't Ask Don't Tell" policy, which prohibited openly gay and lesbian individuals from serving in the military. (This policy was finally repealed as of September 2011.) Employees may also be protected from sexual orientation discrimination by state and local laws, of which there are an increasing number.[9]

Accordingly, Rene could not simply allege, for Title VII purposes, that he had faced discrimination because he was gay. Rather, to state a Title VII case, he was required to allege that he had faced discrimination "because of sex." Had he? That was the question for the trial court – which said no, as did the appellate panel. But, as noted above, the en banc panel disagreed.

## APPLYING THE "BECAUSE OF SEX" TEST IN SAME-SEX HARASSMENT CASES

The "because of sex" issue, elucidated in the Supreme Court's 1998 opinion in *Oncale v. Sundowner Offshore Services*,[10] becomes particularly problematic in same-sex harassment cases in which either or both parties are not gay. But even in these instances, a plaintiff can satisfy the "because of sex" requirement in other ways. Plaintiffs, then, can point to the nature of the conduct and ask the factfinder to infer that sexual touching is always because of the victim's gender.

This point ought to help Rene's case, as he alleges that he was the victim of the same kind of demeaning sexual touching that one thinks of as the basis for a more traditional sexual harassment case. Similarly, the sexual gifts and images Rene was given echo traditional sexual harassment cases in which, for instance, men leave sexual photos and items for women in their workplace to find or view.

Plaintiffs may also rely on a theory of gender policing – that the perpetrator harassed an effeminate man to punish him for stepping outside of traditional gender roles. That, too, can be the basis for an inference that the conduct occurred "because of sex." This theory is facilitated not only by *Oncale* but also by an earlier ruling of the Court, handed down in 1989, *Price Waterhouse v. Hopkins*. There, the Court recognized that the application of a sex stereotype is a form of sex discrimination. Thus, the Court found that illegal discrimination had occurred when an unfeminine woman was turned down for partner at least in part because of the way she dressed and conducted herself. By the same logic, an effeminate man who has been harassed by straight workers may have an actionable claim if he can prove that the harassment he endured was motivated by "gender policing" – that is, by trying to punish or rein in his gender nonconformity. But courts have been wary of "bootstrapping" in this area – remaining reluctant to allow gay or lesbian plaintiffs using sex-discrimination theory to remedy what is at core sexual-orientation discrimination (and thus is not actionable).[11]

Again, this helps Rene. He alleges he was called names that are usually endearments directed toward women, and exposed to the same whistles and blown kisses women are usually the ones to endure. In harassing him as they might harass a woman, Rene can argue, the other butlers were expressing discomfort with his sexuality and punishing him "because of sex."

## THE RULING OF THE EN BANC COURT: RELYING ON THE *ONCALE* DECISION

In a split decision, the eleven-member en banc court upheld Rene's legal theory that harassment may be motivated by sexual orientation but still be actionable under Title VII. Evidence of the plaintiff's sexual orientation, the panel concluded, is irrelevant to his claim.

A plurality of the panel joined an opinion holding that as long as the conduct is sexual in nature, it is "because of sex." Evidence of the victim's sexual orientation is simply irrelevant. Thus because Rene was subjected to physical attacks, "which targeted body parts clearly linked to his sexuality," the harassment of him was "because of sex."[12]

In *Oncale* itself, the *Rene* plurality explained, the plaintiff was a gay man who worked on an oil rig with no women. For the Supreme Court to find his claim actionable, it must have believed that it was enough for him to show he was discriminated against in comparison to other men. Using that approach, the panel concluded that Rene, like Oncale, suffered actionable discrimination.

## THE CONCURRENCE'S DIFFERING APPROACH: GENDER STEREOTYPING HARASSMENT

Three judges concurred in the result, giving the plurality enough votes to overturn the lower court's grant of summary judgment to the employer. But each wrote separately to articulate a different rationale for reaching that result. In Judge

Pregerson's view, the proper characterization of Rene's claim is "gender stereo-typing harassment." Rene was being punished by his male coworkers for failing to live up to their standards of masculine behavior.[13] Gender policing is actionable under Title VII. The Supreme Court gave its imprimatur to such a claim in *Price Waterhouse v. Hopkins*.[14] There, the Court held that Ann Hopkins was a victim of sex discrimination when her employer criticized her for being, in essence, insufficiently feminine, in the way she dressed and conducted herself.

The Ninth Circuit applied *Hopkins* in a case involving a harassment claim by a gay male employee. In that case, *Nichols v. Azteca Restaurant Enterprises, Inc.*, the Court concluded that verbal harassment reflecting hostility toward the victim because he was too feminine constituted illegal sex stereotyping. As a result, the court concluded, such conduct was a valid basis for a discrimination suit.[15]

## THE DISSENTERS' DIVERGENCE: ONLY SEXUAL ORIENTATION DISCRIMINATION, AND NO MORE

Four judges dissented from the result in this case, expressing the view that Rene's claim was invalid under Title VII. The dissenters concluded that Rene could not show he was harassed because he was male, but only because he was gay. And because Title VII does not forbid sexual orientation discrimination, they would have held that he had no case.

On the basis of the evidence, the dissenters reasoned, Rene could not avail himself of any of the different ways of proving the harassment was because of sex. The harassers were not homosexual, and there was no evidence that they were generally hostile to the presence of men in the workplace. In addition, because only men worked on the twenty-ninth floor of the hotel, there was no direct comparative evidence showing that women were treated better than Rene was. Without any of these pieces of evidence, the dissenters suggested, Rene could not make out a valid claim.

The dissenters also cautioned that a case premised on sex stereotyping must be based on the way the victim conducts himself on the job. In their view, a man who is homosexual in his private life but lives up to masculine norms at work cannot recover for harassment based on sex stereotyping.

## WHICH JUDGES GOT IT RIGHT? THE PLURALITY'S QUESTIONABLE REASONING

The plurality put forth a potentially valid theory. Nevertheless, it also made some serious missteps that undermine the opinion.

First, the plurality appears at times to equate the term "sex," as used in Title VII, with "sexual." By using these terms interchangeably, it is easy to conclude that any sexual conduct is "because of sex." But the Supreme Court has made clear that "sex," in this context, is interchangeable with "gender."[16] For Title

VII's purposes, "sex" refers to one's status as male or female, not to sexual activity per se.

Second, the plurality misspeaks when it claims that it is illegal discrimination to treat some men differently from other men, without regard to how women are treated. To the contrary, what makes discrimination illegal under Title VII is that it singles out one sex for worse treatment than the other—or clearly takes sex into account.

Third, the plurality's reading of *Oncale* is probably not warranted, because the Supreme Court in that case did not say that *Oncale* had a valid claim. It only held that the lower court's categorical rejection of same-sex harassment was inappropriate.

Thus, the Court in *Oncale* held that *some* same-sex harassment cases could be based on same-sex harassment, but not that Oncale's own case was necessarily one of them. It then remanded the case to the lower court for a determination whether he was harassed "because of sex." The case settled out of court prior to any determination being made: there has still, in short, been no judicial determination as to whether Oncale's allegations described a case of discrimination "because of sex."

For all of these reasons, the plurality opinion is open to criticism.

## THE BASIC PRINCIPLE BEHIND THE PLURALITY OPINION MAY BE CORRECT

Grabbing a man's testicles, for instance, is something one only does to a man; grabbing a woman's breasts is something uniquely done to women. And in Rene's case, putting a finger into a gay man's anus through his clothes, in a gesture that apparently refers to gay sex between men, occurs not only because the victim is gay but also because he is a man. A woman would be unlikely to face the same treatment, and if she did, it would likely have a different meaning, connoting the harasser's ability to touch her intimately, rather than taunting her for her sexuality. It is thus in most cases appropriate to draw the inference that sexual touching is done "because of sex."

Of course, there may be unusual cases in which such an inference is not warranted –for example, the case of the rare equal opportunity harasser who demands oral sex from both his male and female employees. (See Chapter 17 for more on this rare bird.) Nevertheless, the shortcut the plurality takes, from sexual touching to touching "because of sex," will in most cases be supportable.

### *Judge Pregerson's Concurrence Offers Another Strong Basis for the Result*

There is also another reason to believe the plurality reached the right result, even if its theory has flaws. Judge Pregerson's concurrence puts forth a workable theory for validating Rene's claim, one that supports the plurality's result.

The Supreme Court's validation of sex-stereotyping discrimination in *Hopkins* has been underutilized in the decades since it was issued. In fact, it authorizes a potentially wide-ranging approach to evaluating both opposite- and same-sex harassment claims. When gay men are harassed by their coworkers for being effeminate or womanly, they are being subjected to harassment on the basis of sex. It is because they are men who do not live up to male standards that they are singled out for maltreatment. In the same vein, women who are harassed because they do "men's jobs," or wear "butch" hairstyles, or choose to wear pants and not skirts, are being singled out for their failure to live up to standards for women.

## POTENTIAL LIMITS AND EXTENSIONS OF THE SEX-STEREOTYPE APPROACH TO EVALUATING HARASSMENT CLAIMS

The sex-stereotype theory only works, however, if the victim does in fact defy gender stereotypes. A federal court in New York, in the case of *Martin v. New York State Department of Correctional Services*, dismissed a claim similar to the one in *Rene* because the plaintiff had not proven he was effeminate enough to justify invoking the sex-stereotype theory of harassment.[17] This approach may be what the Supreme Court uses to limit the breadth of the sex-stereotype theory should it decide to hear the *Rene* case.

On the other hand, the sex-stereotype approach could encompass even more than the concurrence lets on. Even more broadly, one could argue that all harassment based on sexual orientation is harassment based on sex, because it involves the application of different expectations to men and women.

Harassing men for being gay singles them out for doing something that women are routinely expected to do – namely, sleep with men. That's sex discrimination, plain and simple.

No court has ever acknowledged this result in the context of sex discrimination. However, the Supreme Court applied similar reasoning in *Loving v. Virginia*, when it declared antimiscegenation laws unconstitutional.[18]

Virginia's law prohibited whites and nonwhites from marrying. Virginia argued that the law did not violate the equal protection clause because it was an "equal opportunity" law: it prevented whites from marrying blacks as much as it prevented blacks from marrying whites. The Court, however, held that the law could constitute race discrimination regardless of the fact that it applied to both races.[19]

Sex orientation discrimination discriminates "because of sex" in the same way that the Virginia law, as the Court held, discriminated "because of race." Sexual orientation discrimination is exemplified by a workplace norm, enforced by harassing coworkers, saying that men should sleep only with women and women should sleep only with men. The Virginia law said, similarly, that whites should only marry whites, and blacks should only marry blacks. Both are discriminatory for the same reason. Both the norm and the law, in prohibiting "mixing," constitute discrimination.

Rene and other homosexual plaintiffs should try this theory, as well as others, when they argue that they have faced discrimination not only due to sexual orientation but also "because of sex."

A version of this chapter appeared on October 8, 2002, at writ.findlaw.com.

*Update: The Supreme Court did not review this case and, in fact, has never revisited the sex-stereotyping theory it approved in the* Price Waterhouse *opinion in 1989. But many scholars have written about these issues, and it continues to be used by both gay and transgender plaintiffs.[20] In 2015, a federal district court in California ruled that sexual orientation discrimination is a form of sex discrimination, regardless of whether the employer's conduct involved the application of sex stereotypes.[21]*

# Late-Night Affairs with David Letterman

David Letterman rocked the late-night television scene on October 1, 2009, with a long and winding on-air confession about a series of intra-office affairs. He revealed little in the way of detail, except to acknowledge that he has "had sex with women who work for me on this show," behavior he described as "creepy." He followed up a few nights later with an apology to his wife, whom he admitted to having "hurt terribly."[1]

The confession was prompted by the indictment and arrest of Robert Joel Halderman, an Emmy-winning CBS producer, for allegedly blackmailing and extorting Letterman. More specifically, prosecutors say that Halderman asked for two million dollars in exchange for his promise not to sell a screenplay based on Letterman's escapades. Media coverage of the scandal turned quickly from Halderman's conduct to Letterman's. In particular, many asked, did Letterman do anything wrong – and, in particular, anything illegal – by having sex with lots of women in his office?[2]

The term "sexual harassment" has been tossed around in the media during the course of the controversy, including by Halderman's lawyer, who claims to have evidence of it. But, legally speaking, did Letterman's conduct – based on what we know about it thus far – constitute unlawful sexual harassment?

## SETTING THE STAGE: THE BASICS OF HARASSMENT LAW

Recall from earlier chapters that sexual harassment can manifest in two forms: quid pro quo and hostile environment. Quid pro quo harassment occurs when a person with supervisory authority takes a tangible employment action (such as demotion or firing) against a subordinate employee who refuses to submit to sexual advances. "Sleep with me or you're fired," is the classic example here. Hostile work environment harassment occurs when an employee is subjected to unwelcome conduct of a sexual nature that is so severe or so pervasive as to create an objectively hostile, abusive, or offensive working environment. An example with which readers might be familiar occurs in the movie *North Country* (which is based on a real case) in which female miners face a range of types of abuse from male coworkers and supervisors at the mine.[3]

## THE LETTERMAN SITUATION

Although there has been plenty of media coverage of the Letterman scandal, we actually know very little about the underlying events. But we do know, based on Letterman's confession, that he had sexual relationships with at least a handful of women who worked for him.

However, when it comes to evaluating the possibility of sexual harassment, what we do not know is more important than what we do. We do not know, for example, how many women in the office he was involved with. We don't know the circumstances of any of the relationships: When did the relationships occur, and are any of them still ongoing? Were they truly consensual, or was there a quid pro quo situation? Were there women who were involved with Letterman who were rewarded or singled out because of the relationships? Conversely, were the women and men who were *not* involved with Letterman adversely affected by the relationships?

## ONE KEY QUESTION: WERE THE RELATIONSHIPS COERCED OR OTHERWISE UNWELCOME?

In order for a sexual harassment case to materialize here, someone would have to complain. For instance, one of the women who was involved with Letterman might, in theory, complain. And if she had been coerced into the relationship with Letterman by promises of job benefits or threats of adverse consequences, she could allege quid pro quo harassment.

Alternatively, if she found the advances unwelcome, but she was not outright coerced or extorted by threat, then she could potentially fall back on a hostile environment claim. Indeed, the first Supreme Court case to acknowledge the existence of the hostile work environment claim, *Meritor Savings Bank v. Vinson*, involved a bank teller who had been in a long-term sexual relationship with her boss that she claimed was voluntary but unwelcome.[4] In the Letterman case, it remains an unknown whether the conduct of the women was coerced or whether Letterman's advances (assuming he, not the women, made the advances) were unwelcome.

Some have argued that sex with the boss is inherently coercive and therefore always inappropriate – but that is definitely not a reflection of the law as it now stands. Still, it is possible to argue that behavior that may not be illegal is nonetheless morally wrong. And the National Organization for Women (NOW) made just such an argument when it issued a press release declaring Letterman's behavior inappropriate. As the statement read:

> Recent developments in the David Letterman extortion controversy have raised serious issues about the abuse of power leading to an inappropriate, if not hostile, workplace environment for women and employees. In the case of Letterman, he is a multi-million dollar host of one of the most popular late-night shows; in that role, he wields the ultimate authority as to who gets hired, who gets fired, who gets raises, who advances, and who does entry-level tasks among the Late Show employees. As "the boss," he is responsible for setting the tone for his entire workplace – and he did that with sex. In any work environment, this places all employees – including employees who happen to be women – in an awkward, confusing and demoralizing situation.[5]

While NOW may well be correct that Letterman's behavior has set an inappropriate or even discriminatory tone, that behavior may not constitute unlawful harassment. Title VII law has, by and large, failed to grapple with the "toxic environment" problem that plagues many workplaces. It focuses on individual incidents and inter-actions, at the expense of stepping back and taking the broader look that NOW calls for. The mere fact that women in an office had sex with the boss does not transform the situation into a provable case of sexual harassment. (When Bill Clinton, while president of the United States, admitted to a sexual relationship with a lowly intern, Monica Lewinsky, there was no talk of unlawful harassment despite the vast power differential.)

When one of the parties to a workplace relationship is the boss, however, it does change the game a bit. First, if actionable harassment is proven, the company's liability should be automatic, as explained below, without the benefit of any defense. Second, when there is such a dramatic power disparity between an alleged harasser and a plaintiff, it will likely be easier to convince a factfinder fact finder that the relationship was coerced or exploitative. In this particular case, however, Letterman's fame and success may have the opposite effect, making it easier to convince a factfinder that the women welcomed or even sought out the relationships, hoping to gain fame, fortune, or some other advantage. Indeed, Letterman's wife was his employee when they first became an item many years ago.

Interestingly, one of the women allegedly involved with Letterman posted the following comment, apparently in a humorous vein, on her own website: "Okay. Here it is. My big comment on Mr. Letterman. It is this: As you can imagine this is a very emotional moment for me because Dave promised me many times that I was the only woman he would ever cheat on." Such a joke seems a very long way from an allegation of sexual harassment.

Of course, the fact that women did not in the past – and have not yet – come out and complained does not rule out the possibility that harassment occurred, or that a valid case could be made. Many victims of harassment fail to complain about harassment for fear of retaliation or for other reasons. In this case, a working comedy writer might prefer to keep on writing, with Letterman as a mentor, rather than to file even a meritorious sexual harassment suit against such a powerful figure. The job is lucrative and interesting, and opportunities for women, unfortunately, are still comparatively few. (Similar problems are raised by the ruling in the *Friends* case, discussed in Chapter 14.)

## WHAT ABOUT A SUIT BY THE OTHER EMPLOYEES?

Assuming the relationships were truly consensual, could the other employees have a cause of action? Many employers ban even consensual relationships at work between supervisors and subordinates (or sometimes between coworkers of any type), but the company employing Letterman and the women he had sex with does not appear to have had such a policy. Could other employees nonetheless sue for discrimination?

As discussed in Chapter 12, courts have struggled with the question whether Title VII's prohibition on sex discrimination is violated when, for example, a supervisor grants preferential employment treatment to a paramour because of their intimate relationship.

The struggle comes because Title VII does not apply to all conduct that is inappropriate, immoral, unethical, distasteful, or even demonstrably unfair; it applies only to *discrimination*. But to answer the legal question whether harassment occurs when an employee is treated worse than the boss's paramour is, more probing analysis is necessary. If sexual favoritism is to be actionable here, it would likely be based on an implicit quid pro quo theory – that he was sleeping with so many subordinates that sexual submission could be understood as a requirement to advance.

While it does seem that "sex with the boss" was widespread at the Letterman show, it is not clear whether favoritism accompanied it. One of the women, for example, reportedly received money to pay for law school while she was involved with Letterman, but the money seems to have been issued as a loan and in fact paid back. The same woman gradually earned an "on-air" presence on the show, even though she had a backstage position. Was that favoritism? Perhaps, but maybe not favoritism that was sufficient to change the entire nature of the workplace for her coworkers – a requirement under the law.

## IF HARASSMENT OCCURRED, IS ANYONE LIABLE?

Perhaps even more important than the definition of harassment is the question of employer liability: Is there someone who can be held accountable for the harassment that is alleged to have occurred? This depends on the nature of the harassment and the managerial power of the harasser. One scenario involves harassment at the hands of a company owner – or someone so high up in the corporation as to be an alter ego of a company. In that situation, liability for both types of harassment is automatic and subject to no defenses. In other words, liability attaches upon proof that actionable harassment occurred.

With this scandal, much of the news focus has been on the responsibility and potential liability of CBS, the network on which the *Late Show with David Letterman* airs. However, Letterman and all the women involved seem to work for an independent production company called Worldwide Pants, Inc. CBS, then, may face no liability for what happened, even if allegations of harassment are made and proven. Worldwide Pants may be in trouble, depending on whether it employs anyone who sues. (David Letterman cannot be sued individually under Title VII, although any judgment against his own company would obviously have financial ramifications for him.)

### ARE THERE PROCEDURAL OBSTACLES TO A LAWSUIT ARISING OUT OF LETTERMAN'S CONDUCT?

If the women involved with Letterman or their coworkers have a viable theory of harassment to pursue on the merits, there may still be procedural obstacles that stand in the way of a successful suit. The statute of limitations is the most obvious potential roadblock. Plaintiffs cannot file a Title VII lawsuit unless they have filed a charge with the EEOC, the federal agency charged with implementing Title VII, within 180 days of the unlawful employment practice they are challenging.

For claims of hostile work environment harassment, this period can be effectively extended if there are a related series of incidents, at least one of which occurs during the requisite period prior to the filing of an EEOC charge.[6] It may well be that, in this case, some or all of the relationships ended too long ago to permit a timely claim today, either by the women themselves or by their co-workers.

### THE BOTTOM LINE: A SEXUAL HARASSMENT CASE REQUIRES SUBSTANTIALLY MORE THAN A SET OF BOSS-EMPLOYEE RELATIONSHIPS

In sum, the news of David Letterman's many affairs with his employees fairly raises the question of whether sexual harassment occurred – and provides a teachable moment on the sometimes damaging consequences of sex at work. Depending on the facts, some of which have yet to emerge, NOW may be justified in condemning Letterman's ethics. But what about the law?

At least so far, it is too soon to pronounce this a situation of sexual harassment. Letterman's conduct may have been inappropriate, inadvisable, and even demeaning, and yet still not rise to the level of unlawful discrimination. That may represent a weakness in existing law, but as of now, that's the framework we must use to analyze the question "Was this sexual harassment?"

A version of this chapter appeared on October 20, 2009, at writ.findlaw.com.

*Update: No lawsuit was ever filed as a result of this scandal, but a former writer for his show, Nell Scovell, gave a tell-all interview to Vanity Fair not long after the story broke. Of sexual favoritism, which the EEOC describes as behavior that can lead to a hostile work environment" and create "an atmosphere that is demeaning to women," Scovell said "that pretty much sums up my experience."[7] After thirty-three years in late-night television, David Letterman retired in 2015. He now sports a long beard that has fueled comparisons to Santa Claus, but he prefers to be likened to Charles Darwin.[8]*

**21**

# Why Herman Cain Has Not Been Able to Talk His Way
# Out of His Exploding Sexual Harassment Scandal

The story of the sexual harassment allegations against GOP presidential candidate Herman Cain, first broken by Politico, just keeps getting bigger. In addition to the two women who filed formal complaints of harassment against Cain while he was head of the National Restaurant Association (NRA) in the late 1990s, a third woman has now come forward to complain that she was also harassed by him, although she did not file a complaint at the time.[1]

The details of the allegations and the settlements received by the two women who did file formal complaints against Cain have been leaking out in fits and spurts. Meanwhile, Cain has denied any wrongdoing and refused to offer any explanatory details. But we still do not have the whole story, in large part owing to confidentiality clauses in the two settlement agreements that prevent the two women who did file suit from talking about their complaints. These two women risk being sued by the NRA for breach of contract if they step up and tell their sides of the story without first securing a waiver of the confidentiality provision.[2]

For this reason, we may never know exactly what happened at the NRA more than a decade ago and whether it constituted actionable sexual harassment. Certainly, we would be premature in drawing any definitive conclusions about Herman Cain's culpability as a sexual harasser. Yet the allegations against Cain raise important questions about the law and practice of sexual harassment in the workplace that deserve to be answered whether or not the whole story ever comes to light.

Ultimately, Cain's own take on the situation raises some of the most important questions of all.

## "THIS BILL OPENS THE DOOR FOR OPPORTUNISTS WHO WILL
## USE THE LEGISLATION TO MAKE SOME MONEY."

So warned Herman Cain in 1991, when he was president of Godfather's Pizza and when Congress was in the process of strengthening federal antidiscrimination

125

law.[3] Through the Civil Rights Act of 1991, Congress created the right of victims of intentional discrimination to seek money damages in court, rather than just equitable relief (that is, a court order or the like). The act also restored various aspects of antidiscrimination law that had been weakened by a series of Supreme Court rulings.[4]

Cain would have been more accurate had he said that the 1991 bill opened the door to women, rather than to opportunists, and allowed them some compensation for wrongdoing, rather than a way "to make some money." Until very recently, women had to suffer in silence as they were routinely subjected to unwelcome sexual advances and other sexual conduct in the workplace, often at the hands of their bosses. In 1979, a novel survey in *Redbook* magazine founded that 88 percent of 9,000 women said they had experienced behaviors that we might now call sexual harassment in the workplace.[5] And in 1981, a large study of federal workers conducted by the U.S. Merit Systems Protection Board reported that 65 percent of women surveyed said they had experienced sexual harassment.[6] There was no clear legal definition of sexual harassment at the time, but the behavior the women reported included touching, fondling, groping, coercing sexual favors through opportunities for promotion or threats of firing, verbal harassment, and being exposed to sexually explicit graphics.

Then, in 1991, sexual harassment was thrust into the public consciousness during Clarence Thomas's Supreme Court confirmation hearings. Law professor Anita Hill accused Thomas of sexually harassing her when she worked for him at the EEOC. Ironically, he was then the head of this agency, which is charged with enforcing federal antidiscrimination laws. The hearings were televised and the allegations widely publicized and discussed. Sexual harassment became a household term.

The Hill-Thomas hearings may have transformed sexual harassment into a mainstream issue, but the law of sexual harassment was already quite well established by 1991. Title VII of the Civil Rights Act of 1964 had made sex discrimination illegal, but the earliest cases left judges mystified. But harassment then developed at a rapid pace, with guidance and reinforcement from the Supreme Court in several key decisions. By the late 1990s, when the alleged harassment by Cain is claimed to have occurred, sexual harassment had made its way into the public eye, into federal and state antidiscrimination law, and into employment policies across the country.

## "IF SPEAKING TO SOMEBODY IS SEXUAL HARASSMENT, GIVE ME A BREAK."

So sputtered a frustrated Herman Cain, when being interviewed by conservative radio personality Sean Hannity about the allegations against him.[7] What does constitute unlawful sexual harassment? Can "speaking to somebody" be against the law? Obviously, it depends on what you say and to whom.

Both quid pro quo and hostile environment harassment violate Title VII, which governs employers with at least fifteen employees. Words can certainly be sufficient. For example, "sleep with me or you're fired" are words that constitute actionable quid pro quo. The words "women are whores and bitches" are also actionable.

Sometimes what is even more important in litigation than the question whether the conduct was actionable is the question whether the employer can be held liable for the conduct at issue. For harassment by a company owner, liability is automatic. Thus, harassment by someone in Herman Cain's position at the NRA exposes the organization to a very high level of risk.[8] Individuals cannot be sued directly under Title VII, however, regardless of their position in a business entity. Thus, Cain himself, as an individual, would not have faced a Title VII suit. This explains why he does not seem to have been a party to the two settlement agreements.[9]

### "I DID A PRETTY GOOD JOB OF KNOWING WHERE TO DRAW THE LINE."

Here, Cain offers the lack of sexual harassment complaints against him at *some* of the jobs he has held as some sort of testament to his line-drawing talent.[10]

At the time he said this, Cain was being interviewed by Greta Van Susteren of Fox News, who had asked him whether he was just one of those "over-complimenters" – her term for a man who just doesn't know what sexual harassment is and thinks they're "you know, complimenting a woman." Cain credits his apt line drawing to knowing "the lady, the individual" and having a "good sense for where you cross the line relative to sexual harassment." He also told Van Susteren, in response to her question whether he had a "roaming eye," "I enjoy flowers, like everybody else."[11]

In fact, even the little we know so far suggests that Cain is not the line-drawing master he believes himself to be when it comes to sexual harassment. Three different women have said he harassed them while he was the highest-ranking employee in the NRA; two of these filed formal complaints and received significant financial settlements; and one of the two, through a statement read by her lawyer (with permission of the NRA), claims that the harassing behaviors involved a "series of inappropriate behaviors and unwanted advances from the CEO" that took place over a two-month period.

At the margins, sexual harassment can involve line drawing that can be exacerbated by gender-based differences in perceptions of social-sexual behavior in the workplace. Some studies have shown a slight difference in the way men and women perceive ambiguous behavior: what men view as flirtatious or invited may feel unwelcome and harassing to women.[12] But gender differences make only a marginal difference in line drawing, and, interestingly, they make no difference at all when the harassment is severe or overt.

In truth, most sexual harassment is pretty unambiguous. Harassers foist their sexual conduct or advances on unwelcoming subordinates or coworkers who feel powerless to stop it. And the law does not look at harassment from the perspective of the harasser, so relying on one's own ability to "draw the line" is dangerous business. Hostile environment harassment can occur even when the harasser has nothing but benign motives. The question is simply whether the victim experienced the conduct as hostile, offensive, or abusive, and whether a reasonable person in her shoes would also have experienced it that way.[13]

Sexual harassment in the workplace cannot be reduced to a problem of over-complimenting; attempting to minimize the issue that way demeans the experience of modern women, 40 percent of whom are still likely to experience some form of sexual harassment in any two-year period.[14] Cain's attempt to claim his alleged ogling of women was akin to enjoying the sight of flowers reflects a similar lack of understanding about the nature, severity, and prevalence of sexual harassment in the workplace, as well as its potentially severe consequences for women.

And no matter how unwelcome sexual harassment is, study after study has shown that victims rarely file formal complaints after being harassed. Empirically, doing so is in fact the least likely response of a woman to an incident of sexual harassment at work. So the idea that women are filing sexual harassment lawsuits at the drop of a hat, as a way to make money, is simply false on the facts. The overwhelming majority of women just want the harassment to stop.[15]

Moreover, victims tend to complain only about severe harassment, and only when they've exhausted all other avenues. They rightly fear retaliation from the harasser and/or their workplace, and they often worry about being socially ostracized at work and even about damaging the harasser's career.

Thus, a man who, like Cain, provoked two formal harassment complaints within just a year or two or each other ought to have his line-drawing license revoked. Such complaints are not lightly made.

## "THIS IS ABSOLUTELY FABRICATION, MAN."

So complained Cain to Sean Hannity. He added, "How many more ways can I say this stuff is totally fabricated?"[16]

This is perhaps the worst of all Cain's responses to the harassment scandal. There is simply no evidence that sexual harassment complaints are frequently fabricated. All the evidence suggests to the contrary, as noted just above: many employees who are victimized by harassment suffer in silence. Filing and pursuing an internal grievance or a lawsuit is grueling, personally intrusive, and very likely to trigger retaliation and job loss. And, ultimately, such grievances are hard to win. It is the rare person who would endure this process in pursuit of a trumped-up claim.

A survey of employers revealed that, in more than 90 percent of internal grievances involving harassment, the victim's allegations are found to be true. Sometimes what she alleges is not a violation of the company's harassment policy or of applicable law, but according to employers' own reports, they are almost never faced with an outright fabrication.

Certainly, then, it would be surprising if the NRA settled two cases close in time, for a significant amount of money, despite its belief that they were both fabricated. It is an insult to all employees that Cain would resort to such feeble attempts to defend himself, without offering any details of the incident that led to the claim – details that might well support the claimant.

A version of this chapter appeared on November 7, 2011, at writ.findlaw.com.

*Update: After a Donald Trump-like rise to the top, Herman Cain's presidential campaign faded quickly and was a distant memory by the time his party nominated Mitt Romney to run against Barack Obama in the 2012 election. Cain went on to host a nationally syndicated talk show. In a 2013 interview, Herman Cain argued that the harassment charges against him were the "work of Satan."[17]*

**22**

# Why Hostile Environment Harassment Is a "Continuing Violation"

The Supreme Court's decision in *National Railroad Passenger Corp. (Amtrak) v. Morgan* resolved an important, though admittedly technical, question relating to the interpretation of Title VII.[1]

The case involved the statute's brief limitations period – which requires that suits be brought within either 180 or 300 days of when the alleged harassment occurred, depending on whether the state in which the suit is brought has a work-sharing agreement with the EEOC; the parties in the *Morgan* case agreed that the relevant period was 300 days.[2]

The question the Court resolved was this: If a pattern of discrimination includes some incidents too early to fall within the relevant period, can those incidents still form part of the basis for a discrimination suit?

## THE UNHAPPY EMPLOYMENT HISTORY OF ABNER MORGAN

This case arises out of the long-standing but troubled employment relationship between an African-American electrician named Abner Morgan and Amtrak. According to Morgan, from the time he was hired as an electrician helper in 1990 until the time he was fired in 1995, he was subject to a series of discriminatory acts at the hands of his employer. Morgan alleges that he was paid differently, punished unfairly, denied union representation in disciplinary meetings, and harassed because of his race. Amtrak, however, disputes many of these claims on the merits.

Amtrak moved for summary judgment on some of Morgan's claims based solely on the theory that they are time barred (that is, too early to come within the relevant statute of limitations). The trial court granted the motion, and dismissed all claims occurring prior to May 3, 1994, 300 days before Morgan filed a complaint with the EEOC. Then the remaining claims went to trial, but a jury found for Amtrak on all counts. That was not the end of the case, however, for the Ninth Circuit Court of

Appeals held that the pre–May 3, 1994, claims should not have been dismissed in their entirety, for they could be actionable as long as they were "sufficiently related to those occurring within the limitations period."[3]

## HOW FILING CHARGES UNDER TITLE VII WORKS

Title VII requires that complainants first seek relief from the EEOC, a federal agency charged with the responsibility of administering the nation's employment laws. Thus, before any potential plaintiff can file a lawsuit, he must first file a charge with the EEOC.[4] That charge must be filed within either 180 or 300 days of when the acts of discrimination are alleged to have occurred.

The EEOC then has the opportunity to review the case, investigate the claims, and decide whether the case has any merit. If it does, the EEOC will sometimes sue on the employee's behalf – or even, if the complaint reveals widespread illegal conduct, on the behalf of a class of employees. No matter what the EEOC's decision may be, the complainant at some point earns the right to bring his own lawsuit in court.[5]

## THE BASICS OF THE CONTINUING VIOLATIONS DOCTRINE

The "continuing violations" question that has plagued many courts in the last decade, and produced a federal circuit split, is this: When Title VII plaintiffs do ultimately make it past the EEOC, should they be able to recover for discriminatory acts that occurred outside the relevant limitations period?[6]

An ABA treatise variously described the existing case law on this issue as "muddled" and "defy[ing] easy description or convenient characterization" – a strong sign that clarification is in order.[7] The treatise also described the Supreme Court's own prior cases as "impossible to reconcile."[8] A brief review of the cases proves the point.

Courts agree that an isolated act of discrimination that occurs outside the charge-filing period is untimely and does not provide a basis for suit. They also generally agree that the doctrine of "equitable tolling" applies. That doctrine can extend the limitations period for fairness reasons – for example, if the employer has made affirmative representations to the victim-employee that lead the employee to miss the charge-filing deadline, or if the employee mistakenly filed the charge with the wrong federal agency.[9]

But suppose there is no basis for equitable tolling, but there are multiple, related discriminatory acts, some of which fall within the relevant time period – a so-called serial violation? Courts disagree on whether suit can be brought on all the acts, or only those that fall within the time period. This split turns on a disagreement about when an unlawful employment practice "occurs."

## THE SUPREME COURT MAJORITY'S COMPROMISE
## IN MORGAN: TWO RULES

In *Morgan*, the Supreme Court answered the question in an opinion authored by Justice Clarence Thomas – himself a former head of the EEOC who, of course, famously got into trouble based on Anita Hill's harassment claims.[10] The Court's answer to the question about the continuing vitality of the continuing violations doctrine was "Yes and no."[11] The result was a victory for victims of sexual and other forms of harassment, but a loss for victims of other forms of illegal workplace discrimination.

The majority struck a compromise between the positions for which the parties advocated. First, it differentiated between, on the one hand, discrete acts of discrimination (like a discriminatory failure to promote or firing), and on the other hand, hostile environment harassment (under which a series of acts of harassment amounts over time to a hostile work environment for the victim). Justice Thomas's compromise preserves some important rights for victims of harassment, while depriving victims of other forms of discrimination of similar protection.

## WHAT THE MAJORITY OPINION IN MORGAN SAID ABOUT
## DISCRETE ACTS OF DISCRIMINATION

Take the fired secretary. With respect such a discrete act of discrimination, the Court held that the limitations period would begin when she was fired. Each such act, the Court reasoned, constitutes an "unlawful employment practice" that occurs at the time the action is taken. When the act concludes, the clock starts to run.

So far, this may sound reasonable. But the Court also held that the "continuing violations" doctrine cannot apply to a series of discrete acts, even when they are very similar. So suppose the secretary is not promoted because she refuses to sleep with her new boss – but, fearing the loss of her job, she doesn't sue. Then two years later, her boss propositions her again. This time when she refuses, he fires her.

Under the Court's logic, the secretary can now sue for the firing but not the earlier failure to promote. Even if discrete acts like the failure to promote and the firing are similar, the Court reasoned, that does not mean they can be treated as a single "unlawful employment practice." Thus, each act's timeliness must be evaluated as if that act stood alone, even if they seem to form a pattern.

The Court did acknowledge, however, that untimely acts may be used as background evidence to support a claim based on timely acts. So our hypothetical secretary, while she could not sue for and receive damages based on the nonpromotion, could at least take evidence to a jury about it.

The Court also recognized that plaintiffs could still invoke equitable doctrines like tolling (which stops a limitations period due to fairness concerns) or estoppel (which stops a defendant who caused a plaintiff not to file from complaining that she filed late). So, for instance, if our hypothetical secretary could prove her boss's intimidation was the reason she failed to sue earlier about the nonpromotion, she might still be able to sue later, on a theory of estoppel or tolling.

All nine justices agreed with this position, though three would have gone further to clarify other important Title VII questions.

### *The* Morgan *Majority, and Dissent, on Hostile Environment Harassment*

Accordingly, the court held that in the case of a hostile environment claim, the illegal practice "occurs" when the combined acts become sufficiently severe or pervasive to alter the conditions of employment by creating a hostile, offensive, or abusive working environment. When that happens, the court reasoned, it makes sense to consider (and allow the plaintiff to sue upon) the whole course of acts, timely or not. All that is required is that at least one act is timely.

One might think this makes sense because a plaintiff could not sue upon the early acts before the harassment became pervasive – so it is unfair to fault her for not suing earlier with respect to these acts, because she could not legally have done so. This logic also suggests that a plaintiff should be barred from her suit on the basis of untimely acts that did occur after the harassment became pervasive.

But the Court went beyond this logic, to allow untimely acts to be sued upon even if the plaintiff could have sued upon them within the 180- to 300-day period. As long as the hostile environment continues, the Court held, each new act means the plaintiff can go back in time to sue on all prior acts that comprised part of the hostile environment – regardless of whether she could also have sued on those acts long ago.

## THE DISSENTERS' FAIRNESS CONCERNS, AND WHY THEY ARE MISPLACED

Four dissenting justices (Rehnquist, O'Connor, Scalia, and Kennedy) would have rejected the continuing violations doctrine altogether – in cases of harassment as well as discrete acts of discrimination. They argued that each act of harassment in either context is an act of discrimination that "occurs" when it happens – and thus that it must be sued upon within the number of days fixed by statute.

If this rule were adopted, a hostile environment plaintiff could only go back 180 or 300 days to look for acts to sue upon. That is only fair, the dissenters argued, because going back further means the claim is harder for the employer to defend.

The majority's rule, the four dissenters pointed out, means an employer may have to defend itself against a harassment suit that has been building for ten years – even though the memories of witnesses who might have supported the employer may have faded and employee-witnesses may have left the company and moved to another state or firm.[12]

An employer that has not intimidated the suing employee into keeping quiet, and has not had a supervisor who did so, in which cases tolling/estoppel doctrines would apply, should not have to contend with this unfairness by facing a belatedly filed claim, the dissenters noted.[13]

This concern, however reasonable it might sound, is no longer realistic. Employer liability is limited in sexual harassment law – time-wise – by the affirmative defense established in *Faragher v. City of Boca Raton*[14] and *Burlington Industries v. Ellerth*.[15] Moreover, courts interpreting the affirmative defense have adopted extremely stringent standards for victim complaints. Some have held that a delay a short as a month or even a week in filing an internal complaint can be sufficient to excuse the employer from liability. Far from worrying about whether an employee waits 180 or 300 days, these courts sometimes will not give the employee 7, or 30, days to wait.[16]

There is thus no chance for the hypothetical employee who waits ten years before filing a complaint to win any resulting lawsuit. The dissenter's argument about unfairness to employers is thus itself unfair. Any employer with minimal knowledge of the law will adopt complaint procedures that will ensure it always has early knowledge of claims, and can always prepare itself to defend against them if it believes they are meritless (or, one hopes, to address them if it finds they have merit).

## QUESTIONS THE MORGAN MAJORITY LEFT OPEN

The Court also left open two questions on which lower federal courts may continue to disagree – questions that the facts of *Morgan* did not directly raise, and thus the Court chose not to decide.

First, it did not resolve whether the doctrine might apply to a so-called pattern and practice case, in which the claim centers on aggregating various acts to prove systemic discrimination.

Second, it did not address whether the charge-filing period should begin for a hidden violation when it occurs or only when the plaintiff discovers that it has occurred. An example of a hidden violation might be a firing that appeared neutral but that comments in the plaintiff's employment file later showed to be discriminatory.

For instance, a worker believes he was fired because he missed a quota, but later learns he was misinformed about the quota; that he had actually met it and that the reason for his firing was different and discriminatory. Does the period start when he is fired, or when he learns about the real reason for it?

The Supreme Court still has not weighed in on this issue. Three justices (Rehnquist, O'Connor, and Breyer) would have reached this question, at least to acknowledge that some form of notice rule should apply to measure when discrimination occurs.

These justices acknowledge the basic unfairness of an employee's being asked to sue for discrimination before he is sure it exists. This further step would have given more rights to victims, and would have avoided putting them in the unfair "Gotcha!" situation of being victimized both by discrimination and its cover-up.

### Did Any Justice Get It Right?

In the end, the approaches taken in the majority and dissenting opinions are both vulnerable to criticism. The Court's 9–0 refusal to recognize the continuing violations doctrine in cases where employees face a series of discrete discriminatory acts – rather than a hostile environment – is probably an error.

The secretary who is not promoted because she won't sleep with her boss, then two years later is fired because she turns him down again, should be able to sue based on both acts. Both the nonpromotion and firing have serious financial consequences, and the secretary should be compensated for both, if they form a pattern, even if she waits until she is fired to sue.

Not a single justice was willing to acknowledge this basic truth: a pattern is still a pattern, even if it does not constitute a hostile environment. Employers who continue to engage in repeated acts of discrimination should not benefit from a statute of limitations designed to give closure to acts that are long since over and done with. Their pattern is not over, and neither should their exposure to lawsuits be.

Portions of this chapter appeared on January 29 and July 2, 2002, at writ.findlaw .com.

# 23

# When Sexual Extortion Is Successful

Suppose a supervisor threatens to fire a subordinate employee unless she submits to his sexual advances but never actually carries out the threat because she gives in. Should the employer be held automatically liable for the supervisor's sexual harassment?

In its recent opinion in *Jin v. Metropolitan Life Insurance Company*, the U.S. Court of Appeals for the Second Circuit addressed this very question.[1] The decision is especially significant because the proper treatment of so-called submission cases has been up in the air since 1998, when the Supreme Court revamped the law of employer liability for sexual harassment.

## THE TRIAL IN JIN: A QUID PRO QUO, BUT NO FIRING OR DEMOTION

The *Jin* case decided by the Second Circuit involved a "quid pro quo" relationship without a "tangible employment action." The evidence showed that the victim was threatened with firing, initially submitted, and then, rather than being fired, ultimately left the company because of trauma from the harassment.

Min Jin was a successful life insurance sales agent for MetLife in New York City. Beginning in 1993, her supervisor was Gregory Morabito. According to the evidence presented at trial, Morabito engaged in a pattern of sexually harassing behavior from the beginning of their supervisory relationship.

Morabito, according to the evidence, made crude sexual remarks and touched Jin's breasts, butt, and legs in a sexual manner. He also required her to attend private Thursday night meetings in his locked office – during which he would threaten her with a baseball bat, kiss, lick, bite and fondle her, attempt to undress her, and physically force her to unzip his pants and fondle him.

Morabito repeatedly threatened to fire Jin if she did not give in to his sexual demands. For several months, Jin submitted for fear of being fired. But eventually she refused, changing her schedule to avoid him. In the end, Jin left the company, and tried to collect disability benefits because of the effects of the harassment. Ultimately, MetLife fired her because, the company said, she had stopped coming to work without having approval for disability leave.

## WAS THE JURY RIGHT TO FIND NO LIABILITY IN JIN'S CASE?

The jury found that MetLife had taken adequate measures to prevent and correct the problem. In addition, it also found that Jin had unreasonably failed to take advantage of corrective opportunities. Accordingly, it entered a verdict of "no liability" on Jin's claim.[2]

On appeal to the Second Circuit, Jin argued (as she had to the trial court) that the jury was wrong: as a matter of law, Morabito's harassment of her *had* resulted in a tangible employment action. Accordingly, she argued that MetLife was not entitled to make use of the affirmative defense – and should, instead, have been automatically liable regardless of whether it could satisfy the defense's two prongs.

Jin argued that one of the tangible adverse actions she had alleged and proved at trial was the requirement that she submit to weekly sexual activity as a condition of keeping her job, thus becoming prey to Morabito's sexual extortion. The Second Circuit ultimately agreed.

## THE PROPER TREATMENT OF SUBMISSION CASES: WHY *ELLERTH* SHEDS LIGHT

Did the Second Circuit do the right thing? The answer is yes, but to see why, it is necessary to understand the law prior to and after the Supreme Court's crucial 1998 decisions in *Faragher* and *Ellerth*.

Before these two decisions, federal appellate courts had split on the proper treatment of submission cases. Most courts agreed that quid pro cases should result in automatic liability for the employer. And several circuits, including the Second Circuit, in its 1994 decision in *Karibian v. Columbia University*,[3] had held that liability should be automatic even when the quid pro quo bargain is completed, and the victim submits to her supervisor's threats rather than refusing and being penalized by him. At least one circuit, however, had held to the contrary, creating a split.[4]

After *Faragher* and *Ellerth*, the split continued, with the few courts to address the question dividing on the issue of whether the employer in a submission case should be able to try to prove the two-pronged affirmative defense, or should be held automatically liable. The Second Circuit, as noted, just adopted the latter view.

*Ellerth* itself was a case in which adverse action was allegedly threatened but not taken. But the court did not squarely address the "submission" issue in its decision. Indeed, it granted review of an entirely different question: What is the proper rule of liability when a victim is threatened but neither submits nor suffers any consequences?[5]

Nevertheless, the Court's opinion in that case is nonetheless relevant to the question at issue in *Jin*. That is because *Ellerth* defines a "tangible employment action" to include (but not to be limited to) any "significant change in employment status such as hiring, firing, failing to promote, reassignment with significantly different responsibilities, or a decision causing a significant change in benefits."[6]

Is being forced to submit to sexual activity as a condition of keeping one's job – as the evidence showed Jin had been – a "significant change in employment status"? The Supreme Court's nonexhaustive list in *Ellerth* certainly leaves open that possibility. It also makes clear that economic harm is not required, leaving open the possibility that Jin's noneconomic harm could suffice. And logic counsels that Morabito's conduct did indeed change Jin's employment status. Through his sexual demands and accompanying threats, Morabito in effect placed an additional condition on her employment: to keep her job, she not only had to sell life insurance and fulfill any other legitimate duties imposed on her by MetLife but also had to allow herself to be fondled by her supervisor. For other employees, simply selling life insurance was all that was asked.

If anyone doubts it is a significant change in employment status, he or she should consider being offered two jobs: one that came with Jin's predicament, one without. Most of us would accept a far lower salary to avoid the sexual extortion Jin endured. And certainly if the job paid the same, we would pick the one without the gross sexual imposition.

EEOC's guidelines on employer liability, which were revised in the wake of *Faragher* and *Ellerth*, suggest the same conclusion. These guidelines state that employers should be strictly liable when an employee submits to her supervisor's demands and consequently obtains a tangible job benefit. The benefit obtained by Jin was retention of her employment, because failing to submit would have caused her to forfeit it.[7]

### Why Strict Liability for Employers Is Crucial in "Submission" Cases

This rule is correct from the point of view of statutory purpose, as well as that of court precedent. Applying a rule of strict liability to submission cases is the only result that will serve the goals of Title VII, which are preventing harassment and compensating victims. Having to sleep with a supervisor to keep your job is just the kind of "arbitrary barrier to sexual equality" that Title VII is designed to break down.

As the Second Circuit recognized, requiring a subordinate employee to submit to sexual activity as a condition of keeping her job is one of the "most pernicious and oppressive forms of sexual harassment that can occur in the workplace." It should be treated as such. Employers who countenance such behavior by hiring, retaining, and failing to monitor supervisors who impose such conditions should not be rewarded with the affirmative defense; rather, they should be held responsible through automatic liability.[8]

Any other approach would be truly ironic, as it would mandate a more lenient rule of liability in instances of successful, than of unsuccessful, harassment. The harasser who was unable to extort sexual conduct would trigger strict liability for his employer. Yet the harasser who was able to achieve his goal would perhaps trigger only a finding of "no liability" – as occurred in *Jin*.

## A SECOND IRONY: LOSSES FOR THE VICTIMS WITH FEWEST RESOURCES TO FALL BACK ON

Another irony would also result – in which emotionally stronger victims with more options who assert themselves would be vindicated in court, whereas emotionally weaker victims with fewer options who feel compelled to submit would not be. The wealthy career woman may get a verdict in her favor; yet the close-to-the-poverty-line single mother, with a job she cannot leave because her children depend on her, will not.

Those who do submit do so because they do not have the power, economic security, or personal strength to refuse the supervisor's demands. Their counterparts with greater resources may suffer serious harms: a lost job, lost income, lost opportunities, a draining court battle to get justice. But the women with fewer resources will suffer far more serious harms, being effectively required to accept molestation, sexual assault, or even rape as part of their work life. As Catharine MacKinnon argued in *Feminism Unmodified*, "[W]omen who are forced to submit to sex must be understood as harmed not less, but as much or more, than those who are able to make their refusals effective."[9]

The Second Circuit thus reached the correct outcome in this case, a victory for sexual harassment plaintiffs everywhere. Let us hope that other courts to consider the same issue will adhere to *Ellerth*'s precedent and continue to recognize a workplace bargain demanding sexual submission for what it is: a tangible, adverse employment action.

A version of this chapter appeared on August 13, 2002, at writ.findlaw.com.

# 24

# The Consequences of Failing to Complain about Harassment

Christine Hawk alleges that her supervisor subjected her to sexual harassment. She had attended an antiharassment training seminar and was aware of the company's antiharassment policy. However, she waited nine months before filing a formal complaint about her harassment with her employer. (She did, however, alert the company earlier than she was experiencing harassment, without providing any details.)

Why did Hawk wait? She says she feared she would lose her job if she complained. She was intimidated by her supervisor, the alleged harasser, and believed he controlled her future with the company.

Does Hawk's delay mean her case must be dismissed? A federal district court in Philadelphia said no in her case, *Hawk v. Americold Logistics.*[1] In so ruling, it joined a number of other courts that have ruled similarly, forming a modest, if important, trend. It also raised other interesting and significant legal questions about how the Supreme Court's framework in cases of alleged hostile environment harassment should be applied.

## HAWK'S ALLEGATIONS

Christine Hawk began work at Americold Logistics in June 1999, as a temporary employee, making pallets. By the end of that year, she was given a permanent position as a forklift driver. During the majority of her employment with the company, Hawk was directly supervised by Jack Bambary.

According to Hawk's deposition testimony, Bambary began a course of harassment that continued from her first month of work to her last. (Bambary denies this.) She says he made sexual comments to her, paged her daily, made unannounced visits to her home, recited his affections for her, called her into the office under false pretenses, questioned her about conversations she had with other men at work, sent her sexually suggestive e-mails, and told her he wanted to have sex with her in his chair. On one occasion, he grabbed her arm and pulled her toward him, insisting she kiss him; on another occasion, he shoved her up against a wall and demanded sex.

Early on, Hawk told another supervisor she was being harassed by someone, but did not name him for fear she would be fired – a risk she could not afford to take, given her financial status and obligations as a single parent. Nine months later, however, she filed a formal complaint with the company's human resources manager.

When the company investigated, it found Bambary had engaged in "unprofessional behavior." However, it did not conclude that he had sexually harassed Hawk. Nonetheless, it forbade him to have further contact with her and disciplined him for his behavior.

Hawk was given the option of moving to a new facility, which she accepted. However, according to her testimony, Bambary tried to poison her new work environment – among other ways, by telling one prospective coworker that she was a "slut" and a "liar." (Bambary denies this.) As a result, a week later, she sent the company a letter indicating she had been constructively discharged (that is, made to work in such hostile conditions that she had no choice but to leave). The company then terminated Bambary's employment and made an offer for Hawk to return to work. She declined the offer.

## THE TWO-PRONG AFFIRMATIVE DEFENSE FOR HOSTILE ENVIRONMENT HARASSMENT

Hawk's case tests the meaning of the second prong of the *Faragher/Ellerth* affirmative defense.[2] That prong penalizes victims who fail to take advantage of corrective measures available to them. In applying this prong, courts often ask questions such as, if the victim failed to complain, was there any justification for her silence? If she waited to complain, for how long, and why?

Courts have found delays as short as seven days to be unreasonable, although the standard may be less strict for less severe harassment. Courts have not been sympathetic to claims that the victim was waiting to see if the behavior continued or to gather more evidence of harassment.[3]

Another question courts often ask is the following: Did the employee comply with internal grievance procedures – by, for example, complaining to the correct person? And did the victim cooperate with the investigation? If the answer to either question is no, the employer is likely to prevail on the second prong of the affirmative defense.

## DOES FEAR OF RETALIATION EXCUSE FAILURE TO USE INTERNAL PROCEDURES?

What if the victim is too afraid of retaliation to avail herself of internal procedures? In the immediate wake of *Faragher* and *Ellerth*, courts were quick to reject claims that a "generalized fear of retaliation" was sufficient to excuse failure to complain, or delay in complaining.[4]

Their logic may have been that because most victims suffer at least some fear of retaliation, anyone could claim that fear, and the whole requirement would be undermined. Of course, that's strange logic – if most victims indeed are too fearful to employ internal procedures (and as I discuss below, empirical evidence shows they are), does it really make sense to make them mandatory? But lower courts may have felt that accepting this logic was necessary for them to conscientiously enforce the Supreme Court's requirement that victims do avail themselves of these procedures.

But more recently, some courts, such as the one that decided *Hawk*, have begun to recognize that, at the summary judgment stage, victims should have the opportunity to prove that the fears they harbored had an objective or reasonable basis. They have asked questions like these: Was there a specific threat of retaliation if the victim complained? Had the victim tried to complain previously, and found the employer unresponsive? If so, the victim might be found to have a good reason not to complain.

On this view, evidence that the victim had a good, *specific* reason not to employ the internal grievance procedure should get the victim to the jury on this issue. That makes sense. Juries are well equipped to assess whether, in the full circumstances of a given workplace, it was reasonable or unreasonable not to complain. Indeed, assessing reasonableness is the very paradigm of what juries are meant to do.

### Victims of Harassment Infrequently File Formal Complaints

Sexual harassment victims have traditionally tended not to utilize internal complaint procedures or otherwise formally report problems of harassment. Fear of retaliation, including retaliatory termination, and fear of ostracism by coworkers are among the most common reasons victims give for not filing a formal complaint with their employers.[5]

Filing a complaint with an employer is in fact the *least likely* response for a victim of harassment. According to a study of federal employees, 44 percent of those who had experienced sexual harassment took no action at all, while only 12 percent reported the conduct to a supervisor or other official.[6]

The low rate of reporting occurred despite the fact that *every* federal agency has an established sexual harassment policy, and 78 percent of survey respondents reported knowing about the formal complaint channels available to them. That suggests the situation in other workplaces, where policies may not be as well publicized, might be even worse. Strikingly, this survey, when compared with prior ones, shows victims of harassment to be almost as unlikely to file formal complaints of harassment with their employers as they were fifteen years earlier.

Thus, despite the growing public awareness about the problem of sexual harassment, and support for efforts to eradicate it, the fear of retaliation remains. Nor is it an unreasonable fear: After all, the retaliation might come at the hands of the harasser himself – when rules don't stop him from harassing, why would they stop him from retaliating? Moreover, a woman who, like Hawk, is a single parent – indeed, any woman who is in a caretaker position where others depend on the income she brings in – may reasonably fear that being fired would be devastating to those for whom she cares.

## VICTIMS TEND TO CHOOSE INFORMAL, NONCONFRONTATIONAL METHODS OF COPING

Rather than file formal complaints, victims tend to respond in a variety of other ways, most of which are informal and nonconfrontational.[7] Participants in laboratory studies seem to believe that they would be able to handle harassing situations themselves. However, real-life victims tend to be less successful. Real victims tend at first to ignore incidents of harassment, and subsequently to respond with mild recriminations such as "I'm not your type." They also tend to find ways to rationalize the harassment and convince themselves it won't recur or is innocuous: "I wore a sexy outfit"; "It was a joke."

Many women choose costly consequences, such as quitting their jobs, to avoid dealing with harassment directly, as Hawk eventually did in this case. Or they may instead try to effect changes in their work assignments, or seek a new job placement, in order to avoid contact with the harasser – even if those changes are professionally undesirable or damaging to their long-term career success. They may try to appease the harasser without direct confrontation. They may also reach out to friends or coworkers for support.

Other women simply endure harassment, using various psychological strategies to do so. They may pretend it is not happening, treat it as some other kind of conflict that isn't as threatening, blame themselves, or detach from the workplace generally.

## A BETTER LEGAL STANDARD: LOOK TO EMPLOYER EFFORTS TO INDUCE VICTIMS TO COMPLAIN

Current courts tend to force victims into a Hobson's choice: they must either complain, and risk retaliation, or lose their cause of action for harassment.

Even sympathetic courts may require a specific, not just a generalized, fear of retaliation for victims to get to a jury with their claims. That's not realistic: this generalized fear is the very reason most victims don't complain. It is "generalized" because it is typical; such fear is present is most workplaces because *retaliation* is present in most workplaces.

Thus, courts should shift their inquiry to ask whether the employer, taking account of the fact that most workplaces induce this kind of fear, has done anything to ensure that its workplace is the exception. Put another way, courts should focus on whether the employer has created an environment that is affirmatively conducive to complaints.

## WHAT KIND OF ENVIRONMENT MAKES VICTIMS FEEL ABLE TO COMPLAIN WITHOUT FEAR?

Although the research in this area is spotty, there has been some effort by academics to study the factors that make victims likely to complain about harassment.

Victims are more likely to report severe or physical harassment than other forms.[8] In addition, individual factors like gender, race, class, and personal assertiveness clearly play a role.[9] But so does the working environment, including past treatment of complainants and gender balance in the workplace. And that suggests that employers can indeed do something to make victims feel more comfortable about availing themselves of internal grievance procedures.[10]

One study showed that women who have less "organizational power" – for instance, those who work in male-dominated areas or those with low-skill or low-status jobs – tended to respond more passively than other women. The law firm associate, for instance, might be more likely to complain than the law firm secretary.[11] In addition, women characterized as having low self-esteem or "low life satisfaction" responded less assertively than others. Thus, the confident, happy associate or secretary may be more likely to complain than her insecure, anxious counterpart.[12]

Studies also show that women respond more assertively when employers take proactive efforts to prevent harassment – including policies, procedures, and training programs – and disseminate information about the issue. These efforts send the message that the employer does not condone harassment, and that victims who file complaints will be protected.[13]

These studies suggest that employers could improve the environment for victim reporting in a number of ways. They include maintaining better gender balance in the workforce; refusing to tolerate highly sexualized work environments; and educating employees about policies and procedures in a way that reinforces the point that victims are *entitled* to a harassment-free workplace.[14]

In sum, studies show that victims do often have good reasons for failing to file internal complaints, and that employers often cultivate an environment that is inhospitable to complaints. The law should account for what social science research tells us about sexual harassment.

## WHY THE PHILADELPHIA COURT IS ON THE RIGHT TRACK

In Hawk's case, the judge's approach made sense, especially in the context of this social science research. The judge found that Hawk's explanation for delay – fear of job loss – was plausible. Indeed, the fact that her initial complaint refused to name names, he noted, was consistent with such fears. (The judge also found that

Hawk provided sufficient details in her complaint and at least one witness who could corroborate the most serious of her allegations – so that she did put her employer on sufficient notice of her claims.[15])

Hawk now will get the opportunity to go to trial and try to convince a jury that, among other things, she had a good excuse for waiting so long to complain. Given the realities of victim reporting, the law should, at the very least, give her that opportunity.

### A Better Approach: Take Unreasonable Failure to File into Account for Damages

An even better approach would be to disregard victim behavior altogether on the question of employer liability. That is, a victim should be able to sue even if she never complained, to account for the reality that many, many victims are reasonably fearful of complaining and yet still have suffered an actionable harm. However, in assessing damages against an employer, the court could take unreasonable delay in filing, or failure to file, into account.

Thus, if an employer can show that its atmosphere was comfortable for victims, and that it would have intervened had it known of the complaint, maybe it should not have to pay damages resulting from *unreasonable* failure to file or delay in filing. But victims who reasonably fail to file, or delay in filing, should not be punished for simply sharing a common and often justified fear.

A version of this chapter appeared on April 8, 2003, at writ.findlaw.com.

# 25

# Who Is Responsible for Sudden, Severe Harassment?

In 1999, Lucianne Walton was working as a pharmaceutical sales representative for Ortho-McNeil Pharmaceutical ("Ortho"). She has sued Ortho for sexual harassment.

Specifically, she alleges that that year, over a two-month period, her supervisor, George Mykytiuk, groped her, fondled her, and repeatedly raped her. While he never explicitly threatened her, she alleges that he committed several of these acts after showing her the gun he kept close at hand.

She says he had the opportunity to harass her in part because much of the company's pharmaceutical sales force works out of home offices, and most contact between supervisors and subordinates takes place on the road or at the supervisor's house. (Most of the alleged incidents, according to Walton, took place at Mykytiuk's home.)

These are obviously extremely serious allegations that deserve to be heard. Sadly, however, this case, *Walton v. Johnson & Johnson*, will never reach a jury. The trial court granted summary judgment to Ortho. And recently, the U.S. Court of Appeals for the Eleventh Circuit affirmed that ruling.[1]

The Court of Appeals' opinion dodged several important issues. Among them was the important issue of so-called sudden, severe harassment. The issue is this: Can an employer be held liable for such harassment as long as the victim pursued reasonable avenues of complaint? Or is the employer off the hook for all the harassment if it took reasonable measures to prevent it from happening, and reasonable measures to correct it afterward?

Put another way, who should pay the price for "unavoidable" harassment – the victim or the employer?

## EMPLOYER LIABILITY UNDER *FARAGHER* AND *ELLERTH*

The new scheme for assessing employer liability for sexual harassment, set forth in *Faragher v. City of Boca Raton* and *Burlington Industries v. Ellerth*, came from a set of

146

logical impulses.[2] The employer should be liable for all acts of its supervisors if they were aided by the power the employer had given them to control their subordinates. After all, the fact that the boss is the boss means that he can force contact with the victim, make his conduct more threatening, make the victim's submission more likely, and make her filing a complaint less likely.

But sometimes, the Supreme Court held, the employer should benefit from an affirmative defense when no tangible employment action was taken against the victim. The first prong of the defense focuses on the employer's preventative and corrective measures, and the second prong focuses on whether the employee failed to take advantage of corrective opportunities. The Supreme Court has made clear that both prongs must be proven for an employer to establish the affirmative defense – they are joined with an "and" in the *Faragher* and *Ellerth* opinions – and avoid liability or damages. But not all federal appellate courts have taken the hint. Instead, some have flagrantly misapplied Supreme Court precedent.

For example, the U.S. Court of Appeals for the Fifth Circuit, in *Indest v. Freeman Decorating, Inc.*, held in effect that satisfying the first prong was enough. There, the employer's response was "swift and effective." But the employee also timely complained, meaning the second prong was *not* satisfied. The case thus should have gone forward. But it did not.[3] Some courts seem to think that as long as the employer does all it can, it isn't liable. But that is simply not the law. Only additional proof that the employee did not timely or properly complain can establish the affirmative defense.

## THE PROBLEM OF SUDDEN, SEVERE HARASSMENT

This framework makes sense in most cases. But what if the harassment is sudden and severe, creating a hostile environment before the victim has a chance to complain?

In such a case, the affirmative defense is difficult to apply.

First, consider the first prong. Did the employer take adequate preventive and corrective measures? Possibly.

But now consider the second prong, also necessary: Did the plaintiff fail to take the opportunity to complain? That can be hard to answer. On one hand, the plaintiff may not have complained (or not complained promptly enough), and she may technically have had the opportunity to do so because a procedure was in place. But even if she fails to complain, shouldn't the employer be liable for the conduct that occurred before she had a chance to complain? In other words, if a woman is raped by her boss the first day on the job, why should the employer be any less liable if the woman fails to report it immediately afterward? The damage is done, after all, and the woman has been irreparably harmed by someone the employer saw fit to endow with supervisory authority.

## WERE THE TWO PRONGS SATISFIED IN THE WALTON CASE?

Consider the Walton case. First, the first prong: Did Ortho take adequate preventive measures? With respect to preventive measures, the company had a formal, written policy prohibiting harassment and specifying complaint procedures.[4] With respect to corrective measures, when Walton complained, Ortho first suspended and ultimately fired Mykytiuk – though not for sexual harassment. Unable to conclusively prove that the sexual interaction was nonconsensual, Ortho fired Mykytiuk for "exercising poor judgment."

Now, the second prong: Did Walton fail to take the opportunity to complain? She waited nearly two months. But should that matter, given that the harassment was sudden and severe? The district court thought so. It held that by complaining earlier, Walton could have avoided "most, if not all of the actionable harassment."

But there's a major problem with that conclusion. The very first incident alleged involved unwanted sexual touching. Thus, Walton had already suffered serious harassment before she had any chance to complain. (Most courts, as well as the EEOC, treat a single incident of physical harassment as actionable, whether or not it happens again.)

In light of this error, the appellate court should have reversed part of the district court's summary judgment grant. At a minimum, Walton was entitled to have a jury hear about that first incident – and any other harassment that she could not have prevented by complaining. But that was not what the appellate court ordered. Instead, it made two major mistakes.

First, the Eleventh Circuit misapplied its own rule about whether parties that fail to raise issues before the district court can then raise them on appeal. (Its precedents say the general rule doesn't apply when the issue is legal, and the failure to address it would result in a "miscarriage of justice." This plainly was a legal issue. And certainly the failure to address it led to a miscarriage of justice: Walton's allegations – of repeated rapes by her supervisor – will never have the opportunity to be aired before a jury.)

Second, it hinted, without holding, that even if it had reached the issue, Walton might not have prevailed. But that simply isn't true. For reasons above, with respect to early harassment, Ortho could not have satisfied the second prong with respect to the initial harassment.

## WHY THE ELEVENTH CIRCUIT'S HOLDING BETRAYS THE IDEA BEHIND THE PRECEDENT

The Eleventh Circuit thus misapplied the law. Its decision was wrong based on the black letter rules set out in *Faragher* and *Ellerth*. Moreover, it also betrayed the idea behind these rules.

The idea of these two cases was to adopt a standard of automatic liability – a standard more stringent than that of mere negligence on the employer's part. The idea was that even a nonnegligent employer might be liable for the actions of its supervisors.

In reality, though, nonnegligent employers are almost always safe. It's easy to satisfy the first prong, the employer need only take reasonable preventive measures (antiharassment policy and procedures) and corrective measures (investigation and discipline, if warranted), and respond to incidents when it hears of them.

But what about the second prong? The nonnegligent employer can usually satisfy that, too. Some employees complain too late, when they could have complained earlier, because the harassment was not initially sudden or severe. In that case, the second prong is satisfied. Some employees do promptly complain when the harassment is not sudden or severe. Often, the employer can then stop the hostile environment almost before it happens – taking down the very first centerfold that's posted in the factory, for instance, may mean there's no actionable harassment claim (and thus no need to even consider the affirmative defense).

But what if the harassment *is* sudden and severe? In that case, liability should truly be automatic. The environment is legally hostile from the outset, and the victim has a cause of action even *before* she complains, as was the case with Walton. Thus, regardless of when the victim complains, the employer should be liable for at least the initial, unpreventable harassment.

## EMPLOYER RESPONSE ALONE SHOULD NOT DEFEAT SUDDEN, SEVERE HARASSMENT CASES

That's the law – as the Supreme Court sees it. But is it correct? Or, put another way, is it a good idea to hold nonnegligent employers liable in cases of sudden, severe harassment?

The answer, I believe, is yes. After all, it is little comfort to the victim of an assault by her supervisor that he is subsequently fired for his behavior; the harm has already been done. The employer may have been nonnegligent, but she has still suffered damage caused by a supervisor it employed.

A rule holding employers liable in such cases correctly allocates the risk of harm between employers – who hire, train, and monitor supervisors – and victims, who have no control over their working environment. It incentivizes employers to make sure their preventive measures are not just superficial mantras against harassment, but real, effective mechanisms for ensuring those to whom they delegate authority do not abuse it to the detriment of subordinate employees.

This allocation is particularly appropriate in a case like Walton's. As noted above, subordinates were often required, in effect, to meet with their supervisors in a private home or on the road, not in an office. Employers have a heightened duty to screen, train, and monitor supervisors when they exert authority without conventional forms of oversight.

Lucianne Walton should have had the opportunity to get her case to a jury. She claims she was the victim of a horrendous series of harassing incidents at the hands of her supervisor. A jury should decide if her claims have merit. Shame on the Eleventh Circuit for preventing her from having her day in court, before a jury.

A version of this chapter appeared on November 4, 2003, at writ.findlaw.com.

*Update: The Supreme Court has never weighed in on this application of the* Faragher/ Ellerth *affirmative defense. In 2004, however, it ruled in* Pennsylvania State Police v. Suders *that an employer is liable for harassment resulting in constructive discharge – a victim who quits rather than continue to face harassment – only if some official, employer-sanctioned adverse action by a supervisor precipitated the resignation.*[5] *The court later narrowed the definition of "supervisor," in* Vance v. Ball State Univ., *as explained in Chapter 28.*[6]

# 26

## Chinks in the Harassment Law Armor

In its opinion in *Baldwin v. Blue Cross/Blue Shield*, the Eleventh Circuit ended Susan Baldwin's attempt to seek legal redress for the sexual harassment she alleges that she suffered at the hands of her supervisor. But this decision is much more than just a blow to a single plaintiff in a single case.[1]

The ruling is a veritable minefield for future plaintiffs. Moreover, from a broader perspective, the ruling exposes fundamental flaws in the doctrine of employer liability for sexual harassment that has been crafted by the Supreme Court. These flaws make it too easy for employers to avoid liability, and too difficult for employees who have experienced actionable discrimination to recover.

### THE HOSTILE ENVIRONMENT ALLEGED BY SUSAN BALDWIN

Baldwin worked for Blue Cross in Huntsville, Alabama, as a marketing representative. In November 2000, Scott Head became her boss when he was promoted to district manager. According to the facts as judged in the light most favorable to the plaintiff (the required stance for an appellate court reviewing a grant of summary judgment to the defendant), Head engaged in two types of conduct that Baldwin found unwelcome and offensive.

First, he used profanity regularly, and used sex-specific derogatory terms to refer to both employees and applicants. Male subordinates were "peckerwoods" and "cocksuckers"; female employees were "bitches" or "babes"; one female applicant was not hired, according to Head, because she was a "slut" and a "tramp." (He apparently reserved "fucking bitch" for his wife, when complaining about her at work.)

The second type of conduct about which Baldwin complained was more serious and targeted directly at her. On July 26, 2001, Head accompanied Baldwin and other marketing representatives to a banquet for Blue Cross managers in Birmingham. During the banquet speech, Head leaned over to Baldwin and invited her to dance, party, and spend the night in his hotel room in Birmingham rather than driving home. "No one will ever know," he promised. She declined the invitation politely and left to return to Huntsville.

While she was driving home, Head called and urged again that she spend the night with him. He said he was driving to her house in Huntsville and that he would be there with beer to pick her up. He called several more times, telling her during one call that he was at her house, waiting. Baldwin told him to go home to his wife and kids.

A few days later, when Baldwin went to Head's office for a meeting, he closed the door, cornered her against a couch, and said "Hey, Babe, blow me." She moved across the room and changed the subject. Head offered a report on his weekend: "Well, you know, we went out partying this weekend and that fucking bitch wife of mine, you know, she got tanked and we got home and she came pretty unglued and she came at me," and "I threw that fucking bitch on the floor." Head continued with more details about his interaction with his wife, leading Baldwin to become very concerned about her own safety around him, particularly given his sexual advance just a few minutes earlier.

In the months that followed this meeting, Head continued to engage in many forms of inappropriate behavior, including several incidents targeted directly at Baldwin. One time, after getting her attention by calling out, "Hey Babe," Head unzipped his pants and began moving the zipper up and down. Other times, he would come up behind her and literally breathe down her neck.

Throughout these months, Baldwin did not report Head's conduct to the employee relations department, as directed by the company's sexual harassment policy. However, she confided periodically to coworkers about his sexual propositions. Finally, on November 8, 2001, after she had two major conflicts with Head, she filed an internal complaint.

## BLUE CROSS'S RESPONSE TO BALDWIN'S COMPLAINT: PUNISH THE VICTIM?

To be more specific, Baldwin submitted a written synopsis of her allegations about Head's behavior. She met with Emma Barclay in the human resources department and gave an oral synopsis, as well.

As a result, Barclay, Rick King, the vice president of human resources, and Sharon Heaton, another human resources employee, traveled to Huntsville to investigate Baldwin's allegations. They interviewed Head and other employees at a local restaurant, ultimately concluding that they could not substantiate Baldwin's allegations.

Because the company deemed the evidence "inconclusive" as to whether Baldwin was harassed, they refused to discipline Head. Instead, they gave Baldwin two options to make her work environment tolerable: go to counseling *with* Head or transfer to an office in another city two hours away. When Baldwin refused both options, she was terminated.

## WAS THERE ACTIONABLE HARASSMENT? THE COURT WRONGLY SAYS NO

The district court had granted summary judgment to Blue Cross, and the Court of Appeals for the Eleventh Circuit affirmed that ruling. Thus, as noted above, Baldwin lost. At the same time, so did other sexual harassment victims who must try their cases within the Eleventh Circuit, which encompasses Alabama, Florida, and Georgia. That is because the ruling dramatically undermines the ability of Title VII to provide such plaintiffs with appropriate legal redress for discrimination they have suffered. Significantly, the court made it harder to prove that harassment is actionable *and* harder to prove that the employer should be held liable:

First, the district court found that the harassment Baldwin alleged, even if true, was not sufficiently severe or pervasive to be actionable. The Court of Appeals did not directly affirm this aspect of the ruling, because the case was disposed with on other grounds. However, its analysis suggests it would have reached the same (wrong) conclusion. Of course, the district court was right that the mere use of profanity at work is not inherently unfair to women. However, the use of derogatory sex-specific terms like "bitch" and "slut" surely is.

It is true, too, that not all jerks are harassers. Yet a jerk of a boss should not be insulated from claims of harassment simply because he also does other obnoxious things in addition to harassing a subordinate. Moreover, and more important, a supervisor's repeated, unwanted sexual advances toward a subordinate are clearly sufficient to be actionable in a court of law. And on the basis of the facts above – the facts the Eleventh Circuit considered for purposes of his decision – Baldwin plainly suffered a string of repeated, unwanted sexual advances.

## DID THE EMPLOYER SATISFY THE AFFIRMATIVE DEFENSE? THE ERRONEOUS "FIRST PRONG" FINDING THAT THE INVESTIGATION SUFFICED

Not only did the Court of Appeals suggest wrongly that the harassment Baldwin suffered was not sufficiently severe or pervasive but it also wrongly found that the employer had established both prongs of the affirmative defense available in cases of supervisory hostile environment harassment. In analyzing Blue Cross's assertion of the *Faragher/Ellerth* affirmative defense, the Court of Appeals made several key mistakes:

First, the Court of Appeals wrongly concluded that Blue Cross established the first prong of the affirmative defense in that they took reasonable measures to prevent and correct harassment. In reaching this conclusion, the court refused to look closely at the deficiencies Baldwin alleged in the internal investigation. Among other things, Baldwin complained about the method and location for interviewing witnesses, and the investigators' dismissal of concerns they themselves had raised that the witness reports seemed "rehearsed." The deficient investigation, she alleged, had serious consequences: the company failed to find that she had been harassed by her supervisor.

Given that the witnesses interviewed were also subordinates of Head's, the possibility is strong that they lied during the investigation to save their own jobs. Also, if they sounded rehearsed, was it perhaps because Head prepped them? Or did they get together on their own to make sure their stories were consistent? These possibilities suggest the need for a much more searching investigation than Blue Cross actually undertook here. Rather than evaluate the investigation for legal sufficiency, however, the court complained: "We already have enough to do; our role under the *Faragher* and *Ellerth* decisions does not include micro-managing internal investigations."

This is a strange complaint from a court charged with implementing federal laws. In *Faragher* and *Ellerth*, the Supreme Court established a framework that made internal investigations the centerpiece of the remedial structure for problems of workplace harassment. Victims who fail to complain lose their right to sue; employers who fail to maintain grievance procedures are subject to strict liability for harassment. With stakes this high, resulting from a line the Supreme Court drew, how can an appellate court refuse to seriously evaluate a company's internal investigation? When victims lose their right to sue, it ought to be because companies provided at least some counterpart of a fair court procedure. If not, then companies can use monkey trials to evade the law.

Indeed, under the Court of Appeals' standard, employers have no incentive to conduct a good investigation, because any old investigation will offer them the same safe harbor from liability. The court specifically wrote that a legally sufficient investigation "may include conducting the inquiry informally in a manner that will not unnecessarily disrupt the company's business, and in an effort to arrive at a reasonably fair estimate of truth." But, again, informal inquiries – like the one here, a chat at a local restaurant – are hardly a substitute for one's day in court.

Second, the Court of Appeals concluded that the "remedial" options offered to Baldwin – go to counseling with the alleged harasser, accept a transfer, or be fired – were reasonable. Recall that, because the court was reviewing a grant of summary judgment to Blue Cross, it was required to assume that the harassment occurred as Baldwin alleged. In light of that assumption, how could the court truly say that these options represented reasonable efforts to correct the problem?

Consider, once again, what those options were: Why should a victim of harassment have to undergo counseling with the man who visited unwanted sexual advances on her? After all, the initial harassment was traumatic enough. Sending the two to counseling, as if they were a squabbling couple, only furthers the harasser's view of their relationship, which is supposed to be collegial, not romantic.

In addition, why should she have to relocate, lose her "book" of business, and start over just to get away from him? And why should she be fired for being unwilling to make a choice between two profoundly unfair alternatives?

These two flaws worked together against Baldwin: because the company conducted a poor investigation, they were not able to corroborate her allegations and refused to take action against the supervisor. Then, because the court refused to review the quality of the investigation, the "remedial" options offered to a plaintiff with unsubstantiated allegations were deemed reasonable. If the witnesses' "rehearsed" descriptions of the work environment had been further tested, perhaps the company would have decided to offer Baldwin more palatable remedies.

## THE ERRONEOUS "SECOND PRONG" FINDING THAT BALDWIN WAS UNTIMELY IN REPORTING THE HARASSMENT

Finally, the court wrongly held that the employer established the second prong of the affirmative defense, as well – the one that focuses on the victim's failure to take advantage of corrective opportunities made available by the employer.

Baldwin, the court said, did not comply with her duty to promptly report harassment she experienced at work. She complained three months after the first sexual advance, which, according to the court, "is anything but prompt, early, or soon."

Why didn't Baldwin complain right away? Her goal, she testified, was to "just go along to get along." Research shows that this is the typical reaction of victims in her situation, who face many deterrents to complaining about harassment, such as retaliation, being ostracized by coworkers, and being labeled a "complainer" to name just a few.[2]

Yet the court deemed Baldwin's behavior unreasonable as a matter of law – rather than simply holding that it raised a genuine issue of fact that a jury ought to resolve. Other federal courts have been similarly stingy in their interpretation of this prong, holding delays as short as a week sometimes to be inexcusable.[3] But these interpretations, too, fail to accord with the reality as to how long it takes bona fide victims to complain. Our society sends deeply mixed messages when it encourages women to try to thrive in a male world yet, through decisions like these, also tells them they must instantly complain at the first sign of potential harassment.

Finally, the court also faulted Baldwin for failing to cooperate with her employer by accepting one of the "remedial" choices they offered her. Given her view of her supervisor, his behavior, and the importance of her own career, it is hardly surprising or unreasonable that she would reject both options.

## A COURT THAT THOUGHT IT HAD BETTER THINGS TO DO THAN ENFORCE THE LAW

The Eleventh Circuit Court of Appeals has, with its decision in *Baldwin v. Blue Cross*, done a disservice to Title VII and all the victims of harassment who deserve its protection. What hope is there for eradicating sex discrimination in the workplace

when a federal court claims it has better things to do than enforce the legal standard
by which it is bound?

A version of this chapter appeared on April 3, 2007, at writ.findlaw.com.

*Update: Although one of the more egregious harassment opinions to come down the
pike, the Eleventh Circuit declined to rehear the case en banc, and the Supreme Court
denied the petition for review.*[4]

# Do Employer Efforts Prevent Harassment or Just Prevent Liability?

An article in the *National Law Journal* praised Mitsubishi Motor Manufacturing of America, a Japanese car company with a significant presence in the United States, for its remarkable recovery from a dark history of sexual harassment and other civil rights violations. It described Mitsubishi as a "corporate model for training employees about the illegality of harassment and discrimination and investigating complaints when they arise."[1]

What's interesting about Mitsubishi's recovery is that it gives us the chance to ask a forgotten question: Do employer's efforts to prevent harassment actually work, or do they just serve to insulate employers from liability?

## MITSUBISHI'S RESPONSE TO THE SETTLEMENT

Just a few years ago, Mitsubishi settled a sexual harassment case with the EEOC, in which widespread and pervasive harassment within the company was alleged. In the settlement, Mitsubishi paid $34 million to the EEOC and paid several million more to private plaintiffs bringing similar complaints. Since then, the EEOC has settled other high-profile, big-money sexual harassment suits. Yet the settlement with Mitsubishi still stands out as a reminder to employers of the tremendous consequences of failing to control the workplace.

Driven partly by court orders and partly by economic fear, Mitsubishi did make a noteworthy effort to end the culture of harassment that had enveloped its plant in Normal, Illinois. The evidence in the lawsuit showed an environment in which harassment was as routine and commonplace as coffee breaks. More than 300 female employees joined the suit, complaining of groping, fondling, lewd jokes and behavior, and obscene graffiti plastered in work areas.

The company's post-lawsuit response began with the hiring of former secretary of labor Lynn Martin, for a multimillion-dollar consulting gig. Martin's job was to oversee a self-audit of the company's EEO practices and environment. The programs and policies that flowed from Martin's work centered on the adoption and implementation of a zero-tolerance policy. The policy was given teeth by the creation of an entirely separate department, the Opportunity Programs Department (OPD), whose sole function is to train employees about the policy and investigate complaints.

As part of its ongoing antiharassment program, Mitsubishi requires each employee to attend sexual harassment prevention training every two years. It also has stepped up investigations of complaints and the imposition of discipline on offenders.

Since the adoption of the policy, the company boasts vastly fewer complaints of harassment than before, and points to the significant discipline that has been imposed for those complaints that were proven to be valid.

## WHY AND HOW EMPLOYERS TRY TO PREVENT AND CORRECT HARASSMENT

Employers have had an incentive to prevent and correct harassment since the earliest cases recognizing both that harassment is an actionable form of sex discrimination that violates Title VII and that employers, at least in some circumstances, can be held liable for it. Those incentives became clearer and more pointed after the Court's decisions in *Faragher v. City of Boca Raton* and *Burlington Industries v. Ellerth*, in which it laid out a very clear path for employers to minimize their exposure to lawsuits and damages awards.[2] As discussed in previous chapters, employers face automatic liability for hostile environment harassment committed by supervisors unless they can make out an affirmative defense. One aspect of the affirmative defense focuses on whether the employer has made reasonable efforts to prevent and correct harassment.

This defense thus creates strong incentives for employers to undertake such efforts, in order to insulate themselves from liability (like that faced by Mitsubishi). Accordingly, an entire industry has grown up around the need for employers to institute these measures. The industry is composed of lawyers, consultants, and human resource professionals who focus on advising and aiding companies to create and improve their programs so that if they are sued, they can successfully invoke the affirmative defense or generally defend against harassment liability regardless of the applicable law or standard. Employers have reacted swiftly to their advice, hastily adopting new policies, procedures, and training programs to comply with the new rules of liability.

The "best practices" for employers working within this legal regime are straightforward. To prevent harassment, employers must adopt a formal, written antiharassment policy, which describes prohibited conduct, states the employer's opposition to it, and outlines potential disciplinary actions if the conduct nevertheless occurs. The policy must be made available to employees – disseminated individually, included in the employee handbook, or posted in a public workspace. Taking these simple measures, which 90–97 percent of all employers have done, operates as "compelling proof" in some jurisdictions of adequate prevention.

Many employers have also instituted antiharassment training programs. Unlike policies, training programs are not required by courts, although employers who institute them are given credit for doing so. More than half of employers today provide some form of antiharassment training.

The emphasis in the law – reflected in how courts evaluate employers' efforts in the context of sexual harassment lawsuits – is on compliance. Employers who have taken appropriate steps to prevent harassment are rewarded via the affirmative defense; those who have not are punished. But little or no emphasis is placed on success – courts rarely ask whether the measures were indeed effective in preventing further incidents of harassment.

That raises the risk of employers' complying with the letter of the law – by taking formal measures to end harassment – but not with its spirit, if the measures do not actually end harassment. It also thwarts Title VII's primary purpose of preventing discrimination from occurring in the first instance.

## DO PREVENTATIVE MEASURES WORK?

Survey data and anecdotal reports make clear that employers, including Mitsubishi, have been quick to respond to the incentives created by the legal regime – as well as to individual lawsuits giving rise to significant damage awards.

But one question that is rarely asked when analyzing the effect of the rules of liability is whether they actually serve to lower the amount of harassment – or whether they simply create a safe harbor for employers who make a few token changes to the workplace environment. Putting up a poster, of course, does not automatically end harassment. Nor does telling employees not to harass ensure that they won't.

One way to consider whether these rules of liability make sense is to examine survey data and other research about the frequency of harassment over time, and about the effectiveness of particular preventative measures. But the troubling truth is that surveys gauging the frequency and severity of sexual harassment have reported a consistent level of harassment over a period of nearly twenty years. There is thus reason to suspect that the preventative measures being routinely adopted are insufficient to get at the real problem. Put simply, the posters and programs have not, it seems, effected a transformation in attitudes and behavior.[3]

Other survey evidence supports this conclusion. A survey of federal employees, for example, reported that 80 percent of them rated the dissemination of antiharassment policies as "among the most effective actions an organization can take to reduce or prevent harassment." But only 68 percent, somewhat ironically, thought policies actually changed the way employees behaved toward one another.[4]

Furthermore, despite the high *perception* of effectiveness, there are no studies showing that exposure to an antiharassment policy or knowledge of grievance procedures actually deters harassers. Harassers, overcome with sexual attraction or used to treating women in demeaning ways or exploiting power differentials, may simply not care if they are violating the policy. Alternatively, they may assume the policy applies to other people, not them: How can the conduct that seemed innocuous to them for years suddenly be illegal?

## WHY TRAINING SEEMS TO WORK BETTER THAN PUBLICIZING POLICIES AND PROCEDURES

Social science data on training – the one aspect of prevention not required by the law – are more promising. Studies show some evidence of a "training effect," which suggests that individuals can change perceptions of harassment after exposure to various types of training programs. These programs may not only teach them about harassment but also cause them to pay more attention to the problem and thus make better assessments of when it is occurring. A harasser might even realize, through training, that behavior he has taken for granted as innocuous is in fact illegal, and change his ways.

But one limitation of training, reflected in social science studies, is that it affects different individuals differently. Women tend to be less affected by training than men are; individuals with a high propensity to harass tend to be more affected than those with a low propensity to harass are.[5]

The studies suggest that more effective training would be adapted not only to particular workplaces but also to particular employees – a level of individualization that the average employer might not be able or inclined to undertake.

## WHY MITSUBISHI IS A GOOD BUT NOT A PERFECT MODEL

From all reports – including those of an independent monitor, the local EEOC lawyers, and internal sources – Mitsubishi has managed to change its workplace culture to stem the proliferation of harassment. But the measures the company has taken, such as paying six employees full-time to do nothing but deal with problems of harassment, are expensive and unlikely to be replicated by most employers.[6]

The law should encourage employers to replicate one aspect of Mitsubishi's program – a serious, internal assessment, using outside consultants, of a company's harassment problem and the measures that are most likely to eradicate it. In addition, the law should begin to focus not on whether the employer took standard preventative measures, but on whether they took *effective* measures.

The culture of compliance needs to shift to a culture of success. Posting policies and creating procedures is one thing; actually ending harassment is another. Employers need to realize that and act accordingly – and the law needs to set up new, clear incentives for them to do so, beyond the rules the Supreme Court has so far set.

The affirmative defense, for instance, should be more difficult to invoke, so that employers must take effective, substantial efforts that are proven to have success. Only with a showing of such accomplishments should an employer be able to avoid liability for harassment at the hands of its own employees.

A version of this chapter appeared on May 7, 2002, at writ.findlaw.com.

# 28

# Who's the Boss?

In *Vance v. Ball State University*, a divided Supreme Court held that a harasser does not qualify as a supervisor unless he or she has the power to "take tangible employment actions against the victim" – colloquially, the power to hire and fire.[1] This matters because the employer's liability under Title VII for workplace harassment committed by supervisors is much stronger than it is for harassment inflicted by coworkers.

Writing for the majority, Justice Samuel Alito opted for a bright-line rule over one that might have provided redress for the harm that employees suffer at the hands of harassers who, despite not having the power to hire and fire, nonetheless dictate many or all aspects of employees' daily working conditions.

## THE FACTS IN *VANCE V. BALL STATE UNIVERSITY*

This case revolves around allegations by Maetta Vance, an African-American woman who worked at Ball State University (BSU), in its kitchen and catering department, that she was racially harassed. Vance began working at BSU in 2001, and she was, for many of the years she worked there, the only African-American employee.

While employed by BSU, Vance complained numerous times of racial discrimination and retaliation. Upon review by the Supreme Court, however, only her complaints involving one employee, Saundra Davis, were at issue. Davis is a white woman who worked as a catering specialist at BSU, while Vance worked as a catering assistant.

In internal complaints and charges with the EEOC, Vance alleged that Davis cornered her on an elevator in a threatening manner and told her, "I'll do it again." And although Justice Alito leaves out these allegations in his description of the facts, Vance also alleged that Davis used the racial slurs "Buckwheat" and "Sambo" to refer to Vance, both in Vance's presence and outside of it. BSU did take some measures in response to Vance's complaints, but none was sufficient to resolve the problem.[2]

According to the Supreme Court's opinion, the parties "vigorously dispute the precise nature and scope of Davis's duties, but they agree that Davis did not have the power to hire, fire, demote, promote, transfer, or discipline Vance."

Vance eventually filed a lawsuit in federal court alleging that she suffered a racially hostile work environment in violation of Title VII. In her complaint, she alleged that Davis was her supervisor and was responsible for creation of the hostile environment.

The federal district court granted summary judgment to BSU, ruling that BSU could not be held vicariously liable for Davis's actions because she was not Vance's supervisor. And under the more lenient negligence standard applied to coworker harassment, BSU prevailed because Vance did not notify BSU of some of the incidents and, with respect to others, BSU's remedial efforts were deemed sufficient. The Seventh Circuit affirmed this ruling, on the theory that supervisor liability only adheres when the harasser has "the power to hire, fire, demote, promote, transfer, or discipline an employee." Because Davis did not meet that standard, BSU was not vicariously liable for any harassment that may have occurred, in the Seventh Circuit's judgment.

## EMPLOYER LIABILITY FOR SUPERVISORY HARASSMENT: A DEVELOPING DOCTRINE

The issue in *Vance* – what makes someone a "supervisor" in the harassment context – turns on a distinction that the Court had created in earlier cases between supervisor and coworker harassment.

The law of employer liability for harassment under Title VII has been developing for almost twenty years now. Most of these cases involve sexual harassment, but the Supreme Court has made clear that the same standards apply to all forms of unlawful harassment under Title VII, which includes racial harassment. In fact, when the court first recognized the presence of a hostile work environment as a basis for a viable theory of discrimination, it described the development of hostile work environment theory in a Fifth Circuit case, *Rogers v. EEOC*, involving racial harassment. There, the court noted that one "can readily envision working environments so heavily polluted with discrimination as to destroy completely the emotional and psychological stability of minority group workers."[3]

Liability for harassment, whatever the type, turns in part on the power of the perpetrator. Although *Faragher* and *Ellerth* both involved harassment by supervisors, the Court also indirectly approved the application of a negligence standard – the standard asking if the employer knew or should have known of, and failed to respond to, claims of coworker or third-party harassment. These cases created as much

confusion as they resolved. The proper scope and application of the affirmative
defense have been hotly litigated. By and large, lower federal courts have interpreted
the affirmative defense in a way that benefits employers, rather than victims.[4] But
it is clear that employers face greater liability for supervisory harassment than for
coworker or third-party harassment. But what makes someone a supervisor? *Vance*
gave the Court one more opportunity to protect – or choose not to protect – victims
of workplace harassment. A broad definition of "supervisor" would bring more
cases under the stricter standard of liability; a narrow definition would do just the
opposite.

### The Ruling in *Vance v. Ball State University*

In affirming the grant of summary judgment to BSU, the U.S. Court of Appeals
for the Seventh Circuit ruled that Davis was not Vance's supervisor. To reach
that conclusion, the court applied a definition of supervisor that encompasses only
"someone with the power to directly affect the terms and conditions of the plaintiff's
employment," with authority that "primarily consists of the power to hire, fire,
demote, promote, transfer, or discipline an employee." The Seventh Circuit held
that Davis was not a supervisor, even if she periodically had authority to direct the
work of other employees. That power, the court reasoned, was not enough to create
a supervisory relationship.

The Supreme Court's likely motivation for agreeing to review the Seventh Circuit's opinion was a circuit split. While the First and Eighth Circuits also used the
"power to hire and fire" definition of supervisor, three other circuits had adopted
a broader definition that also included individuals with the authority to direct and
oversee the victim's daily work.

The circuit split turns on the proper understanding of agency principles – the
basis for vicarious liability in the first place. Is an individual without the power to
make tangible employment actions, but with the power to direct or control day-
to-day activities, acting as an agent of the employer? The EEOC, which issued an
enforcement guidance in 1999 in the wake of *Faragher* and *Ellerth*, took the broader
view of supervisory status. Under that guidance, an employee who has the "authority
to direct [the victim's] daily work activities" or the power "to recommend," though
not personally affect, "tangible employment decisions" qualifies as a supervisor
because his or her ability to harass "is enhanced by his or her authority to increase
the employee's workload or assign undesirable tasks."[5]

The majority in *Vance*, however, disagreed with the EEOC's approach and upheld
the Seventh Circuit's. It described the EEOC's definition as "nebulous" and unpersuasive. It chose instead a narrower standard that is "workable" and "can be applied
without undue difficulty at both the summary judgment stage and at trial." "The
alternative," the majority feared, would require a "highly case-specific evaluation of
numerous factors" that "would frustrate judges and confound jurors."

The majority's substantive defense of the standard lies in the *Faragher/Ellerth* framework. It read those cases as both drawing a sharp distinction between supervisors and coworkers and tying the concepts of supervisory status and tangible employment actions together. In other words, the same harassers who could have taken a tangible employment action against a victim for refusing sexual advances (a quid pro quo) are those who can engender vicarious liability for the employers.

The majority cast off Vance's (and the EEOC's) definition of supervisor as based on "colloquial" uses of the term, which were inconsistent across contexts. The opinion strings together a series of completely random definitions of "supervisor" from Internet dictionaries to the rules governing the administration of Native American schools to the complex rules of Medicaid administration. The point, one supposes, is to show that there is no uniform definition of "supervisor" in the law or in English usage. But, of course, that was not the question before the Court, nor the position urged by both the plaintiff and the United States, which filed an amicus brief urging the Court to adopt the EEOC's position. The question it should have been limited to is this: What is the proper definition of "supervisor" under an antidiscrimination law that holds employers liable when superiors harass their subordinates?

As the majority concedes, "supervisor" is not a statutory term found in Title VII. The Supreme Court crafted the distinction between tangible-employment-action harassment and hostile-environment harassment and created the affirmative defense out of whole cloth. Having invented a term and given it statutory force, the Court's responsibility is now to interpret the term in a way that serves the statute's underlying purposes. But the majority does the opposite: it adopts a narrow, strained definition of supervisor that expands the already broad safe harbor for employers who do little to monitor work environments or to be proactive in preventing and correcting harassment.

The majority also rejects Vance's argument that the narrower definition of supervisor would not have been met in *Faragher* – one of the Supreme Court opinions in which the current structure was established. While the majority claims that she has "misread" the prior decisions, it concedes that one of the "supervisors" in *Faragher* "may have wielded less authority" than the other and was primarily "responsible for making the lifeguards' daily assignment, and for supervising their work and fitness training." Under the "power to hire and fire" rule the Court adopts in *Vance*, this direction of daily work activities would clearly not have been sufficient. Yet the Court treated this as a case of supervisory harassment. The majority's rejection of Vance's argument on this point is not a rejection on the merits of the case before the Court. Rather, the majority says that the parties in that case did not dispute the status of the alleged harassers, or present to the Court "the question of the degree of the authority that an employee must have in order to be classified as a supervisor." It may well be that the Court did not need to decide the supervisor question in that case, but it is a little odd now to decide that a narrow definition of supervisor is implicit in a case in which the definition would likely not have been met.

In the end, the majority is unfazed by any form of argument. It prefers a bright-line rule to a fact-specific one (questioning the ability of jurors and judges to assess facts in ways no more complicated than they do on a daily basis in other cases) and an employer-friendly rule to a victim-friendly one. (Justice Thomas would have gone even further to minimize employee protections. He wrote separately in concurrence because he believes *Faragher* and *Ellerth* were "wrongly decided"; indeed, he believes that employers should never be held vicariously liable for harassment by their supervisors.)

The ruling in *Vance* hearkens back to Justice Alito's majority opinion in *Ledbetter v. Goodyear Tire & Rubber Co.*, in which he took a stringent view of the statute of limitations in pay discrimination cases – a view that not only disregarded long-standing precedent but also ignored the realities of the way pay discrimination is practiced, perceived, and redressed.[6] Congress eventually passed legislation to overrule his ruling in *Ledbetter*, with the Lilly Ledbetter Fair Pay Act, a turn of events that would make sense here, as well.[7]

### IN DISSENT: JUSTICE GINSBURG PERSUASIVELY CRITICIZES THE MAJORITY

Joined by Justices Breyer, Sotomayor, and Kagan, Justice Ginsburg dissented from the majority's holding and argued for the broader definition of "supervisor" that is endorsed by the EEOC and several federal appellate courts. By striking "from the supervisory category employees who control the day-to-day schedules and assignments of others," Ginsburg wrote, the Court "diminishes the force of *Faragher* and *Ellerth*, ignores the conditions under which members of the work force labor, and disserves the objective of Title VII to prevent discrimination from infecting the Nation's workplaces."[8]

Justice Ginsburg's dissent focuses on the realities of the workplace, which were better captured by *Faragher* and *Ellerth* than by the ruling in *Vance*. Ginsburg reasoned as follows:

> Exposed to fellow employee's harassment, one can walk away or tell the offender to "buzz off." A supervisor's slings and arrows, however, are not so easily avoided. An employee who confronts her harassing supervisor risks, for example, receiving an undesirable or unsafe work assignment or an unwanted transfer. She may be saddled with an excessive workload or with placement on a shift spanning hours disruptive of her family life. And she may be demoted or fired.[9]

As Ginsburg demonstrates by citing this array of actions, it is not only the superior with the power to hire and fire who can wield authority that aids him in his efforts to harass – or to get away with it. And in either case, the superior has that power because the employer has given it to him. The narrower view adopted by the majority, Ginsburg wrote, is "blind to the realities of the workplaces" as well as insufficiently sensitive to the expertise of the EEOC, which has been charged with interpreting and enforcing Title VII.

Justice Ginsburg provides a series of vignettes, based on real, litigated cases, in which "in-charge employees" – the types of supervisors that are now exempted from formal supervisor status under the *Vance* rule – show just how much they are able to negatively transform a subordinate's work environment. Here are her examples: a lead driver who forced a trainee into unwanted sex, which she believed was necessary to gain a favorable evaluation. A retail clerk who was told by the manager to "give [him] what [he] want[ed]" in order to get long weekends off. A lead highway worker who forced a subordinate female employee to wash her snowplow in below-freezing weather and prevented another employee from fixing the heating in her truck. In each of these cases, all of which the majority rejects as irrelevant to the issue in *Vance*, "a person vested with the authority to control the conditions of a subordinate's daily work life used his position to aid his harassment." Each harasser would be commonly understood by the employees whose destinies they controlled to be a supervisor. Yet each is relegated to the status of an ordinary coworker, whose conduct is not attributable to the employer.

In the end, Justice Ginsburg notes, "[T]he Court's definition of supervisor will hinder efforts to stamp out discrimination in the workplace." Vicarious liability is designed to give employers an incentive to screen, train, and monitor their supervisors more closely, rather than letting them run amok in a workplace full of employees who feel afraid to resist their supervisor's misconduct. It is already extremely difficult for a victim of harassment to prevail in a Title VII lawsuit. The majority's ruling in *Vance* has made it that much more difficult.[10]

A version of this chapter appeared on June 25, 2013, at verdict.justia.com.

# 29

# Costly Mistakes

In August 2012, titillating reports emerged about the sexually charged atmosphere in the office of New York State Assemblyman Vito Lopez, including his preference that his female employees not wear bras to work. Two women filed complaints against Lopez for sexual harassment, and the Assembly released a letter in which it reported on the resolution of the women's claims. The Ethics Committee censured Lopez, stripped him of his committee chairmanship, and barred him from hiring interns or employees under the age of twenty-one.[1]

There are many disturbing aspects of this story – the flagrancy of the harassment and the raw abuse of power, among others. But perhaps most disturbing is that these were not the first claims of harassment against Lopez. Previous claims had been made, and secretly and expensively settled. Why would the Assembly allow this behavior to continue unchecked? Why would Lopez himself not be deterred by potential consequences to his pocketbook and political career? Forget the desire to ensure a nondiscriminatory work environment for all employees, which we perhaps naively hope that employers harbor. Isn't the fear of costly jury verdicts or settlements sufficient incentive for employers to intervene to stop known harassment problems? That is the question the New York State Assembly ought to be asking itself this week – and over the many weeks and months ahead when the repercussions of Lopez's alleged chain of harassment horror are acutely felt.

Meanwhile, Chrysler, the auto giant, should have asked itself the same question, as it wrote a check for the $3.5 million punitive-damage verdict that was reinstated by the U.S. Court of Appeals for the Seventh Circuit, in a racial harassment case, *May v. Chrysler*.[2]

Are there lessons for other employers in the cases against Lopez and Chrysler?

## THE LOPEZ PROBLEM: WHY WASN'T HE STOPPED EARLIER?

With respect to the claims against Lopez, Assembly Speaker Sheldon Silver reported that, according to an internal investigation, Lopez was guilty of "pervasive unwelcome verbal conduct," as well as unwanted groping and kissing of female staff members. As detailed in the Assembly's letter to Lopez, the committee found substantiated reports of "multiple incidents of unwelcome physical conduct toward one complainant, wherein you put your hand on her leg, she removed your hand, and you then put your hand between her upper thighs, putting your hand as far up between her legs as you could go." An assault of one complainant occurred in the car when she was required to accompany Lopez on a trip to Atlantic City.[3]

Whatever punishment was meted out by the Assembly (censure, etc.) seems warranted – and then some. But why did the Assembly allow Lopez to rage out of control in an unlawfully discriminatory, and perhaps criminal, manner while he was running a public office? These two women were not the first to complain about Lopez. Indeed, as the scandal was unfolding, it was revealed that the Assembly's Speaker had already authorized secret payments of more than $100,000 of state money (plus $32,000 paid directly by Lopez) to settle at least two sexual harassment claims involving Lopez in June 2012. Putting aside the likely impropriety of the Speaker's not referring this claim to the Ethics Committee – the usual procedure for harassment claims – Silver's decision to settle these claims shows that he knew about Lopez's behavior and yet allowed it to continue unchecked.

Once the scandal became public, even more reports about Lopez's inappropriate and unlawful conduct in the office emerged. Many women interviewed reported the same types of conduct: Lopez asked them to dress in a sexual manner (more specifically, in short skirts, high heels, and no bra); questioned them closely about their boyfriends and sex lives; made unwanted sexual advances; and threatened retaliation against those who resisted, a threat that they took seriously because of his reputed bad temper and his wide-ranging connections in state politics. Those who were "well endowed" were encouraged to use it to their advantage.

Lopez's conduct – the type identified in the Assembly's findings, and the type described by women in newspaper interviews – clearly violates state and federal antidiscrimination laws that prohibit sexual harassment. The State Assembly – and ultimately the taxpayers – faced significant liability for allowing a man with such power over his staff to behave so inappropriately. The only repercussion for the conduct by Lopez that led to the secret payout was that Lopez had to attend a sexual harassment workshop. The secret payout, however, is just the tip of the iceberg, as the damages for failing to stop a known problem of harassment are likely to be even higher – that's the lesson of *May v. Chrysler*, discussed below.

## MAY V. CHRYSLER: A DIFFERENT TYPE OF HARASSMENT, BUT THE SAME TYPE OF LIABILITY

The ruling by the Seventh U.S. Court of Appeals for the Seventh Circuit reinstates a $3.5 million punitive damages verdict against Chrysler in a case brought by Otto May, a pipe fitter at Chrysler's Belvedere, Illinois, assembly plant since 1988. May was never groped on a business trip by a supervisor, but he was systematically tormented, threatened, sabotaged, and physically endangered by a band of coworkers who were bound and determined to drive him out of the workforce.

May filed suit in 2002 under Title VII, bringing a claim for a hostile work environment in which he was targeted on the basis of his race, religion, and national origin. As the factual details below will make clear, May's Cuban Jewish background made him a target for abuse at this particular plant. Title VII prohibits hostile environment harassment on the basis of any characteristic that is protected by the statute. Thus, sexual harassment is not the only actionable type of harassment. Racial, ethnic, and religious harassment are equally unlawful and are governed by the same standards for employer liability.

After a trial, a jury awarded May $709,000 in compensatory damages, and $3.5 million in punitive damages. The evidence at trial showed seventy separate incidents of harassment occurring over the course of three years, many of which each individually could create an unlawful hostile environment by itself. Here are the highlights: graffiti around May's area of the plant saying things like "Otto Cuban Jew fag die," and "death to the Cuban Jew"; puncturing the tires on May's bike and car; pouring sugar in the gas tanks of two of May's cars; and placing "a dead bird wrapped in toilet paper to look like a Ku Klux Klansman (complete with pointy hat) in a vise at one of May's work stations."

There is no question that harassment of this type, even if it had been much less severe or pervasive, is actionable. But is Chrysler responsible for it? Because the harassment that May experienced seemed to be at the hands of coworkers (the perpetrators were never convincingly identified), the employer is held only to a negligence standard. In other words, the employer is liable only if it knew, or should have known, of the hostile environment and failed to take prompt and effective remedial action. (For harassment by supervisors, the liability is stricter.) Punitive damages can be awarded if the employer behaves with malice or reckless indifference to an employee's federally protected rights.

Plant management clearly knew about the harassment early on, because the graffiti was painted on workplace walls. May also complained many times to management, as well as to police, the FBI, and the Anti-Defamation League. So Chrysler's liability turns on its response to the harassment. And it was the company's anemic and entirely ineffective response that led the jury to impose such a high amount of punitive damages in its verdict. (It could also be that the jury was disgusted by Chrysler's main defense at trial, which was to suggest that May inflicted the harassment on himself in order to draw others' attention to him.)

## WHY CHRYSLER'S RESPONSE WAS INADEQUATE

The harassment against May began early in 2002, with vandalism to his car and then to the cars he used as replacements. Each incident was reported to local police and to Chrysler in February 2002. Three months later, May drove over a spike hidden in a rag under his tire and again complained to company security and to the police. May got no response at the plant, so he contacted someone in human resources at Chrysler's headquarters in another state. Ten days later, someone in the local human resources office (who was married to an employee who was a suspect in the harassment) called and offered him a parking space in the salaried lot. May objected, however, that many of the cameras on the lot did not work or were not monitored. By late spring, the threatening messages (mentioned above) started to appear – on May's walls, on his coveralls, and on paper left at his workstation. He found a note in his toolbox on September 12 that said, "no one can help you fucken Cuban Jew We will get you Death to the Jews Cuban fag Die." May complained again and again, but got no response.

On September 26, the heads of human resources and labor relations at Chrysler held two meetings with about sixty people who held skilled-trades jobs. At the meetings, they reviewed Chrysler's harassment policy. According to the appellate court's description of this meeting, "Some didn't appreciate the reminder; they were upset that skilled trades was being singled-out and complained that [the HR head] was telling them they could not have 'fun' at work anymore." Moreover, the court noted, the "meeting was just a meeting." The higher-ups did not interview the attendees as part of any investigation into the harassment, nor did they follow up with those who equated prohibited harassment with "fun." And only 60 of the 1,000 people who had access to May's work area were asked to attend.

The harassment continued unabated after the September meeting. The Anti-Defamation league, a civil rights group, contacted Chrysler to implore it to take action to stop the harassment. May also filed a charge with the EEOC, which found that he had reasonable cause for his complaint and encouraged Chrysler to take necessary remedial action.

In January 2003, May was contacted by Scott Huller in Chrysler's corporate diversity office for an interview. May was asked for names of possible suspects; he provided a list of nineteen people, with his reasons for suspecting that each might be involved, ranging from past discipline for assault, racist behavior, or personal antagonism to May. Huller, however, did not interview any of the nineteen. Someone else was supposed to use the list to crosscheck with the nineteen's work attendance on the dates the harassment occurred.

More than a year after May first complained, at which point the harassment still continued, the company finally developed a protocol for handling the incidents. Graffiti was photographed and then cleaned; attendance data were checked. In May 2003, Chrysler hired a forensic document examiner to compare handwriting samples with the graffiti and notes, but his investigation was inconclusive. Three full years after the first incident, May was still being harassed with graffiti, death threats, and vandalism to his car. Obviously, whatever measures Chrysler employed to address the problem were woefully ineffective.

At trial, Chrysler suggested mostly that May fabricated his whole claim and wrote all the disgusting, threatening messages himself. They pursued this strategy despite the fact that the main human resources officer responsible for his case said she saw "no evidence that he did this himself." Obviously, the jury did not believe this was what happened. To the contrary, its $3.5 million punitive damages verdict shows instead that the jurors believed May.

What Chrysler didn't explain at trial was why it responded so slowly during the first months of harassment, and why it didn't step up its response as it became clear that the problem was not going away. Chrysler failed to take even the most basic steps that are called for in this type of situation. It did not properly investigate May's complaints. It did not interview potential witnesses or suspects. It did not impose measures designed to catch the perpetrators. How hard is it, after all, to discover which employees are painting graffiti on the inside walls of a plant during work hours? How about a surveillance camera? The appellate court noted the lack of a single such camera in evaluating Chrysler's response.

The appellate court majority had no trouble upholding the finding of liability after a step-by-step review of Chrysler's response to May's complaints. As its opinion concludes:

> During the first year of written threats and harassment, what had Chrysler done? They held a meeting. They interviewed May. And, one year in, they hired [a handwriting analyst]. Did that amount to a "prompt and adequate" response to multiple racist and anti-Semitic death threats? Especially in light of the gravity of the harassment, the jury was presented with more than enough evidence to conclude that Chrysler had not done enough.

The law required Chrysler to take steps reasonably calculated to stop the harassment. That, it clearly did not do. It fell so short of the bar, the court concluded, that the jury's award of punitive damages was also warranted:

> If it was negligent to respond to weeks and months of death threats with a pair of meetings and documentation, what happens when that inadequate response does not improve over the course of a year? Two years? Three years? At some point the response sinks from negligent to reckless, at some point it is obvious that an increased effort is necessary, and if that does not happen, punitive damages become a possibility.

Chrysler argued, correctly, that a good-faith response to comply with the law can insulate a company from punitive damages for harassment under the Supreme Court's ruling in *Kolstad v. American Dental Ass'n*.[4] But the court saw no evidence of such good faith. A "good-faith effort at compliance," the court explained, "is not a matter of *declarations* about how much the employer cared about a victim of harassment or about how hard certain HR employees say they worked to rectify the situation."[5]

In addition to all the failures already discussed above, the company also gave principal responsibility for the case to a human resources employee who was married to one of the suspects (she did not recuse herself because she "knew he wasn't the person involved") – an insurmountable conflict of interest that would have doomed even a well-conducted internal investigation. There was also ample evidence at trial that Chrysler's primary concern was simply getting rid of May, rather than protecting him from further harassment. The Seventh Circuit thus concluded not only that punitive damages were appropriate but also that the amount of the damages award was not so "grossly excessive" as to be unconstitutional.

## WHAT THE CLAIMS AGAINST LOPEZ AND CHRYSLER HAVE IN COMMON

The claims against Vito Lopez and the claims against Chrysler may seem to have little in common. They involved very different workplaces; perpetrators with very different levels of power; and very different types of harassment. But what they have in common is more important than the ways in which they differ: in both cases, the problem of harassment was made known to those with the power – and the responsibility – to stop it. And those in power did nothing.

Employers cannot just click their heels three times and hope for the best. Law and common sense both dictate basic steps that should be taken in response to any complaint of harassment, as well as steps designed to prevent harassment from occurring in the first place. The State Assembly and Chrysler each made critical mistakes in their handling of these cases, for which they will pay handsomely. Let's hope that other employers learn from these mistakes, before future employees must endure similar workplaces.

A version of this chapter appeared on September 4, 2012, at verdict.justia.com.

*Update: On May 20, 2013 Lopez resigned from his job as state assemblyman. In June 2013, the New York State legislative ethics panel imposed a $330,000 fine on Lopez resulting from at least thirty-three episodes in which Lopez violated state's Public Officers Law. Two of the former Lopez aides settled with the Assembly and Lopez for $580,000 in damages.[6] Two weeks later, Sheldon Silver, then Speaker of the Assembly charged with investigating the complaints against Lopez, was himself indicted for alleged involvement in a bribery and kickback scheme.[7] In 2015, Vito Lopez died of leukemia, and, again, two weeks later, Sheldon Silver was convicted on all counts in his indictment.[8]*

# 30

## Hands Off the Merchandise

The urban dictionary gives two definitions of the phrase "hands off the merchandise": (1) a "protest/order uttered by one of either gender when someone else (usually of the other gender) wants to indulge in a little touchy-feely but [the protester's] not in the mood"; or (2) "Basically 'Don't touch my stuff, punk.'"[1]

Allen Manwaring, a former grocery store manager who was fired for sexual harassment, but reincarnated as a produce vendor for the very same store, might be the rare person for whom both definitions are appropriate. And the entity ordering him to keep his hands off is the U.S. Court of Appeals for the Second Circuit.

Pursuant to a recent ruling by that court, in *EEOC v. KarenKim*, Inc.,[2] the EEOC is now entitled to obtain an injunction that prohibits Manwaring not only from touching the mostly-teenage-girl cashiers who work at the grocery store but also from touching the *produce* or any other merchandise that would bring him physically into the store. In Manwaring's case, the fact section of the Second Circuit's opinion reveals a disturbing pattern of sexual harassment that went unchecked despite numerous complaints to the store owner.

The opinion also underlines the power – and obligation – that courts have to use equitable remedies when they are necessary to end discrimination. (Legal remedies typically consist of awards of money damages; equitable remedies typically consist of commands from a court to do, or cease doing, a certain action, although they can, confusingly in the employment context, also involve the payment of money.)

### THE ALLEGATIONS IN *EEOC V. KARENKIM*: A ROTTEN FOOD TALE

Karen Connors owned and managed Paul's Big M Grocery, a store in Oswego, New York. In January 2001, Connors hired Allen Manwaring as the store manager. Within months, the two began an intimate relationship that produced an engagement in 2006 and a child. But during that time, Manwaring also became a great liability to Connors business-wise. According to evidence presented at trial, he repeatedly and pervasively harassed a number of female employees, most of whom were teenage girls at the time. The harassment was both verbal and physical, and it continued over a period of several years, undeterred by intermittent complaints and reprimands.

Specific examples of the harassment that was the subject of trial testimony give the flavor of the hostile environment at the Big M:

- Victim #1 testified that after she began working there at age sixteen, Manwaring made sexual comments to her on a daily basis and frequently complimented parts of her body; he also suggested he would like to begin a sexual relationship with her and her mother.
- Manwaring told victim #2, also a teenage girl, if he were her boyfriend, he would never let her "out of the sheets"; and if he were "10 years younger, he would be on top of [her]." When she was working alone in the office, Manwaring would brush up against her breast, push his crotch against her buttocks, touch her hips, whisper in her ear, and rub her shoulders, all of which were unwelcome.
- Victim #3 testified that Manwaring discussed his sexual frustrations with her, and promised that one day he would "pick her up" and have sex with her.
- Victim #4 testified that Manwaring would "squeeze" in behind her in a tiny space by the cash register, so they were "body to body almost."
- Victim #5 testified that, even after this lawsuit began, Manwaring tried to console her after she had a fight with her boyfriend by suggesting that she tell the boyfriend that Manwaring had been wanting to have sex with her for a year and a half.
- Victim #6, a high school girl, testified that Manwaring walked up to her and stuck his tongue in her mouth while she was talking on the phone, and then walked away "with a smirk on his face."
- Victim #7 testified that Manwaring had touched her inappropriately and had demanded to know how much she charged for sexual favors.
- Victim #8 testified that Manwaring pulled up her underwear and made sexual comments when she bent over to restock a deli case.

Finally, there were other witnesses – a total of ten – who also testified to similar types of verbal and physical harassment.

## AN EMPLOYER'S FAILED RESPONSE TO A CLEAR PROBLEM OF HARASSMENT

Although it is sometimes the case that victims of harassment, especially minors, are reticent to complain about sexual harassment because they don't know their rights or fear reprisals, most of the women harassed by Manwaring did speak up. They did so despite the fact that the company had neither a sexual harassment policy nor a grievance procedure in place. The victims who complained about Manwaring's conduct were rewarded, variously, by being reprimanded, accused of lying, or fired.

For example, the first employee to complain about Manwaring's behavior was terminated for absenteeism. When this employee, Victim #1, complained to a manager, the manager hurried away and did not follow up on the complaint. After receiving a complaint from Victim #2, a manager confronted Manwaring by telling him he probably "just didn't realize . . . that certain things are inappropriate." Victim #8 complained directly to Karen Connors – the owner of the company (and Manwaring's fiancée). Connors accused the employee of lying and fired her on the spot. Other employees also complained directly to Connors, including one employee who quit and submitted a resignation letter detailing Manwaring's harassment of her over the course of several years.

As one might expect given the number of witnesses who complained about Manwaring's harassment, his behavior was well known to other employees and to store management. One manager testified that she personally witnessed his inappropriate behavior "at least twice a week." Victim #4 testified that Manwaring's behavior was "chattered about on a daily basis," but that she stopped participating in such conversations after being called into the stockroom by Manwaring, who told her she was lucky "he didn't fire [her] right then and there" for spreading "rumors" about his misconduct. Fearing termination, she began to cry. Manwaring consoled her by hugging her, kissing her on the cheek, and reassuring her that "if he was gonna sexually harass anybody, it would be [her]."

Despite how well-known and widespread Manwaring's misconduct was, Connors testified that she recalled only two complaints of sexual harassment and that she believed both were handled "appropriately." With respect to the high school girl who complained that Manwaring had stuck his tongue in her mouth, Connors testified that she believed Manwaring's explanation that he had fallen into her by accident, and that therefore he had not done anything wrong. Nonetheless, she suspended him for thirty days *with* pay and warned him that he would be fired if another complaint was filed against him. Right when the incident happened, the girl, crying hysterically, called a friend's mother, who in turn called the police. Manwaring was charged with, and pled guilty to, second-degree harassment. However, Manwaring testified that in his "heart, [he] always felt it was an accidental joking incident," and he told others the girl was lying.

The other complaint about which Connors admitted knowing involved Victim #5. That woman at first didn't complain because Connors had showed her the resignation letter (mentioned above) and stated that it was full of lies. But eventually she complained to Connors and told her about several incidents of inappropriate touching and sexual overtures. The victim said she was going to quit because of the harassment.

Connors cried (this was, after all, her fiancée who was being accused) and later informed the victim that Manwaring had been fired. By this point, the harassment lawsuit was already pending, so Connors told employees "to lie and tell everybody he was farming" rather than that he had been fired for harassment. Connors also asked this particular victim not to seek a protective order against Manwaring because that would jeopardize Connors and her company.

## WHY KARENKIM, INC., WAS FOUND LIABLE FOR
## SEXUAL HARASSMENT

This lawsuit against the company that owned the grocery store, KarenKim, Inc., was filed by the EEOC, which exercised its power to sue on behalf of the complainant.

Given the facts of this case, it is no surprise that the jury found KarenKim liable for harassment and awarded both compensatory and punitive damages. Manwaring's conduct created a hostile work environment several times over and poisoned the work environment for all the female employees there. The harassment was both severe *and* pervasive, and it was very clearly unwelcome. And given that Manwaring was the store manager, KarenKim was subject to the supervisory standard for liability.

Finally, KarenKim had no chance to prevail on the affirmative defense to liability or damages given that it had no policy or grievance procedure, had never trained its employees on the subject, and, most damningly, had responded to complaints by either ignoring them or punishing the complainants. The company thus would have been liable even under the weaker negligence standard applied to cases of coworker harassment.

### *The Real Fight in This Case: What Should the Scope of the Remedy Be?*

The issue on appeal in this case did not concern the finding of harassment or the imposition of liability on KarenKim. It concerned, instead, whether the lower court should have granted the EEOC's request for an injunction, to ensure that the grocery store did not continue to be plagued by harassment.

Title VII's ban on sexual harassment can be enforced by private victims or by the EEOC on their behalf. In either case, Title VII allows for the imposition of monetary damages – both compensatory and punitive – and various forms of equitable relief and attorneys' fees.

In this case, the EEOC won compensatory and punitive damages for the victims, amounting to a little more than $100,000 for each of the ten victims. But it also requested various forms of equitable relief, on the basis of the contention that the company still had not adopted adequate measures to prevent future harassment. Among other indications of KarenKim's inadequate efforts is the fact that

Manwaring, despite having been fired for sexual harassment, is regularly present in the store by virtue of his new job as a produce vendor. In stark contrast, one of the victims who attempted to buy groceries at the store after the jury issued its verdict was ordered out of the store and told never to return as a customer. Manwaring is also still in a romantic relationship with the store owner, and there is no legal bar to her rehiring him.

The injunction requested by the EEOC was admittedly broad. It sought an order that would last for ten years and include, among other restrictions, the following: (1) prohibit KarenKim from hiring or paying Manwaring in any way, except for purchasing produce from him; (2) prohibit Manwaring from entering the grocery store building and require the posting of a notice of the prohibition; (3) force KarenKim to hire a monitor to review KarenKim's employment practices and to investigate allegations of harassment; and (5) require KarenKim to revise its harassment policy and grievance procedures and conduct annual antiharassment training.

The district court denied the EEOC's request for injunctive relief on the basis that it was unnecessary and overly burdensome. It also objected to the length of the requested relief and the intrusiveness of having both an independent monitor and the EEOC overseeing their efforts. Fundamentally, the district court disbelieved that the future risk of harassment was as great as the EEOC urged. It pointed out in its ruling that the problem was composed of "isolated instances involving a manager who is no longer employed by the company . . . during a period when the company did not have clearly established anti-harassment policies." But now, the district court pointed out, the company has both an antiharassment policy and a "keen awareness of the issue." The court characterized as "specious" the idea that Connors would let her relationship with Manwaring affect her ability to curtail his behavior. The court was thus "hard-pressed to imagine that should complaints by employees concerning sexual harassment or employment discrimination of any other kind arise in the future . . . KarenKim will not take them seriously."

Although the district court has broad discretion to determine whether injunctive relief is necessary to prevent future violations, it cannot blindly refuse to take account of the future risk of harassment. Title VII explicitly grants courts the power to award injunctive relief, and "the bounds of discretion are set by the purposes of Title VII, which are to prevent discrimination and achieve equal employment opportunity in the future."

Applying that standard, the U.S. Court of Appeals for the Second Circuit found an abuse of discretion on the part of the district court. In particular, the Second Circuit held that the district court had failed to account for the strong likelihood of future harassment given Manwaring's relationship with Connors, her record of failing to deal appropriately with his misconduct, and his continued presence in the store. Their relationship was, the Second Circuit reasoned, "the primary reason why Manwaring's harassment went unchecked for years, subjecting an entire class of young female KarenKim employees to a sexually hostile working environment."

Thus, at a minimum, the Second Circuit concluded, the district court was obligated to enjoin KarenKim from employing Manwaring in the future and from allowing him to enter the premises. The district court had the discretion to deny some of the EEOC's more specific and intrusive measures, but could not deny the request to remove the specter of future harassment by Manwaring. A concurring judge on the Second Circuit panel wrote separately to emphasize that injunctive relief is presumptively justified in cases of intentional discrimination, and that the defendant has the burden to prove it is not necessary.

The failure to respond appropriately to problems of sexual harassment can be a costly mistake. And, as this ruling shows, that failure can engender a loss of freedom, as well. Employers simply are not free to turn a blind eye to the actions of a harasser, particularly one whose actions are so rampant and have led to the exploitation of so many victims.

A version of this chapter appeared on October 30, 2012, at verdict.justia.com.

**PART III**

# Pregnant Women and Mothers at Work

ART 3 © Barry Deutsch. Used by permission.

*This isn't the politically correct thing to say, but when we drove the mother out of the home into the workplace and replaced her with the television set, that was not a good thing.*

(Roscoe Bartlett, former congressional representative of Maryland)

*The role of Vice President, it seems to me, would take up an awful lot of her time, and it raises the issue of how much time will [Sarah Palin] have to dedicate to her newborn child?*

(John Roberts, CNN Correspondent)

One might credibly argue that the key difference between men and women in the workplace is women's unique role in the reproductive process. The Supreme Court has drawn this connection many times, observing, for example, in it is 1992 abortion ruling in *Planned Parenthood v. Casey* that the "ability of women to participate equally in the economic and social life of the Nation has been facilitated by their ability to control their reproductive lives."[1]

The uniqueness of women's physical and biological role in reproduction is obvious. Only women use prescription contraceptives. Only women receive fertility treatment. Only women become pregnant. Only women give birth. Only women breastfeed a baby. And only women become mothers – a social role that is imbued with centuries-old and pervasive expectations, realities, and stereotypes. There are workplace consequences that flow from women's physical role in reproduction, as well as the social roles of pregnant woman and mother.

More than 80 percent of women will have at least one child while in the workforce.[2] Women make up nearly half the workforce today, and, today, more pregnant women work through their pregnancies and return to work following childbirth than ever before.[3] The long arc of pregnancy – including everything from contraception to postpartum recovery and continuing through motherhood – has proven the source of frequent and varied conflicts with employers. Those conflicts sometimes reflect the tangible effects of a woman's reproductive role – exacerbated by work settings that were largely designed around the needs and habits of men – and sometimes reflect simple stereotypes or bias. At the heart of many of these conflicts is, as Justice Ginsburg noted in a recent pregnancy discrimination case, the fact that "[c]ertain attitudes about pregnancy and childbirth, throughout human history, have sustained pervasive, often law-sanctioned, restrictions on a woman's place among paid workers and active citizens."[4]

Is the law today any better equipped to help integrate these women into the workplace? That is the question addressed in the chapters that follow.

## THE DEVELOPMENT OF PREGNANCY DISCRIMINATION LAW

Prior to the passage of the Pregnancy Discrimination Act in 1978, it was common for employers to impede pregnant women's access to new or continued employment. The influx of women into the workforce in the 1960s and 1970s spurred the essentially modern conflict between pregnant women and employers. As a matter of both official policy and individual treatment, employers often refused to hire pregnant women, required pregnant employees to leave before a certain point in their pregnancies, and denied them insurance, disability coverage, and leave that were available to other workers. This third problem became even more significant as the workers generally experienced a dramatic increase in such benefits in the 1970s.[5]

The partial or wholesale exclusion of pregnant women from the workforce eventually bore the imprimatur of law, as the Supreme Court ruled that neither the Equal Protection Clause of the federal Constitution nor Title VII (the main federal statute protecting workers against employment discrimination) prohibited discrimination on the basis of pregnancy as a type of discrimination on the basis of sex. In *Geduldig v. Aiello*, the Supreme Court considered a challenge to California's disability insurance program for private employees, which required all employees to contribute 1 percent of their salaries to the program in exchange for coverage. The plan excluded temporary disabilities resulting from dipsomania, drug addiction, sexual psychopathy, *and normal pregnancy*.[6] The plaintiffs in *Geduldig* challenged the exclusion of pregnancy-related disability by citing *Reed v. Reed* and *Frontiero v. Richardson* – two precedents that had established, for the first time, the right to heightened judicial scrutiny under the Equal Protection Clause for sex-based classifications and thus a strong likelihood that the scrutinized statute would be held unconstitutional.[7] These precedents did not apply, however, according to Justice Stewart's majority opinion, because the exclusion of pregnancy did not constitute a sex-based classification. As the Court explained, "There is no risk from which men are protected and women are not. Likewise, there is no risk from which women are protected and men are not.... The program divided potential recipients into two groups – pregnant women and nonpregnant persons."[8] The majority thought it obvious that there was no connection between "the excluded disability and gender."[9]

Obvious? Criticism of the *Geduldig* opinion would soon become a "cottage industry."[10] Justice Ginsburg later called it a "widely criticized conclusion" that some Supreme Court justices are "perhaps embarrassed to cite."[11] But it remains good law and, more important, laid the groundwork for an opinion two years later that would apply the same reasoning to Title VII. In *General Electric Co. v. Gilbert*, the Court held that the statute's ban on sex discrimination did not encompass a ban on pregnancy discrimination, and thus a private employer was free to provide insurance coverage for all "sicknesses and accidents," but not pregnancy.[12] Justice Brennan, in dissent, argued that "it offends common sense to suggest... that a classification revolving around pregnancy is not, at the minimum, strongly 'sex related.'"[13] Moreover, the majority's ruling in *Gilbert* was particularly troubling given that it rejected the contrary interpretations of the EEOC and seven federal courts of appeals.[14]

Outrage over the ruling in *Gilbert* gave rise to the Campaign to End Discrimination Against Pregnant Workers, a coalition that first proposed, and ultimately secured, a new law banning pregnancy discrimination.[15] The Pregnancy Discrimination Act (PDA) of 1978 passed both houses of Congress by wide margins: 75–11 in the Senate and 376–43 in the House.[16] It heralded in a new era for pregnant workers: guaranteed access to the workplace.[17] More specifically, the PDA specifically overruled *Gilbert*'s interpretation of Title VII by amending the statute to define "because of sex" to include "because of pregnancy, childbirth, or related medical conditions" throughout. The PDA contains two separate clauses, each guaranteeing a substantive right. The first is the right against being treated adversely *because of* pregnancy. The second is the separate right to be treated, when pregnant and unable to work, the same as other employees who are also unable to work owing to temporary disability.

One purpose of the PDA was to eliminate pregnancy-related stereotyping. Congress, here, was picking up on a theme ironically endorsed by the Supreme Court in the same term it turned back the plaintiffs in *Geduldig*. In *Cleveland Board of Education v. LaFleur*, the court invalidated policies from several school districts that had forced pregnant teachers to leave work early in their pregnancies (regardless of whether or not they were able to work) and had permitted them to return only three months after childbirth.[18]

What troubled the Court in *LaFleur* (and a related case decided the following year) was the often-inaccurate assumption that all pregnant women suffered similarly in their inability to work during certain phases of pregnancy and during recovery from childbirth.[19] (The school districts did not help their case by arguing that it was "'not good for the school system' for students to view pregnant teachers, 'because some of the kids say, my teacher swallowed a water melon, things like that.'"[20] (One might argue that children who think such things need *more* exposure to pregnant teachers, not less.) The Court invoked the Due Process Clause, with it is long-established protection for rights related to reproduction – for instance, rights related to contraception, abortion, and child rearing – to conclude that policies like these were sufficiently arbitrary to fail constitutional scrutiny.[21]

When Congress enacted the PDA in 1978, it picked up on this constitutional concern about inaccurate classification – or stereotyping – and extended it to private employers. Importantly, the first clause of the PDA (which was embodied as well in a subsequently adopted federal regulation) took aim at traditional policies and practices that had explicitly or implicitly barred women from working through pregnancy.[22]

Together, *LaFleur* and the first clause of the PDA put an end to most formal policies regarding pregnant workers, for both public and private employers. Employers could no longer openly refuse to hire pregnant women, force them to take leave at a particular point during pregnancy, or require them to stay away for a period of time after childbirth – policies that were once commonplace. After the enactment of the PDA, and following *LaFleur*, employers had to junk these policies or risk lawsuits. Moreover, and important, the PDA went further than the Supreme Court had under *LaFleur* – for it created an equality-based right against being treated adversely *because* of pregnancy. Under the PDA, pregnant women have the right to be individually assessed, rather than judged by stereotype, but also the right to be treated just like everyone else.[23]

There is no question that the PDA opened doors to the workplace. To cite just one statistic, the percentage of pregnant women dropping out of the workforce plummeted after the PDA came into force – from more than half before 1978 to less than one third in 1995.[24] Yet the full promise of the PDA has not been fulfilled.

## THE LIMITS OF THE PDA, AS APPLIED IN PRACTICE

The equality right the PDA establishes is theoretically quite broad, but, practically, more limited. Courts have struggled, for example, to figure out when a particular employment decision was *because* of pregnancy rather than simply a decision that affected an employee who happened to be pregnant.

Consider the Seventh Circuit's ruling in *Troupe v. May Department Stores*. There, a pregnant sales clerk was fired just one day before she was scheduled to take maternity leave, after a series of warnings about excessive tardiness.[25] Was she fired because she was often late to work, or as punishment for being pregnant and planning a maternity leave? The court ruled that she had failed to prove that the employer made the decision because of her pregnancy rather than because of her frequent lateness.[26] *Troupe* illustrates some of the limits of the PDA. First, even if a pregnant woman performs up to the employer's standard, she still bears the burden of proving that any adverse decision was made because of her pregnancy. And this can prove difficult. In a typical (nonpregnancy) employment discrimination case, the plaintiff may be able to find a counterpart of a different race or gender who performed similarly, yet was treated differently. However, the likelihood that a plaintiff will find the "hypothetical Mr. Troupe" suggested by the Seventh Circuit – a man who was *not* fired for being chronically late because of a medical condition for which he will soon commence an extended leave – is very low.[27] So is the chance that the employee will happen to find direct evidence of the employer's animosity toward pregnant workers. Second, to the extent that the plaintiff's pregnancy actually made her unable to perform up to the employer's standards, the PDA provides no absolute protection against adverse action. If morning sickness in fact made her late, then the employer could legally have fired her for tardiness (even though it was tardiness caused by pregnancy), as long as there is no reason to believe it would have treated a comparably tardy male employee differently. As this example illustrates, then, the PDA does *not* require employers to accommodate the actual needs of pregnancy.

For instance, an employer who requires employees to lift heavy things can legally force pregnant employees whose doctors forbid such lifting to go on unpaid leave, or even fire them for that temporary incapacity. Perhaps Judge Richard Posner said it best in *Troupe*: "Employers can treat pregnant women as badly as they treat similarly affected but nonpregnant employees."[28]

The bottom line, then, is that while the substantive guarantee of the PDA's first clause is crucial – without it, pregnant women would be living in the dark ages once again – it is insufficient to bring about true equality. It protects pregnant women against the harm of inaccurate classification – that is, it protects them from being assumed disabled when they are actually able, or stereotyped as weak and needy when in fact they are indistinguishable from men. Yet it does little to protect pregnant women during periods of actual disability – or difference. Thus, the uniqueness of women's reproductive role remains a sticking point.

## THE RIGHT OF COMPARABLE LEAVE AND BENEFITS

The second clause of the PDA makes a separate guarantee – the promise that pregnant women are entitled to the same treatment as other temporarily disabled employees.[29] The meaning of this clause was hotly debated with respect to the Supreme Court case *California Federal Savings and Loan Ass'n v. Guerra* – and the case divided the feminist community, which split over the litigation strategy to be employed.[30] One coalition among feminists argued for an "equal treatment" interpretation of the second clause, which would limit pregnant women to the *same* rights as other temporarily disabled workers – no more, no less.[31] Another coalition argued for a "special treatment" or accommodationist approach, which would permit employers to treat pregnant women better than other temporarily disabled workers.[32]

The Supreme Court adopted the latter approach, ruling that the PDA formed a "floor, but not a ceiling" on employers' treatment of pregnancy and childbirth.[33] In practice, *Guerra* means that employers can choose to provide no benefits or leave for disability at all without violating the PDA, but if they do provide benefits or leave, they cannot exempt pregnant women. *Guerra* also means that employers are permitted to provide benefits *only* for disability related to pregnancy, excluding disabilities attributable to all other causes. They are *required* to treat pregnant women at least as well as similarly situated men; they are *permitted* to treat them better.

The "floor" provided by the second clause is a significant one. Many employers provide benefits for temporarily disabled employees, and, at least in theory, pregnant employees are guaranteed access to the same benefits. The only limit is that benefits for pregnant women must be drawn to cover the actual period of physical disability – six to eight weeks for normal childbirth, for example. The PDA's floor may make it possible for many women to continue work through pregnancy and to resume work after childbirth.

The "not-a-ceiling" aspect of the PDA has also been important for pregnant women. The decision of several large law firms to increase their standard maternity leave to eighteen weeks reflects the employer's power to go further than the law requires, by providing special accommodations for pregnancy, regardless of the benefits the employer may provide for other temporarily disabled employees.[34]

However, as with the right guaranteed by the first clause of the PDA, this right is necessary to open doors but insufficient to facilitate full integration of pregnant women into the workplace. For example, an employer can refuse to provide *any* leave for temporary disability. In that situation, a pregnant woman who needs even minimal leave for childbirth and recovery could not invoke the law to demand it – and, indeed, could be fired for missing work. The FMLA of 1993, which allows up to twelve weeks of unpaid leave for self-care (for any illness or disability, including pregnancy-related conditions or childbirth) or new parenting fills in some of the gap at the bottom, but many people work for smaller employers who are not bound by this law or cannot afford to take unpaid leave.[35]

Finally, even where an employer does provide some benefits for temporarily disabled employees, they may or may not be sufficient to meet the needs of most pregnant women. That the PDA does not force employers to accommodate pregnancy is a major shortcoming, one that should be addressed by Congress.

Some of the challenges facing pregnant women at work are not nearly as bad as they used to be; others are worse, particularly as women enter traditionally male-dominated occupations that are more likely to be physically strenuous or dangerous. Progress, however, does not justify complacency. Many pregnant women continue to experience discrimination in the workplace, and those who pursue their claims in court often face insurmountable problems of proof or courts that are hostile to their claims. And, in many instances, the adverse treatment pregnant women experience is perfectly legal. The chapters in this part explore how pregnancy discrimination law intersects with the reproductive lives of women – where it meets their needs as workers and as women and where it falls short.

Chapters 31–36 show the development of the law over time on the question of whether employers who make light-duty assignments available to at least some other employees with temporary disability should have to provide the same accommodation to pregnant women with comparable restrictions. These cases go to the heart of the second clause – what does it mean to be treated "the same" as those "similar in their ability or inability to work"? Through the stories of two truck drivers and several police officers, all pregnant with restrictions and all denied necessary accommodations, we trace the development of the law on this issue until it reached the Supreme Court in 2015. All the court opinions show judges struggling with the scope of the PDA's second clause and drawing the line – often illogically – between comparative accommodation, which the law requires, and special treatment, which the law does not. And between the failed legislative proposal to amend the PDA to provide for a right of reasonable accommodation and the Supreme Court's refusal to give any deference to the EEOC's passage of new regulatory guidance on this issue, we see the often-complicated game of tag between the Supreme Court, the Executive Branch, and Congress on discrimination issues. Blended in with the discussion of pregnancy accommodation cases is a chapter that looks broadly at pregnancy discrimination law from the perspective of women's equal citizenship. Written for the thirty-fifth anniversary of the PDA, the age at which the women themselves are deemed "advanced maternal age," this chapter sketches a theory of equal social citizenship and considers how well the PDA has delivered on it is promise.

Chapter 38 pauses to look back at the treatment of pregnant workers before the PDA – and the lifelong effects of the discrimination they suffered. It analyzes the Supreme Court's ruling in *AT&T v. Hulteen*, a case about whether the phone conglomerate could pay female retirees lower pensions because of pregnancy leaves they took before enactment of the PDA, which were not credited in the same way as other temporary leaves. In a setback for a whole era of women now reaching retirement age, the Court upheld AT&T's pension scheme against the pregnancy discrimination challenge.

Chapter 39 takes leave of the accommodation issue and considers a more old-fashioned case of pregnancy discrimination – a woman who allegedly suffered a barrage of insults and criticisms after she announced her out-of-wedlock pregnancy. Once a rising star in the business office of a major league baseball team, the woman became the target of abuse and hostility. This chapter considers how the law does – and should – treat such a case, as well as the effects of pregnancy bias on women's work opportunity.

Chapters 40–43 consider the PDA's applicability to cases of discrimination on the basis of contraception, infertility, and lactation. The PDA's first clause, which amends Title VII, prohibits discrimination on the basis of "pregnancy, childbirth, *and related medical conditions.*" Just what is included in that prohibition has been the subject of many lawsuits, including a significant one that ended up in the Supreme Court, *UAW v. Johnson Controls*, which set the stage for a broad reading of that clause by treating a woman's ability to become pregnant as equivalent to pregnancy for PDA purposes. Yet courts have struggled – as the cases in these chapters make clear – to figure out how the PDA should be applied to other aspects of the reproductive process.

Chapters 44 to 46 consider the so-called maternal wall, of which actual pregnancy is just the first brick. Mothers and other caregivers face two types of problems at work: (1) the lack of leave necessary to care for themselves during pregnancy and childbirth and to care for children afterward; and (2) discrimination in the form of harassment, wage penalties, unfair terminations, and everything in between, based on hostility toward working mothers or stereotypes about their weak attachments to the labor force. These chapters first consider the role of the FMLA in providing job security for pregnant women and mothers and, with lesser success, in equalizing the caregiving responsibilities between mothers and fathers. The final chapter takes a broader look at discrimination against caregivers in the workplace and the "best practices" for an employer that wants to minimize it is occurrence.

# 31

## Pregnant Truckers and the Problem of Light-Duty Assignments

On her application for a job driving a truck, Amanda Reeves wrote that she could lift seventy-five pounds and carry that weight for fifty-six feet, and that she could lift sixty pounds over her head. She was hired. But in her first three months on the job, she never, in fact, had to unload a truck herself (or carry anything weighing seventy-five pounds).[1] At that point, Reeves discovered she was pregnant. Her doctor wrote a note restricting her to "light work," and indicated that she should not lift more than twenty pounds. When she showed the note to her employer, her supervisor said they had no "light work" for her to do and sent her home. The company then continued to deny her daily requests for light work, citing its policy that only on-the-job injuries merited light-duty assignments, and eventually fired her.[2]

Is this illegal pregnancy discrimination? The U.S. Court of Appeals for the Sixth Circuit ruled, in *Reeves v. Swift Transportation Company, Inc.*, that it is not.[3] In so holding, the Sixth Circuit joined two other fairly politically conservative federal circuits, the Fifth and Eleventh, which have reached the same conclusion in similar cases.[4] More politically liberal circuits, such as the Second and Ninth, have yet to weigh in.

This case is an important reminder of the limited rights pregnant women have against discrimination. If workers like Reeves are to be protected, it seems that Congress, state legislatures, or individual cities may have to pass new laws and regulations, or extend existing ones, in order to help them.

Under the Pregnancy Discrimination Act of 1978, employers must treat pregnant women at least as well as nonpregnant workers with similar ability or inability to work.[5] This comparative right of accommodation means that an employer only has to provide leave for childbirth, for example, if it provides leave for other temporary disabilities. That left a serious gap in protections for pregnant women: most biological mothers require at least a short period of leave for childbirth and recovery. But if they took that necessary leave, and if their employers did not provide leave (paid or unpaid) for disability, then they could legally lose their jobs.

In 1993, the FMLA partially filled that gap. Under the FMLA, employees are entitled to twelve weeks of unpaid leave per year if needed for pregnancy- or childbirth-
related disability, or to care for a newborn or newly adopted child.[6] (The FMLA also
provides this leave for an employee's own serious health condition, or to provide care
for an immediate family member with a serious health condition.[7]) Unfortunately,
this leave is unpaid, and therefore not feasible for many employees to take. But at
least it provides pregnant women who are covered by the FMLA (an issue discussed
in Chapters 44 and 45) who need childbirth leave with benefits during their leave
and with job security: they no longer can be legally fired for simply doing what's
necessary.

## IS THERE A RIGHT TO "LIGHT-DUTY" WORK FOR PREGNANT WOMEN? REEVES'S CASE

Even with these two important federal laws on the books, pregnant women often
find it difficult to successfully combine working and reproduction. One recurring
issue is work during pregnancy itself: What happens when a woman is temporarily
unable to carry out some or all of a job's duties because of pregnancy?

That was the case for Amanda Reeves, who sought temporary dispensation from
the lifting requirement in order to continue working as a truck driver throughout
her pregnancy. Her employer, however, denied the request, citing its express policy
of providing "light-duty" assignments only to employees who were injured *on the
job*. Pursuant to this policy, workers who suffered disability because of pregnancy –
or any other off-duty cause – had to either continue work as usual or risk losing their
jobs.

In other circumstances, an employee like Reeves might have taken unpaid FMLA
leave to cover at least part of her pregnancy. To be eligible for FMLA leave, however,
an employee must have worked 1,250 hours for the same employer in the previous
year;[8] Reeves had begun work only a few months earlier. After being fired, Reeves
sued her employer, Swift Transportation, under the Pregnancy Discrimination Act.
She argued that Swift's policy was expressly discriminatory, in that it provided light-
duty assignments to employees who could not perform heavy lifting but not to
*pregnant* employees who could not perform heavy lifting.[9]

The trial court granted summary judgment to Swift, and the appellate court
affirmed. Swift's policy, both courts ruled, was "pregnancy-blind." It simply distinguished between disabilities incurred at work (covered) and disabilities incurred
elsewhere (not covered).[10] Presumably, then, pregnancy-related disability would be
covered only if it resulted from an on-the-job rape.

To establish that Swift's policy – and the company's actions pursuant to it – was
unlawful, Reeves had to show discriminatory intent. She argued that the "neutral"
policy was a pretext for discrimination against pregnant women. However, Swift
explained its policy in neutral terms (the on-the-job/off-the-job distinction), and the

court held that Reeves failed to prove that the company acted with discriminatory intent when it adopted the policy or when it applied the policy to her.[11]

## WAS REEVES REALLY ASKING FOR "PREFERENTIAL" TREATMENT, AS THE COURT SUGGESTED?

According to the Sixth Circuit, Reeves was essentially asking not for equal treatment, but for preferential treatment. She wanted to be granted a light-duty assignment, even though other employees who became disabled off duty would be denied one. The court held, however, that as long as the company treated pregnant women no worse than it treated employees with comparable disabilities, its actions did not violate the PDA.[12]

Arguably, the problem with the Sixth Circuit analysis is that it assumes a comparison group that may not be the correct one: it compared the treatment of Reeves with the treatment of employees with temporary disabilities incurred off duty and found she was treated no worse. But what if the comparison group were, instead, employees with temporary disabilities, with no consideration as to the source of injury? Reeves *was* treated worse than at least some of these employees – the ones who incurred on-the-job injuries. Nevertheless, the Sixth Circuit held that it was, in effect, up to the employer to choose the relevant comparison group: as long as the employer is not motivated by discriminatory intent, the law permits it to select any neutral criteria for limiting the availability of light-duty assignments.

## FEDERAL LAW SHOULD BETTER PROTECT PREGNANT WORKERS

Federal law does not require even minimal accommodation for pregnancy-related disability, as long as the employer treats pregnant employees at least as well as other temporarily disabled employees. In *Reeves*, the employers adopted a "neutral" policy that differentiates between on-duty disabilities (which do not include pregnancy) and off-duty disabilities. And, for this particular court, this ostensible neutrality was a powerful defense. Let's assume this is a legally tenable position (later chapters suggest that it is not) and that an employer can categorically refuse to accommodate *any* disability resulting from pregnancy through the adoption of policies on pregnancy-neutral grounds. Won't that make it difficult for women to succeed at many jobs? More than half of the women who give birth are employed at the time.[13]

It's true that the FMLA affords some protection, by guaranteeing many employees the right to a period of unpaid leave. But it also has important limitations, discussed in Chapters 44 and 45. Many women cannot afford to take unpaid leave, and only employees of larger employers who have worked nearly full-time for the previous year are eligible.

Pregnancy is not inherently disabling. Many women can continue their jobs without any accommodations at all. (Being a pregnant law professor, for example, is typically not a problem.) But even with a normal pregnancy, there are often limitations on specific physical movements, such as heavy lifting. One problem with a legal framework that does not *require* employers to accommodate pregnancy-related disability is that it exacerbates the deeply entrenched gender segregation in jobs that require physical strength, such as truck driving, construction, and law enforcement.

Pregnancy discrimination charges with the EEOC experienced a meteoric rise in the first decade of this century. In 2006, Verizon settled the second-largest pregnancy discrimination lawsuit, which resulted in the payment of millions in damages and the restoration of "service credits" to employees who were docked them because of pregnancy many years ago.[14]

Might it be time to rethink the law's approach to pregnancy discrimination? While the current law is a huge improvement over the era in which pregnant women faced open, legal discrimination, pregnancy is still an unfair obstacle to women's success in the workplace.

A version of this chapter appeared on June 13, 2006, at writ.findlaw.com.

# 32

# A Big Win for Pregnant Police Officers

Recently, a New York jury in ruled in favor of six female police officers who had alleged that the Suffolk County Police Department (SCPD) discriminated against them when they were pregnant.[1] The monetary awards are small – between $5,000 and $23,000 for each plaintiff – but the vindicated principles are huge.[2] Fair treatment of pregnant workers is an essential component of workplace equality for women.

## THE UNFAIR TREATMENT ALLEGED AND PROVEN IN THIS CASE

Prior to 2000, the SCPD had permitted officers with disabilities *of any origin* to request and obtain so-called light-duty assignments – that is, alternatives to patrol that required less physical exertion and posed less risk of injury. Such assignments included desk jobs, but also positions as academy instructors, drug program instructors, and, perhaps most appealing, beach patrol officers.[3] Many pregnant officers made use of this policy: 45 percent of light-duty assignments awarded to officers injured off duty were given to pregnant women, and 75 percent of the light-duty assignments taken by women because of an off-duty disability were because of pregnancy. These assignments averaged fewer than six months in duration.[4]

But in 2000, the SCPD adopted a new policy that light-duty assignments would only be available to officers who became disabled while on duty.[5] As a result, many pregnant officers were forced to take unpaid leave and to suffer a concomitant loss of benefits, seniority, and opportunities for advancement. In some cases, they ended up using all available sick and vacation time during pregnancy, and then had none left to recover from childbirth.[6]

There was strong evidence in the record that the policy not only had a discriminatory impact but also reflected discriminatory intent. (The plaintiffs sued on both theories.) For instance, plaintiff Sarah MacDermott alleged that she was denied a light-duty assignment while pregnant, even though a male officer who had been injured off duty *after* the new policy was adopted was given just such an assignment.[7] And Sandra Lochren, who had been working as a drug prevention instructor for four years when she told her supervisor she was pregnant, was transferred to a different precinct and ordered to go on patrol.[8] Moreover, the SCPD did not have, and did not acquire, bulletproof vests that fit most women in the later months of pregnancy.[9] So even if the plaintiffs had wanted to remain on patrol, they would have lacked proper safety precautions. Unwilling to either give pregnant women "light-duty" assignments or outfit them properly to go on patrol, the SCPD, in effect, took the view that they belonged barefoot and in the kitchen.

## THE PLAINTIFFS' LEGAL THEORIES: DISPARATE TREATMENT AND DISPARATE IMPACT

The plaintiffs sued under Title VII, as amended by the PDA, and under an analogous New York law. As noted above, they alleged two types of illegal discrimination: "disparate treatment" and "disparate impact."[10]

"Disparate treatment" is defined as intentional discrimination toward an employee on the basis of a protected characteristic such as sex. By virtue of the Pregnancy Discrimination Act of 1978, pregnancy discrimination is sex discrimination. Thus, employers cannot lawfully make decisions on the basis of sex or pregnancy.[11] Disparate treatment theory can be used to attack a policy that is explicitly discriminatory, or to attack individual employment decisions or actions that are taken because of an employee's sex (or race, ethnicity, religion, etc.).[12] Disparate impact" discrimination, in contrast, is the theory used to attack a policy that is neutral on its face but that has a disproportionate and adverse impact on a protected group, such as women.[13] This type of situation – challenging a policy in a male-dominated profession with norms unintentionally designed around a prototypical male officer – is exactly why disparate impact theory exists. The plaintiffs were wise to use both theories, given bad precedent like *Reeves* on the validity of an on-the-job/off-the-job distinction.

## THE EEOC'S FINDING AND THE JURY'S ULTIMATE DECISION

In 2003, the federal Equal Employment Opportunities Commission (EEOC) found that the SCPD female officers had probable cause to sue for pregnancy discrimination under Title VII. The suit then advanced to federal court, where it was tried to a jury. After a three-day deliberation, the jury ruled in favor of the plaintiffs.[14] While a jury verdict is not as revealing as a written judicial opinion, it appears that the plaintiffs prevailed, at least in part, on both theories of discrimination.[15]

Two plaintiffs were found by the jury to have proven intentional discrimination.[16] Evidence, from cases like Sarah McDermott's, that the light-duty policy was ignored when noneligible men made requests but strictly enforced when pregnant women did was no doubt important to the jury's finding. Indeed, no pregnant woman successfully garnered a light-duty assignment after the policy changed in 2000, while there were several examples of other deviations from the policy. Bending the rules for others, but not pregnant women, smacks of intentional discrimination.

A finding of intentional discrimination was not entirely surprising, particularly because the SCPD is already governed by a broad consent decree that resulted from a lawsuit twenty years ago alleging race, gender, and ethnicity discrimination within the department. Together, these suits suggest that the climate for women in the SCPD has in the past been, and maybe still is, less than ideal.[17]

## THE MOST IMPORTANT ASPECT OF THE VERDICT: THE DISPARATE IMPACT FINDING

What really makes this case important, however, is not the finding of intentional discrimination. After all, police and fire departments have a long history of being sued for different forms of intentional sex discrimination, including discrimination in hiring and sexual harassment.[18] It is the disparate impact theory that sets this case apart from other recent ones. Disparate impact theory says that even if the SCPD can show that the policy is gender and pregnancy neutral, and that it did not adopt the new policy in order to disadvantage pregnant officers, the plaintiffs can still prove it unlawful.

Under disparate impact theory, plaintiffs begin with the burden to show that a facially neutral policy has a statistically disproportionate impact on a protected group.[19] Using the statistics noted above, plaintiffs were easily able to carry this burden. The burden then shifts to the employer to show the business necessity for the policy.[20] The SCPD, too, carried its burden: it said that it wanted to reduce corruption and the abuse of light-duty assignments. Apparently, it feared officers would fake or exaggerate off-duty injuries to get light work even though they were not genuinely disabled.

In this case, both of these burdens were met. That meant that the burden shifted back to the plaintiffs: to win, they had to show that the proclaimed business necessity could be met in a less discriminatory manner. The jury found that it could be. And no wonder: while officers might be able to fake off-duty injuries, it is very hard to fake pregnancy! The jury rightly found that the SCPD could work around its concern with the abuse of light-duty assignments, without imposing such a significant and recurring penalty on female officers, most of whom will bear children during the formative stages of their careers.[21]

## LEGISLATIVE SOLUTIONS TO THE PROBLEM OF PREGNANCY- AND CHILDBIRTH-RELATED DISABILITY: CALIFORNIA'S PROGRESSIVE APPROACH

Is there a solution? First, under federal law, employers should be required to accommodate pregnancy-related disability, just as they are required to accommodate permanent disabilities under the Americans with Disabilities Act. (See Chapter 37's discussion of the proposed Pregnant Workers' Fairness Act.)

California law already does this. It defines an "unlawful employment practice" to include an employer's refusal to "temporarily transfer a pregnant female employee to a less strenuous or hazardous position for the duration of her pregnancy if she so requests, with the advice of her physician, where that transfer can be reasonably accommodated."[22] Had this type of law been in effect in New York, the SCPD case would never have arisen because light-duty assignments would have been made available where *necessary* to pregnant women.

Second, employers or the government should provide at least some paid leave for pregnancy-related disability, childbirth, or parenting. Again, California stands out as a model: it enacted a law in 2002 that uses the state disability insurance program to provide some paid leave to workers who have to take time off to care for an ill family member, or to bond with a new child. Under this law, employees can receive at least partial wage replacement for up to six weeks a year for any covered purpose.[23] (A similar law has been introduced in the New York legislature.[24])

## THE NEED FOR GREATER ACCOMMODATION OF PREGNANCY AND CHILDBIRTH

The basic legal framework governing pregnancy and family leave at the federal level is simply inadequate. Under the Pregnancy Discrimination Act, employers are under no obligation to accommodate any disability resulting from pregnancy or childbirth. Pregnant women's rights are limited to a right against biased decision making, and a comparative right of accommodation. Under the FMLA, employees have an absolute right to twelve weeks of unpaid leave per year for new parenting or one's own serious health condition. However, 40 percent of the workforce is ineligible for leave under the terms of the act, and many more cannot afford to take unpaid leave. There is no federal law that requires employers to provide paid leave for pregnancy-related disability, childbirth, or infant care.

Together, these rules mean that an employer can say to a pregnant woman that she must either perform all her job duties, despite medical advice to the contrary, or take unpaid FMLA leave that she cannot afford. And if she doesn't fall within the FMLA, the employer can simply fire her for failing to meet job requirements.

California has taken a progressive stance on these issues, implementing a mandatory accommodation law. Other states – and, ideally, Congress – should follow California's lead to guarantee pregnant women the leave they need. As it is, pregnancy discrimination operates as a real limit on the ability of women to achieve workplace equality. This is particularly so in traditionally male occupations such as law enforcement. And it shouldn't be that way. The law currently is too far toward one extreme, letting pregnant women workers fend for themselves financially and medically, despite genuine disabilities and hardships.

The other extreme, too, would be wrong. It would do a disservice to women to demand work relief for all pregnant women, regardless of their jobs and regardless of their individual ability to work. Indeed, a policy automatically relegating pregnant women to light-duty work, despite the determination by a doctor that they were fit to continue their normal duties, is another kind of discrimination – one that was successfully challenged and, in theory, eliminated decades ago.

In sum, the law should do its part to ensure that women can become mothers and still remain workers – whether that means continuing in their normal duties or taking necessary leave and returning to their jobs later. It is not too much to ask that the law reflect the realities of pregnancy and childbirth. But as of now, it does not.

A version of this chapter appeared on June 27, 2006, at writ.findlaw.com.

*Update: The New York bill passed the State Assembly in 2007 but died in committee in 2008. A similar bill was introduced in 2011, and was referred to the Committee on Senate Labor in June 2012.[25] In 2015, however, the legislature passed a pregnancy accommodation bill, as part of the larger Women's Equality Agenda, which requires employers to provide reasonable accommodations for pregnancy-related disability as long as they do not impose an undue hardship on the employer.[26] To date, at least sixteen states have enacted some form of a pregnancy accommodation requirement into law.[27]*

# 33

## Undue Burden

It was a case of exquisitely bad timing. Akema Thompson, an officer with the New York City Police Department, was scheduled to take the sergeant's exam on October 19, 2013. But she was also scheduled to do something else that day – give birth to a baby. Because fetuses don't take requests, Officer Thompson requested an accommodation from the city that would have allowed her to take the exam on another day in the event she needed to reschedule because of a conflict with childbirth or immediate recovery from it. Her request was denied, despite the fact that promotional exams were routinely rescheduled for other reasons.[1]

Officer Thompson has filed a charge of discrimination against the City of New York, alleging that the testing accommodation policy, administered by the Department of Citywide Administrative Services (DCAS), was unlawful as applied to her.[2] She claims that the denial of her request for an accommodation is invalid under federal, state, and local discrimination laws. While her case has yet to be adjudicated at any level, her situation is all too common among pregnant working women. Employers routinely deny costless accommodations that impose no hardship and that, in many cases, are made available to other workers because of circumstances or conditions that conflict with workplace obligations. Officer Thompson is just the latest victim of a system that fails to see pregnancy as a condition worthy of even minor accommodation. The consequences of this mind-set for individual women, like Officer Thompson, and women in general is devastating.

### THOMPSON V. CITY OF NEW YORK: THE CHARGES

Officer Thompson is challenging the denial of a testing accommodation as a form of unlawful discrimination. Officer Thompson filed a charge with the EEOC, alleging denial of her requested accommodation constitutes sex, pregnancy, and disability discrimination. In her charge, she details the request she made and the various responses she received from DCAS. This agency regulates and administers testing for all city jobs – not just those at the NYPD. Thus, the NYPD was not responsible for the denial of Officer Thompson's request. Although the facts have not been adjudicated by an agency or court, the charge filed appends copies of the written correspondence back and forth between Officer Thompson and DCAS regarding her request.[3]

In January 2013, Officer Thompson learned that the city had scheduled a sergeant's promotional exam for the following October. Although this might seem like a routine event, these exams are scheduled only "as needed" and can be spaced apart by several years. Officer Thompson immediately paid almost $800 to a test prep company for a review course. The next month, Officer Thompson became pregnant and informed the NYPD of her condition shortly thereafter. Her due date was, as mentioned above, the exact same day as the exam.[4]

In June 2013, Officer Thompson registered for the exam, paying an additional $83. Because of the conflict with her due date, she contacted DCAS to request that she be allowed to take the exam on another day. She provided medical documentation of her due date and the number of weeks she would need to recover medically from childbirth. She requested the accommodation numerous times both in writing and over the phone. In one of these communications, Officer Thompson mentioned that the NYPD had told her to request to take the exam on an alternative testing day already set aside for those whose religious observances conflicted with the scheduled date. At some point, Officer Thompson sought assistance from the Patrolmen's Benevolent Association (PBA), the union for patrol officers in the NYPD, and the PBA requested an accommodation on her behalf.[5]

The request for accommodation was flatly denied. She was told, in one piece of correspondence, that her "request to postpone this test due to the possibility that you may give birth on, or shortly after the test date, is not approvable."[6] In another e-mail, she was informed that city policy *does* allow the promotional exam to be rescheduled, but only for conflicts due to (1) military duty, (2) DCAS error, (3) required court appearance (in any type of proceeding), (4) physical disability incurred on the job, or (5) the death of a close relative.[7] She was also told in other correspondence tests could be rescheduled to accommodate religious observance.[8]

Three days before her due date, Officer Thompson went into labor. She was hospitalized that day, October 16. While in labor, she alleges she received a telephone call from a representative at DCAS, who reiterated that she could not postpone the test because of childbirth and offered her a cushion to sit on during the exam or two additional hours to complete it.[9]

Neither a cushion nor extra time was going to make it possible for Officer Thompson to sit for the sergeant's exam. She had an emergency C-section on October 16 and was not released from the hospital until October 20, the day after the exam was given. And while other candidates may well have taken the October 2013 exam at later dates because of "approvable" conflicts, Officer Thompson was denied the opportunity. It might be years before the opportunity surfaces again.

## REASONABLE ACCOMMODATION FOR
## PREGNANCY-RELATED RESTRICTIONS

Under federal law, employers have no absolute duty to accommodate pregnancy, but they cannot refuse to accommodate pregnancy when offering accommodations for people with similar limitations. And employees may also have rights under state or local pregnancy discrimination laws. The New York Human Rights Law protects against pregnancy discrimination in a manner similar to the federal PDA.[10] And as of January 30, 2014, New York City offers pregnant workers more expansive protections under the Pregnant Workers Fairness Act (PWFA).[11] The local PWFA (distinguished from a proposed federal bill by the same name, discussed in Chapter 37) applies to employers with at least four employees. The law requires employers to provide "reasonable accommodation" necessitated by pregnancy or childbirth unless doing so would cause an "undue hardship" on the employer.[12] The types of accommodations contemplated by the law include light-duty assignments (e.g., one without heavy lifting); changes to the work setting (e.g., to avoid toxins); more frequent breaks to eat, drink, or use the bathroom.[13]

In Officer Thompson's case, she is challenging the city's refusal to accommodate her pregnancy by allowing her to postpone the sergeant's promotional exam. Under the new PWFA in New York City, the city's denial would almost certainly be unlawful. Asking to postpone an exam that provides the opportunity for significant career enhancement and is offered very infrequently is a reasonable request. It would be all but impossible for the city to prove that postponement imposed an undue hardship given that it already offers the same accommodation to at least five other groups of workers (noted above). All that Officer Thompson asked is that an existing accommodation be extended to her – an accommodation that would be effectively costless to the city.[14]

But this law did not take effect until January 30, 2014, several months after the test Officer Thompson missed because of childbirth. Unless the law is applied retroactively, it will not help her. However, the New York City Division of Human Rights, which implements antidiscrimination laws, has taken the position publicly that it considered pregnancy a disability even before this law took effect.[15] Moreover, she should have been granted the accommodation under the federal and state laws in existence at the time of her request. And it is worth noting that despite the change in city law, the DCAS testing accommodation policy remains in effect today.[16]

Even without the protection of local law, however, Thompson should have a claim under the PDA, as interpreted by the Supreme Court in *Young v. UPS*.[17] This is the perfect case to test the court's benefits-versus-burdens analysis. DCAS admits that it provides such accommodations to a wide variety of workers – including some with far less dire conflicts with the test than childbirth on the same day – while withholding them from pregnant officers. For example, it allows candidates to postpone the promotional exam if a close relative has died within a week of the exam date.[18] While this is a humane rule that correctly assumes officers need time to grieve and tend to the burial of a deceased relative, it is not clear that these officers could not show up for the scheduled exam if no alternative were given. But for Officer Thompson, both her predicted due date and her actual delivery date posed a direct and insurmountable conflict with the exam. She could not be in two places at once – a hospital maternity ward and an administrative testing room. The allegation that she was telephoned while in the hospital and offered a cushion to sit on while she took the test, if proven, would be nothing short of mockery of her situation.

The law does not require DCAS to provide testing accommodations, but it does prohibit the agency from withholding an otherwise available accommodation from pregnant candidates. And even if the policy didn't facially violate the PDA, it imposes a disparate impact on female officers, who are disproportionately likely to have their careers hindered by this policy. Neutral policies that cause a disparate impact must be justified by business necessity and, even then, cannot be followed if there is a less burdensome alternative.[19] Given that the promotional exam can be postponed for a host of other reasons, it will be impossible for the city to show that the refusal of postponement to pregnant candidates is necessary to the operation of the business and/or that no less burdensome approach could be taken.

## WHY THE DCAS RULE REFLECTS BAD POLICY

Even if DCAS could successfully argue that its nonaccommodation rule comports with federal and state pregnancy discrimination law, why would it want to deny a minor and costless accommodation to a valuable employee? The answer can only be in the undervaluing of female officers. Although this particular accommodation did not relate to Officer Thompson's ability to perform her existing job, it did prevent her from seeking a promotion. Had she done well on the exam and earned a promotion, wouldn't the city be better off by advancing someone proven qualified for a higher position? And for many pregnant women, the refusal of minor accommodation will affect their ability to carry out some aspects of an existing job. An employer's refusal to accommodate in such a case can mean that the employee is forced to quit or take unpaid leave. (And because DCAS administers testing for all city jobs, its stingy accommodation policy cuts a wide swath.) While the most significant consequences will be borne by the employee, suddenly deprived of income and perhaps health insurance, the employer will suffer as well in the costs of rehiring, retraining, and, perhaps, not replacing with the same quality employee.

Pregnant women generally are physically able to engage in paid work, just as they are physically able to carry out other responsibilities in their lives. (Pregnant mothers don't suddenly stop caring for other children because a new one is on the way.) But there can be conflicts between the physical effects of pregnancy and the demands of a job. Just as the conflicts will vary by woman, by pregnancy, and by work environment, the accommodations needed to keep a pregnant woman at work will vary, as well. But often, as was true for Officer Thompson, the conflicts can be alleviated with a minor and inexpensive, or even costless, accommodation. Yet employers still deny them. They should be taken to task for this as a matter of social policy, as well as a matter of law. Whether the law requires them to or not, employers should take the steps necessary to integrate pregnant women into the workforce – in all jobs and at all levels. Pregnancy and childbirth are temporary, but a talented employee could be there for a lifetime.

A version of this chapter appeared on April 1, 2015, at verdict.justia.com.

*Update: In July 2015, New York City settled Thompson's case for $50,000 in damages and the opportunity to take a makeup test. The City also promised, as part of the settlement, to pay Thompson's legal fees and, more importantly, to change its policy to allow employees with pregnancy- or childbirth-related disability to take makeup exams along with others eligible to do so.[20] The new pregnancy accommodation law in New York, discussed in the previous chapter, may also help women who face these kinds of conflicts in the future.*

# 34

## Hard Labor

*New Pregnancy Discrimination Guidance from the EEOC*

Pregnancy discrimination in the workplace is an intractable problem, one that has resulted in a startling number of claims each year to the EEOC – rising at a faster rate than women are joining the workforce – and increased media attention.[1]

What do these statistics capture? As a threshold matter, we can be confident that EEOC charges represent only a tiny fraction of instances in which a worker actually experiences bias based on her pregnancy. Research firmly establishes that most workers who experience discrimination never take any formal action or seek redress of their injuries.[2] But does the increase in complaints reflect a rise in the incidence of pregnancy discrimination, or simply greater awareness by employees of their legal rights? Probably both. A sixfold increase in monetary payouts related to EEOC charges – from $5.6 million in 1997 to $30 million in 2007 – suggests greater enforcement or a greater percentage of well-founded complaints.[3] And the $30 million figure does not even include damages awarded in subsequent lawsuits.

At the same time, however, there is reason to think the rise in complaints also reflects greater awareness of rights against pregnancy discrimination. As a recent *Wall Street Journal* article reports, nonprofit advocates for women have been receiving increasing numbers of calls for assistance with problems of pregnancy bias or discrimination. Among other things, however, these calls indicate workers' confusion about their legal rights. Some erroneously believe they have a right to paid childbirth leave. Others erroneously believe that no adverse employment action (such as firing, demotion, or a decrease in pay) can be taken against a pregnant woman. Others are not sure whether they are entitled to return to the identical position they previously occupied at work after an approved pregnancy or childbirth leave.[4]

Greater awareness, greater confusion, and more discrimination all call for the same remedy: greater clarity on the law of pregnancy discrimination. The EEOC has responded to this need with a new Enforcement Guidance on pregnancy discrimination – its first in several decades – to explain its interpretation of applicable statutes.[5] This chapter explains key aspects of the guidance as well as its potential relevance to *Young v. UPS*,[6] a pregnancy discrimination case currently pending before the Supreme Court.[7]

## THE EEOC'S NEW ENFORCEMENT GUIDANCE: WHAT IS "PREGNANCY"?

As discussed in the preceding chapters, the meaning and scope of the Pregnancy Discrimination Act of 1978 has been an endless source of controversy and litigation. The EEOC Guidance first tackles the question that has plagued courts of what falls within the category of "pregnancy, childbirth, and related medical conditions." Work can potentially conflict with all aspects of the reproductive process. Lawsuits have raised specific questions about whether discrimination on the basis of contraceptive coverage, infertility, and lactation fall within the PDA. (These lawsuits and issues are discussed in greater detail in Chapters 40 to 43.)

The Guidance takes an appropriately broad approach to defining discrimination under the PDA, given the text of the statute and the Supreme Court's prior opinions. While an employer is not liable for pregnancy discrimination if the woman's condition was neither revealed nor obvious, it is liable for adverse decisions based on stereotypes or assumptions about a pregnant woman's capacity to work, as well as for decisions motivated by a past pregnancy. Even before a pregnancy occurs, employers cannot discriminate on the basis of potential pregnancy – fertility – or reproductive risk. They also cannot discriminate on the basis of a woman's intentions to become pregnant, or her seeking of fertility treatment to become pregnant. This does not mean that employers must facilitate employee efforts to become pregnant – it tacitly approves court decisions holding that the exclusion of fertility treatments from employer-provided insurance does not violate Title VII – but only that they cannot single out or punish employees on the basis of false assumptions about how an existing or future pregnancy might impact a woman's capacity to work or because of animus against an employee who has made these decisions. Employers must also, under the second clause of the PDA, provide leave, benefits, or accommodations for these conditions to at least the same degree it provides them for comparable medical conditions.[8]

The Guidance also weighs in on contraception, an issue that has been controversial under discrimination law and also in recent litigation about Obamacare. In the Guidance, the EEOC concludes, as several federal courts have, that an employer's exclusion of prescription contraceptives – all of which are used by women only – from an otherwise comprehensive insurance plan constitutes illegal sex discrimination. With respect to lactation, the Guidance concludes that discrimination against an employee because she is breastfeeding is actionable and that the comparative right of accommodation means that employers must accommodate lactation at least to the same degree they accommodate similar medical conditions. Finally, although the PDA expressly states that employers do not have to provide insurance coverage for abortion, the Guidance concludes that they cannot take adverse action against a woman for seeking an abortion or encourage her to get one in order to keep her job.

## THE ENFORCEMENT GUIDANCE AND DISCRIMINATORY LIGHT-DUTY POLICIES

A second key question covered by the Guidance relates to an employer's failure to accommodate pregnancy-related incapacity despite accommodating similar incapacity for at least some other workers. In the past decade, there have been a number of lawsuits raising questions about the scope and meaning of the second clause of the PDA. (Typical cases are discussed in Chapters 31 to 34.) The objectionable policies do not, by their words, exclude pregnancy, but they are drawn in a manner such that workers with pregnancy-related disability cannot obtain light-duty accommodations. This is so even when the workers who do receive light-duty accommodations are, in every way, "similar [to pregnant women] in their ability or inability to work."[9] Yet, despite the obvious violation of the PDA's second clause, several federal appellate courts have upheld light-duty policies of this nature. Taking a misguided approach to the PDA, courts have searched for discriminatory intent rather than seeing the policy itself as a formal policy of facial discrimination. The type of reasoning on which courts have relied is the death knell for the right of comparative accommodation. It effectively allows employers to revert to a pre-PDA world, in which they can single out pregnancy from among other disabilities for adverse treatment. This is precisely what the PDA was enacted to eliminate.

The new EEOC Guidance, fortunately, tackles the light-duty issue head-on. It concludes that a pregnant worker "may still establish a violation of the PDA by showing that she was denied light duty or other accommodations that were granted to other employees who are similar in their ability or inability to work." Comparative evidence that pregnant workers are treated worse than others similar in their ability or inability to work, as a matter of policy or actual practice, is sufficient to establish a violation of the PDA whether or not the employer bore animus against pregnant workers. Therefore, the plaintiff need not use pretext analysis to smoke out discriminatory intent. A policy or decision that denies light duty to a pregnant worker while making it available to someone injured on the job or someone with a qualifying disability under the ADA is prima facie evidence of discrimination.

Moreover, the Guidance continues, "an employer cannot lawfully deny or restrict light duty based on the source of a pregnant employee's limitation. Thus, for example, an employer must provide light duty for pregnant workers on the same terms that light duty is offered to employees injured on the job who are similar to the pregnant worker in their ability or inability to work." This is an important response to the appellate court rulings, including the one in *Young*, which have held that discrimination based on *source* of injury is "pregnancy neutral" as long as pregnancy is not the only condition excluded.

## CONCLUSION

The new EEOC Guidance tackles other issues related to pregnancy discrimination, as well: the proper use of disparate impact theory, the impropriety of forced leave policies, and, importantly, the interaction between other federal statutes such as the FMLA and the Americans with Disabilities Act (including the latter's 2008 amendments). Across the board, the EEOC takes an approach designed, as Congress intended, to allow pregnant women to begin work, continue working, and return to work throughout the reproductive process. The Guidance shows sensitivity to the most common types of employer policies and practices that continue to stymie the careers of women who have been or might be pregnant, and it urges employers to go beyond even what the law requires where necessary to level the playing field. Were employers to both comply with the law and follow the recommended "best practices," pregnant women would find a very different workplace indeed.

A version of this chapter appeared on July 22, 2014, at verdict.justia.com.

# 35

## Forceps Delivery

*The Supreme Court Narrowly Saves the Pregnancy
Discrimination Act in Young v. UPS*

By a vote of 6–3, the Supreme Court ruled in favor of Peggy Young, a UPS driver who claimed she was illegally discriminated against when she was denied a workplace accommodation that was made available to other employees with similar physical restrictions. In an opinion by Justice Breyer, the Court concluded that her case should not have been dismissed on summary judgment; rather, she should have had the opportunity to prove that UPS, by refusing her an accommodation it made available to many other restricted workers, committed pregnancy discrimination. Justice Alito agreed that UPS's victory on summary judgment should be vacated and the case remanded, but based on a different interpretation of applicable law.[1]

This ruling caps off more than a decade of controversial litigation over the application of the Pregnancy Discrimination Act to accommodation claims. And while the Court's reasoning raises many questions, the holding restores protection that pregnant workers should have had by statute but that they have been denied by many federal courts.

### HARD LABOR: PEGGY YOUNG AND UPS'S LIGHT-DUTY POLICY

When Peggy Young finally became pregnant after a series of miscarriages, her doctor imposed a restriction on how much she could lift. At the time, she worked as an "air driver" for UPS, a delivery driver who carried lighter letters and packs for United Parcel Service that had arrived by air. UPS decided that it could not continue to allow her to work unless she could lift the amount listed in her job description, even though she rarely if ever was asked to lift things that heavy. She requested a light-duty assignment but was denied, despite the fact that UPS made such accommodations available to three large groups of employees: those who were injured on the job, those who were eligible for an accommodation under the Americans with Disabilities Act, and those who had lost their commercial driver's licenses because of a medical condition such as a diabetic complication or a legal condition such as the loss of a license after a drunk driving conviction. Young, however, was denied a similar accommodation. She was forced out of her job, lost her health insurance, and was allowed to return to work only after giving birth.[2]

## YOUNG'S RIGHTS UNDER THE PDA

Peggy Young sued, claiming that UPS had violated the PDA. The second clause – the one at issue in *Young* – provides that pregnant women have the right to be treated the same as others who are "similar in their ability or inability to work," but "not so affected" by pregnancy.[3] This approach has been criticized for giving pregnant workers only a comparative, rather than an absolute, right of accommodation. But even setting aside that limitation, courts have struggled for years over what this clause means and how to define the proper comparison group. This disagreement was at the heart of the *Young* case, as well as several other similar cases over the past several years. (See Chapters 31 to 33.)

Both the trial and appellate courts held that UPS had not violated the PDA because the UPS light-duty policies did not exclude *only* pregnancy; there were at least some temporarily disabled employees who, in theory, might need accommodation but would not receive it. As long as the policy was "pregnancy-blind," it did not run afoul of the PDA. This type of reasoning essentially read the second clause out of the PDA, because the first clause already expressly forbids employment actions taken "because of" pregnancy. In so doing, the Fourth Circuit joined several other circuits, although most were dealing with less egregiously discriminatory policies than UPS's.[4]

## SPLITTING THE BABY: THE SUPREME COURT'S RULING IN *YOUNG V. UPS*

Peggy Young argued that UPS's policy was discriminatory because it permitted light-duty accommodations to some workers – potentially many – who had similar types of work restrictions but did not allow the same accommodation for her. Under the second clause of the PDA, she argued, UPS must grant her the same accommodations available to other workers with similar restrictions.[5] UPS argued that no policy could violate the PDA if it was pregnancy neutral – that is, if it did not single out pregnancy as the only condition that did not merit some particular accommodation.[6]

The majority opinion split the baby. It rejected the interpretations offered by both parties. With respect to Young's interpretation, Breyer wrote that pregnant women were not entitled to "most favored nation" status, under which they could demand an accommodation that was offered to *any* other worker. This, the majority wrote, was too broad a reading of the second clause. (At least Justice Alito, who otherwise took a more narrow approach to clause two, avoided the oddly abstract and impersonal "most favored nation" terminology and instead referred to "most favored employees.") With respect to UPS's interpretation, the majority reasoned that such an interpretation would collapse the second clause into the first, in violation of an important principle of statutory construction. And even more damningly, this reading would have allowed the employer's policy in *Gilbert* – which covered all sicknesses and accidents – to be upheld despite the incontrovertible fact that the PDA was enacted expressly to overrule that opinion.[7]

The majority, instead, crafted a new approach to applying the Second Clause of the PDA, which, it claims, "minimizes the problems [of the parties' interpretations], responds directly to *Gilbert* and is consistent with longstanding interpretations of Title VII."[8] The court's approach makes use of the so-called *McDonnell-Douglas* test,[9] which is used to smoke out discriminatory intent by employers accused of unlawful disparate treatment. Under that test, a plaintiff must first make out a prima facie case, demonstrating that she was treated differently from someone similarly situated but outside the protected class.[10] The district court in Young's case had held that she failed to make out a prima facie case because none of the proposed comparators were "similarly situated" – she hadn't been injured on the job, she did not qualify for ADA protection, and she hadn't lost her commercial driver's license. The policy, in other words, was used in its own defense – she was not similarly situated to anyone covered by the policy because she was not covered by the policy.[11] Brilliant.

Fortunately, Justice Breyer's opinion rejects this application of *McDonnell-Douglas*. A plaintiff can establish a prima facie case of pregnancy discrimination simply by showing that "she belongs to the protected class, that she sought accommodation, that the employer did not accommodate her, and that the employer did accommodate others 'similar in their ability or inability to work.'"[12] This alone will fix a number of the problems in lower court rulings, where courts had found a variety of different ways to prevent light-duty claims from reaching the next stage.

Upon establishment of the prima facie case, the burden of production then shifts to the employer, who must articulate a legitimate, nondiscriminatory reason for its differential treatment. Here, the Court interposes another rule to protect pregnancy discrimination plaintiffs. "[C]onsistent with the Act's basic objective, that reason normally cannot consist simply of a claim that it is more expensive or less convenient to add pregnant women to the category of those ('similar in their ability or inability to work') whom the employer accommodates."[13] Those reasons animate many policies that restrict light-duty accommodations and, indeed, the "employer in *Gilbert* could in all likelihood have made such a claim."[14]

After the employer articulates a legitimate, non-discriminatory reason for its treatment of the plaintiff, the plaintiff has the opportunity nonetheless to reach a jury by "providing sufficient evidence that the employer's policies impose a significant burden on pregnant workers, and that the employer's 'legitimate, nondiscriminatory' reasons are not sufficiently strong to justify the burden, but rather – when considered along with the burden imposed – give rise to an inference of intentional discrimination."[15] This, too, is new, and gives pregnant workers the opportunity to force the real question underlying all these cases: Why would the employer categorically exclude pregnant women from an accommodation that it provides to potentially large numbers of other workers?

For Young, the Court wrote, she could prevail on remand by showing that UPS does not have a sufficiently strong reason for refusing to accommodate pregnant employees with lifting restrictions while accommodating nonpregnant employees with lifting restrictions – "to the point that a jury could find that its reasons for failing to accommodate pregnant employees give rise to an inference of intentional discrimination."[16] This was a clear victory for Peggy Young – the ruling below was vacated – but it invites more litigation in pregnancy discrimination cases, as the standard is far from clear or categorical. But it is certainly better than the alternative approach, under which several federal appellate courts upheld blatantly discriminatory policies that excluded pregnant women from routinely available, and sometimes costless, accommodations for no apparent reason. (See Chapter 31.)

## THE BABY GROWS UP: THE FUTURE OF PREGNANCY DISCRIMINATION ACT CLAIMS

The Court's opinion leaves several issues that will have to be sorted out as pregnancy discrimination claims move forward in the lower courts. What are the most likely issues?

### How "Many" Comparators Does It Take to Support an Inference of Discrimination?

As the Court explains the PDA, an inference of pregnancy discrimination may arise from the nonaccommodation of pregnancy despite the accommodation of "many" – but not all – workers with non-pregnancy-related disabilities.[17] Lower courts will now have to parse exactly what this means. This should not require a pregnant worker to identify numerous specific individuals whose conditions the employer treated more favorably. Because the ultimate question is, as the court says, "the extent to which an employer's *policy* treats pregnant workers less favorably than it treats non-pregnant workers similar in their ability to work"[18] (emphasis added), it should be enough for a plaintiff to show that the more favorable treatment extends to numerous nonpregnancy *conditions*. The fortuity that few individuals may have actually presented with the conditions favored by the employer's policies should not defeat a pregnancy discrimination claim if such conditions would be accommodated under the employer's policies.

For example, if an employer's policy gives paid time off for a wide range of illnesses but not pregnancy, a pregnant worker should still be able to make out a discrimination claim even if, by good fortune, few of the employer's employees had become ill and taken advantage of the policy. Similarly, if the employer has never before had a disabled employee with a lifting restriction, but its policies make clear that it would accommodate such a (nonpregnant) worker, that too may support the plaintiff's prima facie case. The bottom line is, where an employer's policies by their own terms treat a broad range of conditions more favorably than pregnancy – as distinguished from a singular exception or fluke – that should suffice to support an inference of pregnancy discrimination.

### What Counts as a "Legitimate Nondiscriminatory Reason"?

Clearly, the employer must do more to meet this burden than merely coming up with a way to describe an exclusionary policy in pregnancy-neutral terms. As the Court points out, that kind of formalism is exactly what Congress repudiated in enacting the PDA.[19] Even the General Electric policy in *Gilbert*, covering illness and accident, can be stated in pregnancy-neutral terms: the policy covers illness and accidents, and pregnancy does not qualify as either.[20] Similarly, as the Court explains, it is not enough to defend the unfavorable treatment of pregnancy by reference to the fact that it would cost more to include it or create added administrative burdens. These explanations too could have supported the General Electric policy. Rather, the employer must provide a reasoned justification of the unfavorable treatment of pregnancy that does not discriminate against pregnancy as the source of the condition causing the work-related effects.[21]

This understanding of the legitimate nondiscriminatory reason (LNDR) makes sense of the Court's examples of permissible reasons for treating nonpregnant workers more favorably: where such favorable treatment is meted out according to job class, the employer's needs, age, or seniority. In any of those cases, the source of the condition affecting the employee's ability to work – pregnancy or not pregnancy – is not the reason for the conferral or denial of the accommodation.

While this means that preferential treatment of employees in some jobs, such as the court's example of more dangerous assignments, may be an LNDR, it does not follow that preferential treatment of all on-the-job injuries will necessarily qualify as an LNDR. The latter discriminates on the basis of the source of condition (pregnancy is not an injury, nor is it incurred on the job), while the former does not. Nor do the justifications for singling out employees who hold dangerous jobs for preferential treatment extend to blanket policies limiting accommodations to on-the-job injuries. Many on-the-job injuries result from mundane, everyday misfortunes that could occur anywhere and are not the product of particular dangers on a job. Consider a friend who holds an office job in marketing at a bank. This otherwise graceful woman stood up from sitting at her computer without noticing that her foot had fallen asleep; she inadvertently landed on her foot wrong, breaking several bones. Hers was classified as an on-the-job injury, triggering her employer's policies for such conditions. Blanket rules accommodating all on-the-job injuries but not pregnancy necessarily discriminate by source of condition and are not necessarily (at least when framed as a blanket rule) nondiscriminatory responses to dangerous conditions or special risks on the job.

## What Proof Is Required to Show Pretext?

Much of the time, the *McDonnell-Douglas* proof method comes down to the pretext stage. Here, the plaintiff has the opportunity to rebut the employer's nondiscriminatory justification by exposing it as a pretext for discrimination. Under the ruling in *Young*, that means showing that the employer lacks reasons that are "sufficiently strong" to justify the "significant burden" on pregnant workers.[22] Although Justice Scalia's dissent accuses the majority of mistakenly conflating the disparate treatment claim with proof of disparate impact and an absence of business necessity,[23] the Court's approach better fits the theory of the PDA. A core lesson of the PDA, and the history behind it, is that the disfavored treatment of pregnancy often rests on the devaluation of pregnant employees as future mothers and unreliable workers, and the view that pregnant employees are not worth the same investments as other workers needing accommodations for other reasons.[24] Too often, employer refusals to accommodate pregnant employees, despite accommodating other workers with similar impairments, and without good business reasons for such distinctions, rest precisely on the kind of stereotyping that amounts to intentional discrimination. The Court's test should provide meaningful protection to pregnant workers to challenge the very practices that the PDA intended to eliminate.

## THE EEOC'S POWER TO PERSUADE

As mentioned above, the Court in *Young* rejected the plaintiff's interpretation of the second clause of the PDA, which would have found a per se violation of the statute whenever an employer provided for accommodations for some workers, but denied them to similarly restricted pregnant women. This was not just a theory she invented. It is supported by the plain text of the statute. Moreover, the EEOC took that exact position in its formal pregnancy discrimination guidelines. Although the Supreme Court sometimes takes agency interpretations into account, it refused to do so here. The guidelines did not, in the court's view, have the power to persuade.[25]

The court's disrespect for the EEOC's position stems from its conclusion that the most recent guidelines were enacted *after* the court granted the petition for certiorari in this case.[26] They thus seemed strategic rather than reasoned, to the majority anyway. The reality is that the EEOC has taken a consistent approach to pregnancy accommodation since even before the PDA was enacted. Regulations adopted in 1972 provided that "[d]isabilities caused or contributed to by pregnancy . . . are, for all job-related purposes, temporary disabilities and should be treated as such under any health or temporary disability insurance or sick leave plan available in connection with employment."[27] And post-PDA guidance was consistent with this early statement and added the additional clarification that "[i]f other employees temporarily unable to lift are relieved of these functions, pregnant employees also unable to lift must be temporarily relieved of the function."[28] But, in the Court's view, this guidance did not resolve the question posed in *Young* – whether a pregnant employee is entitled to an accommodation offered to *any* other employee, or only to those offered to numerous other employees. In the majority's view, this "post-Act guidance . . . does not resolve the ambiguity of the term 'other persons' in the Act's second clause. Rather, it simply tells employers to treat pregnancy-related disabilities like nonpregnancy-related disabilities, without clarifying how that instruction should be implemented when an employer does not treat all nonpregnancy-related disabilities alike."[29]

The EEOC's more recent guidance – promulgated in July 2014 – does address this question specifically, providing that "[a]n employer may not refuse to treat a pregnant worker the same as other employees who are similar in their ability or inability to work by relying on a policy that makes distinctions based on the source of an employee's limitations (e.g., a policy of providing light duty only to workers injured on the job)."[30] Examples make clear that the EEOC would have required UPS to grant someone like Peggy Young a light-duty accommodation given that it made the same accommodation to other employees with a different source of injury. It is this interpretation that the *Young* majority refused to follow because it found difficulties with timing, consistency, and thoroughness of the agency's consideration of the issue. In part, it was troubled by the fact that the federal government has taken a different position when defending itself against a pregnancy discrimination claim in court.[31]

This rejection of the EEOC's position merits three brief notes. First, it is hardly fair to attribute the government's self-serving litigation position (in a case, *Ensley–Gaines v. Runyon*,[32] in which postal service workers sued the federal government for pregnancy discrimination) to the agency in its rule-making and administrative enforcement capacity. Inconsistency is to be expected between those two very different contexts, and from different departments of government. Second, the EEOC's clarification in July 2014 was not in any way contrary to the interpretation it has urged since the PDA's initial passage – and its position on pregnancy discrimination even before 1978. While it did address a specific example at issue in the *Young* case, that same issue had been the centerpiece of several federal appellate decisions dating back almost twenty years. Third, the Court's decision not to follow the interpretation suggested in one example should not undermine the rest of the EEOC's pregnancy discrimination guidance, which provides a comprehensive interpretation of the PDA. All but the one sentence mentioned above should continue to have the full force of an agency interpretation.

## CONCLUSION

It is not uncommon for the Supreme Court's employment discrimination rulings to invite more litigation, and the *Young v. UPS* ruling is no exception. The Court, however, has set the stage for broader protection for pregnant workers – and a more disciplined approach to ensuring their rights under the PDA are enforced.

Portions of this chapter appeared on March 31, 2015 and April 20, 2015, at verdict.justia.com, and were coauthored by Deborah L. Brake.

*Update: Like most Supreme Court rulings on discrimination law,* Young v. United Parcel Service, Inc., *raised more questions than it answered. As lower federal courts begin the task of analyzing the next set of questions, advocacy groups have taken the lead in educating employers and pregnant women on accommodation law. A new site, Pregnant@Work.org provides a wealth of resources for doctors, lawyers, employers and pregnant women.*[33]

# 36

## The Pregnancy Discrimination Act Reaches
## Advanced Maternal Age

October 31, 2013, marked the thirty-fifth anniversary of the passage of the Pregnancy Discrimination Act (PDA) of 1978. Signed into law on Halloween that year by President Jimmy Carter, the PDA was instrumental in ending a long-standing era of the lawful exclusion of pregnant women from the workforce. The act ushered in an era of unprecedented access for women to jobs before, during, and after pregnancy. This was, and still is, cause for celebration. Yet pregnant workers today continue to face high levels of discrimination and, more important, lack some basic legal protections that are necessary to enable some women to continue working throughout pregnancy.

In human years, thirty-five is a turning point when "advanced maternal age" sets in, and most conversations with one's obstetrician start with, "Well, because of your age, we need to...." It marks the beginning of the end of one's fertility and the increase in the likelihood of pregnancy complications and fetal abnormalities.

We might say that the PDA has reached a similar stage. After a robust start, in which the PDA was effectively used to eliminate the most common types of policies and decisions used to exclude women from the workplace entirely or marginalize their participation, attorneys and the women they represent have together struggled in recent years to ensure that the PDA is useful to the pregnant workers whom it should benefit. The complication here is not, of course, the biological clock, but, rather, the mind-set of judges, who cannot give the act its due, and who perhaps feel that its time is done and gone. But we should not stop pushing for pregnant workers' rights until those workers have been fully integrated into the workplace and do not suffer discrimination.

This chapter considers gaps in current law that still render pregnant women second-class citizens in the workplace and argues that we should work toward a new standard of equal inclusion, rather than just equal access.

## THE PROMISE OF THE PDA: EQUAL CITIZENSHIP FOR WOMEN

When Congress approved the PDA, it did so in response to a long history of open discrimination against pregnant women in the workplace, and, more immediately, to two recent Supreme Court decisions that were highly adverse to pregnant women and that seemed to reinforce the lawfulness of that history.

The legislative history of the PDA focuses a great deal on overruling the specific effects of *General Electric Co. v. Gilbert* – a step that was necessary to open the basic protections of Title VII to pregnant and childbearing women. But peppered throughout the committee reports and floor debates relating to the PDA is talk of broader goals – the desire, among others, to guarantee women equal "citizenship." As one witness testified to a congressional subcommittee, "Pregnant workers and workers who are new mothers are, fundamentally, workers. They should not be relegated to second class citizenship in employee rights or benefits."[1]

It is common for advocates or legislators to invoke notions of citizenship – or, more specifically, the desire to avoid relegating a group to "second-class citizenship" – when pushing for new civil rights laws. It is a powerful rhetorical device that calls immediately to mind disturbing periods in history when particular groups were deprived of important rights – suffrage, jury service, the right to own property, and so on – despite having the same formal status as U.S. citizens.

Although such citizenship references are often purely rhetorical, the notion of full and equal citizenship can provide a powerful normative framework for assessing the degree to which a group has become integrated into society or, in the alternative, remains marginalized. "Citizenship" is obviously a term used most often to describe nationality, or one's formal status in a country. But it has also been used more broadly by scholars to describe a multidimensional concept that connotes inclusion, participation, or belonging.[2] "Equal citizenship" or "full citizenship" thus describes the set of rights and benefits that accrue to full members of society.

One dimension of citizenship – social citizenship – is particularly useful when examining the experience of pregnant women in the workplace. The connection between work and citizenship is multifaceted but undeniable. Work provides individuals with the independence necessary to exercise political rights and with an important forum for interacting with other members of society. Work also, as scholars like Vicki Schultz have argued, is deeply connected to self-identity and dignity.[3] Perhaps most importantly of all, work provides the pathway to economic security and the ability to provide for one's family.

The claim made here, in the context of the battle against pregnancy discrimination, is that the tradition of social citizenship, which seeks equal access to paid work, must encompass at least some protection for a pregnant woman's right to work *despite the potential physical limitations of pregnancy*. On this theory, the state, at a minimum, should facilitate pregnant women's access to work through reproductive episodes by defining "discrimination" to include the failure to provide reasonable and necessary accommodations for pregnancy-related disability.

## WHY CURRENT LAW FALLS SHORT OF DELIVERING ON
## THE PROMISE OF EQUAL CITIZENSHIP

Today, pregnancy discrimination law, the cornerstone of which is the PDA, opened many doors for pregnant women, starting a long-term trend toward women working more and longer during pregnancy and resuming work more quickly after child-birth.[4] Yet it has still has serious gaps in its protections. Namely, the law fails to deal coherently with situations in which pregnant women are able to work but are experiencing some diminishment in capacity due to their condition.

This failure is manifested in many ways, including, to take just three examples, when courts uphold employer policies that offer light-duty assignments but exclude pregnant women from them;[5] when courts permit pregnant women to be fired or put on forced unpaid leave because they cannot perform exactly the same set of tasks as they could before and after pregnancy;[6] and when courts refuse to use disparate impact law to police harsh-but-neutral policies that disproportionately disadvantage pregnant women and are of dubious business necessity.

The PDA grants rights based primarily on a pregnant woman's capacity. The law protects many women against "pregnancy discrimination," but it provides absolute rights only to the extent a pregnant woman is able to work at full capacity, uninterrupted by pregnancy, childbirth, or related medical conditions. The law does not generally permit employers to refuse to hire pregnant women or to make *assumptions* about their inability to carry out certain tasks. This right against stereotyping is important, but it provides no protection when the assumption that the pregnant woman has job-related limitations is correct.

Indeed, current federal law does not insist that employers provide accommodations to enable a woman to continue working through her pregnancy, and permits employers to fire employees who suffer a full or partial temporary loss in capacity due to pregnancy, subject only to the very minimal protection provided by disparate impact law. The pregnancy discrimination framework, which ties rights to capacity, fails to account for the actual effects of pregnancy on women's bodies and work capacity and thus fails to meet the needs of many pregnant working women today, especially those who labor in nontraditional jobs that can be physically strenuous or hazardous.

## SUPPLEMENTING ANTIDISCRIMINATION PROTECTIONS WITH
## AN EQUAL CITIZENSHIP IDEAL IS THE PATH THAT WILL
## ULTIMATELY GIVE PREGNANT WOMEN TRUE EQUALITY

As a normative ideal, equal citizenship calls for all members of society to have the opportunity to make use of their natural talents and abilities, and to participate in all aspects of private and public life. Justice Ruth Bader Ginsburg invoked this concept in *United States v. Virginia*, in which the Supreme Court struck down the all-male admissions policy of the Virginia Military Institute. She wrote that the government does not act "compatibly with equal protection when a law or official policy denies to women, simply because they are women, full citizenship stature – equal opportunity to aspire, achieve, participate in and contribute to society based on their individual talents and capacities."[7] The treatment by employers of pregnant workers, because of the common conflicts between pregnancy and work and the law's failure to adequately address them, still falls short of this ideal. Let's take the anniversary of the PDA as an occasion to recommit to gender equality and take the steps necessary to achieve it.

Portions of this chapter appeared on October 28, 2008, at writ.findlaw.com, and on October 29, 2013, at verdict.justia.com.

# 37

## The Pregnant Workers' Fairness Act

### A *Time for Change?*

In May 2012, Democrats in the House of Representatives introduced the Pregnant Workers Fairness Act (PWFA). The bill would guarantee pregnant women the right to reasonable accommodation when the short-term physical effects of pregnancy conflict with the demands of a particular job, as long as the accommodation does not impose an undue hardship on the employer.[1] This chapter examines the ways in which courts have unjustifiably narrowed protection under existing statutes and the realities of the situations of pregnant women at work that make existing interpretations of the law insufficient.

#### UNDERSTANDING PREGNANCY DISCRIMINATION
#### RIGHTS IN PRACTICE

The most significant impact of the Pregnancy Discrimination Act (PDA) of 1978, at least initially, was to invalidate widespread formal policies that told pregnant women when they could and could not work, and in which sorts of jobs. The PDA forced employers to shift to a more individualized model under which pregnant women could not be fired, not hired, or otherwise disadvantaged just for being pregnant. Decisions about employment now had to be made based on capacity to work, rather than pregnancy status.[2]

The second and important impact of the PDA was to force changes to standard employer benefit and leave policies, many of which excluded pregnancy altogether. Under the second clause of the act, employers must treat pregnant employees at least as well as they treat other temporarily disabled workers. Employers thus must, for example, provide paid or unpaid leave to pregnant women who medically require it if they would do so for something who needed it because of some other temporary disability.[3]

In practice, the PDA protects some pregnant women, some of the time, as follows:

- For a pregnant woman who *can* work at full capacity – that is, she has no physical effects that interfere with her job responsibilities – the PDA can be effective in protecting her against the stereotypes and animus her employer might harbor about pregnant women generally. If a pregnant woman is able to perform all aspects of her job, she cannot be assumed to have limitations that, in fact, she does not have, nor can she be denied the opportunity to work just because she is pregnant.
- For a pregnant woman who temporarily *cannot* work because of the physical effects of her pregnancy, the particular demands of her job, or the interaction between the two, the PDA guarantees that she will have the same access to leave and benefits as other temporarily disabled workers do. If the employer is generous, she may be well protected; if the employer provides meagerly in this regard, then she will be less well protected. She may also have access to twelve weeks of unpaid leave under the FMLA if her employer is large enough and she works enough hours per year.[4]
- For a pregnant woman who *could* work, but only if the employer made certain accommodations to her assigned tasks or work environment, the PDA provides a comparative right of accommodation. Under the second clause of the act, such a woman is entitled to whatever accommodation her employer grants to other temporarily disabled employees. If no such accommodation is granted, the pregnant woman has no absolute right to medically necessary accommodations and can be discharged for failure to perform her job, subject only to the very limited protection offered by disparate-impact theory. (Disparate impact theory is the basis for challenging employment actions that are not on their face discriminatory, but differentially affect a particular class of employees.[5])

## THE PDA'S LIMITATIONS

Pregnant women with partial incapacity due to pregnancy are the least well protected by the PDA, which provides only a comparative right of accommodation. This limitation is built into the structure of the statute. But courts have taken a modest right of accommodation and turned it into a barely detectible right of accommodation, through a series of cramped, and often indefensible, interpretations of the PDA.

One such narrowing is in the definition of pregnancy. The PDA prohibits discrimination because of pregnancy, childbirth, and related medical conditions.[6] Although the Supreme Court interpreted this language quite broadly in *International Union v. Johnson Controls*, to include "potential pregnancy,"[7] lower federal courts have ignored this ruling and taken a narrower approach.

As discussed in Chapter 43, a federal court in Texas just ruled in *EEOC v. Houston Funding* that lactation is not "related" to pregnancy under the PDA and, thus, a woman can be fired for breastfeeding.[8] Some courts have also ruled that neither contraception nor infertility is "related" to pregnancy under the PDA, which means that employers can refuse insurance coverage or otherwise discriminate on those bases.[9] A second type of narrowing of the rights of pregnant women comes from courts' resistance to drawing an inference of pregnancy discrimination. Plaintiffs often have trouble convincing courts that an adverse action they suffered was taken because of the status of pregnancy, as opposed to because of its disabling effects (which is permitted by law) or for some neutral reason.

A classic and troubling case is *Troupe v. May Department Stores*, discussed briefly in the introduction to Part III, in which a pregnant sales clerk was fired one day before she was scheduled to begin maternity leave. She was frequently late because of morning sickness. Her employer claimed she was fired for excessive tardiness, not because she was pregnant and planning to take maternity leave.[10] The court agreed with the employer – concluding that it is not pregnancy discrimination if she was fired for being late, even if she was late because she was pregnant.[11] The court is right – pregnancy is not an excuse for failing to perform according to the demands of the job. But without an obvious comparator – a man who was excessively absent and *not* fired one day before a scheduled leave – the court refused to entertain the possibility that the tardiness did not motivate the firing, but that the pregnancy itself or the planned maternity leave did.[12]

The third, and most damaging, type of narrowing of rights against pregnancy discrimination comes in denial-of-accommodation cases. In a growing number of cases, courts have effectively read the second clause out of the PDA. They do this in different ways, but here are the highlights:

- Courts have upheld light-duty policies that restrict such assignments to workers with on-the-job injuries. Rather than take the PDA's second clause at its word (again, it states that pregnant women are entitled to the same accommodations as those "not so affected but similar in their ability or inability to work"), the courts allow employers to define the comparison group based on any criterion that is "pregnancy neutral" such as the source of the injury. Pregnant women who need leave because of their level of incapacity encounter this same problem – being denied access to paid leave or other benefits because they were "injured" off the job.[13]

- When analyzing formal policies such as these, courts employ "pretext" analysis to smoke out animus against pregnant women. When they do not find animus, they conclude that no discrimination has occurred.[14] But the second clause of the PDA does not merely ban ill-motivated decisions that harm pregnant women. That's the job of the first clause. The second clause requires, affirmatively, that employers treat pregnant workers no worse than other temporarily disabled workers who are "similar in their ability or inability to work." In *Young v. UPS*, the Supreme Court clarified the meaning of this phrase, but it remains to be seen how much protection the new interpretation will provide.

- Courts have refused to allow pregnant women to compare themselves – when invoking the comparative right of accommodation – with employees who receive accommodations mandated by the Americans with Disabilities Act (ADA). (The ADA mandates, for employees who meet the definition of "disabled," reasonable accommodations that do not impose an undue hardship on employers.[15]) Courts have ruled that "ordinary pregnancy" is not a disability within the meaning of the ADA; pregnant women thus cannot seek accommodations directly under the ADA.[16] But neither can they compare themselves with disabled workers, apparently, when enforcing the comparative right of accommodation. This situation is now more troubling than it once was, given amendments to the ADA in 2008 that have been interpreted by the EEOC to protect many types of temporary disability, including those whose only limitations are back pain and restrictions on lifting.[17] Yet, the EEOC still takes the position that pregnant women cannot be treated as "disabled" for purposes of requesting reasonable accommodations, even if their restrictions are identical to another worker who is not pregnant.[18] Who is left for pregnant workers to compare themselves with now?

## THE PREGNANT WORKERS FAIRNESS ACT (PWFA): A PROPOSED LAW THAT SHOULD NOT BE AS NECESSARY AS IT IS

The recently introduced bill HR 5647, the Pregnant Workers Fairness Act, is styled as a bill "[t]o eliminate discrimination and promote women's health and economic security by ensuring reasonable workplace accommodations for workers whose ability to perform the functions of a job are limited by pregnancy, childbirth, or a related medical condition."[19]

The bill focuses on the lack of a meaningful right of accommodation for pregnant women under existing law. The lack of such a right is caused in part by a limitation introduced by design in the PDA. But much of that lack is caused by erroneous judicial rulings that refuse to give the PDA's second clause its intended scope.

The PWFA would, if enacted into law, makes it unlawful to:

- Refuse to "make reasonable accommodations to the known limitations related to the pregnancy, childbirth, or related medical conditions of a job applicant or employee" without demonstrating "undue hardship" to the employer.
- Deny employment opportunities to a woman in order to avoid making required accommodations.
- Force a woman to accept an accommodation she does not want.

- Force a woman to take leave "under any leave law or policy... if another reasonable accommodation can be provided" instead.[20]

The PWFA would be administered as part of Title VII, which means it would apply to employers with at least fifteen employees, would require the filing of an EEOC charge as a prerequisite to filing a lawsuit, and would allow an employee to seek money damages for any violation.[21] Its substantive approach, however, is modeled on the ADA, which grants covered employees an affirmative right of reasonable accommodation regardless of how others are treated.

## CONCLUSION

If enacted, the PWFA would provide protection for many pregnant women who struggle to navigate jobs and working environments that were typically not designed with them in mind. An absolute right of accommodation would be particularly helpful for those women working in traditionally male-dominated occupations that tend to involve greater physical demands and hazards than traditionally female occupations. This bill could thus help break down the entrenched occupational segregation in the American economy. But whether or not the PWFA becomes law, courts should pay closer to attention to existing pregnancy discrimination law, which provides many of these protections already. And employers should, whether the law requires them to or not, take the steps necessary to integrate pregnant women into the workforce. Short-term accommodations can have long-term payoffs.

A version of this chapter appeared on May 11, 2012, at verdict.justia.com.

*Update: On May 14, 2013, the Pregnant Workers Fairness Act was introduced in the U.S. Senate and reintroduced in the U.S. House of Representatives.[22] As of the date of publication of this book, it has yet to pass either body of Congress.*

# 38

## The Supreme Court Deals a Blow to
## Once-Pregnant Retirees

Is it permissible to penalize retiring women for pregnancy-related disability leaves that they took before the law required employers to treat such leaves like all other disability leaves? In its 7–2 ruling in *AT&T v. Hulteen*, the Supreme Court said yes, leaving in place a disturbing relic of a discriminatory past with real present-day consequences.[1]

### PREGNANCY AND PENSIONS AT AT&T

*Hulteen* involves a group of female employees who took unpaid leaves for disability related to pregnancy between 1968 and 1974.[2] Pursuant to AT&T's policies in place at the time, an employee who took "disability" leave from work received full service credit (that is, credit for having worked for the full period during which he or she was disabled), no matter how long the leave. In contrast, an employee who took leave related to pregnancy – even if she was temporarily disabled by the pregnancy – could receive service credit for no more than thirty days. (An uncredited leave resulted in the employee's "start date" at AT&T being adjusted forward to the extent of the leave.) In 1977, the company adopted a new policy, which entitled employees with pregnancy-related disability to receive both benefits and service credit for six weeks, but neither benefits nor credit thereafter. Again, employees who took other disability leaves were entitled to full service credit.[3]

Like many other companies, AT&T amended its leave policy in 1979 to comply with the newly enacted Pregnancy Discrimination Act (PDA).[4] Prior to the PDA's enactment, the Supreme Court had ruled, in *General Electric Co. v. Gilbert*, that Title VII's ban on sex discrimination in employment did not include pregnancy discrimination.[5] It was perfectly legal for an employer to treat employees differently because of pregnancy. *Gilbert*, though, was overruled by the PDA, giving pregnant employees, among other things, the right to be treated the same as comparably disabled employees with respect to all benefits, including seniority calculations.[6]

Thus, AT&T could no longer grant less credit and fewer benefits to workers who took pregnancy-related disability leave than it did to those who took leave for other types of disability without violating federal law (although it could freely deny leave to both). AT&T thus amended its policy to provide equal service credit for all disability leaves, including those necessitated by pregnancy.[7] AT&T did not, however, take any action to pay benefits or restore service credit to women who took pregnancy leaves under the differential system.[8]

### *AT&T V. HULTEEN*: THE ISSUE BEFORE THE SUPREME COURT

Four of these women – Noreen Hulteen and three others – sued AT&T. They did not take issue with the decades-old injury they had suffered when they were deprived of benefits extended to others on disability leave. But they did challenge their loss of service credit during their pregnancy leaves, which means today, and for the rest of their lives, they are entitled to lower pensions at retirement.[9]

The four women who sued AT&T alleged that its use of an adjusted start date, which affects, among other things, the level of pension benefits they receive, is discriminatory in violation of Title VII, the main federal antidiscrimination law.[10] The federal trial court ruled in favor of the plaintiffs, holding that post-PDA retirement calculations could not be lawfully based on rules differentiating service credit on the basis of pregnancy from other service credit, whether or not those rules had been lawful at the time.[11] An en banc panel of the U.S. Court of Appeals for the Ninth Circuit agreed and affirmed the judgment, splitting with both the Sixth and Seventh Circuits, which had ruled to the contrary.[12]

### THE COURT'S DECISION: RULING FOR AT&T BASED ON ITS "BONA FIDE SENIORITY SYSTEM"

The Supreme Court, however, reversed, and ruled in favor of AT&T. The majority opinion, authored by the retiring Justice David Souter, turns on its determination that AT&T's pensions were set based on a "bona fide seniority system," and therefore were subject to special protection under Title VII.[13]

Title VII defines an "unlawful employment practice" as discrimination "against any individual with respect to his compensation, terms, conditions, or privileges of employment, because of such individual's . . . sex."[14] To challenge an unlawful practice under Title VII, an employee must file a charge with the Equal EEOC within 180 days of its occurrence.[15]

Hulteen argued that the unlawful discrimination occurred when AT&T used the differential service credits to calculate pensions at retirement. The court relied, however, on section 703(h) of Title VII, codified at 42 U.S.C. 2000e-2(h), which immunizes employers' decisions if they are based on a "bona fide seniority system," as long as those decisions are not "the result of an intention to discriminate because of race, color, religion, sex, or national origin."[16]

The question before the court, then, was whether the express exclusion of pregnancy leaves under AT&T's earlier policies reflected "intent to discriminate."[17] The majority said no because, at the time the relevant leaves were taken, (i) pregnancy discrimination was legal (the PDA had not yet been enacted); and (ii) pregnancy discrimination was not considered a form of sex discrimination (thanks to the Court's ruling in *Gilbert*).[18] A majority of the justices thus concluded that AT&T was entitled to exclude pregnancy leaves from service credit calculations in the first instance and, once the company had done so, those calculations could be carried forward as part of a "bona fide seniority system" without triggering future liability.

The majority relied on the Court's 1977 ruling in *Teamsters v. United States*, which upheld a seniority system that disproportionately advantaged white employees because the employer had, prior to Title VII's enactment, favored them in job assignments.[19] Under 703(h), the Court ruled in that case, the seniority system was not tainted by the prior discrimination and was therefore immune from challenge, even though it perpetuated the long-standing disadvantage to minority workers.[20] In the *Hulteen* majority's view, AT&T's system is on par with the one challenged in *Teamsters* and therefore is valid.

## THE PROBLEMS WITH THE REASONING OF THE *HULTEEN* MAJORITY

The problem with the majority's reasoning, here, is twofold. First, the discrimination in this case was part of the seniority system itself – the system provided the rules for calculating service credits – rather than being merely reflective of other employment policies or practices.[21] The *system* thus reflects an "intent to discriminate" that was not present in *Teamsters*. Second, section 703(h) does not say that the employer must intend to *illegally* discriminate in structuring its seniority system – only that the employer must have the "intent to discriminate."[22] It thus should not matter whether pregnancy discrimination was unlawful or not when those policies were in place. Either way, one thing is clear: AT&T did intend to discriminate on the basis of pregnancy, which current law does not permit.

The stickier question is whether the early policies resulted from intent to discriminate on the basis of sex (as opposed to pregnancy). The answer to this question turns on how one reads the effect of *Gilbert*. The *Hulteen* majority rules, in essence, that once *Gilbert* was decided, pregnancy discrimination could not be considered a form of sex discrimination at any time prior to the enactment of the PDA in 1978.[23] (Justice Ginsburg disputes this point in her dissent, which is described in greater detail below.) And the majority also concludes that the "intent to discriminate" must have been present at the time when the service credits were determined, rather than in the present day, when the credits were used to calculate pension benefits.[24]

By its own admission, the Court in *Hulteen* has permitted employers to continue implementing a seniority system that penalizes classes of workers that are protected by current law.[25] The result is to add insult to injury for the once-pregnant employees, for whom the consequences of an initial instance of unfair treatment will now reverberate throughout the duration of their retirements.

## JUSTICE GINSBURG'S DISSENTING OPINION: ACKNOWLEDGING THE HARM OF DIFFERENTIAL TREATMENT OF PREGNANT WORKERS

In Justice Ginsburg's dissenting opinion in *Hulteen*, which was joined by Justice Breyer, she disagrees with the majority's crabbed interpretation of the PDA, which would permit the plaintiffs, and others like them, to be penalized in perpetuity for taking pregnancy-based disability leaves earlier in their careers.[26]

While the PDA did not require employers to compensate women for prior disadvantage on the basis of pregnancy, it does "protect women . . . against repetition or continuation of pregnancy-based disadvantageous treatment."[27] Continuing or repeating such treatment, moreover, would violate the PDA's "core command" that disadvantageous treatment on the basis of pregnancy in the employment context "must cease."[28] Justice Ginsburg thus concluded that AT&T had committed a current violation of Title VII by using a pregnancy-based classification to set pension benefits post-PDA.[29]

Justice Ginsburg also thought that it was at least arguable that AT&T's pre-PDA policies were not lawful in the first instance. After all, the EEOC had issued guidelines in 1972 that required employers to treat pregnancy-related disability the same as all other temporary disabilities for all employment-related purposes. In *Gilbert*, the Court ignored these guidelines, as well as the unanimous view of federal appellate courts that pregnancy-based classifications were a form of sex discrimination.[30] The favorable law pre-*Gilbert* and Congress's swift repudiation of the ruling make it at least arguable that AT&T was not entitled even before 1978 to single out pregnancy-based leaves for disadvantageous treatment.[31]

The dissent's reasoning has a key leg up on the majority's: it is developed in context, rather than in a vacuum. Justice Ginsburg interprets the PDA against a long (and in some cases, continuing) history of adverse treatment against pregnant women – treatment that has jeopardized women's workplace equality more broadly. The *Hulteen* plaintiffs each suffered the loss of only a few months of service credits because of their pregnancy leaves. But the denial of those credits is just one example of the innumerable ways in which pregnant women's access to the workplace on equal terms has been – and continues to be – threatened. The adverse treatment of pregnant workers, based often on mistaken assumptions about their capacity to work, has been repeatedly acknowledged by the Supreme Court in prior opinions.[32]

## THE LIKELY EFFECT OF THE *HULTEEN* RULING

The unfair treatment of pregnant workers has consequences. As is explored further in Chapter 36, workplace inequality dooms women to a type of second-class citizenship, which prevents them from capturing the rights and benefits of societal membership. Justice Ginsburg tapped into this concern about equal citizenship in her *Hulteen* dissent, observing that "[c]ertain attitudes about pregnancy and childbirth, throughout human history, have sustained pervasive, often law-sanctioned, restrictions on a woman's place among paid workers and active citizens."[33]

The ruling in *Hulteen* may not have broad-ranging consequences, although it surely will have tangible effects on those women now reaching retirement age who labored in the era before a statutory and constitutional right of sex equality. But it is a mistake to interpret statutes without attention to the purpose for which they were enacted. The PDA is an essential component of protecting women's workplace equality; it should be given its due. The remedy sought in *Hulteen* could be granted without unsettling the expectations of other AT&T employees covered by the same seniority system. They seek only equal benefits going forward, for equal work done in the past. This is not too much to ask.

A version of this chapter appeared on May 26, 2009, at writ.findlaw.com.

# 39

## If She Does Not Win It Is a Shame

Leigh Castergine was the first woman to become a senior vice president in the front office of the Mets, a once-beloved but now-losing Major League Baseball team in New York. She was in charge of ticket sales and was rewarded over the years for innovations and successes to the tune of multiple $50,000 raises and a $125,000 bonus. But she met her glass ceiling when she, an unmarried woman, announced her pregnancy in 2013.

According to the complaint she just filed in federal court, the Mets's chief operating officer, Jeffrey Wilpon, looked none too favorably upon her pregnancy. She alleges that he humiliated and embarrassed her, making no secret of his disdain for her decision to have a baby without being married. And when she complained to human resources about his behavior, she was fired.

This chapter considers the nature of the discrimination alleged in this case and explains why it is part and parcel of a matrix of biases and stereotypes that pregnant women still face in the workplace.

### THE ALLEGATIONS IN CASTERGINE'S COMPLAINT

An Ivy League graduate and former Division 1 student athlete, Castergine had worked her way up from low-wage ticket sales jobs with other clubs to a high-ranking position in the Mets's front office. She specialized in data analytics and pricing strategy, key skills for a team with high costs and a waning fan base. The job was a challenge, given the team's poor performance over many years and what she describes as "a series of public relations blunders that too frequently led to the franchise being ridiculed in the sports pages."[1] Often told her job was like selling "tickets to a funeral" or "deck chairs on the Titanic,"[2] Castergine persevered and was recognized repeatedly and lucratively for excellent work.

When Castergine announced that she was pregnant in September 2013, the whole tenor of her work life changed. Before revealing her pregnancy, Castergine sat in on a meeting where her superiors discussed another woman who had recently given birth. They complained that she "hasn't been the same since she had children" and discussed moving her to a different department.[3]

Upon revealing her pregnancy, Castergine, who had once been profiled in an industry publication and described as "the next female President in the sports industry,"[4] was subjected to a strong of torments by Wilpon, who became "fixated on the idea that Castergine would have a child without being married."[5] (All facts mentioned in this chapter are based on the allegations in Castergine's lawsuit; the defendants have publicly denied them and stated that they are opposed to all forms of discrimination.) He would repeatedly and obviously look at her finger for an engagement ring and told her expressly she would make more in salary and bonuses if only she would get a ring.

Wilpon's alleged comments were often made to or in front of others. He told one colleague he is "old-fashioned" and thinks she "should be married before having a baby."[6] He told another "she is a senior vice president now; people would respect her more if she was married."[7] He announced at a meeting that there were "two rules" regarding her pregnancy: "don't touch her belly and don't ask how she's doing; she's not sick, she's pregnant."[8] He later told her: "I am as morally opposed to putting an e-cigarette sign in my ballpark as I am to Leigh having this baby without being married."[9] Although six other senior executives were present, including the team's general counsel, no one objected to Wilpon's comment.

Castergine complained to her immediate supervisor about Wilpon's comments. He acknowledged the conduct (some of which he had heard in person) but took no action. She alleges Wilpon's treatment of her became more hostile after the complaint, rather than designed to remediate the situation. She later complained to the executive director of human resources, Holly Lindvail, who urged Castergine to quit.

After a difficult pregnancy, Castergine gave birth in March 2014 and returned to work three months later. In July she again approached Lindvail about the hostile environment, and Lindvail again urged her to quit. In August, citing "issues" with "her performance," the Mets fired Castergine. Wilpon claimed she failed to meet her sales goals, but he also shared his belief that "something changed" when she gave birth, and she was no longer "as aggressive as she once had been."[10]

Castergine filed suit alleging violations of the federal FMLA, the New York State antidiscrimination law, and the New York City antidiscrimination law. She alleges interference with her right to take job-protected leave for childbirth, discrimination against her on the basis of pregnancy, and retaliation.

## A CLASSIC CASE OF PREGNANCY DISCRIMINATION: "ANIMUS" AND HOSTILITY TOWARD PREGNANT EMPLOYEES

The hostile response of Castergine's superiors to her pregnancy is not unique. It was exactly this type of animus and bias against pregnant, working women that led

Congress to enact the PDA of 1978.[11] Many state fair employment statutes, including New York's, have done likewise, banning discrimination because of pregnancy, alongside other forms of prohibited discrimination.[12]

While courts have long struggled to determine whether some forms of the unequal treatment of pregnant women are discriminatory (more on that below), Castergine's allegations, if proven true, are precisely the kind that courts have most easily grasped as discriminatory. The different treatment of an employee once she is known to be pregnant, combined with derogatory remarks about her pregnancy, register easily as discriminatory and present the easiest cases for plaintiffs to win.

Stereotypes about pregnant working women are both persistent and pervasive. They result at least in part from a complicated gendered ideology of motherhood and a cultural ambivalence about combining work and motherhood that sometimes translates into more explicit forms of pregnancy bias in the workplace. For example, one study compared the benevolent treatment of pregnant retail customers with the hostile treatment of pregnant retail job applicants, suggesting that the hostility was aroused by the image of a pregnant *worker*, rather than just a pregnant *woman*.[13] Another study found greater hostility to pregnant applicants in more masculine-type jobs.[14] Pregnant workers are routinely subjected to lower ratings of competence and suitability for promotion, held to higher performance standards, and recommended for lower salaries.[15] There is also a well-established wage penalty for working mothers.[16]

In cases decided under the federal PDA, plaintiffs are most successful with claims involving a discernible anti-pregnancy "animus," typically involving explicit statements by decision-makers making derogatory comments about the plaintiff's pregnancy. With this type of fact pattern, courts can't help seeing the employer's negative reaction to the plaintiff's pregnancy, combined with an adverse employment action resulting from it, as a form of pregnancy discrimination. So if the allegations are true, the case is a home run.

## A COMMON CORE OF STEREOTYPING, BUT INCONSISTENT RESULTS

But courts do worse when examining forms of pregnancy discrimination that do not neatly fit this precise paradigm, despite their underlying similarities. While many pregnant women, like Castergine, are punished for becoming pregnant, despite their undiminished ability to do the job, others require some – often modest – accommodation to keep working while pregnant, and seek equal treatment in how the employer treats nonpregnant employees in similar need of accommodations. In this class of cases, courts have done a terrible job of recognizing the unequal treatment of pregnant workers as unlawful discrimination, despite clear language in the PDA directing them to do so and despite the similarity in stereotyping that lies behind the treatment of pregnant workers in both types of cases.

These cases often involve women in much-lower-paying jobs than Castergine, jobs with rigidly structured workdays and no flexibility, where pregnancy requires modest allowances to continue working. In one such case, a pregnant store clerk needed – but was refused – permission to carry a water bottle on her shift, per her doctor's orders.[17] In another, a pregnant stocker sought, but was denied, a shift change to be permitted to stock only lighter-item shelves.[18] The refusal-to-accommodate cases also arise frequently when women hold nontraditional jobs, jobs held predominantly by men and with a history of excluding women, and become pregnant. As seen in Chapters 31–36, police work, firefighting, and construction work are common settings for this class of pregnancy discrimination cases.[19]

In all of these cases, the pregnant worker seeks the kind of accommodation that the employer would have provided to a nonpregnant worker with a limitation that has a similar effect on the employee's ability to work. Sometimes the employer accommodates similarly situated but nonpregnant workers because of the employer's own policy (as in policies granting light-duty work for on-the-job injuries), sometimes because of an agreement with the union, and sometimes because of another legal mandate (as with the Americans with Disabilities Act, which requires reasonable accommodations for a broad range of disabilities, even temporary ones, but has been interpreted not to cover normal pregnancy). But whatever the employer's reason for accommodating the limitations of nonpregnant workers, the PDA specifically directs them to treat pregnant workers no worse than they treat other employees similar in their ability to work. Oddly, courts confronted with an employer's refusal to provide such equal treatment have refused to recognize it as unlawful pregnancy discrimination.

What makes the courts' myopia so stark is not just that the statute clearly prescribes the equal treatment of pregnancy, or even that the cases predominantly involve lower-wage workers and women holding nontraditional jobs – precisely those workers most in need of the protections of the law. Especially anomalous in the courts' very different approaches to the unequal accommodation cases versus the type of discrimination Castergine alleges is that the very same gender stereotyping and gender ideologies underlie both types of discrimination. They should not be seen as occupying opposite ends of the spectrum but as flip sides of the same coin. In both classes of cases, stereotypes about women, work, and maternity are at the heart of the matter.

Recognizing the continuity between overtly pushing women out of their jobs when they become pregnant and accomplishing the same result more subtly by denying pregnant workers the same benefits and treatment afforded nonpregnant workers with similar work capacity, Congress proscribed both forms of discrimination in the PDA. The latter is encapsulated in the PDA's second clause, which requires pregnant workers to be treated "the same . . . as other persons not so affected but similar in their ability or inability to work."[20] As Congress rightly understood, that clause was necessary because denying pregnant workers the same benefits, privileges and accommodations available to other workers with conditions similarly affecting work functioned to push pregnant workers out of the workforce as effectively as more blatant discriminatory exclusions. That such discriminatory policies were justified by "cost" rather than outright animus was of no matter; "cost" predictions themselves for pregnant workers were often tainted by stereotypes predicting that women would eventually leave the workforce or be less competent workers on becoming mothers.

Historically, employer policies that denied accommodations for pregnancy but provided them for other conditions similarly affecting work were based on both descriptive and prescriptive stereotypes. Descriptively, such policies were predicated on stereotypes about pregnant workers as fungible, less valuable, and less deserving of accommodation than nonpregnant workers.[21] Prescriptively, the differential treatment of pregnancy reinforced a judgment that women should not combine work and maternity, or if they do, not at the same level of workplace attachment as the worker held before the pregnancy.[22]

Such stereotypes continue to have force in the differential treatment of pregnant workers today. Scholars who study work and pregnancy have found that pregnant workers' requests for even minor accommodations – accommodations readily available to others with similar work capacity – are often met with outright hostility. They are treated as fungible, not worth the kinds of investments routinely made in other workers.

## CONCLUSION

As is the case with so many of the issues profiled in this book, stereotypes are at the heart of pregnancy discrimination. Courts need to be on the lookout – not only in cases of blatant hostility, such as Castergine's treatment in the Mets's front office, but also in more subtle cases, as well. Her claim should be an easy run around the bases, but other pregnant women, suffering just as much because of society's expectations of pregnant women, may not be so lucky.

A version of this chapter appeared on September 16, 2014, at verdict.justia.com, and was coauthored by Deborah L. Brake.

*Update: In March 2015, Castergine and the Mets released a joint statement that they had agreed to settle the case and dismiss the lawsuit, but the terms of the settlement were not made public.[23] The long-losing Mets, meanwhile, turned things around in dramatic fashion and ended up in the 2015 World Series, where they lost 4-1 to the Kansas City Royals.*

# 40

## Must Employers Who Cover Prescriptions Cover Contraception?

In 2007, the U.S. Court of Appeals for the Eighth Circuit ruled that an employer need not provide insurance coverage for prescription contraceptives, which are only used by women, in order to comply with Title VII's guarantee of sex equality.[1] This ruling directly contravenes a ruling by the EEOC.[2] A significant loss for women, this case showcases the need for federal regulation of contraceptive coverage.

### ACCESS TO CONTRACEPTION AS A WOMEN'S ISSUE

Around the turn of the twenty-first century, most women did not have insurance coverage for birth control. Indeed, studies estimated that two-thirds of large group insurance plans did not provide any coverage for oral contraceptives, the most commonly used reversible method of birth control, and nearly half did not cover any prescription contraceptive drug or device. Many plans do (and did), however, cover surgical sterilization for both men and women.[3]

The class of prescription drugs and devices currently available to prevent pregnancy – birth control pills, Depo Provera, and intrauterine devices, to name the most common ones – are exclusively used by women. Women are, therefore, the ones hurt by the lack of insurance coverage for contraception, poor women most of all. And, obviously, the lack of access to contraception may result in unwanted pregnancy, a consequence that imposes disproportionate and unique burdens on women. It is for these reasons that access to contraception has figured prominently on the agenda for women's rights advocacy during the past decade. Fortunately, that effort has brought about many successes.

## THE EEOC'S VIEW ON CONTRACEPTIVE
## COVERAGE EXCLUSION: IT IS PREGNANCY
## DISCRIMINATION, PLAIN AND SIMPLE

Insurance coverage for contraceptives has remained an important issue on the feminist agenda. The EEOC's decision came after eighteen months of pressure from advocates for women's and workers' rights. In June 1999, a conglomerate of public interest organizations representing those and other interests requested that the EEOC issue a policy guidance taking a position on insurance coverage for contraception. Specifically, the advocates asked that the EEOC declare that an employer's failure to provide insurance coverage for birth control is pregnancy discrimination – and so it did, though through an opinion in an individual case rather than a policy guidance.

In that ruling, the EEOC made clear that it agreed with the public interest organizations that omitting contraceptive coverage from employee insurance is illegal.[4] The EEOC held that an employer's failure to provide insurance coverage for prescription contraceptives was a form of illegal pregnancy discrimination.

How did it reach that result? The starting point is the PDA of 1978, which amended Title VII to say that discrimination on the basis of "pregnancy, childbirth, or related medical conditions," is sex discrimination, and that women so affected are entitled to equal treatment.[5] That promise of equal treatment applies to all aspects of employment including, the Supreme Court held in an early case interpreting the PDA, the doling out of benefits like insurance.[6]

To reach the result it did, the EEOC had to establish two things: first, that a classification based on contraception is a classification based on pregnancy, and, second, that the insurance plans at issue impose unequal (and therefore unlawful) treatment on the basis of pregnancy.

The first of these hurdles is the harder one, in that it requires one to believe that being pregnant and avoiding being pregnant are essentially the same thing. The EEOC made this leap based on the Supreme Court's third PDA case, *International Union, UAW v. Johnson Controls*. There, an employer had only permitted infertile women to hold certain jobs involving lead exposure. The Court held that the PDA prohibits discrimination not only on the basis of pregnancy itself but also on the basis of fertility – that is, a woman's potential for pregnancy.[7]

The EEOC relied on *Johnson Controls* to pull contraception within the PDA. What that decision means, the EEOC reasoned, is that employers cannot discriminate against women who try to control their ability to get pregnant. Because prescription contraception is one way in which women exercise that type of control, the EEOC concluded that excluding contraceptive drugs and devices from insurance coverage is pregnancy discrimination.[8] In other words, when an employer refuses to pay for prescription contraceptives, it draws a pregnancy-based classification. The fact that only women (and generally only fertile woman, who have the potential for pregnancy) use prescription contraceptives is important to the ultimate conclusion that such contraception is pregnancy related.

The second question is whether such a classification is unlawful: Are women without insurance coverage for contraception being denied equal treatment on the basis of pregnancy? To answer that question, the EEOC examined the other insurance benefits offered by those two particular employers, to see whether the plans in question singled out pregnancy for disadvantageous treatment.[9]

The comparison the EEOC drew was between prescription contraceptives, which were excluded from the plans, and other prescription drugs designed to prevent rather than cure disease, which the plans covered. Because the plans covered vaccinations, preventive dental care, and a variety of drugs to prevent the development of certain medical conditions, the EEOC found that women were being denied equal treatment.[10]

## THE EEOC'S RULING AND COURT DECISIONS HAVE RESULTED, IN PRACTICE, IN GREATER INSURANCE COVERAGE FOR CONTRACEPTION

Six months after the EEOC ruled, a federal district court in the State of Washington reached the same conclusion as the EEOC, in the case of *Erickson v. Bartell Drug Co.*, the first court ruling requiring employer-based insurance to cover prescription contraceptives under Title VII.[11] In *Erickson*, the district court noted that "[a]lthough the plan covers almost all drugs and devices used by men, the exclusion of prescription contraceptives creates a gaping hole in the coverage offered to female employees, leaving a fundamental and immediate healthcare need uncovered. . . . Title VII requires employers to recognize the differences between the sexes and provide equally comprehensive coverage, even if that means providing additional benefits to cover women-only expenses."[12]

With the EEOC and *Erickson* rulings in hand, many female employees nationwide were able to convince their employers to voluntarily begin covering contraception in order simply to comply with the law, or else, more pragmatically, to avoid future litigation or liability.[13]

Since *Erickson*, many more district courts have had occasion to consider the contraceptive coverage issue.[14] The results have been roughly split between finding a violation of Title VII and refusing to find one. Then came the Eighth Circuit's ruling – the first federal appellate decision on the issue.

## THE EIGHTH CIRCUIT'S RULING: A SIGNIFICANT LOSS FOR FEMALE EMPLOYEES

The Eighth Circuit case began when Brandi Standridge and Kenya Phillips filed suit challenging their employer's refusal to provide insurance coverage, under the employee health plan, for prescription contraceptives. They represented a class of women employed by Union Pacific Railroad Company, and alleged that the coverage omission constituted illegal sex discrimination under Title VII.[15]

The employees' insurance plan provided coverage for a broad-range of prescription drugs, but excluded coverage for contraceptives when used for the sole purpose of preventing pregnancy. (Oral contraceptives would, for example, be covered if used to regulate menstrual periods or control acne.[16])

At issue was whether Union Pacific's failure to provide insurance coverage for prescription contraceptives violates Title VII, as amended by the PDA. The district court ruled in favor of the employees. Following *Erickson*, it held that the exclusion of all prescription contraceptives violates Title VII because it "treats medical care women need to prevent pregnancy less favorably than it treats medical care needed to prevent other medical conditions that are no greater threat to employees' health than is pregnancy."[17]

The Eighth Circuit reversed, however, and ruled in favor of Union Pacific. With respect to the PDA claim, the court reached two key conclusions. First, it concluded that contraception is not "related" to pregnancy for PDA purposes. It distinguished *Johnson Controls* on the grounds that "fertility" is covered because it involves the potential to become pregnant; contraception and infertility, on the other hand, by definition do not involve such potential. In so reasoning, it relied on an earlier Eighth Circuit ruling, a 1996 case in which the panel held that the PDA does *not* require employers to provide insurance coverage for infertility treatments.[18] Like infertility treatment, the court observed, contraception is only indicated – not required – prior to pregnancy, and thus is not covered by the PDA.[19] Second, the court concluded that because contraception generally is used by both men and women, the decision whether or not to provide insurance coverage is also gender neutral. Employers, the court ruled, are thus free to refuse coverage without implicating Title VII's prohibition on pregnancy discrimination.[20] The Eighth Circuit flatly refused to follow the EEOC ruling on the contraceptive coverage issue. In the court's view, such a ruling need only be followed by courts to the extent it has the "power to persuade." Finding it unpersuasive, the court just disregarded it.[21]

The Eighth Circuit also considered whether Union Pacific's insurance plan constituted sex discrimination. Here, the court considered whether the plan treated men, as a class, better than women, as a class. In concluding that it did not, the court criticized the lower court's decision to compare contraception with other treatments designed to prevent disease. Instead, the court explained, the court should have limited the comparison to the category at hand: contraception.[22]

Because the plan did not cover any contraceptive drug or device, whether used by men or women, the Eighth Circuit concluded, it did not treat one sex more favorably than the other. (It is hard to fathom that this provides any meaningful comparison, because all prescription contraceptives are for female-only use, and insurance doesn't generally provide any coverage for nonprescription drugs or devices, ranging from over-the-counter cough medicine to condoms.)

## INSURANCE COVERAGE FOR PRESCRIPTION CONTRACEPTIVES: THE NEED FOR LEGISLATIVE PROTECTION

From a gender equality standpoint, the Eighth Circuit's ruling in *Union Pacific* is cause for concern. Admittedly, the language of the PDA is ambiguous, but the failure of employers to provide equally comprehensive coverage to male and female employees clearly violates Title VII's ban on sex discrimination.

Moreover, contraceptive inequity is just another unequal burden borne by working women. Women's out-of-pocket health costs already significantly exceed those of men, and the need to pay full price for contraception only exacerbates that gap. Access to contraception is essential for women to be able to exercise control over their ability to become pregnant; that control, in turn, is an essential aspect of gender equality.

The uneven results achieved in litigation thus far, and the ambiguous language of the PDA, make it important for advocates – while perhaps also continuing to battle on in the courts – to pursue other avenues to secure contraceptive equity. Indeed, perhaps the most significant activity surrounding the issue of contraceptive insurance coverage in the last decade has been going on outside of courtrooms, and in state legislatures.

Since 1998, for example, more than half the states have adopted laws mandating that insurers include coverage for prescription contraceptives if they cover other prescription drugs.[23] Also in 1998, Congress voted to provide contraceptive coverage to federal employees; it has renewed that coverage every year since.[24]

These state laws have made a significant difference in the number of women who have access to coverage for prescription contraceptives, but their force is limited in two respects. First, under a federal law, ERISA, employers who self-insure are exempt from state-mandated benefits laws. Many large corporations provide insurance benefits in this way, leaving as many as half of all employees outside the protection of state-level laws – though potentially within the scope of new federal ones that could be enacted.[25] Second, these state laws apply only to group-based health plans, so people who purchase individual health insurance policies are not protected.

Even with these limitations, the protection provided by these laws is a big improvement over the pre-1998 landscape. Still, with some states providing no mandate, and others' having their mandate undermined by ERISA, there is a genuine need for Congress to pass a statute guaranteeing women's access to contraception.

A committed group of federal legislators has tried, so far unsuccessfully, to bring that about. The Equity in Prescription Insurance and Contraceptive Coverage Act (EPICC) has been introduced in every Congress since 1997. Most recently, it was introduced in both the House and Senate in early 2007, as part of a broader bill to expand access to preventive health care services. If enacted into law, EPICC would require employer-based health insurance plans to provide coverage for prescription contraceptives. The current versions of the bill are pending before committees in both branches of Congress.[26]

Rulings like the Eighth Circuit's in *Union Pacific*, combined with the uneven protection available under state law, make the need for federal regulation more acute. If women cannot rely on courts to enforce Title VII's broad mandate for sex equality, federal regulation is needed to provide complementary protection via targeted federal statutes.

A version of this chapter appeared on April 17, 2007, at writ.findlaw.com.

*Update: The availability of insurance coverage for contraceptives has changed dramatically in the past several years. By 2010, nine in ten employer-provided insurance plans covered prescription contraceptives, compared with only three in ten a decade earlier. Most importantly, regulations under the Affordable Care Act (Obamacare) now require health insurance plans to provide FDA-approved contraception methods and contraceptive counseling at no cost to patients.[27] The scope of the religious exemption contained in these regulations is the subject of ongoing litigation and controversy, including a decision from the Supreme Court in* Burwell v. Hobby Lobby Stores, Inc., *which allowed a for-profit, closely held corporation to claim a religious exemption to the contraceptive mandate based on the religious beliefs of the owners.[28] Although the Hobby Lobby decision is the subject of significant and piercing criticism, its reach seems to be expanding rather than contracting. The Supreme Court agreed to review another case on the scope of the religious exemption during its October 2015 term.[29]*

# 41

# Fertile Ground for Discrimination

The United States Court of Appeals for the Second Circuit recently issued an important decision on federal antidiscrimination law in *Saks v. Franklin Covey Co.* There, it held that an employer can deny insurance coverage for infertility procedures done only to women. Doing so, according to the court, constitutes neither pregnancy nor sex discrimination. While the opinion has some persuasive qualities, there is a strong argument to be made that the wrong result was reached.[1] The decision is the first appellate ruling on an issue that has been brewing in lower courts, and it is likely to have an unfortunate effect.

Because infertility treatments are costly, and insurance coverage is spotty, many women already find themselves pushing employers to include fertility benefits in their insurance plans. Others find themselves fired owing to absences or sickness related to fertility treatments.

Infertility treatment should be addressed, under the law and insurance plans, in the same way pregnancy-related expenses are now treated. In addition, infertility-treatment-related absences and sick leaves should be treated in the same way as pregnancy-related absences and sick leaves. It only makes sense: for many couples, infertility treatment is a necessary step on the road to pregnancy.

## THE FACTS OF THE CASE

For four years, Rochelle Saks worked as a store manager for Franklin Covey. During her tenure there, she unsuccessfully tried to conceive a child with her husband. Over the course of several years, she underwent progressively more invasive fertility treatments – including intrauterine inseminations, oral and injectable fertility drugs, hormone injections, and in vitro fertilization (IVF). She became pregnant twice using these methods, but she miscarried both times.[2]

Saks sought reimbursement for these costly procedures through her employee health plan. The plan guaranteed coverage for "medically necessary" procedures –

those required "for the diagnosis or treatment of an active illness or injury." Pregnancy was considered an "active illness" under the plan.[3] The plan covered some infertility products, including ovulation kits, oral fertility drugs, and even penile implants. It also covered surgery to correct conditions causing infertility, such as endometriosis or tubal blockages. But it expressly excluded much more expensive "surgical impregnation procedures," such as artificial insemination, IVF, and two other procedures known as GIFT and ZIFT. Accordingly, the plan denied Saks reimbursement for all but a few of her expenses.[4]

## INFERTILITY: MOST SOLUTIONS ARE VERY COSTLY AND OFTEN UNREIMBURSED

Up to 6 million Americans are "infertile," a label assigned after a couple engages in unprotected intercourse for one year without achieving pregnancy. About 40 percent of the time, the cause of infertility is attributable to a male factor, 40 percent to a female factor, and 20 percent to a "couple factor" (such as an incompatibility between the male and female) or to some unknown factor.[5] Only half of those who are infertile seek treatment, and cost is a significant factor for those who forgo it. That's not surprising, for the cost of fertility treatments is staggering. For instance, a single round of IVF can cost up to $12,000, and the procedure may have to be repeated several times before pregnancy is achieved.[6]

Insurance coverage for infertility varies tremendously. According to a 1996 survey, about 40 percent of large employers covered some form of advanced fertility treatment, like IVF. But only 19 percent of HMOs paid for IVF, and some large insurance plans have stopped covering such treatments in recent years because of the cost and increasing demand.[7]

About a quarter of the states require health plans to provide coverage for at least some fertility treatments. New York, for example, requires insurers to cover infertility drug treatments, as long as they cover prescription drugs generally, and surgeries or treatments designed to correct a problem creating infertility. But it does not require coverage of the more expensive procedures like IVF.[8]

Mandated benefit laws, like New York's, are of limited usefulness, however. As discussed in Chapter 40, ERISA, a federal law governing employee pensions and benefits,[9] preempts mandated benefit laws with respect to companies that operate a self-insured health plan.[10] For example, Franklin Covey, Rochelle Saks's employer, was located in New York and thus might have been subject to the states mandatory coverage laws. But because it operated a self-insured plan, it was probably exempt. That left Saks with only one option: to challenge the plan's exclusion, not under state mandatory benefit statutes, but rather under antidiscrimination law.

## SAKS'S FIRST LEGAL THEORY: PREGNANCY DISCRIMINATION

First, Saks argued that the plan's failure to reimburse her for all her fertility expenses violates the PDA.[11] As with challenges to the exclusion of prescription contraceptives, the issue is whether an employer can omit infertility benefits while offering an otherwise comprehensive insurance plan. Specifically, does infertility qualify as a "pregnancy, childbirth, or a related medical condition," because it relates to women's intention or potential to become pregnant? Case law affords some guidance on this point.

Most important, case law, as discussed in Chapter 40, has established that pregnancy discrimination can precede conception and be asserted by a plaintiff who is not pregnant and, indeed, who is trying *not* to become pregnant. Thus, it is far too late in the day to claim, for example, that only pregnant women can invoke the protections of the PDA.

The idea of the PDA, then, is not to give special rights to pregnant women. It is to ensure that women's capacity to bear children, and their choice whether or not to do so, do not subject them to unfair discrimination in the workplace. On this theory, the PDA should extend to infertility, as well. If a woman is fired, or denied insurance coverage, because pregnancy, in her case, requires infertility treatments, then she has suffered pregnancy discrimination within the meaning of the PDA.

Unfortunately, the *Saks* court concluded otherwise. The PDA only reaches pregnancy discrimination as a form of sex discrimination, it pointed out, and both sexes suffer from infertility, in roughly equal proportion. (Pregnancy, in contrast, affects only women.) Thus discrimination on the basis of infertility, the court held, does not constitute unlawful pregnancy discrimination.[12]

The *Saks* court's ruling on this point is in some tension with the Supreme Court's ruling in *UAW v. Johnson Controls*.[13] That case said it is pregnancy discrimination to impose an employment rule that turns on a woman's childbearing capacity. But Saks's insurance plan does that: it excludes coverage to some women based on their childbearing capacity. Under *Johnson Controls*, that is arguably a form of pregnancy discrimination.

## SAKS'S SECOND LEGAL THEORY: SEX DISCRIMINATION

Second, Saks argued that her insurance plan's exclusion of surgical impregnation procedures constituted sex discrimination pure and simple – prohibited not only by the PDA's logic, under which pregnancy discrimination is a kind of sex discrimination but also by Title VII, which prohibits sex discrimination in itself.[14] Such procedures, Saks pointed out, are performed only on women. And similar procedures on men – for instance, surgery to remove a blockage in the vas deferens, which is the conduit for sperm – were covered under the plan.[15]

Again the court ruled against Saks. It reasoned that surgical impregnation was equally likely to be a remedy for either male or female infertility, and thus both sexes were "equally disadvantaged" by the exclusion.[16] The court ignored the fact, however, that the surgical impregnation procedures are *performed* only on women, whatever their cause may be. And that means that men, under a plan like Saks's, are covered for every single medical or surgical infertility treatment performed on them, and women are not. That is plainly sex discrimination.

A version of this chapter appeared on January 28, 2003, at writ.verdict.com.

# 42

## Can a Woman Be Fired for Absenteeism Related to Fertility Treatments?

Like many other women, Cheryl Hall was afflicted with infertility. After taking one leave from work, and requesting a second, to undergo IVF, she was fired. Does Title VII prohibit an employer from firing an employee under these circumstances? In a recent ruling, Hall v. Nalco, the U.S. Court of Appeals for the Seventh Circuit said yes.[1]

### CONFLICTS BETWEEN REPRODUCTION (INCLUDING INFERTILITY TREATMENT) AND WORK

As many previous chapters have shown, pregnant women sometimes face challenges at work, whether posed by environmental conditions, like chemicals, radiation, or infectious disease; by physical movements that can be difficult to perform, like standing for long periods of time, stooping over, climbing stairs or ladders, or lifting heavy objects; or, finally, by job conditions, like irregular hours, shift work, or psychological stress. For some women, the potential conflicts between reproduction and work start even earlier – while they attempt to become pregnant. For those who struggle with infertility, balancing work with the often invasive and time-consuming procedures used to try and achieve pregnancy can be a significant challenge. For instance, IVF, an increasingly common procedure, requires a difficult series of procedures and injections that will require most, if not all, women to take time off from work. Many will also suffer side effects from IVF drugs or the procedures that may interfere with a woman's full working capacity.

### WHAT PROTECTION DO WOMEN HAVE WHEN REPRODUCTION CONFLICTS WITH WORK?

The PDA is the primary source of protection against discrimination on the basis of reproductive capacity. But its application to infertility treatments, as demonstrated in

Chapter 41, has been uncertain. The question in *Hall*, a matter of first impression in the Seventh Circuit, was this: Does infertility qualify as a "related medical condition" because it relates to women's intention or potential to become pregnant?

Cheryl Hall, the plaintiff in the recent case that came before the Seventh Circuit, did require leave from work while undergoing in vitro fertilization. Although her case had not yet reached a factfinder when it was appealed, the parties agreed that Hall took a monthlong leave of absence in March 2003. She did not become pregnant through that round of IVF and requested a second leave of absence in August 2003. Before she was scheduled to begin the second leave, however, her supervisor informed her that the company was reorganizing and retaining only one of the two people with her title, and she was terminated.[2]

Hall filed a charge with the EEOC, alleging that she was fired because she took leave to undergo fertility treatments, and that this was in violation of the PDA. She alleges that her supervisor told another supervisor Hall had "missed a lot of work due to health" and wrote "absenteeism – infertility treatments" on her performance review. She also noted that the employee who kept the remaining position of the original two was a woman who is incapable of having children.[3] The district court granted summary judgment to Hall's employer on the ground that "infertile women" are not a protected class under Title VII. Because both men and women can experience infertility, the court reasoned, it is a gender-neutral condition. However, as the Seventh Circuit explained on appeal, this reasoning does not comport with case law interpreting the PDA.[4]

Hall's case was helped by the *Johnson Controls* ruling, in which the Supreme Court held that it violates the PDA to deny women certain jobs (there, jobs with lead exposure) simply because they are fertile and because the working conditions might pose risk to a fetus later conceived.[5]

As courts have made clear, the PDA grants no special rights to pregnant women. Rather, it exists to ensure that women's capacity to bear children and their choice whether or not to do so do not subject them to unfair discrimination in the workplace.

## IS IT DISCRIMINATION FOR EMPLOYERS TO PUNISH TIME OFF FOR INFERTILITY TREATMENT WHEN BOTH MEN AND WOMEN CAN EXPERIENCE INFERTILITY?

There's a second issue, however, which is trickier. If both men and women can experience infertility, is it "pregnancy discrimination" to fire a woman because she takes time off to treat it?

Here, again, *Johnson Controls* is instructive. The opinion said that the employer's rule violated the PDA because it was not based on "fertility alone," but rather was based on "gender and childbearing capacity."[6] The argument to be made in Hall's case is that only women will undergo assisted reproductive procedures to become pregnant. The Seventh Circuit thus concluded that Hall, if her allegations are true, "was terminated not for the gender-neutral condition of infertility, but rather for the gender-specific quality of childbearing capacity."[7]

This ruling is in some tension with the Second Circuit's ruling in *Saks v. Franklin Covey Co.*, discussed in Chapter 41, which held that discrimination on the basis of infertility does not constitute unlawful pregnancy discrimination.[8] But perhaps the proper way to understand the difference between the two cases is in terms of status versus effects – the PDA does not require that employers accommodate reproductive need, but it does not allow them to punish people simply for engaging in the reproductive process.

To the extent the rulings are in tension, the appellate court in *Hall* has the better of the argument, however, and the few lower courts to consider the precise issue have ruled similarly. As one of those courts explained, "It makes sense to conclude that the PDA was intended to cover a woman's intention or potential to become pregnant, because all that conclusion means is that discrimination against persons who intend to or can potentially become pregnant is discrimination against women, which is the kind of truism the PDA wrote into law."[9]

## WILL CHERYL HALL WIN ON REMAND?

While Hall won this round of her case, obtaining the important appellate ruling that fertility-treatment discrimination can be a form of pregnancy discrimination under the PDA, she still has obstacles to surmount. The grant of summary judgment to her employer was reversed, but now she must proceed to trial.

Let's assume for a moment that Hall's employer did just as she alleged – that is, it fired her for absenteeism related to infertility treatments. Is that an unlawful form of discrimination? It depends. If her employer fired her because it bore animosity or hostility against women because of their pregnancy status (including those actual pregnancy, potential pregnancy, or inability to achieve pregnancy), then the termination would certainly constitute unlawful discrimination.

But if her employer did not seek to penalize her because of her potential pregnancy and simply disliked her absenteeism, what then? Under the PDA, women have no absolute right to accommodations for disability related to pregnancy or childbirth. Her employer could fire her for absenteeism, even if the cause was her fertility treatments, as long as it would have fired a man under comparable circumstances. She would then be no better off than the plaintiff in *Troupe*, discussed in the introduction to Part III. Hall's ultimate burden will be thus to prove that they singled her out for adverse treatment because of her fertility treatment, or to allege and prove that a strict absenteeism policy has a disparate impact on pregnant or potentially pregnant women.

Regardless of whether Cheryl Hall is able to prove liability at trial, this appellate ruling vindicates an important right of gender equality. It is also an important reminder that the burden of juggling reproduction and work falls almost exclusively on women. The law should do more to accommodate that reality, but the Seventh Circuit's ruling is at least one step in the right direction.

A version of this chapter appeared on August 19, 2008, at writ.findlaw.com.

# 43

## Is Lactation Related to Pregnancy?

A prominent contributor to Rick Santorum's 2012 presidential campaign startled audiences by suggesting that Bayer aspirin could be used as a reliable method of contraception. The contributor, Foster Friess, in an interview with MSNBC host Andrea Mitchell, insisted that "back in [his] day," aspirin was a surefire way to prevent pregnancy.[1]

How exactly would that work? Friess explained, "The gals put it between their knees." In other words, aspirin-clenching knees would prevent conception by preventing sex. An added bonus: this aspirin method of contraception, claimed Friess, "wasn't that costly."[2] Friess was, of course, joking, although I doubt that many women were laughing. But the recent fight over the scope of the religious exemption to the provision of the federal health care reform law – which requires comprehensive insurance plans to provide coverage for prescription contraceptives at no cost to the user – is no joke. It's a dead serious, highly contested issue.

The new federal law mandates that insurance plans must cover prescription contraceptives at no cost to the women who use them.[3] The mandate resulted from a report by the Institute of Medicine finding that access to contraception is essential to women's health, and that contraception is insufficiently accessible to many women.[4]

Beginning in August 2012, contraception will be one of several preventive health services that must be included in health insurance plans, at no cost to the user. The Catholic Church strenuously objects to the mandate, and has been locked in a bitter battle with the Obama administration over the scope of the religious exemption. The exemption, as embodied in a final ruling of the Department of Health and Human Services in December 2011, was narrow – applying only to churches and other houses of worship.[5] However, the Obama administration backtracked a bit after a furious backlash ensued. The administration has now agreed to a compromise that will guarantee employees of religiously affiliated organizations (such as certain hospitals and universities) access to prescription contraceptives at no cost, but will also ensure that the insurance company, rather than the employer, foots the bill.

Putting the religious issues aside, though, this controversy about the federal mandate for contraceptive coverage is merely the latest battle in a long-running war – variously involving employers, employees, insurance companies, state governments, and the federal government – about whether women, alone, should bear all the consequences, costs, and hardships of reproduction.

One focal point of this debate has been the courts, which have been asked repeatedly to decide whether employers' failure to provide insurance coverage for prescription contraceptives constitutes either sex discrimination or pregnancy discrimination.

Now the very same legal issue is at the core of a recent ruling by a federal judge in *EEOC v. Houston Funding II, Ltd.*, that lactation discrimination is not actionable under Title VII or the PDA because lactation, the judge reasoned, is not related to pregnancy.[6] This case, like those involving contraceptive coverage and infertility discrimination, raise important questions about how far the law goes – and should go – to protect women against reproductive discrimination.

## LACTATION DISCRIMINATION IN EMPLOYMENT: A FEDERAL JUDGE HOLDS THAT SUCH A CLAIM IS NOT ACTIONABLE AS EITHER PREGNANCY OR SEX DISCRIMINATION

The plaintiff in the lactation-discrimination case was Donnicia Venters. Venters was hired by Houston Funding in 2006. Two years later, on December 1, 2008, she took a leave of absence to give birth. The company had no maternity leave policy and was too small to be covered by the FMLA, which guarantees up to twelve weeks of unpaid leave for a variety of reasons, including childbirth and newborn parenting, for employees of companies with at least fifty employees.[7]

Venters gave birth on December 11. A few days later, she spoke with the company's vice president, Henry Cagle, who asked her when she planned to return to work. She said that she did not know, and that she was waiting for her doctor to advise her on that subject. During January and early February 2009, Venters communicated regularly with people at her office, including team leaders, and continued to pay her insurance premium. She never provided an exact return date, but she repeatedly expressed her desire to return soon.[8]

During a meeting held on February 10, a group of employees, including Cagle, met and together decided to fire Venters. A few days later, Venters's doctor advised her that she could return to work. On February 16, Venters left a message informing Cagle that she had been cleared to work. The next day, February 17, Venters called again; told Cagle she was ready to return to work; and asked if she could use a back room to pump breast milk. Cagle informed her that they had replaced her because they had not heard from her about firm plans to return to work. Only then did the company send her a letter firing her – purportedly for job abandonment. Venters received that letter – which was dated February 16, the day before Venters had asked to be able to pump breast milk in a back room at work – on February 26.[9]

The EEOC sued Venters's employer on her behalf. It claimed that the company had fired Venters because she wanted to pump breast milk at work. However, the federal district judge who heard Venters's case ruled that even if Venters was right that the company had, indeed, fired her because of her request to pump breast milk, firing her for that reason was not a legally actionable form of discrimination.[10]

"The law," the judge wrote, "does not punish lactation discrimination." Lactation discrimination is not pregnancy discrimination, according to the judge, because it is not "pregnancy, childbirth, or a related medical condition" under the PDA.[11]

The EEOC also contended, on Venters's behalf, that to fire Venters had constituted sex discrimination. But the judge deemed that argument worthy of but one single, conclusory sentence: "Firing someone because of lactation or breast-pumping is not sex discrimination."[12]

## LACTATION IS, OF COURSE, A CONDITION RELATED TO PREGNANCY AND CHILDBIRTH – AND COURTS SHOULD SO HOLD

The cases dealing with contraception, infertility treatment, and lactation all raise the same question: What is the intended scope of the phrase "related medical condition" in the first clause of the PDA? Or, to ask the same thing a slightly different way, can an employee be fired because of her childbearing capacity? Work-related conflicts with reproduction do not neatly coincide to the nine months of pregnancy; rather, they stretch to the outer edges, including both pre-conception and postpartum periods.

Venters alleged not that she was refused time or space to pump breast milk, but that she was *fired* for even asking to pump breast milk at work. The judge in that case rejected her pregnancy discrimination claim, offering the following reasoning:[13]

> Discrimination because of pregnancy, childbirth, or a related medical condition is illegal. Related conditions may include cramping, dizziness, and nausea while pregnant. Even if the company's claim that [Venters] was fired for abandonment is meant to hide the real reason – she wanted to pump breast milk – lactation is not pregnancy, childbirth, or a related medical condition. She gave birth on December 11, 2009. After that day, she was no longer pregnant and her pregnancy-related conditions ended.[14]

This reasoning is preposterous from virtually any perspective.

Scientifically, of course, it would be ridiculous to argue that lactation is not a "related medical condition" regarding pregnancy or childbirth, because the production of milk is an involuntary, physiological response to giving birth. No childbirth, no lactation.

Logically, as well, the reasoning can't be followed, because it would mean that a woman who suffers any number of childbirth-related complications is not protected by the PDA if those complications happened to occur after, rather than before, the birth.

Legally, too, the judge's reasoning is absurd. It violates both the text and spirit of the PDA. The PDA was enacted to strike at the broad spectrum of employer policies and practices designed to keep women of reproductive age out of the workplace. It was enacted to stop employers from reacting on impulse and stereotype about the capabilities and talents of pregnant women and to force them to assess women as individuals. As written, the PDA prohibits employers from subjecting women to any employment decision because of pregnancy, childbirth, or related medical conditions. Firing a new mother because she seeks to breastfeed is exactly the type of discrimination the PDA was intended to eradicate. If employers could legally fire employees for lactating, that would be an easy way to rid the workplace of many of its women. Moreover, singling out employees for adverse treatment, based on a characteristic that afflicts only one members of one sex, is sex discrimination, plain and simple. Only women give birth, and only women lactate.

Note, in this case, that the plaintiff, Venters, did not request any time off or change in her duties to accommodate her desire to pump milk. The PDA, particularly as interpreted by federal courts, is quite stingy regarding the right to insist on workplace accommodations for pregnancy, childbirth, or related medical conditions. As discussed in earlier chapters, employers need only accommodate such needs if they offer accommodation for other temporarily disabled employees. Venters's employer may well, thus, have been able lawfully to refuse her request.[15]

But Venters, the plaintiff in Houston Funding, was simply asking not to be fired after revealing that she planned to breastfeed (and pump milk) after returning to work. She deserved the chance to prove that her employer had fired her for just that reason – and thus to vindicate her right against this form of discrimination. Health care reform may resolve the important and long-standing problem with contraceptive access in this country, but even though this important battle has been mostly won, we must not forget about other aspects of the reproductive process that still leave women especially vulnerable in the workplace.

## CONCLUSION

Importantly, each of these issues – access to prescription contraceptives, treatment for female infertility, pregnancy, childbirth, and lactation – is unique to women. Thus, the way an employer deals with any of these issues can raise the specter not only of pregnancy discrimination but also of sex discrimination.

In an ideal world, the workplace would be structured to accommodate reproduction, as it is an essential aspect of human life. But historically, most workplaces were designed with male workers in mind, and the evolution of a more inclusive and accommodating structure has been slow. Law has played an integral – though, disappointingly, not yet sufficient – role in protecting women as they try to navigate the many potential conflicts between reproduction and work.

A version of this chapter appeared on February 21, 2012, at verdict.justia.com.

*Update: The district court's ruling in EEOC v. Houston Funding, was reversed on appeal by the Fifth Circuit.[16] In a brief opinion, the court wrote that "lactation is a related medical condition of pregnancy for purposes of the PDA. Lactation is the physiological process of secreting milk from mammary glands and is directly caused by hormonal changes associated with pregnancy and childbirth." Judge Edith Jones concurred, but wrote separately to emphasize that Venters could not have prevailed if her complaint was that she was denied "special facilities or down time during work to pump or 'express' breast milk."[17]" As with contraceptive coverage, lactation discrimination has been affected by the Affordable Care Act. The act requires hourly workers to be provided regular breaks and a space other than a restroom to express breastmilk.[18]*

# 44

# A Victory for Families, but Hardly a Panacea

In *Hibbs v. Department of Human Resources*, the Supreme Court upheld the FMLA as constitutional when applied to the states. Among other things, that means that sufficiently large employers must grant twelve weeks of unpaid maternity and paternity leave per year.[1]

The decision is important, and ironic, for several reasons. For one thing, surprisingly, it was a pro-federal power decision authored by Chief Justice Rehnquist – a committed conservative with a history of upholding states' rights against the exercise of federal power. For another thing, from a civil rights perspective, the decision may offer little tangible benefit, and even take away more than it gives.

At the same time that Rehnquist's majority opinion validates the FMLA's exercise of federal power, the decision cements the Court's recent efforts to hamstring Congress in other ways. For instance, the decision reiterates that Congress cannot define the substantive equality guarantees of the Fourteenth Amendment. In addition, it operates under the assumption that Congress cannot enact substantive entitlements pursuant to its powers under Section 5 of the Fourteenth Amendment.[2] While the Court's conservative block had laid the groundwork for this in recent cases involving Eleventh Amendment challenges to other federal civil rights statutes intended to apply to the states (which the Court did not ultimately allow), *Hibbs* gave Justice Rehnquist the opportunity to reinforce and apply that precedent while appearing to promote civil rights.

Thus, while approving this relatively narrow civil rights law, the Court preserved its ability to strike down other, broader acts, at least to the extent they are applied to the states.

## MR. HIBBS GOES TO WASHINGTON

Mr. Hibbs, the plaintiff, was an employee in the Welfare Division of the Nevada Department of Human Resources, a unit of Nevada's state government. He sought unpaid leave from his job to care for his ailing wife. Nevada granted him the leave under FMLA, as well as under a "catastrophic leave" policy, but later fired him anyway. (The parties disputed, among other points, whether the two kinds of leave should be concurrent or consecutive.[3]) Hibbs sued under the FMLA, but Nevada argued for dismissal because of the sovereign immunity provided by the Eleventh Amendment. The trial court agreed with Nevada, but the U.S. Court of Appeals for the Ninth Circuit agreed with Hibbs.[4] Meanwhile, seven other federal appellate courts had also held that sovereign immunity had been abrogated, but only one case involved the same provision of the FMLA.[5]

## THE FMLA, THE ELEVENTH AMENDMENT, AND THE SUPREME COURT'S BOTTOM LINE

The FMLA – a federal statute enacted in 1993 – requires employers with more than fifty employees to give employees twelve weeks of unpaid leave when that leave is necessitated by an employee's serious illness, by birth or adoption of a child, or by the serious illness of a close family member.[6] At the end of the leave period, the employee must be reinstated. If the employer does not comply, the employee may be able to sue for damages. Thus, in the *Hibbs* case itself, William Hibbs invoked the FMLA to sue his employer, the State of Nevada, for allegedly refusing to reinstate him after he took time off to care for his sick wife.

The State of Nevada argued that the Eleventh Amendment meant Hibbs's suit had to be dismissed. That amendment prohibits Congress from making states amenable to suits for money damages, unless it both has the power to abrogate their sovereign immunity and clearly does so.[7] "Sovereign immunity" is a concept imported to America from English law, under which the king could not be sued. In the United States, however, the "sovereigns" are the people, and the question is whether the governments that represent them can be sued. The Court has held that sovereign immunity is the default rule – meaning that states have it until Congress can and does take it away. In *Hibbs*, the Court said that Congress could, and did, abrogate state immunity under the FMLA. Now that these issues have been resolved in Hibbs's favor, the case can proceed forward in the court below.[8]

## THE BASIS CONGRESS CLAIMED FOR AGGREGATING SOVEREIGN IMMUNITY

It was quite obvious in the *Hibbs* case that Congress was unmistakably trying to take away states' sovereign immunity with respect to FMLA claims and to allow them to be sued. After all, a provision of the FMLA states specifically that states and their subdivisions are bound by it.

That left only one question: Did Congress have the power to take away their immunity? To answer this question, in accord with its prior precedents, the Court looked to the constitutional provision that was the source for Congress's power to enact the FMLA.

In this case, it didn't have to look far. The legislative history of the FMLA contains plain statements that Congress was drawing on its power under Section 5 of the Fourteenth Amendment, as well as its power under the Commerce Clause. Section 5 authorizes Congress to "enforce" the Constitution's guarantee of equal protection with "appropriate legislation." This provision, the Court has held in the past, gives Congress the authority to abrogate Eleventh Amendment immunity, provided it exercises that power in an appropriate way. (In contrast, the Court has refused to allow Congress to abrogate immunity when it acts pursuant to the Commerce Clause or the Spending Clause.[9])

## THE COURT'S HOLDING THAT CONGRESS WAS, INDEED, EXERCISING SECTION 5 POWER

That leads to another question: Congress said it was acting under Section 5, but was its action valid? The Court has said that Section 5 allows Congress to enact statutes prohibiting unconstitutional behavior by the states. But in this case, the Constitution did not guarantee twelve weeks' leave in particular, as the FMLA does, so simply denying that period of leave was not inherently unconstitutional. In addition, it might not be unconstitutional for a workplace to give greater maternity leave than paternity leave, because mothers are still recovering from pregnancy, and fathers, obviously, are not. But the FMLA gives both sexes twelve weeks equally.[10]

Fortunately for Hibbs, however, the Court had also said that Section 5 empowers Congress to enact statutes that prohibit constitutional behavior – such as, here, denying twelve weeks of leave – to the extent necessary to prevent and deter unconstitutional conduct. To do so, however, Congress must both act based on a history of constitutional violations and design a remedy that is both proportional and congruent to the identified injury. Put simply, Congress must be acting to remedy *actual, past* constitutional violations by the states.[11]

In *Hibbs*, the Court both found the required constitutional violations and approved Congress's remedy for them. Specifically, the *Hibbs* opinion found that states had long committed acts of sex discrimination against female employees, often based on "pervasive sex-role stereotype that caring for family members is women's work." In addition, it found that the FMLA was enacted to promote sex equality by responding to that discrimination.[12]

## A HISTORY OF SEX DISCRIMINATION WHEN IT COMES TO WORKING WOMEN

The Supreme Court's solicitude in *Hibbs* for Congress's findings regarding the history of state-sponsored sex discrimination is heartening. As the Court recognized, there was copious evidence to support these findings.

For the better part of the twentieth century, states enacted and maintained laws designed to limit the rights of working women. Illinois refused to permit women to act as lawyers.[13] Michigan refused to allow women to tend bar.[14] Oregon limited the number of hours women could do wage-earning work.[15] Florida encouraged women to avoid jury service on the theory that it would interfere with their duties as mothers.[16] Repeatedly, when women tried to seek relief from the U.S. Supreme Court, it turned them away, making the Court's own recognition of this discrimination all the more significant as an implicit repudiation of past judicial mistakes.

Even today, Congress found evidence that states continue to rely on outmoded gender stereotypes in the workplace. And these stereotypes were particularly strong with respect to the administration of caregiving and parental leave. States, the record showed, like private sector employers, tend to offer maternity leave but not paternity leave. Or even worse, they offered no leave at all. Either way, they furthered the stereotype of women as primarily responsible for family caregiving needs, parental or otherwise. Denying paternity leave but allowing maternity leave (beyond any actual period of disability associated with childbirth) assumes that men are not interested in child care, and places the whole burden on women. Meanwhile, offering no leave at all tends to force women to quit in order to become full- or part-time caretakers. In either case, women become less attractive to employers because they are likely to cost more and stay for less time.

Currently, the Supreme Court applies a "heightened scrutiny" standard for gender-based classifications.[17] Under that standard, these state-enacted laws and state-administered policies, like their predecessors from earlier in the century, would be struck down as violations of the Equal Protection Clause.

Accordingly, this evidence solidly established a history (past and present) of unconstitutional, discriminatory policies. This was the history that Congress relied on in enacting the FMLA. Given this history, and the limited scope of Congress's response to it, the Court concluded that the FMLA – as a remedy for constitutional injury – was both congruent and proportional.[18]

The FMLA entitles both mothers and fathers to leave for caregiving, on the same terms. In so doing, it should eliminate any disincentive for employers to hire women. In addition, it should encourage fathers to become more involved in caregiving. More broadly, through these measures, the FMLA seeks to promote equality between women and men as workers, and between women and men as parents. By equalizing leave for both sexes, the Court said, it "attacks the formerly state-sanctioned stereotype that only women are responsible for family caregiving." In addition, it targets the "fault line between work and family," where "sex-based generalization has been and remains strongest."[19]

## CONCLUSION

While it is a victory for sex equality that the FMLA was upheld, it is a relatively small victory, in practical terms. As taken up in Chapter 45, the FMLA has fallen short of its promise in many ways.

A version of this chapter appeared on June 3, 2003, at writ.findlaw.com.

*Update: In a later case,* Coleman v. Ct. of Appeals, *the Supreme Court held that Congress had not successfully abrogated sovereign immunity for purposes of suits brought under FMLA's self-care provision.*[20] *Justice Ginsburg dissented, arguing, among other things, that the gender-neutral, self-care provision also combats the history of sex discrimination in the workplace by accommodating women's need for leave during pregnancy and for childbirth without singling them out as workers in need of special treatment. "It would make scant sense," she argued, "to provide job-protected leave for a woman to care for a newborn, but not for her recovery from delivery, a miscarriage, or the birth of a stillborn baby. And allowing States to provide no pregnancy-disability leave at all, given that only women can become pregnant, would obviously 'exclude far more women from the workplace.'"*[21] *In a somewhat surprising, but long overdue, turn of events, paid leave has become a key issue in the 2016 presidential campaign.*[22]

# 45

# A Small Step in the Right Direction

## The Family and Medical Leave Act at Twenty

Twenty years ago, Congress passed the FMLA,[1] the first federal law to guarantee (some) workers unpaid leave when they are forced to take time off to care for themselves or close relatives when seriously ill, or to care for a newly born or adopted child. The bill that ultimately became law had been fought over for eight years and, during that time, had suffered a series of withering cuts until it was anemic enough to gain majority support in Congress.[2]

The FMLA added important protections for eligible employees, but it fell short of its aspiration to force employers to provide at least minimal accommodations for workers' caretaking obligations and serious illnesses. Many workers are not eligible for FMLA leave, and those who are often cannot afford to take it.[3] And although it provides men and women the same opportunity to take caretaking or parenting leave, it has done little to alter the disproportionate burden of caretaking that falls on women in most families.[4] Nor did it improve the lives of workers enough to rescue the United States from its dismal ranking among industrialized countries when it comes to workers' medical and caretaking leave.

After twenty years, it's time to expand the FMLA's protections to facilitate broader access to affordable leave in times of need. The current system has proved helpful in that it has established a norm that employees should not risk job loss due to leave necessitated by short-term health crises or the new obligations of parenting. It has also proven that the wildly exaggerated fears about the burden on employers of the cost of accommodating such leave, which drove much of the eight-year debate before the FMLA finally passed, were just that – wildly exaggerated. Employers report that they can administer FMLA leave with little cost or trouble. It's now time to take the next step.

### THE FMLA: WHAT IT DOES AND DOESN'T OFFER

The FMLA gives eligible employees the right to twelve weeks of *unpaid* leave per year such leave is needed to care for a newborn or newly adopted child, to care for a seriously ill family member, or to attend to one's own serious health condition.[5] To be eligible, an employee must have worked at least 1,250 hours in the previous year[6] for an employer who employs at least fifty workers within a seventy-five-mile radius of where the employee requesting leave reports to work.[7]

What does it mean to have a right to unpaid leave? Fundamentally, the FMLA is a job-security law. A person who is allowed FMLA leave has the right to be restored to the same position following the period of leave, as long as the employer would not otherwise have fired the employee or eliminated the position during that period.[8] The leave-taking employee also has the right to the continuation of benefits throughout the leave,[9] and the right not to be retaliated against for taking leave.[10]

The wrongful denial of FMLA leave or retaliation against a leave-taker can be challenged through a private lawsuit or through an administrative action by the Department of Labor. As discussed in Chapter 44, two lawsuits over the constitutionality of allowing private lawsuits against state employers have reached the Supreme Court, with different results. In *Nevada Department of Human Resources v. Hibbs*,[11] the Court held that state employees could sue to enforce the family-care (sick relative) provision of the act; but in *Coleman v. Court of Appeals of Maryland*,[12] the Court held that employees cannot sue to enforce the self-care provision because the states' sovereign immunity under the Eleventh Amendment was not successfully abrogated.

## THE SUPREME COURT'S VISION OF THE FMLA IN *HIBBS*

In *Hibbs*, the Court held that Congress validly exercised this power when it enacted the FMLA in order to promote equality for women in the employment context. The FMLA requires that employers offer caretaking leave to men and women on equal terms. This, in itself, promotes sex equality, at least formally. But the FMLA was also supposed to go further: under the Court's vision, once men and women were offered leave on equal terms, they were supposed to take it on more equal terms. Men would thus share the burden of caring for children. And women would achieve equality not only as parents but also as workers, as employers would lose the incentive to prefer men over women based on the idea that women would be likely to take more leave.[13]

Twenty years have passed since the FMLA was enacted, and the data points do not support this vision. The good news is that most employers covered by the FMLA have complied with its terms and made caretaking leave available on gender-neutral terms. But the bad news is everything else.

Generally, men still don't take caretaking leave.[14] Generally, as they did prior to enactment of the FMLA, women take caretaking leave whether they are guaranteed reinstatement or not. And generally, employers continue to view women as more costly – and therefore less desirable – as employees, because employers expect that women will take more leave than men, whether or not they actually do.

## THE LEGISLATIVE PROCESS: A BILL TO
## ACCOMMODATE MOTHERHOOD

As noted above, the Supreme Court attributed a very broad vision of equality to Congress when it considered and passed the FMLA. In fact, however, the FMLA's legislative history suggests something much less inspiring – a bill to accommodate motherhood, rather than one to induce equal parenthood.

The FMLA was the first law signed by President Clinton, just sixteen days after he was first inaugurated.[15] Prior family leave bills had either failed in Congress or been vetoed by President George H. W. Bush. Thus, although the FMLA was substantially weaker than previous bills (it offered shorter periods of leave and covered fewer employers), it was hailed as a victory for families and workers. There was little public discussion of its impact on gender equality.

Congress's formal findings with respect to the FMLA do include a statement that "it is important for the development of children and the family unit that fathers and mothers be able to participate in early childrearing."[16] Yet most other evidence in the legislative record suggests that Congress understood that the parenting leave provided under the law, although available to men, would still be used primarily by women.

Both sides of the debate professed to have the goal of preventing discrimination against women. Meanwhile, both also operated with the implicit assumption that women would continue to be the primary caretakers of children and thus the ones to take FMLA leave. Republicans claimed that if the FMLA were *passed*, women would suffer discrimination at the hands of employers who would then refuse to hire them at all.[17] They cited to a Gallup poll reporting that 40 percent of employers said they would be less likely to hire women of childbearing age if a law mandating leave for them was enacted.[18]

As one representative warned, speaking "as the father of four daughters," the FMLA would "legislate women into unemployment," because "the primary responsibility for child care still falls mainly to women; [and] women will be the predominate ones using mandated leave."[19] On the other hand, Democrats argued that if the FMLA *did not pass*, women would suffer discrimination at the hands of employers who would refuse to take them back following leave for childbirth, parenting, or other caretaking commitments. One proponent advocated for passage of the FMLA to eliminate discrimination against "working parents, and especially against working women who are still the primary care givers for most American families."[20]

Even feminist advocates, who initially conceived of and drafted the FMLA, seemed, for reasons of political expedience, to become complicit in the assumption that women would be the main leave-takers. Indeed, they ultimately pitched the bill in family-friendliness terms, and appealed to men's desire for job protection during their own serious illnesses – not for job-guaranteed paternity leave.[21]

## CARETAKING AND LEAVE-TAKING BEFORE THE
## FMLA: A GENDERED STORY

The data available during debate about the FMLA supported the assumptions about women's caretaking, leave usage, and employer hostility. Women in 1992 – as they do today – performed the majority of caretaking tasks for children, even in two-income households.[22] And, unsurprisingly, this allocation of childrearing responsibility induces gendered leave-taking patterns: If women must do most or all of the caretaking, it is difficult or impossible for them also to work without the ability to take leave if necessary. Before the FMLA, leave was made available and taken on distinctly gendered terms. Four states passed FMLA-like legislation, but a comprehensive 1988 study by the Families and Work Institute showed the laws had almost no effect on the rate at which mothers took childbirth or parenting leave.[23]

It also showed that, even before the state statutes were passed, 83 percent of employers surveyed reported that they already offered women an average of eleven weeks unpaid leave for disability related to childbirth, and an additional eight weeks for parenting leave.[24] In sum, motherhood was accommodated even before doing so was legally mandatory.

Before mandatory leave laws, the needs of biological fathers were accommodated to a lesser extent. Sixty percent of employers reportedly offered some unpaid leave to fathers, but very few had a formal program for allowing it.[25] Fatherhood was thus not accommodated to anywhere near the degree that motherhood was. In the states that began to mandate paternity leave, a slightly greater number of fathers utilized it. But the average leave increased in length only from 3.7 to 4.7 days – most of which was taken as paid vacation or sick leave rather than unpaid parental leave.[26] Other studies have found similar leave-taking patterns for men. For instance, a 1986 survey conducted by Catalyst revealed that not a single male employee took available paternity leave in 85 percent of the establishments that offered it.[27]

Congress had little reason to suspect the FMLA would alter the patterns seen under state-mandated leave laws. Indeed, a report of the U.S. General Accounting Office, predicted that – under an earlier, stronger version of the FMLA – while men would make half of the leave requests under the FMLA, none of the requests would be made so that the men could care for newborn or newly adopted children.[28]

Why don't men take leave? The answer is cultural and financial. Men often make more than their female partners do – a reality that itself is largely the product of sex discrimination. As a result, taking unpaid leave costs them more. Meanwhile, traditionally, men have not been involved in caregiving. They feel pressure, reinforced by widely held sex stereotypes, both to maximize their career opportunities and dissociate themselves from family-centered work. In addition, they fear retaliation from employers for availing themselves of leave offered. Women often have little choice but to take at least some maternity leave and their doing so fits sex stereotypes. In contrast, men can opt not to take paternity leave, and they defy sex stereotypes by taking it. Men thus reasonably may have a greater fear than women that their employer may hold their taking leave against them, or simply be less accustomed to experiencing consequences at work flowing from parenthood.

These disincentives appear powerful. The numbers are so stark – almost no men take leave, even if it is available, and those that do average a leave of five days – that some scholars have suggested that the FMLA ought to make leave mandatory for both men and women.[29] Alternatively, other reforms – such as subsidizing FMLA leave through unemployment insurance – might induce higher-earning men to take leave. In addition, such reforms may also enable more women to take advantage of the leave period despite financial constraints.

### THE IMPACT OF THE FMLA: A MIRROR OF THE PAST

Two-thirds of covered employers made some change to their leave policies because of the FMLA.[30] Yet very little else has changed. A 2000 report of the Department of Labor provides the most recent data on the use of FMLA leave by employees. (The FMLA established the Commission on Family and Medical Leave, and gave it the responsibility for studying the impact of the legislation on both employers and employees.) According to the 2000 survey, 16.5 percent of all workers took leave for an FMLA reason.[31] An additional 3.5 million employees needed leave, but were not able to take it, most often because they could not afford to take unpaid leave.[32]

Parenting obligations actually triggered a relatively small percentage of total leaves taken. Only 7.9 percent of leave-takers used the time for a pregnancy-related disability; 18.5 percent used it to care for a newborn, newly adopted, or newly placed foster child; and 11.5 percent used it to care for an ill child.[33] In contrast, more than 50 percent of leaves were taken because of an employee's own serious illness.[34]

Unfortunately – and very surprisingly – the official data do not show the length of parenting leaves by gender. Thus, it is difficult to draw firm conclusions about gender-based leave-taking patterns post-FMLA. But some inferences, at least, can be made.

According to the survey, parenting leaves by both sexes tend to be relatively short – more than half of them last fewer than ten days.[35] These data suggest paternity leaves are probably not much longer than before. (Women often characterize their leave as maternity-disability, so the shorter parenting leaves are in many cases taken by men.) There are no data to show that men are taking leave more often, or for longer periods of time, in order to parent their children.

The FMLA was pushed as a complement to then-existing laws regarding childbirth and parental leave. More than thirty states had their own leave laws on the books when it was passed. And many employees had the protection of the PDA as well. But that law did not (and does not) mandate that employers provide any leave at all – only that if they did, the leave policy had to be at least as generous for pregnant women as it was for comparably disabled employees.[36]

The FMLA fills some gaps in existing law. It deprives most employers of the right to provide no leave for disability related to pregnancy or childbirth. And by doing so, it makes it less likely women will drop out of the work force, of necessity, when they have children.

It also mandates that employers provide parenting leave, not just leave associated with the disability of childbirth. But against a backdrop of a culture in which women are in fact primary caretakers – and pushed to continue in that role – these protections do little to induce a reallocation of parenting responsibilities toward men. Moreover, for women who provide the bulk of caretaking within the family, the FMLA is insufficient to protect their needs. For example, when women experience pregnancy-related disability, they often use up their entire allotment of FMLA leave before the baby even arrives. They are then left with neither salary replacement nor job protection if they stay home for any period of time with the baby. Women also disproportionately hold part-time jobs, which means they are less likely to be covered by the FMLA.

## RETHINKING THE FMLA: GOING BEYOND ACCOMMODATING MOTHERHOOD

To promote equality, an amended FMLA would need to do more than simply accommodate motherhood, as the current FMLA does. The current FMLA at least forces employers to accommodate motherhood – so women who become parents cannot be deprived of the opportunity to come back to work. To be effective in promoting gender equality, an amended FMLA would also have to eliminate the incentives employers have to discriminate against female employees who are or are likely to become mothers. This is where the current FMLA's vision of equality falls short. Providing fathers with the formal opportunity to take parenting leave – in a society in which social, cultural, and economic forces make it unlikely they will do so – does little to force equal parenthood.

Indeed, what is most disappointing about the current FMLA is that it seems that no one involved in its passage believed it would have that effect. At best, they hoped the FMLA would provide job security for women as they continued not only to give birth to children (a biological imperative) but also to be their primary caregivers.

The gender neutrality of the FMLA – a feature that endured from the first bill proposed to the final one enacted – is, then, purely symbolic. A congressional mandate for paternity leave may refute commonly held stereotypes about women's caretaking obligations. But a better law would aim to change the behavior that makes the stereotypes true.

The FMLA's gender-neutral approach to mandatory leave is part of what makes it safe from Eleventh Amendment challenges – and that approach should not be changed. But other amendments to the statute should address the reality that real equality for working mothers remains elusive. The state-sponsored discrimination against women – both in terms of sex-specific leave policies and the refusal to allow leave at all – was surely one obstacle to women's equality. But social norms and gender-based pay disparities in the workplace are obstacles, as well.

The FMLA should be reevaluated – and potentially amended – on the occasion of this anniversary. The goal should be to see whether there is a way in which it could make paternity leave – and paternal caretaking – more enticing. Paid leave for both sexes would be a significant improvement but not a panacea. It's time to go back to the drawing board.

## WHERE THE FMLA FALLS SHORT: COVERAGE, PAY, AND GENDER EQUALITY

When the FMLA was signed on February 5, 1993, it was read as a symbol of Washington's change in power, for it was the first bill introduced into the House of Representatives in the session that began as Bill Clinton was inaugurated to the presidency. It was heralded as proof of the promised "end of gridlock," and as an endorsement of Clinton's "People First" campaign platform.[37]

The act may indeed have been emblematic of those things. But a significant factor in its easy passage through Congress was how little it offered employees, especially as compared with its earlier versions, which had suffered a variety of fates – including failure in either or both houses of Congress or, twice, a presidential veto.[38] The enacted version was a compromise that reduced the number of weeks of leave,[39] eliminated the possibility of taking full-length leaves for illness and parenting during the same year, and drastically reduced the number of employers bound by the FMLA by raising the minimum size of the businesses that would be bound by the statute from those with just one employee to those with at least fifty.[40]

The costs of this compromise are well documented. As detailed above, the law does little to alter the existing, gendered patterns of leave-taking. But there are other costs, as well. First, the law does not protect a sufficient number of employees. Nearly 40 percent of employees in the United States are not eligible for FMLA leave either (1) because the employers they work for are too small, or (2) because they do not work sufficient hours to qualify.

Second, unpaid leave does not help employees who cannot afford to go without pay. While many employees take FMLA leave, many more are eligible but do not take it. A survey administered in the year 2000 by the Department of Labor to study implementation of the FMLA found that 3.5 million employees needed FMLA leave but did not take it. The most common reason cited by employees for not taking leave was the inability to afford unpaid leave, and almost 90 percent of the non-leave-takers reported that they would have taken leave if at least some of it had been paid. Even among those who do take FMLA leave, almost none take it more than once,[41] and most such leaves are short – more than half, in the 2000 survey, lasted fewer than ten days, and fewer than 10 percent extended past eight weeks.[42]

### NEXT STEPS: MORE EMPLOYEES, LONGER LEAVES, SOME PAID LEAVE

The United States is remarkable in its failure to support workers or their families. No other high-income country fails to provide paid leave for newborn care, and most others provide lengthy periods of paid leave and even longer periods of job protection. In the United States, without a legal requirement of paid leave, the vast majority of employers do not provide it. Professional workplaces like law firms and high-tech companies are the most likely to provide generous paid-leave allotments; low-wage workplaces almost never do. And lower-income workers are least likely to have savings or other resources that allow them to forgo their wages for any period of time.

A small handful of states have established systems to support short-term, paid parenting leave. The state systems are set up differently, but each is modeled on a short-term disability-insurance system to which employees contribute. They provide a model for the expansion of the federal FMLA, which could use the same model to add a paid-leave component.

The easiest next step for the FMLA – one that has been proposed in Congress many times – would be simply to reduce the minimum number of employees necessary for FMLA coverage. A reduction to twenty-five or fifteen (the number used in most federal anti-discrimination laws) would vastly expand the number of employees who work for FMLA-covered employers. And while the business lobby has – and will continue to – object to any such change, the lesson from the passage of the FMLA in 1993, and our subsequent, successful experience with its implementation, is that we shouldn't always believe critics of leave laws when they say that the sky is falling.

The Department of Labor surveys have made clear that, despite their fears, employers have had no trouble implementing the FMLA. Indeed, a majority of employers surveyed reported that they were able to implement the required leave policies with minimal cost or administrative difficulty, and with "no noticeable effect" on productivity or profitability. Now that the evidence is in, and cutting strongly in favor of more leave, let's urge Congress to take the FMLA – and the United States – to the next level.

Portions of this chapter appeared on October 7, 2003, at writ.findlaw.com and on March 5, 2013, at verdict.justia.com.

*Update: After many failed efforts to amend the FMLA, it seems clear that change is more likely to come at the hands of states (see Chapter 33) or the voluntary actions of employers. Several tech companies made headlines in 2015 with announcements of new family-friendly leave policies, and Mark Zuckerberg, co-founder and CEO of Facebook, took a 2-month paid paternity leave upon the birth of his first child in December 2015.*[43]

# 46

## "Best Practices" to Promote Work-Family Balance

Recently, the EEOC issued a "best practices" document for employers on work-family balance.[1] This "technical assistance" document is designed not only to promote compliance with antidiscrimination laws that relate to or affect employees with caregiving responsibilities but also to encourage employers to adopt policies that go beyond legal minimum requirements.

This document is not binding on employers, yet it is notable for reflecting both the increasing challenges faced by employees with caregiving responsibilities, and the low likelihood of successfully addressing such problems through mere compliance with existing law. As acting EEOC chairman Stuart J. Ishimaru stated in a press release accompanying the document, "Today we take another step forward, articulating not just the bare minimum required to avoid unlawful discrimination, but also thinking broadly about the ways in which family-friendly workplace policies can improve workers' ability to balance caregiving responsibilities with work."[2]

### CHALLENGES FOR EMPLOYEES WITH
### CAREGIVING RESPONSIBILITIES

The notion of "caregivers" comprising a special class of employees is of relatively recent origin. What separates these employees descriptively from others is that they, in addition to doing paid work, are also engaged in significant caregiving outside of the workplace. Obviously, the biggest subcategory of caregivers is parents, but caregivers also include those engaged in the care of aging parents or relatives with disabilities. These caregiving responsibilities pose a variety of challenges that fall under the general "work-life balance" heading.

These caregiving responsibilities are not distributed evenly across the working population. As the EEOC's best practices document notes, the care of children and other dependents is disproportionately provided by women, and even more disproportionately by women of color.[3] Men's role in parenting and other caregiving has increased, but is still vastly outweighed by women's. At the same time, women's workforce participation has dramatically increased, so that women account today for 46 percent of the workforce, and women's earnings are increasingly important.[4] These trends may be further exacerbated by the recessionary economy, in which the vast majority of layoffs have fallen on men (who tend to work in hard-hit industries such as construction and investment banking), and, thus, women's job security and earnings are even more important to family support. There is thus a significant overlap between women's rights and caregivers' rights.

Although every employee faces different challenges in trying to balance work and family, there are common pitfalls for those who engage in both paid work and significant family caregiving. For many caregivers, inflexible workplace policies and insufficient access to leave present the biggest obstacles to their successful balancing of work and family responsibilities. To make matters worse, stereotyping about caregivers is prevalent: women caregivers are often thought to be less committed to their paid work or to be likely to be less competent because of their actual or likely role in caregiving. Meanwhile, men are thought to be ill suited for caregiving and thus not in need of parental leave or a flexible work schedule. Prevalent, too, are instances of employer animus or hostility against workers who reveal anything other than a single-minded and uninterrupted commitment to paid work.

## THE LEGAL TREATMENT OF "CAREGIVERS"

The EEOC acknowledged caregiving employees as a group in 2007, when it issued its *Enforcement Guidance: Unlawful Disparate Treatment of Workers with Caregiving Responsibilities*.[5] This enforcement guidance – unlike the best practices document – is specifically tailored to explain, and assist in compliance with, existing law. Its express purpose was to "assist investigators, employees, and employers in assessing whether a particular employment decision affecting a caregiver might unlawfully discriminate on the basis of prohibited characteristics."[6]

No existing law creates a special, protected status for "caregivers." Title VII, however, bans discrimination in the employment context on the basis of sex or pregnancy, and it is sometimes the case that "caregiver discrimination" is in fact sex or pregnancy based and thus unlawful.[7] In addition, the Americans with Disabilities Act of 1990 (ADA) prohibits "discrimination because of the disability of an individual with whom the worker has a relationship or association, such as a child, spouse, or parent."[8] The enforcement guidance identifies six circumstances in which discrimination against a caregiver may violate Title VII or the ADA.

- Sex-based disparate treatment of female caregivers, including a wide range of conduct from asking only female applicants about marital or parenting status, to steering female caregivers toward lower-paid jobs, to stereotyping female caregivers about their workforce commitment or competence, to imposing a wage penalty on mothers.

- Pregnancy discrimination, including the application of stereotyped assumptions about a pregnant woman's work capacity, insistence on preemployment pregnancy tests without complying with relevant ADA principles, engaging in "benevolent" protection of pregnant employees, and treating pregnant workers less favorably than other temporarily disabled workers who are similar in their ability or inability to work.
- Discrimination against male caregivers, including denying male employees' requests for parental leave while granting similar requests from women, penalizing men for making use of available caregiving leave, and denying men access to flexible work schedules.
- Discrimination against women of color, including the disproportionate application of stereotypes about female caregiving to women of color.
- Unlawful caregiver stereotyping under the ADA.
- Hostile work environment harassment, including harassment leveled against pregnant workers, mothers, or disabled workers.

The enforcement guidance also addresses retaliation law, which generally protects individuals against retaliation for invoking their federal antidiscrimination rights. Retaliation is prohibited if it would be reasonably likely to deter an employee from complaining. Caregivers, however, may be swayed more than other employees by particular threats. As the Supreme Court noted in a recent retaliation ruling, which I discuss in Chapter 9: "A schedule change in an employee's work schedule may make little difference to many workers, but may matter enormously to a young mother with school age children."[9]

## WHAT THE "BEST PRACTICES" DOCUMENT ADDS TO THE MIX

The EEOC's enforcement guidance comprehensively identifies the types of employment practices with respect to caregivers that are most likely to run afoul of existing law. The best practices document takes this project a step further – to suggest particular workplace policies that will not only help employers avoid violating existing law but also promote better work-life balance for employees with such responsibilities. Part of the EEOC's justification for prompting employers to exceed legal requirements in this regard is research showing that family-friendly workplace policies enhance productivity and aid in employee retention, both components of lowering employer costs.

The best practices document is grouped into three categories: general; recruitment, hiring, and promotion; and terms and conditions. Within each category, it suggests specific policies that promote work-life balance.

In the first category, the EEOC recommends that employers adopt a formal EEO policy that expressly addresses "caregivers" as a class. It recommends that the policy describe common stereotypes or biases about caregivers, and provide examples of prohibited conduct. It also recommends that managers be trained specifically about the range of federal laws that potentially bear on the rights of caregivers, including not only Title VII and the ADA, as mentioned above, but also the PDA, the Equal Pay Act, the FMLA, and others. Finally, it recommends that managers be trained and incentivized to support employee efforts to balance work and family responsibilities, to respond to caregiver discrimination complaints effectively, and to avoid unlawful retaliation.

In the second category, the EEOC focuses not only on purging the hiring process of unfair stereotypes about caregiver-employees but also on encouraging employers to take more proactive efforts to entice and fairly evaluate them. It suggests, among other things, that employers review current hiring practices and pay scales to make sure they do not disadvantage caregivers, ensure that job opportunities are communicated equally to caregivers, engage in targeted recruitment of caregivers, identify and remove barriers to reentry for workers who have experienced caregiving-related career interruptions, and increase transparency in employment decision making.

Finally, in the third category, the EEOC suggests a number of policies designed to alleviate common conflicts faced by caregiving employees. At the top of the list is better use of flexible work arrangements that allow employees to better blend their home and work responsibilities. Flexibility can be added through variable start and end times to the workday, compressed work weeks, telecommuting, and greater availability of part-time positions. The document suggests that required overtime should be "as family-friendly as possible,"[10] and that voluntary overtime should be used if possible. It also suggests greater use of light-duty assignments for pregnant workers, which, as discussed in Chapters 31 to 37, current law does not go far enough to provide. The document also suggests, importantly, that employers provide reasonable personal or sick leave to facilitate caregiving obligations. The leave mandated by current law is clearly insufficient to meet the needs of most pregnant women and parents.

In conclusion, the best practices document cites research demonstrating "that flexible work policies have a positive impact on employee engagement and organizational productivity and profitability."[11] And certainly, such policies have the potential to benefit employees, particularly women, who shoulder disproportionate responsibility for both parenting and elder care.

## THE BOTTOM LINE: THE EEOC HAS MADE IMPORTANT PROGRESS FOR CAREGIVERS

The EEOC has taken an important step here to push employers beyond the mandates of existing law. Decades of antidiscrimination law have been extraordinarily important to the removal of formal barriers to the workplace faced by women and minorities. Yet until now, the law has proven relatively ineffective in striking down the more subtle, yet equally entrenched barriers that remain.

As long as workplaces remain structured around the norm of a male worker without caregiving responsibilities, and as long as women continue to do most of the caregiving work, equal employment opportunity will remain elusive. Proactive measures, such as the ones suggested in this document, are likely to be much more effective than the narrow right to sue for unlawful discrimination.

A version of this chapter appeared on May 12, 2009, at writ.findlaw.com.

# PART IV

# Female Breadwinners and the Glass Ceiling

ART 4 © Paul Fell/CartoonStock. Used by permission

*And I'll take 69 cents on the dollar, or whatever the current feminist myth is about how much we make, just to never have to pay for dinner. That seems like a fair deal to me.*

(Ann Coulter)

*It was very humiliating to learn that I was being paid so much less than my white-male peers for doing the exact same job and doing it well. . . . ! I didn't want anybody to give me anything. I didn't want any special treatment. I just wanted the opportunity to have the job, to do the job and to get compensated.*

(Lilly Ledbetter)

The general theme of this book has been that despite many gains, gender continues to define many aspects of the workplace, especially for women. We have seen the persistence of biased decision making, the continued impact of sexually harassing behavior, and an almost laughable inability of many employers to deal with pregnant workers. But now it is time to get down to brass tacks: How do women today fare in terms of equal pay and advancement? As the chapters that follow reveal, women continue to struggle for parity on these most basic issues. Equal pay has proved elusive, as has equal access to the highest echelons of ladder – across the political, public, corporate, and other sectors. And damning stereotypes about women continue to pervade not only the workplace but also the public and political consciousness.

## PAY EQUITY AND THE GLASS CEILING

Although the gender wage gap today is narrower than the 1970s' measure of fifty-nine cents on the dollar, the bulk of the change occurred during the 1980s, and studies show little additional progress since 1990.[1] Moreover, the disparity in men's and women's wages extends, with some variation, throughout the employment life cycle. Women in their forties and fifties earn salaries more disparate from their male counterparts than do women at the beginning of their careers.[2] When earnings over a longer period of time are aggregated, the gap is even starker. In their prime earning years, women earn only 38 percent of what men earn over a fifteen-year period.[3]

Although there are plausible nondiscriminatory reasons for pay differences between men and women, none of them, even in the aggregate, explains the entire gap.[4] For example, differing degrees of labor force attachment cannot explain the large gap in wages between men and women who both work year-round and full-time during at least twelve of fifteen consecutive years.[5]

Differences in the number of hours worked also fail to explain the gender disparity in wages. Hour for hour, women earn less than men do.[6] Similarly, differences in education explain little of the wage gap.[7] Most important, when studies simultaneously control for multiple variables such as education, occupation, hours worked, and time away from the workplace because of family care responsibilities, a significant gender gap remains.[8] The remaining gap, once these factors are eliminated from the analysis, is caused by discrimination.

Discriminatory pay decisions are not an isolated event. Rather, they continue to reverberate throughout a woman's employment life. Even small pay disparities are typically magnified by percentage-based pay adjustments and morph over time into a devastating disadvantage. Indeed, in "Women Don't Ask: Negotiation and the Gender Divide," Linda Babcock and Sara Laschever found that a $4,000 (7.6 percent) starting pay disparity between a male and a female employee, followed by 3 percent annual raises, would evolve into a $15,000 annual disparity by age sixty. That means the female employee may lose a total of $361,171 over her employment life, while the male employee gains a staggering $568,834 assuming he earns even a modest 3 percent in interest on the difference.[9]

Women's advancement is another lens through which to view workplace equality. But here, the story is no rosier – and the solutions no more obvious. In 1984, Gay Bryant, the editor at *Working Woman* magazine, coined the term "glass ceiling" to describe the invisible yet real limit on women's advancement to higher positions. "Women have reached a certain point – I call it the glass ceiling," Bryant observed, "in the top of middle management and they're stopping and getting stuck."[10] The term stuck and became a catchphrase to describe women's seeming inability to reach the "upper echelons of power."[11] Part of the Civil Rights Act of 1991, discussed at various places in this book, was the establishment of the congressional Glass Ceiling Commission, which issued a report in 1991 confirming the existence of barriers to the advancement of women and minorities.[12] It found, for example, that while women and minorities composed two-thirds of the population and more than half the workforce, they held only 3 percent of senior management positions at Fortune 1000 companies. One can find similar statistics in almost every walk of life. And, as Christine Jolls has argued, the invisible barrier to advancement is in large part of the product of "uncontroverted sex discrimination in labor markets."[13] The glass ceiling continues to be a common lens through which to view women's progress, though little headway has been made in breaking it.

The problem of pay inequity – and the law's often-inadequate response to it – is explored in Chapters 47 to 51. The focal point is Lilly Ledbetter's pay discrimination case against Goodyear Tire & Rubber Company. Although she lost her case in the Supreme Court, the ruling led to a new law in her name, designed to fix the damage the court had done. Her story provides a window into the nature of pay discrimination, its practical and legal consequences, and the balance of power between the Supreme Court and Congress. Chapter 51 considers National Pay Equity Day and why women wear red to mark the occasion.

Chapters 52 to 57 explore the glass ceiling by examining the way in which women have been held back in a variety of contexts. Unlike most of the chapters in this book, these six do not explore court rulings or new laws that shed light on a particular cause of action or claim. Rather, they look more broadly at the progress of women – and the continuing obstacles they face – in setting like the legal profession, the federal workforce, sports, and American politics.

# 47

## The Supreme Court Slams the Door on Pay Discrimination Claims

The Supreme Court issued a 5–4 decision in *Ledbetter v. Goodyear Tire & Rubber Co.* that will be devastating for plaintiffs who have suffered pay discrimination and seek to sue under Title VII, the main federal anti-employment-discrimination statute.[1] It interpreted the statute of limitations in a way that will make it difficult, if not impossible, for women to challenge pay discrimination, an intractable problem, effectively. Unless Title VII is robustly enforced, that discrimination will persist. But the Supreme Court has just erected a substantial obstacle to enforcement.

### THE FACTS AND THE RULINGS BELOW

Lilly Ledbetter worked as a production supervisor at Goodyear Tire & Rubber's plant in Gadsden, Alabama. She took early retirement in 1998, nearly twenty years after she began working for the company and after being transferred against her will to a less desirable job on the production floor. Ledbetter filed a charge of discrimination in 1998 with the EEOC, alleging various forms of sex discrimination.

At trial, Ledbetter proved to the jury that she had suffered illegal pay discrimination. She was paid less than the lowest-paid male in the same job – so much less that her salary sometimes fell below the minimum salary set by the company's pay policy for her position. Goodyear did not dispute the pay disparity, but it argued (unsuccessfully) that it resulted from her consistently poor performance, which, it claimed, dictated her unusually small or absent annual pay raises. Ledbetter offered evidence that performance evaluations were falsified; that she received a "Top Performance Award" one year; that the company's policy with respect to pay raises was not followed; that there was widespread discrimination against female managers at the plant; and that plant officials bore discriminatory animus against female employees. On this record, the jury awarded Ledbetter $223,776 in back pay and more than $3 million dollars in punitive damages. (This award was reduced by the court to

$300,000, however, because Title VII limits total damages to $300,000 for claims against employers of this size – a cap that was set when the law first provided for money damages in 1991.)

On appeal, the employer, Goodyear, claimed that Ledbetter was entitled to nothing because her lawsuit was filed much too late. Plaintiffs cannot file a Title VII lawsuit unless they have filed a charge with the EEOC within 180 days of the unlawful employment practice they are challenging, or 300 days in states that enter a work-sharing agreement with the EEOC.[2] (The limitations period is 300 days in states with a state employment agency with authority to grant relief. The rationale behind this slightly longer period is to give states a chance to solve employment discrimination issues first prior to federal involvement.)

But when does that 180 days begin to run in a pay discrimination case? Goodyear said that the clock was ticking as soon as the decision to pay the employee less on the basis of sex was first made. But Ledbetter claimed it started ticking anew every time she received a paycheck reflecting (and implementing) the earlier discriminatory decision. The U.S. Court of Appeals for the Eleventh Circuit agreed with Goodyear and reversed the jury's verdict. It said that a plaintiff alleging pay discrimination can reach no further back than (and possibly not even as far as) the most recent pay decision prior to the beginning of the charge-filing period.[3]

## THE SUPREME COURT'S RULING: DISCRIMINATORY PAY DECISIONS ARE DISCRETE ACTS

The issue presented by Ledbetter's case is when pay discrimination claims must be brought in order to be timely. No one disagrees that the applicable statute of limitations is 180 days. But 180 days from when? There are three possible answers: (1) from the day of the pay *decision* that sets a discriminatory wage, (2) from the day an employee *learns* her pay is discriminatory (in the law, this is called a "discovery" rule), or (3) from the date of any *paycheck* that contains an amount affected by a prior discriminatory pay decision (this is deemed a "paycheck accrual" rule).

The Supreme Court sided with Goodyear and opted for the first approach, which means that a plaintiff has 180 days after the pay decision that sets the discriminatory wage to file her charge with the EEOC in compliance with Title VII's statute of limitations. The majority declined to consider whether a discovery rule, the second approach, might be used to extend the statute of limitations for discrimination that is unknown to the employee. In addition, it flatly rejected the paycheck accrual rule, the third approach, even though the court had endorsed just such an approach in previous cases.

This case turned primarily on the court's interpretation of its own precedent, a 2002 ruling in *Amtrak v. Morgan*, which is discussed in Chapter 22 for its effect on sexual harassment lawsuits.[4] In that ruling, the court held that "discrete" acts of discrimination must be challenged within 180 days of their occurrence. In so doing, it rejected the so-called continuing violations doctrine – under which some lower federal courts had permitted plaintiffs to challenge a series of related acts of discrimination, as long as at least one had occurred within 180 days prior the filing of an EEOC charge.

In *Morgan*, the court carved out an exception for "hostile environment" harassment since, by its very nature, the claim accrues over time and through the aggregation of multiple incidents of misconduct that together create the hostile environment. (Imagine, for example, the progression from a single unpleasant, sexist remark, directed to the lone woman in an office, to a situation in which such remarks become routine and unavoidable.) For such claims, a plaintiff can challenge harassment as long as at least one of the acts that together created the hostile environment occurred within the 180-day, charge-filing period.

Thus, the issue in *Ledbetter* was whether pay discrimination claims – for statute of limitations purposes – would be treated like claims based on, say, discriminatory firings, where the clock clearly starts ticking immediately, or like hostile environment claims, where the clock starts ticking with the final act alleged.

In an opinion written by Justice Samuel Alito, the *Ledbetter* Court ruled that the "discrete" act rule, rather than the harassment rule, applies to pay discrimination claims. This ruling departs from the longstanding position of the EEOC, the agency charged with enforcement of Title VII, which followed the paycheck accrual rule instead – the third approach, which allows the plaintiff to sue within 180 days of her last discrimination-tainted paycheck.[5] It also rejected the position taken universally by federal appellate courts.[6]

The Court's rejection of Ledbetter's claim turned on two basic conclusions. First, the Court ruled that under *Morgan*, a discriminatory pay decision is a discrete act that triggers the statute of limitations. Second, it ruled that a paycheck containing a discriminatory amount of money is not a present violation, but, instead, is merely the effect of a prior act of discrimination. "[C]urrent effects alone cannot breathe life into prior, charged discrimination," the Court wrote, as "such effects have no present legal consequences."[7]

## THE PRECEDENTS THE COURT CITED AND THOSE IT IGNORED

To reach the second conclusion, the Court relied on *United Air Lines v. Evans*, in which it had dismissed the discrimination claim of a flight attendant who had been wrongfully terminated and then rehired – without seniority – years later.[8] The Court refused to permit her to challenge the loss of seniority, because it held that that was just an "effect" of the prior, uncharged wrongful termination.

The Court also relied on *Delaware State College v. Ricks*, in which a librarian who had been denied tenure, allegedly on the basis of race, was not permitted to sue within 180 days of his departure from the college, because the notice of the tenure denial had been communicated to him a year earlier.[9] Again, the Court held that the actual termination was merely an effect of the allegedly illegal denial of tenure, rather than a present violation of Title VII.

In relying on these precedents, the Court in *Ledbetter* effectively ignored another line of precedents in which it had applied a different rule to pay claims. For example, in *Bazemore v. Friday*, all members of the Court joined Justice Brennan's separate opinion, in which he wrote: "[e]ach week's paycheck that delivers less to a black than to a similarly situated white is a wrong actionable under Title VII."[10] This case involved a challenge to a race-based pay structure that was implemented prior to Title VII but continued after the law's enactment. The decision to pay black employees less was legal at the time it was made, but the employer could not continue to pay those amounts now that race discrimination was against the law.

The Court in *Ledbetter* attempted to distinguish *Bazemore* on the theory that the employer had carried forward a discriminatory pay *structure* rather than a discriminatory pay *decision*. But this is the least persuasive of the Court's justifications for its harsh rule, for a paycheck that is deflated because of a decision to pay an *individual* woman less because of her sex is no less a discrete instance of discrimination than one that is deflated because of a decision to pay *all* women less because of their sex.

As Justice Ginsburg argues in dissent, the majority's opinion in *Ledbetter* means that "[a]ny annual pay decision not contested immediately (within 180 days) . . . ! becomes grandfathered, a *fait accompli* beyond the province of Title VII ever to repair." An employer could pay a woman less than her male counterparts for her *entire* career, and admit that the reason for doing so is because she is female, as long as the decision to set the discriminatory wage happened at least six months earlier. This rule places untenable burdens on employees and circumvents Title VII's substantive protection against pay discrimination.[11]

## PERCEIVING DISCRIMINATION: AN OBSTACLE TO ENFORCING SUBSTANTIVE RIGHTS

In order to prevail on a pay discrimination claim after *Ledbetter*, a victim must quickly perceive that she has suffered discrimination and promptly report it. But that is a rare occurrence in the typical case, and surely discrimination law should address the typical cases where real-life plaintiffs suffer discrimination, not just the rare ones.

There are many obstacles to bona fide victims' perceiving discrimination generally, and pay discrimination in particular. For example, social psychologists have shown that women are reluctant to perceive themselves as victims of sex discrimination because it conflicts with deeply ingrained beliefs that the world is meritorious and individuals are responsible for their own fate. Women also tend to compare themselves with other women – not to similarly qualified, similarly skilled men – in evaluating their treatment.[12]

For example, working women tend to evaluate the fairness of their current pay by reference to what other women earn, and what they themselves have earned in the past. Such within-gender comparisons by women lead to diminished salary expectations. In studies where men and women are asked to set their own rates of pay for performing a specified task, men typically pay themselves one-third more than what women pay themselves for the same task. Recognizing that one's wage is deflated, and the product of discrimination, is thus difficult.[13]

In addition, the limited availability of information, paired with limits on the way people process the information that is available, further thwarts people's ability to quickly perceive sex discrimination. Studies have found that people resist perceiving individual instances of sex discrimination under normal conditions of information gathering – in which information trickles in piece by piece, showing individual instances of different treatment. People are much more likely to perceive discrimination when information regarding disparities is presented all at once – showing across-the-board, organization-wide comparisons between men and women. Because employees almost never have access to that kind of global, synthesized information (at least until they have filed a lawsuit and gain information through discovery), individual instances of discrimination frequently go unnoticed.[14]

While these problems make perceiving sex discrimination difficult in general, the problems are greatly compounded for pay discrimination. Employers rarely disclose company-wide salary information, and workplace norms often discourage frank and open conversations among employees about salaries. As a result, employees rarely know what their colleagues earn, much less what raises and adjustments are given out to others with each and every pay decision.

That's a major problem from the perspective of eliminating discrimination, because an employee who learns that she will receive a 5 percent raise will have little reason to suspect pay discrimination, without knowing, at the very least, what raises others have received. Indeed, the discriminatory pay gap may begin with no change at all in an employee's pay, but rather with a decision to increase the pay of a male colleague, while leaving her pay unchanged for a discriminatory reason.

Unless corrected, a discriminatory pay decision or starting wage will be perpetuated and magnified by subsequent percentile pay adjustments. Even if an employee is aware of a minor disparity between her own pay and her colleagues' pay, relatively minor disparities may go unnoticed until, over the years, the disparity becomes too large to ignore. But by that time, under *Ledbetter*, the employee will have lost long ago the right to complain.

The Court's rule thus effectively immunizes employers from Title VII liability for pay discrimination in many cases.

## CATCH-22: COMPLAIN IMMEDIATELY, BUT NOT TOO SOON!

Perhaps the most troublesome aspect of the Court's opinion is the dilemma it creates for employees who, under the Court's ruling, must file a charge alleging suspected pay discrimination within 180 days of when it begins or lose forever the right to challenge it. One might think, at first glance, that employees should respond by filing with the EEOC the moment they suspect discrimination. However, in a cruel catch-22, an employee who complains to her employer too soon, without an adequate factual and legal foundation for doing so, may find herself in an even worse position: out of a job because she complained, and with no legal recourse for the retaliation she suffered.

Under *Clark County School District v. Breeden*, the Supreme Court held that an employee who opposes what she believes (inaccurately) to be unlawful discrimination is protected from retaliation only if she had a "reasonable belief" that the practice she opposed in fact violates Title VII.[15] (Retaliation doctrine under Title VII is also discussed in Chapters 9 to 11.) The plaintiff in *Breeden* internally complained about a sexually explicit colloquy between her supervisor and a coworker during a meeting that she found offensive. She was subsequently assigned to less desirable job duties and relieved of her supervisory responsibilities – as a result, she alleged, of her speaking out.

Title VII outlaws not only discrimination but also retaliation done to punish those who speak out about it. Yet the Supreme Court rejected Breeden's retaliation claim on the ground that even if she had experienced retaliation in response to her complaint, no reasonable employee could have believed that the sexual dialogue would, *without more*, create a hostile environment in violation of Title VII. In other words, if Breeden had waited until further offensive comments were made on other occasions to speak out, then she might have been able to win her retaliation claim.

This standard leaves employees unprotected from retaliation if they oppose an employment practice too soon. Lower courts have applied this standard harshly, leaving plaintiffs unprotected for acting on their subjective beliefs that certain employer conduct is discriminatory without sufficient factual and legal support for proving an actual violation of Title VII.

The dilemma for pay discrimination claimants is especially poignant: it may take a pattern of substantial pay disparities in order to establish an inference that the gap in pay is attributable to gender bias, rather than to some legitimate nondiscriminatory reason such as performance or experience. If the plaintiff waits too long, she loses her ability to challenge continuing discrimination in pay, even as the gap increases through neutral, percentage-based raises. Yet if she complains to her employer at the first sign of a pay gap, she risks lacking an adequate foundation for a "reasonable belief" that the gap is attributable to gender discrimination – leaving her vulnerable and unprotected from retaliation in response to her complaint. This is the essence of a catch-22.

The only way out of this dilemma is for the employee to immediately file a charge with the EEOC at her very first suspicion of pay discrimination, without saying a word to her employer or anyone in the workplace – because *Breeden*'s reasonable belief standard applies only to forms of "opposition" short of the formal EEOC charge-filing process. Once a formal EEOC charge is filed, protection from retaliation kicks in, regardless of whether the plaintiff reasonably or unreasonably believed a violation occurred. (The relationship between the "opposition" and "participation" retaliation clauses in Title VII is discussed in Chapter 11) One of the stranger results of the *Ledbetter-Breeden* dilemma is to encourage employees to avoid precisely the kind of informal, prompt resolution and conciliation of disputes that the majority in *Ledbetter* insists Title VII intends. Rather than risk speaking out to improve the situation within a given company, employees may go straight (and silently) to the EEOC.

Employees unfamiliar with the strange and unexpected landmines now embedded in Title VII law may find themselves injured – bringing suspected pay discrimination immediately to the attention of their employer, only to find themselves punished for their forthrightness and without protection from retaliation. Yet the Court's opinion reflects an utter lack of concern for the dilemmas now confronting pay discrimination plaintiffs.

## IMPLICATIONS FOR VICTIMS OF PAY DISCRIMINATION

Pay discrimination victims can also file claims under the federal Equal Pay Act of 1963, which may enable them to challenge pay discrimination under a different tolling rule than the Court adopted in *Ledbetter* for Title VII claims. The Equal Pay Act requires employers to pay men and women equally if they do substantially similar work, with possible defenses for pay disparities resulting from merit-based systems, seniority systems, or a factor other than sex. A plaintiff may challenge an ongoing violation of the Equal Pay Act at any time and may seek recovery for the prior two years of discrimination (or three years, if the violation is "willful").[16]

However, the existence of an alternative statutory remedy for sex discrimination in pay does not fully solve the problem, because some pay discrimination that violates Title VII is not covered under the Equal Pay Act. The Equal Pay Act is limited to cases where the plaintiff can point to a comparator of the opposite sex who does the same work in the same job for more money. Title VII, in contrast, reaches all claims of intentional pay discrimination, regardless of whether there is an opposite-sex comparator who earns more. For example, a woman in a workplace where she holds a unique job, or simply a job that is not the equivalent of any job performed in that workplace by a higher-earning man, will have no hope of prevailing under the Equal Pay Act, even if she can clearly prove that the employer paid her less because of her sex.

The unfortunate consequence of the Court's ruling in *Ledbetter* is to effectively nullify Title VII's broader reach by imposing a harsh and unrealistic filing deadline, leaving women only the protection of the narrower Equal Pay Act. This is an odd result, given that Title VII was passed after the Equal Pay Act and was intended to broaden preexisting federal legal protection from sex discrimination.

The consequences are even harsher for victims of pay discrimination on bases other than sex: they are not protected by the Equal Pay Act at all. Victims of race-based pay discrimination, for example, will have no recourse if their claims are more than 180 days old. Women of color, in particular, who already have difficulty sorting out the "race" from the "gender" components of bias in court cases, will have a particularly tough road to navigate. This seems especially unfair, as women who may be suffering two types of pay discrimination that converge may end up having no viable case at all.

What the Supreme Court has done in a single case will take much effort to undo. But equality and the rights Title VII was designed to protect demand that it be undone.

Portions of this chapter appeared on November 14 and 27, 2006, and June 4, 2007, at writ.findlaw.com, and was coauthored by Deborah Brake.

# 48

# A Call for Congressional Action to Remedy Pay Inequality

The Supreme Court made a mess of pay discrimination law with its ruling in *Ledbetter v. Goodyear Tire & Rubber, Inc.*[1] Congress should override the ruling – and should also take the opportunity to amend Title VII, the centerpiece of federal protection against employment discrimination, in other ways, as well. The *Ledbetter* decision requires employees to file a Title VII pay discrimination claim within 180 or 300 days of when the discriminatory decision was first made and communicated to the employee.

As discussed in Chapter 47, the Court's ruling will have disastrous consequences for victims of pay discrimination, who are likely to suffer from salary discrimination that compounds throughout their careers. Moreover, the court failed to effectively address the problem that many discrimination victims are not likely to be immediately aware that their paychecks are affected by discrimination. Congress should step in to restore Title VII protections for pay discrimination victims, as well as to take further measures to ensure that Title VII protects all employees against discrimination.

## LEDBETTER'S SILENCE ON WHEN TO START AND TOLL THE CLOCK: DISCOVERY RULES AND EQUITABLE TOLLING

The *Ledbetter* Court dismissed as "policy arguments" the concerns raised by the dissent about the hardship for employees who do not learn about pay disparities until it is too late. The Court ignored the elephant in the room: What kind of information suffices to place an employee on notice that she has a potential pay claim, so as to start the 180-day clock ticking? The majority simply states that the clock starts to run when the "discriminatory pay decision was made and communicated."[2]

But exactly what information must be communicated to the employee in order to trigger the statute's short limitations period? Is it enough for the employer to simply specify the employee's new pay level? If so, then Title VII pay claims have just been relegated to the dustbin of civil rights history. Perhaps, more charitably, the majority meant that the time period will start running once the employee learns that she will receive an amount that is less than some of her male comparators who perform similar work will receive? Or perhaps it meant that the time period starts running when she learns she will receive a specified percentage raise that is less than the raises received by others? Yet even the communication of that more detailed salary information, providing comparisons to other workers, is unlikely to actually place an employee on notice that she has a potential pay discrimination claim, without additional facts pointing to some basis for believing that discrimination entered into the decision.

Instead of answering, or even entertaining, such questions, the Court simply reiterated that it has never specified whether or not a "discovery rule" applies to Title VII claims. (A discovery rule, if adopted by courts, operates to delay the onset of the statute of limitations until a plaintiff has "discovered" her injury.) By its silence, the Court invites lower courts to fashion their own approach, a worrisome prospect, especially in conservative federal circuits hostile to discrimination claims.

Some lower courts have rejected a discovery rule altogether. Others have applied a narrow discovery rule that starts the clock when the plaintiff first learns of an employment-related injury, not when the plaintiff has reason to suspect discrimination. In an age discrimination case, *Cada v. Baxter Healthcare Corp*, for example, the U.S. Court of Appeals for the Seventh Circuit ruled in 1990 that the clock starts ticking from the time the employee learned he was fired, not when he later learned that he was replaced by a younger worker and began to suspect age discrimination.[3]

Such interpretations make the discovery rule an ineffective tool for protecting employees who do not have reason to suspect discrimination. To be meaningful, a discovery rule must reflect the realities of the workplace, with sensitivity to the types of information necessary to apprise employees that they have suffered pay discrimination. The information sufficient for a reasonable person to suspect pay discrimination should include not just the concrete numerical changes in the employee's own pay, but also organization-wide comparisons of salary by gender, accompanied by the employer's explanation of any gender disparities. Only if an employee knew all this could we accurately say that she was on notice that she might have suffered pay discrimination.

In lieu of a robust discovery rule, another device called "equitable tolling" could be used to delay the limitations clock where an employee does not have reason to suspect discrimination. (The idea of "equitable tolling" is that, at times, for fairness reasons, it serves justice to consider the ticking statute of limitations clock to have paused during a particular period of time.) While courts generally acknowledge the availability of this device in Title VII, its typical application is too limited to have an impact in most cases. Many courts do not toll the limitations period based on the employee's lack of information unless the employer actively concealed relevant facts or actively misled the employee into believing she did not have a claim. And, of course, they are right do so: deceptive conduct like this is an excellent reason to invoke equitable tolling. But it is not the only just reason to do so. Moreover, in reality, employer concealment of wrongdoing is not the main reason victims fail to perceive pay discrimination.

Equitable tolling rules have other limitations, as well. For example, pursuing a discrimination allegation through an employer's internal complaint process does *not* toll the limitations period. Thus, an employee who first pursues a suspicion of discrimination through the employer's internal procedures in an effort to find out what happened and try to resolve it internally will be foreclosed from filing a Title VII charge if she waits until that process ends, and the 180-day time period passes.

The failure to toll the limitations period while employees pursue internal procedures for redress creates an incentive to channel employee complaints into lengthy internal procedures, and run out the clock so that employees lose their chance to file a formal claim. Refusing to toll the limitations period also goes against the Supreme Court's own hope that some claims will be resolved internally, and emphasis that companies need to have a chance to be alerted of and address claims. The absence of a meaningful discovery rule and of fair equitable tolling rules, in combination, makes plaintiffs' compliance with the *Ledbetter* rule all the more impossible, Title VII's guarantee of employment equality all the more elusive, and the need for Congress's intervention all the more pressing.

## PROPOSED FIX #1: ADOPTING THE PAYCHECK ACCRUAL RULE

Justice Ruth Bader Ginsburg closed her dissent in *Ledbetter* with the exhortation that "[o]nce again, the ball is in Congress' court." Ginsburg was referring to the Civil Rights Act of 1991, a federal law that overturned a spate of harsh Supreme Court decisions adopting unnecessarily narrow interpretations of Title VII and other civil rights statutes.[4]

One of the decisions overturned by the 1991 act was *Lorance v. AT&T Technologies*.[5] The Court in *Lorance* took a near-identical approach to filing requirements for challenging a discriminatory seniority system, as *Ledbetter* more recently did for pay discrimination. In the *Lorance* ruling, the Court held that employees had to challenge the discriminatory seniority system within 180 days of when it was first adopted, rather than within 180 days of when it was first applied to them.

Congress specifically overturned the *Lorance* ruling in the 1991 act, correcting the injustice of barring employees from challenging discrimination that was perpetuated each time the seniority system was applied. Although the statutory correction was specifically directed to seniority systems, the legislative history reflects Congress's broad disapproval of the reasoning and the result. In fact, an interpretative memorandum written by Senator Danforth, a key player behind the 1991 act, disapproved the application of *Lorance* to contexts outside of seniority systems.[6]

In *Ledbetter*, however, the Supreme Court ignored this legislative history, and instead relied on the now-repudiated *Lorance* to support its similar approach to pay claims. As Justice Ginsburg points out in her dissent, the Court has "not once relied upon *Lorance*" in the "more than 15 years" since Congress passed the 1991 act, and "[i]t is mistaken to do so now."[7] The Court's failure to take the lessons of the 1991 Act to heart makes the need for Congress to revisit its teachings all the more pressing. Specifically, Congress should restore the paycheck accrual rule – permitting employees to challenge pay discrimination that extends into the filing period, regardless of when it first began – that lower courts had applied before *Ledbetter*. The point is simple and just: as long as an employees' paycheck is still tainted by discrimination, she should not be time-barred from challenging it.

## PROPOSED FIX #2: LENGTHENING THE STATUTE OF LIMITATIONS

At the root of the problem for claiming rights under Title VII is the unusually short statute of limitations. Under current law, a victim of employment discrimination must file a charge with the EEOC within 180/300 days "after the unlawful employment practice occurred."[8]

When Title VII was first enacted in 1964, the statute of limitations was a mere ninety days. That provision of the law merited little discussion, beyond the occasional reference to the problem of stale claims.[9] Congress extended the limitations period to 180 days in 1972 to bring Title VII into line with the National Labor Relations Act, the federal law that regulates unions. Although Title VII's statute of limitations is two to three *years* shorter than the applicable period for most civil lawsuits, no serious effort was made to extend it again until 1990.[10]

The Civil Rights Act of 1990, a bill that was never ultimately passed, included a provision extending the statute of limitations to two years. This time, the proposed extension was intended to bring Title VII into line with other federal antidiscrimination laws, such as Section 1981, which prohibits race discrimination in employment contracts. The House report accompanying the bill criticized the existing limitations period because of the "substantial time" it takes for an individual to realize discrimination has occurred, to become educated about what remedies are available, and to seek the assistance of counsel. Opponents repeated familiar concerns about "stale claims."[11]

A very similar bill was introduced in 1991, again including a two-year limitations period for discrimination claims brought under Title VII.[12] But this provision was contested and ultimately removed from the bill enacted into law as the Civil Rights Act of 1991. Opponents cited concerns about Title VII's goal of "prompt resolution" and the foreseen expansion of liability for businesses.[13] Since 1991, no serious effort to extend Title VII's statute of limitations has been made. Yet such an extension would alleviate many of the unfair pressures currently placed on discrimination victims. Time, it turns out, is important to the realization of discrimination and the willingness to complain, not to mention more mundane steps like figuring out how to file a complaint, finding a lawyer who will take the case, and so on.

Put simply, there is no good reason why a person who slips in a grocery store aisle because of an uncleaned spill should have two years longer than a person who suffers pay discrimination to figure out what happened, who is to blame, and how to enforce her rights.

### PROPOSED FIX #3: LIFTING THE CAPS ON DAMAGES

Justice Ginsburg also noted in her dissent in *Ledbetter* the unfairness that arises from the nonuniformity among federal civil rights laws. Women, for example, may be able to seek redress for some types of pay discrimination through the Equal Pay Act, thereby avoiding the court's harsh rule in *Ledbetter*. But victims of pay discrimination based on race, for example, will not have that option. And even for women, the Equal Pay Act is inadequate to fill the gaps in Title VII's protection that have been created by *Ledbetter*.

In addition, there is another kind of inequity resulting from the nonuniformity of our federal civil rights laws that is also blatantly apparent from the *Ledbetter* case. Because *Ledbetter* involved a claim for sex discrimination under Title VII, the plaintiff's damages were capped by the statutory limit of $300,000 applicable to large employers. The $300,000 limit applies to combined compensatory and punitive damages and to all claims in the case. Thus, even an employer that violates the statute in numerous ways – for example, by retaliating against the employee as well as engaging in discrimination and harassment – cannot be liable for more than $300,000 in combined damages on all claims.[14] The cap applies to Title VII violations *except* for claims challenging conduct covered by Section 1981, which bars race discrimination in the making and enforcement of contracts, including employment contracts. Thus, damages from sex discrimination are capped under Title VII, while damages for race discrimination are not.[15]

The *Ledbetter* case is a good illustration of how the caps work in practice. The jury awarded Ledbetter more than $3.5 million, which included a substantial punitive damages award to punish Goodyear for its gross misconduct. But that award was reduced to $360,000, representing the $300,000 maximum allowable combined compensatory and punitive damages, plus an award of $60,000 in back pay. Thus, a company such as Goodyear stands to lose very little (compared with its total profits, that is) by violating Title VII, even if its conduct is blatant and egregious.

Even when adopted in 1991, a $300,000 cap on damages (lower for smaller employers) was ill-advised for a statute purportedly designed to deter employers from violating Title VII. Sixteen years later, it is obviously insufficient to deter violations of the law. Surely, one of the lawyers at Goodyear could have easily discovered that the Gadsden plant paid its only female manager a substantially lower salary than each of its fifteen male managers, and, indeed, had never paid a female manager equally to a man. If the penalties for violating Title VII were more substantial, companies like Goodyear would have more incentive to be proactive, and to make sure that they complied with equal pay requirements. Congress should thus lift the statutory cap on damages in Title VII, so as to permit plaintiffs full recovery for intentional employment discrimination and impose sufficient incentives on employers to deter discrimination in the first place.

## IF CONGRESS ACTS NOW, IT CAN TEACH THE COURT A NEEDED LESSON ABOUT TITLE VII

Congress should accept the *Ledbetter* dissent's invitation to correct this unnecessarily narrow reading of Title VII and to grant employees a fair chance at challenging unlawful pay discrimination. In so doing, Congress can not only advance justice for discrimination victims but also send a strong message to the Court – and lower federal courts – that crabbed interpretations of Title VII are not in line with Congress's intent.

This is a court that is sorely in need of such a reminder. The paramount goals of Title VII are, and always have been, to prevent discrimination and provide make-whole relief to the individuals harmed by it – not to protect employers from "stale" challenges to ongoing discrimination. But one would not know that from a decision such as *Ledbetter*.

A version of this chapter appeared on July 10, 2007, at writ.findlaw.com, and was coauthored by Deborah Brake.

# 49

## The Lilly Ledbetter Fair Pay Act of 2009

Using a different pen for each letter of his name (to maximize the number of souvenir pens available for those involved in the bill's passage), President Barack Obama signed the Lilly Ledbetter Fair Pay Act into law on January 29, 2009.[1]

That the nation's first black president was signing his first bill into law marked an important civil rights moment, but the bill itself marked another. Former president Bush had preemptively refused to sign such a law when it was first proposed almost two years ago, just as he had with a variety of other pieces of antidiscrimination legislation.[2] (As discussed in Chapter 19, similar threats were issued against the Employment Non-Discrimination Act, which would have banned employment discrimination on the basis of sexual orientation.)

President Obama's decision to proudly sign the Ledbetter Act thus signals not only more robust protection against pay discrimination but also the potential for further improvements and expansion to our nation's civil rights laws. As Obama declared in his speech at the Ledbetter signing, the bill sends "a clear message that making our economy work means making sure it works for everybody."[3]

Through her loss at the Supreme Court – and her will to fight for other women in her situation – Lilly Ledbetter became a sort of folk hero.[4] She waged the fight invited by Justice Ginsburg, who lamented in dissent that "[o]nce again, the ball is in Congress' court." She was inviting Congress to step in, as it had in 1991, to overrule stingy readings and narrow interpretations of anti-discrimination laws.[5]

CONGRESS HEEDS JUSTICE GINSBURG'S CALL:
THE LEDBETTER FAIR PAY ACT OF 2009

Although *Ledbetter* dealt with a rather technical rule, it promised significant adverse effects for victims of pay discrimination. It effectively immunized employers from Title VII liability for pay discrimination in many cases.

Within just a few weeks of the *Ledbetter* decision's issuance, the House Education and Labor Committee convened a hearing as a first step toward considering whether to take corrective legislative action to correct the Court's interpretation. Congress ultimately considered two versions of a bill to restore the paycheck accrual rule – the Lilly Ledbetter Fair Pay Act and the Fair Pay Restoration Act. However, these efforts stalled through the end of the George W. Bush administration, given his promises to veto any such bill. A new version of the bill, the Lilly Ledbetter Fair Pay Act of 2009, was introduced in the Senate on January 8, 2009.[6] It passed 61–36, after supporters successfully fought off hostile Republican amendments. It then passed the House, five days later, by a vote of 250 to 177. President Obama signed the bill into law two days later.

### How the Ledbetter Fair Pay Act Changes the Law – and Affects Age Discrimination and Disability Discrimination Victims, as Well

The Ledbetter Act is narrowly focused on undoing the damage wrought by the Supreme Court's decision. Among Congress's findings was that the *Ledbetter* ruling "significantly impairs statutory protections against discrimination in compensation that Congress established and that have been bedrock principles of American law for decades."[7]

The new law adds a provision to Title VII, which states:

> An unlawful employment practice occurs, with respect to discrimination in compensation in violation of this title, when a discriminatory compensation decision or other practice is adopted, when an individual becomes subject to a discriminatory compensation decision or other practice, or when an individual is affected by application of a discriminatory compensation decision or other practice, including each time wages, benefits, or other compensation is paid, resulting in whole or in part from such a decision or other practice.[8]

The amendments also apply to other antidiscrimination laws like the Age Discrimination in Employment Act and the Americans with Disabilities Act, which borrow Title VII's limitations period. The act is made retroactive to May 28, 2007, the day before the Court issued its ruling in *Ledbetter*.

In effect, the act takes a broad view of the employment practices that trigger the limitations period under Title VII. There will certainly be litigation over the meaning of "other practices," but the law's application to straightforward pay discrimination claims is clear. Employees will still face obstacles to enforcing their substantive rights against pay discrimination – lack of knowledge of disparate pay or its causes, cognitive obstacles to the quick perception of discrimination, as well as fear of, and insufficient protection from, retaliation. But the Ledbetter Act makes sure that employees are not additionally hampered by the Court's crabbed interpretation of Title VII's already-short limitations period.

*A Victory for Working Women – though Not for Lilly Ledbetter Herself*

In sum, while the Lilly Ledbetter Fair Pay Act is not a panacea for all that ails federal antidiscrimination law, it is an essential step in the right direction – toward the promise of equal work opportunity for all. As President Obama noted in his signing speech, the bill honors women like Lilly Ledbetter who have worked hard, have been treated unfairly, and have stood up for the principle of equality. Sadly, and ironically, Ledbetter herself will receive no compensation at all as a result of the law passed in her name. Her jury verdict remains vacated, and the ultimate judgment in Goodyear's favor remains final and unappealable. Yet Ledbetter can know, at least, that her fight will make the world just a little bit better for the working women who follow in her footsteps.

A version of this chapter appeared on February 13, 2009, at writ.findlaw.com.

# 50

# Taking Stock

## Is the Ledbetter Act Working?

In just the first year since the passage of the Lilly Ledbetter Fair Pay Act, courts have struggled with its implementation. While it clearly has undone the damage of the Supreme Court's decision in *Ledbetter v. Goodyear Tire & Rubber Co.*, the first round of cases under the act reveal some open questions – and some cause for concern.

To date, the biggest issue to date is this one: How broadly should courts construe the act's coverage of employment decisions that discriminate in compensation? What constitutes a "discriminatory compensation decision or other practice" as defined in the act?[1] One case from the Third Circuit is a good vehicle for exploring these questions.

### MIKULA V. ALLEGHENY COUNTY: THE FACTS OF THE CASE

A recent ruling from the U.S. Court of Appeals for the Third Circuit, *Mikula v. Allegheny County*, illustrates some of the difficulties courts have confronted in applying the Ledbetter Act.[2] In that case, the same panel of appellate judges twice considered the scope of the Ledbetter Act's coverage of pay discrimination claims, with different results each time.

The plaintiff, Mary Lou Mikula, was hired as a county grants manager in 2001. In September 2004, she petitioned the county to change her title to "grants and project manager" and to increase her salary to equal or exceed that of the male "fiscal manager," who earned $7,000 more annually than she did. The county did not respond. In October 2005, Mikula again lobbied for a pay increase and change in her job title. But the county again failed to respond. In March 2006, Mikula filed an internal complaint with the county's human resources department, in which she compared her job responsibilities with those of the higher-paid fiscal manager and claimed that the pay discrimination began when she was first hired. In an August 2006 letter, the county responded to her complaint, finding her allegations unfounded and stating that her title and salary were "fair when compared with similar jobs." In April 2007, Mikula filed a Title VII charge for pay discrimination with the EEOC.

The district court dismissed Mikula's claim as untimely under *Ledbetter*, holding that the unlawful practice occurred in 2001, when Mikula was first hired at a lower salary than her male counterpart.[3] A "discovery" rule would not have helped Mikula, the court held, because she had discovered the pay disparity at least three years before filing her EEOC charge in 2007. (For employees in Pennsylvania, Title VII charges must be filed within 300 days of their occurrence to be timely; Mikula thus had less than one year to file from whatever date it was on that the statute of limitations had begun to run.)

## THE POST–LEDBETTER ACT RULINGS IN THE *MIKULA* CASE

While Mikula's case was on appeal, however, Congress passed the Ledbetter Act. Moreover, it made the act retroactive with respect to cases, such as Mikula's, that were pending on or after May 28, 2007, the date the Court decided *Ledbetter*.

Surprisingly, a panel of Third Circuit judges at first affirmed the district court's dismissal of the Title VII claim notwithstanding the intervening act. The court concluded that the county's August 2006 letter – which was sent within 300 days of when Mikula filed the charge – was not a "compensation decision or other practice" under the act, because it merely reported the results of the county's investigation into Mikula's complaint. Further, the panel treated that letter as merely a failure to answer a request for a raise, which it also did not view as a compensation "decision" under the act.[4]

In her initial appeal, Mikula had represented herself, but, fortunately, she obtained counsel and plentiful amici curiae support in time to file a petition with the court to reconsider her case. On rehearing, the same Third Circuit panel issued a revised opinion, this time reversing the lower court's dismissal of Mikula's Title VII claim as untimely. Yet, still, the appellate court took an unduly cramped and narrow view of the scope of the Ledbetter Act.

On rehearing, the court viewed its initial error as the refusal to treat an employer's failure to answer a request for a raise as a compensation decision under the act. This time around, the court recognized that an employer's refusal to answer a request for a raise has the same result as an outright denial (which, the court admitted, would clearly be a "compensation decision"). Thus, the court concluded that employers should not be given the incentive to ignore raise requests as a "safe harbor" way of denying such requests for discriminatory reasons.

Thus, the court concluded, Mikula should have been able to sue for any discriminatory paychecks she subsequently received, within the 300-day period before she filed her EEOC charge in April 2007.

The errors in the court's initial decision, however, go much deeper, and not all of them were corrected in the September 2009 decision. Oddly, the court continued to treat the county's August 2006 letter defending Mikula's salary as outside the "compensation decisions" covered by the Ledbetter Act, reasoning that employers should not be penalized for responding to internal discrimination complaints.

## THE WAY IN WHICH THE THIRD CIRCUIT MISUNDERSTOOD THE LEDBETTER ACT

The court's view that treating the August report as a compensation decision would somehow penalize the county for responding to a discrimination complaint reflects its lack of understanding of the scope of the Ledbetter Act. With or without the August report, the Ledbetter Act would treat any paycheck that paid Mikula less because of her sex as a timely basis for her claim if she received it within 300 days before filing the charge.

Indeed, even if Mikula had never filed an internal discrimination claim, or had never even explicitly asked for a raise at all, her claim should still be timely based simply on her allegations that the paychecks she received after June 20, 2006 (300 days before she filed the charge), paid her less than the county would pay a similarly situated male. This would be the correct result under the act even if the pay discrimination began when she was first hired in 2001 and no additional pay decisions followed, nor any requests for raises.

At the core of the Third Circuit's cryptic opinion seems to be a misunderstanding – and perhaps outright rejection – of the paycheck accrual rule that the Ledbetter Act adopted. By tying the timeliness of Mikula's claim to the county's refusal to respond to her requests for a raise, the court seems to require some additional employer practice or compensation decision aside from the initial decision – however old – to pay an employee less on the basis of sex. But the Ledbetter Act legislates expressly to the contrary.[5]

Even if Mikula had never requested a raise or filed an internal complaint, her claim should have been timely because she alleged that she continued to receive lower pay because of her sex into the charge-filing period. Thus, while it reached the correct result in this particular case, the court's opinion suggests a troubling misunderstanding of exactly what the Ledbetter Act accomplished.

The *Mikula* court also seems to misapprehend the remedies available in pay discrimination cases after the Ledbetter Act. Although the opinion is ambiguous, the court appears to limit Mikula's recovery to only those discriminatory paychecks received within 300 days prior to her EEOC charge. The court is correct that the actionable paychecks are limited to this time period. However, in terms of the available relief under the Ledbetter Act, the act explicitly allows up to two years' back pay for pay discrimination that is "similar or related to" the unlawful pay discrimination that occurred within the charging period.[6]

As a result, if Mikula proves that the paychecks she received after June 20, 2006, were tainted with sex discrimination, then she should be able to recover back pay for similar or related pay discrimination in her paychecks going back as far as April 17, 2005. Yet the court's discussion of pre-*Ledbetter* case law, which it viewed the Ledbetter Act as restoring, wrongly seems to preclude any relief beyond the 300-day limit – a result that conflicts directly with the terms of the Ledbetter Act.

A version of this chapter appeared on September 29, 2009, at writ.findlaw.com, and was coauthored by Deborah L. Brake.

# 51

## The Lady in Red

You may not even know that April 17, 2013, is a holiday. It's neither a federal holiday nor one made up by Hallmark to sell cards. It is Equal Pay Day, a day designated by the National Committee on Pay Equity (NCPE) each year since 1996 to signify how long into a new year – the date is usually mid-April – a woman must work to earn what her male counterparts had already earned by the end of the previous year.[1] Equal Pay Day also falls on a Tuesday, to signify when men need to start every workweek to end up with the same pay as women by the end of that week. And to honor the holiday, we should all be wearing red, the official color of Equal Pay Day, to signify that women's paychecks are "in the red."

Equal Pay Day is one of many reminders that pay discrimination remains an important source of gender inequality – one that threatens women's independence and financial security throughout their entire working lives and into retirement. Women continue to make less than eighty cents for every dollar men make, a disparity that cannot be accounted for by labor force commitment, voluntary job choices, or time off to care for children.[2] Indeed, virtually every economist who has crunched the numbers, regardless of his or her ideological slant or background, has concluded that the gender wage gap is at least partially created by pay discrimination – which means paying women less to do the same job simply because they are women.

Despite the entrenched reality of the wage gap, efforts to close it have been largely unsuccessful. And people like Wisconsin governor Scott Walker would be happy to see it grow larger. Walker signed into a law a bill repealing the state's 2009 Equal Pay Enforcement Act (EPEA), which had allowed employees to seek damages in state court for gender-based pay discrimination.[3] This chapter considers the current status of the gender wage gap, some of the obstacles to remediation of pay discrimination claims, and efforts to bolster (or inhibit, as in Wisconsin) women's right to equal pay.

## THE PERSISTENCE OF THE GENDER WAGE GAP

The gender wage gap – the fact that women earn less than men – is a persistent and well-documented reality in the United States. Researchers disagree about the size of the wage gap, but not about its existence or significance. The wage gap is much larger for African-American women and Latina women, who earn even less than white women do, when compared with white men.[4] And it exists at every level of earnings. The percentage gap is highest at the top of the spectrum – female "physicians and surgeons" earn only 63 percent compared with men in the same category[5] – but it is perhaps most significant at the bottom of the spectrum, where even the male wage is startlingly low. The gap grows over the life cycle, leading one study to find that, in their fifteen prime earning years, women earned only 38 percent of what men earned.[6]

As women have increased their labor force commitment, shouldn't this gap have disappeared? One might think so, but the numbers do not reflect this. Although the wage gap has narrowed from the 1970s measure of fifty-nine cents on the dollar to today's seventy-five to eighty cents on the dollar, the bulk of the change occurred in the 1980s and little progress has been made since.[7]

## EXPLAINING THE WAGE GAP: DISCRIMINATION CLEARLY PLAYS A ROLE

According to an article in the *Daily Beast*, the lead supporter of the effort to repeal Wisconsin's EPEA, state senator Glenn Grothman, insists that any wage gap that exists between men and women can be explained entirely by women's greater involvement in child rearing, at the expense of their careers.[8] In a two-lawyer marriage, Grothman speculates, the male lawyer is "working 50 or 60 hours a week, going all out," while the female lawyer is taking "time off," raising kids, and "not go, go, go." When the male lawyer ends up with a $200,000 salary, while the female lawyer ends up with a $40,000 salary, this is, Grothman suggests, because there was "a different sense of urgency in each person."

Grothman also conjectures that men and women have different goals in life, which can also explain the wage gap: "[M]oney is more important for men," he argues. In support of his wild conjecture, Grothman cites Ann Coulter, who he claims has "looked at this" and proven that marriage, and the gender-role divisions that ensue, explains the entirety of the wage gap. (Coulter's view on the wage gap is captured in her quote in the introduction to Part IV, in which she offers to trade equal pay for the right not to pick up the tab at dinner.)

Coulter's baseless reassurances aside, every economist who has examined wage gap data has concluded that it persists to some degree *even when all plausible explanations are controlled for*. Accordingly, no reasonable person can come to any valid conclusion but one that holds that some portion of the gap must be attributed to pay discrimination. For example, part of the wage gap is sometimes attributed to differing degrees of labor force attachment between men and women. (This is another way to phrase Grothman's theory that men care more about money and jobs, while women care more about raising children.) Yet women who work year-round and full-time during at least twelve of fifteen consecutive years still earn only 64 percent of what men with a similar attachment to the labor force earn.[9]

Likewise, differences in the number of hours worked also fail to explain the gender disparity in wages. Hour for hour, women earn less than men do.[10] Differences in educational attainment provide similarly little by way of explanation. The wage gap only goes down a percent or so when comparing men and women with similar levels of college education.[11] Even in the aggregate, these differences do not explain the bulk of the wage gap. When studies simultaneously control for multiple variables such as education, occupation, hours worked, and time away from the workplace because of family care responsibilities, a significant gender gap still remains.

Beyond the statistical analyses, other evidence also supports the persistence of pay discrimination. Studies have shown, for example, that employers penalize women for expected leave-taking beyond the leave most women actually take.[12] There is also a well-documented "wage premium" for married men – probably reflecting the assumption by employers that married men are more stable and have an incentive to work harder to provide for their families – and, correspondingly, a wage penalty for women with children, regarding the converse assumptions that are applied to such women as a class (they will prioritize children first, work second).

The EEOC, which enforces federal antidiscrimination laws including Title VII and the Equal Pay Act, collects millions every year from employers in administrative proceedings that are brought to challenge pay discrimination. Major companies have settled multimillion-dollar lawsuits for pay discrimination. In fiscal year 2011, the EEOC collected $23 million in settlements of Equal Pay Act claims.[13]

For all these reasons, there is absolutely no question that pay discrimination still exists, nor any question that it has harmful effects on women. Even a small pay disparity early in a career can blow up into an enormous one over time, particularly when raises are doled out as a percentage of salary.

## PAY DISCRIMINATION LAW: THE EQUAL PAY ACT

A public service announcement from the late 1960s tunes in to Batman and Robin tied up while a bomb ticks ominously in the background.[14] Fortunately, Batgirl barges in. Batman yells, "Quick, Batgirl, untie us before it's too late." But Batgirl tells them, "It's already too late. I've worked for you a long time, and I'm paid less than Robin."

"Holy discontent," says Robin, surprised by Batgirl's uppity remark. As for Batman, he tells Batgirl that this is "no time for jokes." Batgirl persists: "It's no joke. It's the federal equal pay law: same employer means equal pay for men and women." Now

Batgirl has Robin's attention; he exhorts, "Holy Act of Congress!" But Batman is not so impressed and tries to put Batgirl off, asking if we can "talk about this later." The scene ends as the narrator asks: "Will Batgirl save the dynamic duo? Will she get equal pay? Tune in tomorrow or contact the wage and hour division listed in your phone book under the U.S. Department of Labor."

The law that is being advertised in this clip is the centerpiece of the federal effort to eradicate pay discrimination. Enacted in 1963, the Equal Pay Act guarantees equal pay for equal work for men and women who do the same job for the same employer.[15] The Equal Pay Act is an important source of protection against pay discrimination. A plaintiff may challenge an ongoing violation of the Equal Pay Act at any time, and may seek recovery for the prior two years of discrimination (or three years, if the violation is "willful").

The act, however, has some limitations. For example, it allows for several affirmative defenses even when unequal pay is proven. One such affirmative defense is based on the contention that the wage gap is due to "a factor other than sex."[16] And what can count as such a factor has been broadly construed to include factors that are themselves the product of sex discrimination sometimes such as prior salary. Even more shocking, there is support for the idea that a salary set by mistake can be justified as a factor other than sex.[17]

Moreover, an employee cannot win an Equal Pay Act claim without a comparator – that is, an actual man to whom she can point who is working for the same employer, doing the same job, and earning more than she is. A woman who holds a unique job in a workplace, or simply holds a job that is not the exact equivalent of any job performed in that workplace by a higher-earning man, will have no hope of prevailing under the Equal Pay Act, even if it can clearly be proven that the employer paid her less because of her sex.[18]

The Equal Pay Act does not permit awards of compensatory or punitive damages. Prevailing plaintiffs are limited to back pay and certain other, more limited, types of relief. This limitation is why state laws – like the one Wisconsin just repealed – play an important supplementary role in enforcing equal pay mandates. Before the Wisconsin law was enacted, Wisconsin had a disproportionately large gender-based wage gap as compared with other states. But its ranking had begun to improve, perhaps as employers took note of the state's equal pay requirements.[19]

## PAY DISCRIMINATION: TITLE VII AND THE LEDBETTER CASE

In addition to the Equal Pay Act, Title VII also prohibits pay discrimination. Moreover, as explained in Chapters 47 to 49, Title VII encompasses a broader-range of cases than the Equal Pay Act does. Title VII prohibits employers from taking any employment action "based on sex," which includes decisions that set salaries or grant raises. Thus, any adverse pay decision in which sex was taken into account can be challenged under Title VII.[20]

Title VII has its own limitations, one of which was revealed by Lilly Ledbetter's pay discrimination lawsuit against her employer, and fixed by Congress two years later. The Ledbetter Act was an important fix for the Supreme Court's bad ruling. But it only brought equal pay law back to where it had started. Equal pay laws have been on the books for almost fifty years, and yet the problem of gender-based pay discrimination continues more or less unabated.

One reason for the persistence of gender-based pay discrimination is the difficulty that employees face in learning that pay discrimination has occurred in the first place. Pay decisions are largely made in secret. Even though it is illegal to do so, many employers have policies prohibiting employees from discussing pay with their coworkers.[21] Moreover, many pay decisions are not obviously or inherently adverse: an employee might not even realize that a starting salary or a raise decision reflects discrimination at all, without information that is unavailable to him or her – information, for example, about how the decision was made, or how other similarly situated or slightly senior or junior employees were treated. There are also complicated cognitive biases at work, which lead women to expect lower pay (and thus not to suspect discrimination) and to downplay the possibility that discrimination is the explanation for an adverse employment outcome. And even when pay discrimination is obvious or is discovered, both the Equal Pay Act and Title VII impose procedural obstacles that make it difficult for the victim to enforce her substantive rights. In addition to the improvements recommended in Chapter 48, Congress should focus on other means to eradicate pay discrimination and the more complicated problem of occupational segregation (in society's eyes, there are still "men's jobs" and "women's jobs," and the "women's jobs" pay less), which accounts for a great deal of the gender wage gap. A recent GAO report found that while women represent 49 percent of the overall workforce, they comprise 59 percent of the low-wage workforce.[22] But efforts to enact comparable worth or other means to eradicate occupational segregation have universally failed.

## THE BOTTOM LINE: WE NEED STRONGER FAIR PAY LAWS, OR THE GENDER-DISCRIMINATORY PAY CAP WILL PERSIST

Women do not get paid less because they prefer lower-paying jobs or because they take their work less seriously. They do get paid less because they suffer from intentional pay discrimination. Studies have shown this beyond a shadow of a doubt, and it is too late in the day to reasonably disagree.

Moreover, fair pay laws are not, as Glenn Grothman argues, too burdensome for employers, who are asked simply to look to employees' performance and not their gender when determining starting salaries, raises, and bonuses. Fair pay laws are, however, too burdensome for the class of people they purport to protect – the employees. Even provable pay discrimination often goes unremediated because of procedural obstacles to enforcement, and much pay discrimination goes completely undiscovered. Equal Pay Day is a reminder that unequal pay, despite Batgirl's best efforts, is not a relic of the past. It is alive and well – and in need of superhero-style rescue by Congress, state legislatures, the EEOC, and analogous state agencies.

A version of this chapter appeared on April 17, 2012, at verdict.justia.com.

*Update: Yvonne Richards, the actress who played batgirl, died in 2015.*[23] *But shortly thereafter her legacy was honored by passage of fair pay laws in California and New York, designed to reduce pay secrecy, remove obstacles to pay discrimination claims, and otherwise fill in gaps left by federal equal pay law.*[24]

# 52

# Unfinished Business

A flurry of recent events invites consideration of why gender still matters. To some, this may be surprising: if we are in what some call a post-identity age, in which one's sex, race, or ethnicity does not – or should not – matter, then why still speak about gender? Talking about gender is important for at least one fundamental reason: there is still a gap between ideals of sex equality and of equal citizenship and the reality of many women's lives. Growing attention to the persistence of gender inequality – both in the United States and globally – provides a perfect moment for addressing, and working to close, that gap.

## THE OBAMA PRESIDENCY: A MOVE BEYOND IDENTITY POLITICS?

When Barack Obama was elected in November 2008, after winning a hard-fought battle with Hillary Clinton in the Democratic primary, many were ready to proclaim our arrival at a post-race society. As William Bennett remarked in election night media coverage, "I hope it closes a chapter in American history. The great stain. Obviously you don't change American history. The notion that some people say, well, if you're born black in this country there's just things you're limited from doing, this is the biggest job of all. Think of what you can say to children now. Every child of every race."[1]

Hillary Clinton's near-success in obtaining the Democratic primary nomination and the choice of then-governor Sarah Palin as the vice presidential candidate on the Republican ticket also speak to the state of gender in our society, but, here, the message may be more complicated. Clinton's bid for the nomination, while ultimately unsuccessful, reenergized feminists and caused many people to grapple with the role of gender in politics and as an aspect of leadership. The battle between Clinton and Obama for women's votes reopened debates about essentialism, and revealed not only a generational divide among women but also divides on the basis of other, often complicated, identity categories.

Trying to explain the disappointment, and even anger, that some women felt – and the resulting threats to vote for John McCain that some reportedly made – when Clinton lost to Obama, Susan Faludi wrote of "second place citizens" and the frustration that, eighty-eight years after women's suffrage advocates secured the right to vote, women still hit the glass ceiling in reaching the highest political office.[2]

The gender divides were tapped anew with McCain's selection of Palin as his running mate, in what Faludi described as an "unabashed bid" to court some of Clinton's alienated supporters. Palin invited women to support her candidacy to "shatter that glass ceiling once and for all."[3] With headlines like "Feminist Template Obliterated" and "From Seneca Falls to . . . Sarah Palin?," media commentators grappled with "what women want" and "the puzzling politics of gender."[4] Could women who supported Clinton and felt taken for granted by their party simply "cross out 'Hillary' and write 'Sarah,'" when Palin held a wide variety of beliefs that are at best inhospitable to gender equality, and at worst completely contrary to it?[5]

In the end, despite the disappointment of many female Clinton supporters, exit polls indicated that women's votes clinched Obama's victory, with women's perceiving Obama as speaking directly to women's economic concerns.[6] And African-American women's votes played a significant role in key battleground states. There is thus no doubt that President Obama's election is historic and carries undeniable symbolic power, particularly for Americans old enough to remember earlier civil rights struggles. When Obama himself refers to his life exemplifying the American dream, it is a reminder of the steady evolution in American history toward a more complete realization of founding principles about liberty and equality.

Perhaps the most credible view of the state of race and gender in our society is that the election of Obama signals the *beginning* of a new era in terms of racial equality and justice, rather than a sign that such goals have already been fully achieved. Obama, after all, was the only African American in the Senate when he was elected president.

And, in turn, Clinton's strong campaign does not elide the continuing underrepresentation of women in political office. Rather, it reveals both challenges to, and the persistence of, gender stereotypes that code political leadership as masculine. Faludi, for example, contended that by casting herself as a fighter and winning the support of white male voters, Clinton had "stepped across an unstated gender divide," but crossing this divide seems to be due to her success at being perceived as sufficiently tough and "man enough" for the job. Ironically, loosening of these stereotypes may come from what some have called President Obama's "unisex" presidency, which embraces a "feminine" managerial style emphasizing communication, inclusion, consensus, and collegiality.

## JUSTICE SONIA SOTOMAYOR'S CONFIRMATION: A CONTEMPORARY EXAMPLE OF WHY GENDER – AND ETHNICITY – MATTER IN PUBLIC LEADERSHIP

One important measure of the gender gap between men and women is their representation in high office (both elected and appointed). The problem of political representation, and of ambivalence about women in positions of political power, is by no means restricted to the United States. Women are underrepresented in the law-making bodies of the world's states. Indeed, according to the most recent Global Gender Gap report, there is still a "political empowerment gap" between men and women, measured in terms of "political decision-making at the highest levels."[7] They are certainly underrepresented on the U.S. Supreme Court, to which only three women have ever been appointed, and no more than two have ever served concurrently.[8]

The recent nomination and confirmation of Justice Sonia Sotomayor to the Supreme Court illustrates the tension between the sense of our being in a post-identity age and the sense that identity often still matters deeply. Sotomayor's endlessly quoted statement in a speech – "I would hope that a wise Latina woman with the richness of her experiences would more often than not reach a better conclusion than a white man who hasn't lived that life" – brought issues of identity to the fore.[9]

Why is it important that there be more than one woman on a nation's highest court? Why is it important that a Latino sit on the bench, when the Court has never before included a Hispanic justice? What difference does difference make? Justice Ruth Bader Ginsburg, the second woman appointed to the High Court, gave an interview to Emily Bazelon in which she addressed such questions. When asked about Sotomayor's above-quoted statement, Ginsburg replied, "I'm sure she meant no more than what I mean when I say: Yes, women bring a different life experience to the table. All of our differences make the [judicial] conferences better. That I'm a woman, that's part of it. That I'm Jewish, that's part of it, that I grew up in Brooklyn, N.Y., and I went to summer camp in the Adirondacks, all these things are part of me."[10]

Justice Ginsburg also took on the equal representation issue, suggesting that having more than one woman on the Court had symbolic importance for the public's perception of the Court. As she remarked, "It just doesn't look right in the year 2009" for her to be the sole woman on the Supreme Court (which she became after Justice Sandra Day O'Connor retired in 2006).[11]

Justice Ginsburg also expressed the belief that the lack of gender balance on the court makes a difference. During Judge Sotomayor's confirmation process, the media aired debates over what difference "difference" makes. Justice Ginsburg recalled that although she and Justice O'Connor frequently disagreed, they were always in agreement in the Court's gender discrimination cases. (And studies indicate that this may be one area of difference between female and male judges.[12])

There is another reason, too, that diverse representation and life experience matter. Recollections by various justices – and legal scholars – suggested that the mere presence of a justice with a different life experience (such as Justice Thurgood Marshall, the first African-American justice) exerted a persuasive force. Justice Marshall's stories about experiences of racism and discrimination also broadened the knowledge of the Court, even though he was often in the dissent in later years, as the tide of the Court became more conservative.

Speaking of her own presence on the Court, Justice Ginsburg herself suggested that her male colleagues may not have initially appreciated, as she did, the humiliation experienced by a thirteen-year-old girl subjected to a strip search when school officials thought she might be carrying prescription drugs.[13] Justice Ginsburg also raised a similar point in dissenting from the Court's recent opinion in *AT&T v. Hulteen*, a case in which the majority failed to acknowledge the adverse consequences for women caused by pregnancy discrimination.[14] On the tendency to see pregnancy as unrelated to gender, Justice Ginsburg quoted an earlier federal court opinion: "It might appear to the lay mind that we are treading on the brink of a precipice of absurdity. Perhaps the admonition of Professor Thomas Reed Powell to his law students is apt; 'If you can think of something which is inextricably related to some other thing and not think of the other thing, you have a legal mind.'"[15] (The Court's ruling, and Justice Ginsburg's dissent, in *Hulteen* are discussed in Chapter 38.) Is it easier for women, than it is for men, to see that pregnancy and gender are inextricably linked?

In her confirmation hearings, Justice Sotomayor distanced herself from her famous "wise Latina" remark, explaining that she did not believe any group had an advantage in judging, and that "every person has an equal opportunity to be a good and wise judge, regardless of their background or life experiences."[16] Moreover, she stressed that, as a judge, she is impartial and follows the rule of law. But her life experiences will no doubt inform her own experience as a justice and also enrich the experiences of her colleagues on the bench. Justices sitting in a bench together, as Justice Souter has observed, "are supposed to influence each other, and they do."[17]

Regardless of whether her gender and ethnic identity influence her decision making, the symbolic importance of Sotomayor's nomination and confirmation – not only because she is a woman but also because she is a Latina and a person whose life story embodies the American Dream – is evident from the jubilant celebrations of her confirmation.

Of course, not all women think the same way, but the continuing gender gap in elected and leadership positions denies the opportunity for women's voices to be heard. Some nations have been more aggressive than the United States in trying to close the political gender cap, making use of electoral gender quotas.[18] These quotas, while sometimes criticized as discriminating against men, have been a key component in many countries to overcome barriers to women's office-holding. The refusal to consider these measures may be one reason the United States has comparatively low women's rates of office-holding, despite robust formal legal and political commitments to sex equality.

## NEXT STEPS: THE WHITE HOUSE COUNCIL
## ON WOMEN AND GIRLS

Gender inequality continues to warrant attention in the United States. Toward that end, President Obama announced in 2009 the creation of the White House Council on Women and Girls, to make sure that all federal agencies "take into account the particular needs and concerns of women and girls" and that they "are treated fairly in all matters of public policy."[19] He referred to his earlier signing of the Lilly Ledbetter Fair Pay Act (discussed in Chapters 49 and 50) as one step, but he noted that making progress on many more issues – including economic security, work-family balance, health care, and preventing violence against women – would be an "important measure of whether we are truly fulfilling the promise of our democracy for all our people."[20] The president stressed that these issues are not only "women's issues" but also "family" and "economic" issues. The new council is a small but important step toward focusing anew on the lingering issues of gender inequality and unequal citizenship in the United States.

A version of this chapter appeared on August 31, 2009, at writ.findlaw.com, and was coauthored by Linda C. McClain.

# 53

# Will ABA's Proposed Solutions for Gender
Inequity Work?

In 2001, the ABA's Commission on Women in the Profession issued its third report on the status of women lawyers, "The Unfinished Agenda: Women and the Legal Profession."[1] The commission identifies significant obstacles to the success of women lawyers and makes suggestions for eliminating them.

The ABA report delivers a timely and important message – that equality continues to elude women lawyers. It concludes that while women lawyers continue to be undercompensated, undervalued, sexually harassed, and victimized by discrimination and bias, the overarching perception is nevertheless that they have attained full equality.

The report makes useful suggestions for future research, which may be helpful in developing future ways women can overcome the profession's obstacles. But, unfortunately, some of the report's current proposals for changing the profession do not account for legal disincentives and cultural barriers that make them unlikely to work when applied in the real world.

## OBSTACLE #1: MYTHS ABOUT MERITOCRACY

To begin, the report should be lauded for suggesting research that may debunk the myth that equality has already been achieved, and that the legal profession is already fully meritocratic. Despite hard evidence of persistent and entrenched gender inequality in the legal profession, many fail to see it. This barrier, which Professor Deborah Rhode has identified elsewhere as the "'No Problem' Problem," is perhaps the most insidious.[2] The failure to perceive inequality leads to complacency about gender issues and a corresponding failure to invoke problem-solving mechanisms. To combat these misperceptions, the ABA report encourages better and more systematic assessment of gender inequality problems.

Among the type of assessment suggested are surveys designed to assess the experience of women lawyers with respect to a variety of benchmarks (compensation,

promotion, leadership, work structure, and satisfaction). The push for surveys makes
sense. Surveys and studies can aggregate and publicize the individual, private experiences of women – and that, in turn, can convince lawyers, judges, and the public
that there is a problem to be reckoned with. For example, surveys about sexual
harassment in employment and education – conducted long before "sexual harassment" became a household phrase – certainly had this effect. (See the discussion in
the introduction to Part III of this volume.)

### OBSTACLE #2: GENDER STEREOTYPES

Another important barrier to women's equality arises from persistent gender stereotypes. This barrier, which is certainly not unique to the legal profession, takes several
forms according to the ABA report. The legal profession offers a catch-22 to women,
according to the report: traditionally female characteristics are undervalued by the
profession, yet women tend to be penalized for exhibiting masculine traits.[3]

For example, a woman who is traditionally feminine may be seen as too timid to
be a litigator even though she is adept at settlement. A woman who is an aggressive
litigator, on the other hand, may be seen as a "bitch." In addition, women are held
to higher standards than men are, and rated as less competent than men even where
they are objectively equal. Women are also evaluated using subjective criteria that
validate gender biases, so that, in a sense, they are doomed to fail before they are
even evaluated.

To undercut the effect of negative gender stereotypes, the ABA report identifies
tools for eliminating gender bias in performance evaluations. The report's suggestions include monitoring evaluations for stereotypical remarks, and teaching eval-
uators how to make objective performance reviews.[4] The ABA report is correct
that performance evaluations could certainly be conducted more fairly. But both
law and the reality of law firm culture make that unlikely. Law firms rely almost
exclusively on partners' subjective evaluations of associates in making partnership
decisions. And employment discrimination law not only permits them to do so but
also as a practical matter, insulates such decisions from allegations of discrimination.
Because of these realities, employers have very little incentive to adopt the practices
identified by the ABA as ideal.

The ABA report also advocates placing greater reliance on objective, "outcome-
related" criteria in women's performance evaluations.[5] Ironically, early on women's
advocates urged law firms to rely less on objective criteria, such as the prestige of the
law school a woman attorney attended, or her service on the law review, because such
criteria disadvantaged women. Now, however, the ABA is suggesting that reliance
on objective criteria will enhance fairness.

But it is not clear that women would fare better in a system that puts more weight
on objective "outcome-related criteria." In the context of private practice, many of
the potential objective measures, like rainmaking or trial experience, would work

against women, due in part to other forms of discrimination and stereotyping. For example, a woman may not get trial experience as an associate, because she is stereotyped as being likely to be better at brief writing – then have her lack of trial experience held against her when she is up for partner. Or a woman may find she is less successful as a rainmaker because male clients prefer to work with men, or because male partners prefer to send business to younger male lawyers – then have her lack of rainmaking held against her when she is up for partner, or when, as a young partner, her compensation is determined.

## OBSTACLE #3: LACK OF MENTORING AND SUPPORT NETWORKS

A third important obstacle to women is the lack of role models, mentors, and support networks for women lawyers. This has been identified as a persistent problem by every study of women in the legal profession. That part is easy. What is difficult is figuring out why it happens, and how to combat it. One explanation certainly lies in the numbers: there are fewer women in positions of leadership to be mentors to younger women.[6] Other explanations lie in culture and attitudes. Men may avoid mentoring women because they fear accusations of sexual harassment, because they feel more comfortable with men, because they take men more seriously – or even, in some instances, because their wives dislike their working with women. Women who themselves attain success in law sometimes fail to mentor younger women to avoid drawing attention to their own gender, or because they feel those women should have it as hard as they did. The ABA report recommends formal mentoring programs, though it recognizes that assigned relationships often don't prosper. (Unfortunately, assigning someone a mentor is often like "assigning" them a friend – an attempt to create a compatibility that may not exist naturally.)

Another, perhaps more promising, recommendation in the report is to encourage women's networks across organizations. Women's bar associations, support groups, and executive golf groups can all serve this purpose. Interestingly, sex discrimination law has thus far had very little to say about mentoring – although it can, by policing other forms of discrimination (such as in hiring and partnership), help greater numbers of women reach the top.

## OBSTACLE #4: FAMILY RESPONSIBILITIES

By and large, places where women practice law make it hard to fulfill both family and professional responsibilities. And it is, of course, not news that women tend to be more burdened with family responsibilities than men or that work-family conflicts are pervasive.

Law firms and other employers have responded to widespread complaints about women's work-family conflicts (and laws telling them they have to respond) by enacting a variety of policies designed to ease women's burdens. Accordingly, most firms report that they have some family-friendly policies on the books, like part-time schedules or generous family and medical leave. But the gap between policies and practice is tremendous. Very few women utilize these opportunities, and those that do often lose opportunities for advancement.

The ABA report identifies "best practices" like flex-time, telecommuting, and generous leave policies as ways to reduce the impact of work-family conflicts on women.[7] But, ultimately, the commission has the same problem that feminist lawyers and scholars have – there is no easy way to reconcile rigorous careers with the demands of motherhood. Until men begin to really share the burdens of childrearing, working women will continue to struggle.

## OBSTACLE #5: SEXUAL HARASSMENT

No report on the status of women would be complete without at least a nod to the problem of sexual harassment – and the ABA report is no exception. Predominantly suffered by women, sexual harassment takes an incredible toll on physical and emotional health, career advancement, and economic well-being. And, as many studies and cases reveal, sexual harassment continues to be an entrenched problem in the legal profession.

The ABA report calls for employers to enact effective policies that provide effective, safe grievance mechanisms for victims of harassment, and that are calculated to punish harassers. But Title VII, the federal statute under which employers can be held liable for sexual harassment committed by their employees, already gives employers the incentive to take those actions.[8] Yet surveys continue to report widespread harassment in almost every employment setting. Whether antiharassment policies have any effect on the incidence of harassment – or simply serve to insulate employers from big damages awards by allowing them to use the policy as part of their defense – needs to be explored. And clearly, more needs to be done to combat the problem of sexual harassment than the enactment of policies alone.

## OBSTACLE #6: GENDER BIAS IN THE JUSTICE SYSTEM

In focusing on gender bias in the judicial system, the ABA report picks up on two decades of work by federal, state, and local task forces designed to study that problem. These task forces – and the ABA report – cite many types of bias: disrespectful treatment of women by judges and opposing counsel; valuation of the credibility of women lawyers, litigants, and witnesses below that of their male counterparts; and judges' reliance on demeaning stereotypes about gender in deciding cases. The ABA report points to a model plan for combating gender bias drafted by the National Judicial Education Program.[9] Among other things, the plan calls for ongoing monitoring of gender bias problems, antibias education, codes of conduct, and bias complaint mechanisms. These proposals may be a more effective tool than the law, which has so far failed to get at the problem of gender bias in courts.

## CONCLUSION

The ABA Report comes at the same time as news that more than 50 percent of incoming law students are now female – a sign taken by some to mean that the trends in legal education and the profession are changing.[10] But studies also show that women in the law school setting – faculty, administrators, and students – fare worse in law schools in every measurable category. Perhaps the best place for the profession to start combating discrimination is in their training grounds: law schools.

A version of this chapter appeared on May 22, 2001, at writ.findlaw.com.

# 54

## Equality Still Elusive for Women in the Federal Workforce

The workplace depicted in the 1980 movie *Nine to Five* (described in detail in the introduction to this book) is a veritable wonderland of sex discrimination.[1] Sexual harassment, pay discrimination, rampant stereotyping, and family-unfriendly policies, to take just the most obvious examples. How much difference has thirty years made? To read this book, one might conclude not much. A recent study of the federal workforce depicts a similarly dismal scene, in which female federal employees labor on unfair terrain and continue to experience what might seem to be dated problems of discrimination.[2]

### GENDER AND THE FEDERAL WORKFORCE

In 2010, the EEOC convened a working group to "identify the obstacles that remain in the federal workplace that hinder equal employment opportunities for women."[3] The EEOC is broadly charged with implementing federal antidiscrimination laws in the workplace, in both the public and the private sector. Although federal employees have the same substantive protections as other employees, they are subjected to different procedural requirements for claiming them. There is, thus, a separate office within the EEOC to deal with the federal workforce, and it is this office that convened the working group as part of the EEOC's "overall mission to eradicate discrimination in both the federal sector and private sector workplace."[4]

Given that the federal government is the nation's largest employer – employing nearly four and a half million people[5] – it makes sense to focus a bright light on the challenges that still face female employees. (By comparison, even Walmart, the nation's largest private sector employer, employs only 1.3 million people in the United States.[6]) The working group gathered together federal EEO directors, federal "affinity" groups like Federally Employed Women, nonfederal advocacy groups, and a social scientist from Harvard. Together, these "dialogue partners" considered the most serious impediments to women's equality and came up with suggestions for eliminating them.

In broad brush, the working group found that while women have made significant advances in the federal workforce, they still experience inequality on a variety of fronts. The report highlighted six "obstacles" to equal opportunity, as follows:

- Inflexible workplace policies create challenges for women in the federal workforce with caregiver obligations.
- Higher-level and management positions remain harder to obtain for women.
- Women are underrepresented in science, technology, engineering, and mathematics fields in the federal workforce.
- Women and men do not earn the same average salary in the federal government.
- Unconscious gender biases and stereotypical perceptions about women still play a significant role in employment decisions in the federal sector.
- There is a perception that federal agencies lack commitment to achieving equal opportunities for women in the federal workplace.

## WOMEN AND CAREGIVING RESPONSIBILITIES

The report documents the basis for each conclusion and the collateral consequences, and identifies proposals for change. For example, with respect to inflexible workplace policies, the report notes that while the number of women (and mothers) in the workplace has dramatically increased, their caregiving responsibilities have hardly changed at all – they are still the primary caregivers in most families. This leads to greater conflicts for women than for men between caregiving and work and, according to a GAO report from 2003, a greater chance for women of foregoing advancement or greater earnings in exchange for positions with more flexibility.[7]

Inflexible workplace policies, the report concludes, lead to a variety of consequences, including dissatisfaction for female employees; dampened productivity, morale, and attendance; difficulty in the recruitment and retention of women; and leaves of absence while women tend to caregiving responsibilities that can hinder their ability to acquire necessary training and experience for advancement.

The report thus recommends that federal agencies should add flexibility to jobs, including flexible start and end times, job sharing, telecommuting, and more generous leave and benefits. (For what it's worth, Lily Tomlin's character in *Nine to Five* was a big advocate in the movie of job sharing.) It also recommends that training and other measures should be undertaken to ensure that those who take advantage of flexible features should not be "penalized or stigmatized for doing so."[8]

The problem of conflicts between caregiving responsibilities and work is not unique to the federal government. The EEOC has tried more broadly to tackle these issues with the adoption in recent years of an enforcement guidance on caregiver discrimination, and a list of "best practices" designed to eliminate the most common features of the workplace that disproportionately impact women with caregiving responsibilities.[9] Likewise, many advocacy groups and academics have worked hard to bring attention to these issues and to propose model workplace policies that would make for a more level playing field for women.

## WOMEN, UNEQUAL PAY, AND THE GLASS CEILING

The report also focuses attention on the problem of unequal pay and the difficulty that women have in ascending to the highest levels of management. Within the federal workforce, women comprise 43 percent of the workforce, but only 37 percent of GS-14 and GS-15 positions and only 30 percent of senior executive service positions. The average grade for women is a full level below the average for men. And women are paid, on average, eleven cents less on the dollar.[10]

Neither the pay gap nor the glass ceiling is unique to the federal government. Indeed, the problems seem to be worse in the private sector and common across all fields. As discussed in Chapters 47 to 51, the gender wage gap remains both stark and stagnant. Researchers disagree about the size of the wage gap, but not about its existence or significance. Likewise, the glass ceiling is a real and documented reality in virtually every field, leading to a "pyramid" formation for women in many of them. (Women hold only 4.6 percent of CEO positions in Fortune 1000 companies.[11])

The working group report focuses on possible solutions to these problems in the federal workforce. It recommends specific measures to increase the availability and effectiveness of mentoring and networking. It encourages agency-by-agency self-audits to identify specific obstacles to women's advancement. With respect to unequal pay, the report encourages better and more data collection about the particularized problems. It also encourages an amendment of the Equal Pay Act to allow for attorney's fees and costs, the lack of which currently makes it difficult for discrimination victims to find lawyers.

Finally, and perhaps most important, the report concludes that "the federal government should take on the role as the Model Employer and implement a strategy to eliminate the gender pay gap among federal employees."[12] As the nation's largest employer, the federal government should assume this role in all respects. Pay discrimination in many workplaces goes undetected because employees do not have access to the information that would reveal the disparities; and even when such disparities are detected by employees, employees face many obstacles in trying to enforce their substantive rights.

Moreover, there is nothing in antidiscrimination law that gives employers any incentive to take proactive measures to ensure equal pay. There's no reward for implementing fair-pay practices when setting starting salaries, nor any for conducting self-audits that would reveal unintended, but discriminatory, pay patterns. To the contrary, looking for problems might set employers up for lawsuits, creating incentives not to do so. If the federal government were to make good on this recommendation, it would set an example for other, smaller employers that might make a real difference in pay equity.

## UNCONSCIOUS BIAS AND RETICENCE TO ENFORCE ANTIDISCRIMINATION NORMS

The final two obstacles to equality that were identified in the working group report are (1) the persistence of unconscious gender bias and stereotyping, and (2) the perception by employees that federal agencies are not truly committed to equal employment opportunity. The report notes that "prejudiced actions are often the unconscious manifestation of mental processing and stereotypical associations," which may result in management's "viewing female applicants and current employees in predetermined ways."[13] One particular practice identified in the report is the "mini-me" syndrome, in which hiring employees are unknowingly in search of candidates with similar characteristics to their own. Unless the hiring employees are themselves diverse – recall the glass ceiling problem, however – this results in unequal opportunities at the hiring and promotion stages. The report recommends measures such as unconscious bias training – and the use of something called the Implicit Association Test – to bring these biases to the conscious level and make those who are hiring employees more attuned to their own prejudices.

Evidence of a lack of commitment to equal opportunity included the failure by some agencies to fund EEO programs, failure to comply with existing regulations and directives, and the failure to hold agencies accountable when discrimination is proven. Although the problems identified were specific to the federal government, many other private sector employees have a similar perception of their own employers, and feel that trying to enforce their rights against discrimination will be futile. For the federal workforce problems, the report suggests a variety of specific responses, including funding guarantees, audits to assess compliance, adequate punishment of offenders, and publicizing findings of discrimination. Other private sector employers would be wise to do their own self-audits and figure out how to clean up their own shops. The failure to do so, as we see in highly publicized cases of discrimination and harassment, can be costly.[14]

## CONCLUSION

The most important thing about this report is that it exists. All employers – particularly those employing millions of workers – should take stock of the role that gender continues to play in their workplaces. If we simply count heads – for example, how many women are in the workforce, how many are the sole or primary breadwinner in the family – we might reach the mistaken conclusion that equality is damn near achieved. But the true state of gender equality turns not on whether women are hired, but whether they can succeed once they have been hired. This report suggests that we still have some distance to travel.

A version of this chapter appeared on January 7, 2014, at verdict.justia.com.

# 55

## "Girlie Men"

During the 2004 Republican National Convention, Arnold Schwarzenegger brought the cheering crowd to its feet when he declared: "And to those critics who are so pessimistic about our economy, I say: Don't be economic girlie men."[1] The term "girlie man" came from a *Saturday Night Live* skit, in which two Schwarzenegger-imitating weightlifters used the term to mock those they considered their physical inferiors – those with less disproportionately huge biceps.

Schwarzenegger first used the "girlie men" term to attack those California legislators with whom he was stalemated over the state's budget. Some of those who were offended asked for an apology – on the ground, for example, that the term was often used to derogate gay men. But no apology was forthcoming. Indeed, a spokesperson for Schwarzenegger described the comment as an "an effective way to convey wimpiness."[2] And later, Schwarzenegger argued that people should just lighten up about his remarks, for he had merely meant the term as "a joke."

Even Democrats have started using the term. Maureen Dowd, in her column in the *New York Times*, quoted a Democratic insider who had complained that Senator John Kerry had "turned into a girlie-man."[3] And some of the very same California legislators targeted by Schwarzenegger's earlier invective proudly attended fellow legislator Rico Oller's fund-raising event, "Rico's Road Kill Rally – No Girlie Men Allowed."[4]

The increasing use of the term "girlie men" is no joke; it's an example of offensive yet powerful sex stereotyping. The term wrongly assumes that women and girls are weak and ineffective – men's physical inferiors and (by implication) simply their inferiors. These stereotypes continue to wreak havoc not only in the political arena but also in our courtrooms – when, for example, women lose discrimination cases because they do not conform to gender stereotypes – and our workplaces.

## VICE PRESIDENT CHENEY'S "SOFTER SIDE" REMARK: ANOTHER IMPLICIT SLUR ON WOMEN

With women serving effectively in the military, and young women (even girls) excelling in the Olympics, America is flooded with proof that being a girl or a woman is not to be equated with being weak or ineffective. Indeed, the U.S. women's teams brought home more gold medals from Athens than the men's teams did – showing their strength, speed, courage, and stamina in the process. Yet this stereotype continues.

And, sadly, the use of the "girlie men" term isn't the only time that this very message of women's supposed inferiority and weakness has been sent during the campaign season. Consider Vice President Cheney's convention speech, which mocked John Kerry's call for "a more sensitive war on terror."[5]

Cheney barbed sarcastically: "As though Al Qaeda will be impressed with our softer side."[6] Cheney's comment implied, of course, that Kerry's war on terror would be too womanly, and, in his mind, too weak and tentative. When a man has a "soft side," after all, it's typically deemed his feminine side.

## A "GIRLIE MAN" SUPPOSEDLY LACKS NOT ONLY PHYSICAL STRENGTH BUT NERVE AND GUTS

Putting Schwarzenegger's "girlie men" remarks in context helps to illuminate the stereotypes they further.

First, consider his attack on the California legislators. Schwarzenegger argued, "They cannot have the guts to come out there in front of you and say, 'I don't want to represent you. I want to represent those special interests: the unions, the trial lawyers'. . . I call them girlie men. They should get back to the table, and they should finish this budget."[7] A "girlie man," in this view, lacks "guts" because he is beholden to special interests. His "girlieness" is a kind of "wimpiness" – a lack of nerve, a lack of strength, and an inability to speak with an independent mind, and get things accomplished. Conversely, the phrase implies, "real" men have guts, courage, strength, and the capacity for strong leadership that serves the people directly. So given the choice, the phrase implies, we should prefer "real men" over "girlie men" as our political leaders.

That's not the only choice we have, of course: we could also elect actual women, as Schwarzenegger and others who have used the term seem to forget. It's damaging for America to continue to identify maleness with the qualities we hope for in political leaders – and, indeed, in business leaders. We will continue to see women in disproportionately small numbers in leadership positions in government and in business as long as this stereotype reigns.

And even when – and if – more women are among the ranks of elected officials, and women legislators simply cannot be ignored, it's doubtful that the stereotyping will stop. Instead, it's likely that a persistent, equally offensive distinction will emerge.

The distinction could, for instance, contrast "girlie women," who are seen as being weak, indecisive, and typical of their sex, with "manly women," who are seen as departing from their gender to mimic the way men think and act. The former would be seen as weaklings, the latter, as pretenders. Walking the line would be difficult, if not impossible, and women shouldn't be expected it to walk it, in any case.

## PLAYING INTO EXCEPTIONALLY DAMAGING HISTORICAL STEREOTYPES

The same equation of femaleness with weakness and dependence that Schwarzenegger and Cheney so casually adopt has tainted our history since the early days of the republic. For example, one repeatedly offered rationale for limiting the right to vote to propertied white men – and thus excluding free women, enslaved men and women, and men without property – was that only propertied men were capable of the independence prerequisite for citizenship. Ignored was the fact that women's and enslaved persons' dependence was legally enforced. Legally, both were economically dependent on their husbands and subject to their authority.

Historically, notions of physical and intellectual differences between the sexes meant that women were confined to the domestic sphere, while men operated in the commercial and public spheres. Decades of civil rights laws and constitutional equality litigation have worked at limiting the law's tolerance of such stereotypes. But if a juror still clings to a stereotype – perhaps because society itself does, and its leaders do – then the legal system cannot effectively correct for that bias. The jury, after all, is still often a "black box" characterized by secret decision making.

## NOT JUST A JOKE: HOW THE "GIRLIE MEN" SLUR HAS BECOME AN UGLY POLITICAL TACTIC

But aren't we taking this all too seriously? After all, Schwarzenegger's term was borrowed from a *Saturday Night Live* sketch. True, but it wasn't *repeated* by him in an *SNL* sketch. Instead, it was used in a political speech, calculated to serve a particular goal crucial to the California governor's ability to push his agenda through. Then it was used again – and this time, the use clearly was calculated, not off the cuff – in a political speech at the Republican Convention. That speech was crucial to Governor Schwarzenegger's political future; whether he got a strong reception, he knew, would help decide what his prospects might be. Under pressure, the governor resorted to stereotypes.

If there were any doubt Schwarzenegger meant to stereotype rather than just joke with this term, it was eliminated at the convention when he contrasted these "girlie men" with President Bush, whom he described as "a leader who doesn't flinch, who doesn't waver, and does not back down."[8] (The choreography of the Republican Convention, meanwhile, brought to mind for many commentators the images of president as cowboy or president as Western gunslinger. No images of a Marlboro Woman were invoked.)

The message is clear: women equal weakness. (Notwithstanding the strong, powerful female bodybuilders Schwarzenegger doubtless has known in his career; notwithstanding Linda Hamilton, the actress who survived punishing physical training to work with him in *The Terminator*; and notwithstanding the strong, powerful women politicians who represent the people of his home state.)

## ANOTHER DAMAGING STEREOTYPE: MILITARY SERVICE IS A PROXY FOR LEADERSHIP ABILITY

Meanwhile, on both sides of the aisle, another pernicious equivalence is being put forward. On this view, masculinity, which itself is equal to strength and honor, is shaped by military service, and both are prerequisites for effective political leadership. Senator Kerry, for instance, opened his acceptance speech by stating that he was "reporting for duty." In so doing, Kerry placed first among his qualifications for leadership the one that he no doubt thought would give him a decided edge over President Bush: his record of military service and his status as a decorated war hero. In drawing on his Vietnam experiences with his "band of brothers," Kerry relied on a qualification that was totally unavailable to women of his generation: active combat duty during wartime. Meanwhile, President Bush continues to trumpet and rely on his war on terror as a strong "plus" in his campaign. A view like this sees those who dwell on Iraq's thousand dead U.S. soldiers and thousands of Iraqi casualties as weak and self-indulgent – in a word, womanly.

Decades ago, Georgetown professor Wendy Williams observed that among our deepest cultural myths about men and women is that of man as the aggressor in war and sex, and woman as mother and nurturer. This myth, too, reared its ugly head this campaign season, as a battle over each candidate's war credentials – and hence, really, over each's manliness – was waged.

Worse, the term "girlie men" and the mockery of "sensitivity" as a dangerous form of softness implies that those who are antiwar are weak. Masculinity, these days, seems to require acting forcefully and relentlessly, heedless of the consequences: shoot first, ask questions later, and never look back. Thus, to question whether military action is necessary, or whether it is being conducted in a justifiable manner, is unmanly. The man who argues for peace is not a statesman, but a "girlie man." The woman who argues for peace is simply illustrating the weaknesses of her gender.

## BUSINESSES AND UNIVERSITIES, AT LEAST, HAVE BEGUN TO VALUE "FEMALE" WORK STYLES

Ironically, even as these stereotypes about leadership hold sway in political rhetoric, businesses and universities have come to appreciate models of leadership associated with more supposedly "feminine" styles – such as consensus building, cooperation, careful listening, and the like. In addition, works such as Anne Crittenden's recent book, *If You've Raised Kids, You Can Manage Anything*, argue the case that the skills involved in parenting, such as developing patience and a sense of empathy, translate effectively into the world of work and management.

Nevertheless, old stereotypes die hard: a woman's years of child raising are still typically seen as a resume gap, not an extra qualification.

## SCHWARZENEGGER'S HYPOCRISY: AMERICANS ARE EQUAL, AS LONG AS THEY'RE NOT "GIRLIE"

Schwarzenegger's "girlie men" remarks aren't just offensive in themselves – they also undermine his other promises to his electorate. Elsewhere in his convention speech, Schwarzenegger characterized America as a nation where difference doesn't matter and that brings out the best in people, "no matter the nationality, no matter the religion, no matter the ethnic background." In this America, he contended, everyone should have the same chances and the same opportunities. By contrast, he said, terrorists hate democracy, hate religious freedom, and "hate the progress of women."

Let's take Schwarzenegger at his word: he suggested that difference, presumably including sex difference, truly should not affect one's chances and opportunities in a free and equal America. He also suggested that "the progress of women" is a quintessentially American ideal. But if the governor wants women to truly be equal, he must stop equating being a woman with being weak.

A version of this chapter appeared on September 21, 2004, at writ.findlaw.com, and was coauthored by Linda C. McClain.

*Update: The Women's World Cup final on July 5, 2015, in which the United States beat Japan by a score of 5–2, was the most-watched soccer game in American history. With more than 26 million viewers, this soccer game was watched by more people than recent NBA basketball finals and the 2014 World Series. See Richard Sandomir, Women's World Cup Final Was Most-Watched Soccer Game in United States History, N.Y. Times, July 7, 2015, at B8. As for Arnold Schwarzenegger, after serving two terms as the governor of California, he returned to acting, starring in the 2015 dud* Terminator: Genisys, *as Pops, an elderly robot.*

# 56

## Playing "Too Womany" and the Problem of Masculinity in Sport

With forty years under its belt, Title IX is rightfully lauded for having not just leveled, but transformed the playing field for women and girls. Title IX, passed as part of the Education Amendments of 1972, provides that "no person in the United States shall, on the basis of sex, be excluded from participation in, be denied the benefits of, or be subjected to discrimination under any education program or activity receiving Federal financial assistance."[1] Simply put, Title IX bans sex discrimination by educational institutions that take federal money.

Congress's aim in passing Title IX was to provide women and girls with equal opportunity in education in an era when they were blatantly discriminated against in terms of admission, especially to professional schools; had their enrollment numbers capped; or were admitted but were subjected to entirely different (and worse) treatment.

Title IX indeed has changed the face of education. It has been invoked to protect students against sexual harassment by teachers and peers, to ensure fair treatment of pregnant and parenting students, to remove obstacles to women's education in nontraditional fields like science and math, and to curtail the use of single-sex education that was rooted in stereotype. But Title IX is most known for its impact on athletics, even though that was probably the furthest thing from the legislators' minds when they enacted it. (The legislative history suggests little more than some chuckling over the prospect of coed football and coed locker rooms.)

Title IX's transformative effect on women's sports is undeniable. One year before Title IX's passage, there were fewer than 300,000 female high school athletes. Today, there are more than 3 million. A girl's likelihood of playing high school sports has gone from one in twenty-seven to nearly one in two. Female college sports have seen dramatic growth as well – from 32,000 women playing in 1971 to more than 200,000 playing today.

There is no question that sports have changed women. Female sports participation has proven positive effects that are related to academic achievement; job success;

positive self-esteem; reduced incidence of self-destructive behaviors like smoking, drugs, sex at a young age, and teen pregnancy; and physical and mental health benefits. By and large, sports have been empowering and have even changed, in fundamental ways, what it means to be a woman.

But have women changed sports? Why is it that despite the widespread participation of women and girls in sports, a team of ten-year-old boys would be told by their male trainer (as recently happened to one of my sons) the reason they lost their soccer game is because they "played too womany"? (No, "womany" is not a word, but that's beside the point here.) And why is it that this remark strikes so few people as offensive? Has women's participation in sports changed the norms of femininity for women, but not the norms of masculinity for men?

## THE MASCULINE ORIGINS OF SPORT

Sports have always been a place where masculinity is learned and practised. Sports were introduced in American schools out of fear that boys were becoming too womanly when the shift from an agrarian to an industrial labor force, along with limits on child labor, left them at their mothers' apron strings rather than their fathers' boots. For athletic boys, sports are a path to success and popularity. Conversely, too, boys who lack athletic interest or ability risk remaining on the periphery of masculinity. Indeed, sports are so typed as masculine that they are sometimes pushed as a cure for homosexuality in the pseudo-psychological/religious programs designed, on false pretenses, of course, to supposedly turn gay kids straight. The same message surfaces in more mainstream programs, as well. As reported in one lawsuit, when a student complained to the principal that he was experiencing antigay harassment, the principal reassured him, "You can learn to like girls. Go out for the football team."[2] The message is endemic to American boyhood: an athletic boy is a real boy.

Sport is a rite of passage for boys, and an institution that reinforces a hierarchy of masculinity. The very nature of sports, as developed in schools and at other competitive levels, is associated with core tenets of masculinity – physicality, aggression, competition, and winning. The more a sport revolves around these features, the more masculine it is perceived to be. And the more it emphasizes violence, aggression, or brute strength over aesthetics, the more masculine it is perceived to be. The more masculine it is, the more money gets poured into it, the more fans it has, and the more it reinforces traditional norms of masculinity. No one would, for example, question the relative placement of football or basketball to diving or gymnastics on the masculinity scale.

## THE COST OF PRIZING MASCULINITY IN SPORT

The reinforcement of traditional norms of masculinity through sport has its costs. For example, the allocation of resources to the most masculine male sports – football and basketball – consumes the lion's share of most institutional athletic budgets, leaving all other men's sports to scramble for the leftovers. Recent data show that Division I colleges and universities spent about 88 percent of their total men's sports budget on football and basketball.[3] (And despite conventional wisdom, the vast majority of these sports do *not* generate a profit, especially when all costs and expenditures are actually accounted for.) The huge rosters for football also take spots from "less masculine" sports. With seventy to eighty or more football players on the roster, there are fewer resources to fund other teams.

The money devoted to football and basketball has a cost for all such "less masculine" sports – both men's and women's. With no end in sight to their bloated budgets, the over-allocation has to be taken from somewhere. Women's sports, along with the less masculine men's sports (the so-called nonrevenue sports), take the hit. Title IX offers little resistance. It does *not* require equal funding of men's and women's sports; funding is just one factor in a qualitative comparison of the overall men's and women's programs. Even then, actual equality is mostly a pipe dream at the highest competitive levels. Regardless of how winning or well-known a women's team is, it is unlikely to receive the perks that are taken for granted in the most-valued men's sports. Women's teams rarely, if ever, see the luxury of hotel accommodations on nights before home games, high-tech video and digital display equipment in locker rooms, travel by chartered jet, being coached by someone paid more than the university president, and money lavished on recruits.

There are other costs, as well, to a system that encourages and rewards extreme performances of masculinity in male athletes. With masculinity comes a presumption of heterosexuality, and an expectation of unfettered sexual access to women. The culture of men's sports creates an atmosphere of entitlement in which sex is one of the perks. This sets up a dynamic in which men who do not live up to these norms are hazed or harassed; and other men feel entitled to behave in sexually aggressive, even assaultive, ways. Indeed, there have been several recent cases showing how expectations of sexual access can be part and parcel of a high-profile men's sports program, which I discuss below.

## MASCULINITY'S COLLATERAL DAMAGE

In one of the more notorious of these cases (although it is more of a variation on a theme than a breaking of the mold), the University of Colorado was sued for collaborating in a football recruiting program that supplied female students as euphemistically named "ambassadors" to show high school senior football recruits a good time during their visits to campus. The lawsuit arose from the gang rape of two female students by football players and recruits during one of these visits. In *Simpson v. University of Chicago Boulder*,[4] a federal court of appeals held that the university was accountable for failing to supervise its recruiting program, despite its knowledge of the risk of sexual assault.

In a similarly egregious case against the University of Georgia, a female student alleged that she was gang-raped by a group of football and basketball players. Again, a federal appeals court allowed the suit to proceed based on the university's knowledge, prior to admitting him, that the athlete who led the gang rape had committed prior sexual assaults and harassment. The university also displayed deliberate indifference in taking a full *eight months* after receiving the police report to conduct an investigation. And, in the end, the university never punished the assailants.[5]

Other cases involve male athletes whose hypermasculine aggression is not reserved for women. In several cases, schools have been sued for their inadequate responses to cases of male-on-male hazing and assault. In one of the earlier cases, *Seamons v. Snow*,[6] a male high school football player was tied, naked, to a horizontal towel bar with athletic tape; his former girlfriend was then invited in to see him. The coach viewed this as a normal part of athletic culture – "Boys will be boys" – and when the victim complained, the coach accused him of betraying the team. The victim should have, the coach explained, "taken it like a man." The victim was told to apologize to the team for tattling, and, when he refused, he was dismissed from the team. Unfortunately, the federal appellate court reviewing this case upheld the dismissal of the complaint, concluding that the "qualities Defendants were promoting, team loyalty and toughness, are not uniquely male." And there was no proof, the court noted, that a female victim would have been treated better. More recent cases have done a better job discerning sex stereotyping in such hypermasculine performances in male locker-room culture, and have allowed Title IX claims to proceed.[7] These cases show some promise in using Title IX to challenge the extreme excesses of male sports culture. But their impact so far has been limited.

What all these cases have in common is the exaltation of men's athletics to the point where it becomes untouchable by the rest of the university, however outrageous the behavior being condoned. The phenomenon of "what happens in athletics, stays in athletics" is far too prevalent in the big-time men's sports programs, where ranks close to preserve the privilege and status of the program above all else. Even the worst examples of bad behavior being covered up fail to provoke the kind of momentum necessary to truly change the culture of privilege in the university that the most elite men's programs enjoy.

It is not just women and less privileged boys and men who pay the price of a male sport culture gone awry. The masculinity of sport has costs even for the men who attain the highest privilege in sports. Sport sociologists have identified a "toxic jock" identity that men in the highest-status sports often assume, which leads to an overidentification with the role of athlete, and an indulgence in harmful and dangerous high-risk behaviors. Men who overidentify with sport prioritize athletics over academics, which leaves many of them with little education and dim job prospects. Needless to say, most college athletes do not go on to be professional athletes.

## THE CHALLENGES OF CHANGING SPORT CULTURE

While female athletes have made great strides under Title IX, their success has done little to change the masculine culture of sport. And yet this is a challenge that Title IX must take up if women are ever to attain equal status in sport. The masculinity that sport confers on boys and men depends too much on separating the masculine, which is prized, from the feminine (whether it appears in girls or less masculine boys), which is reviled. Insulting male athletes for playing "too womany" is an ungrammatical variation on an old theme, the time-tested insult that a boy "throws like a girl." The language can be updated in myriad ways, and for extra punch, accompanied by vulgar references to female anatomy, but the underlying message is the same as it was in the pre–Title IX era. And, remarkably, the adults who are entrusted to teach sports to our boys see little problem with that message (except perhaps in its most vulgar linguistic form).

In asking what, if anything, Title IX can do about this state of affairs, one possibility might be to rethink the law's allowance of sex-separate competition. The insult of playing like a girl might lose its sting if boys grew up learning to fear a female opponent who bends the ball like a young Julie Foudy. While we would not advocate radical changes to Title IX's baseline of allowing sex-separate teams, which has placed crucial pressure on schools to expand girls' and women's sports in order to keep up with their growing interest, we see no reason why community sports programs, especially in the younger years, shouldn't encourage more coed play. Learning to respect all athletes, both male and female, at a young age could go a long way toward inoculating male athletes against the more problematic aspects of male sports culture that we have addressed here.

Even greater inroads might be made if boys had greater exposure to women as coaches. Most of the attention to the underrepresentation of women in coaching has focused on women's sports. The trajectory for women coaches is a mirror image of that of female athletes in the post–Title IX era: while women used to be well over 90 percent of the coaches of women's sports, they are now just over 40 percent.[8] The turnaround is staggering, and is often lamented as an unintended consequence of Title IX. In fact, the causes are complex, but as women's sports gained greater resources, the coaching jobs became more desirable to men, and the old-boy networks in athletics worked to their advantage. But the story of women coaches in men's sports is one of continuity, not change: the percentage of female coaches of men's sports has held constant, at a meager 2–3 percent. With the legions of accomplished female athletes and teachers out there, surely "the best man for the job" of coaching boys' and men's teams is not always, necessarily, a man. If more women coached male athletes – and more male coaches interacted with them as colleagues and competitors – perhaps a way could be found to motivate male athletes that did not depend on devaluing or dehumanizing half the human race in the name of coaching.

A version of this chapter appeared on September 17, 2013, at verdict.justia.com, and was coauthored by Deborah L. Brake.

*Update: After being chastised by the team coordinator for using gender slurs in coaching, the trainer began complaining that the boys played "like Muppets." Meanwhile, Carli Lloyd, the breakout star of the 2015 Women's World Cup, scored three goals (the third from more than fifty yards away) in the first sixteen minutes of the championship game, the fastest hat trick in World Cup history.*

# 57

## Binders for Women, Blinders for Romney

It was a welcome moment in the second presidential debate, held October 16, 2012, at Hofstra University, when one of the town hall participants asked a question about pay equity. The first debate, after all, had ignored all women's issues, despite the fact that such issues have been at the center of several national political controversies and reveal stark ideological and practical differences between the two candidates for president, Mitt Romney and Barack Obama. And, of course, it is no secret that women comprise well more than half the electorate and an even greater proportion of the much sought-after "swing" and "undecided" voters.

At Hofstra, Katherine Fenton directed her question at President Barack Obama. "In what new ways," she asked, "do you intend to rectify the inequalities in the workplace, specifically regarding females making only 72 percent of what their male counterparts earn?"[1]

This was something of a softball for Obama, who has an excellent record on women's issues and on pay equity in particular. The very first bill he signed as president was the Lilly Ledbetter Fair Pay Act (discussed in Chapter 49), which restored the protection to victims of pay discrimination that had been gutted by the Supreme Court in its 2007 ruling in *Ledbetter v. Goodyear Tire & Rubber Co.*[2] And Obama's health care reform law contains many provisions designed to ensure that women have access to essential medical care such as mammograms, Pap smears, and contraception.

The interesting part of this segment of the debate began when Romney opened his mouth. In his nonanswer answer, Romney revealed that he fundamentally does not understand – or care about – issues like pay inequity that face women in the workplace. And his efforts to suggest that he does were ill informed, irrelevant, and, in some cases, downright offensive.

## "BINDERS FULL OF – OF WOMEN"

To Candy Crowley's lead-in, "Governor Romney, pay equity for women," Romney responded with praise for the "important topic," one that he "learned a great deal about" as governor. His learning came when trying to "pull together a Cabinet and all the applicants seemed to be men." "Well, gosh," he said to his staff, "can't we – can't we find some – some women that are also qualified?"[3] Enter the binders full of women. Romney says he went to women's groups for help in finding qualified women to be considered for his cabinet. As he continued on at the debate, he commented, "And I brought us whole binders full of – of women."[4]

In the twenty-four hours since it was first uttered, this phrase has gone a long way towards infamy. A Tumblr site went up almost immediately featuring image after image mocking it.[5] The images include binders full of dancing women, party girls, and beleaguered office help, and more than one play on the hit song "Single Ladies," inviting Romney to put "three rings on it." (As I'm a longtime fan of the movie *Dirty Dancing*, my favorite is a classic photo of Patrick Swayze with the tagline: "No one puts baby in a binder.") A Democratic PAC bought the domain name bindersfullofwomen.com and filled it immediately with tidbits and quotes from Romney on a wide range of women's issues, many of which show the hypocrisy of statements he has made in both debates and elsewhere while on his last-minute attempt to appear moderate on social issues.[6]

But putting this humorous commentary aside – though a welcome diversion from an otherwise uninspiring and gloomy campaign season – this comment, and the explanation that came with it, reveals Romney's dated and uninformed conception of women's position in the workforce. News reports after the debate suggest, moreover, that Romney did not go in search of qualified women – the binders were sitting there when he took office, the product of an effort by MassGap, a nonpartisan coalition formed to put more women in senior positions in government. And some have rightfully questioned why a man with his experience and connections didn't already have some women in mind, or why he thought qualified women were in short supply. Romney was taken to task for this mind-set in 1994, when he tried unsuccessfully to unseat Senator Ted Kennedy. When was asked why the private equity firm he founded had fewer than 10 percent female partners, he cited their lack of interest in the profession and the fact that elite business schools graduate "only a handful" each year. (Harvard Business School, according to an article in Huffington Post, graduated 30 percent women in 1995.[7])

But let's give Romney the benefit of the doubt and assume that he was at least receptive to the idea of putting women into senior positions in his cabinet if presented with binders full of them from which to choose. Kudos to him, although one study reports that the number of women in senior positions went down during his governorship and up under his successor.[8] Certainly, the glass ceiling that prevents many women from reaching the upper echelons of government and private industry is very real, and it takes proactive efforts, perhaps including binders, to overcome the old-boy network that continues to put white men into these positions in numbers that are disproportionate to their numbers in the qualified labor pool.

But what does this have to do with pay equity and the entrenched gender wage gap that was cited by the questioner? Women continue to make less than eighty cents for every dollar men make, a disparity that cannot be accounted for by labor force commitment, voluntary job choices, or time off to care for children. Indeed, virtually every economist who has crunched the numbers, regardless of his or her ideological slant or background, has concluded that the gender wage gap is at least partially created by pay discrimination – which means paying women less to do the same job simply because they are women. The wage gap is even larger for women of color and exists at every level of earnings – from surgeons to lunch ladies. And even as women have increased their labor force commitment, little progress has been made in reducing the gap since the 1980s. The wage gap threatens women's independence and financial security throughout their entire working lives and into retirement.[9]

Pay discrimination is illegal under both the Equal Pay Act of 1963[10] and Title VII of the Civil Rights Act of 1964.[11] But women have had notorious difficulty enforcing their substantive rights under these laws, due in part to a series of procedural obstacles, among them timely filing rules that require them to quickly identify pay disparities (despite the fact that such information is usually kept secret) and challenge those disparities despite a significant risk of adverse consequences for doing so.

The Ledbetter Act signed into law by Obama eliminated one such obstacle by establishing that each paycheck containing a discriminatory wage triggers a new statute of limitations. Romney has refused on many occasions to answer the question whether he would have signed the Ledbetter Act into law – strongly suggesting that he would not have but he does not want to pay the penalty of alienating female voters. And his running mate, Paul Ryan, actually voted against the act.

The Ledbetter Act addresses only a small component of pay discrimination law. Much broader changes are needed to eradicate intentional pay discrimination and to tackle the even more complicated problem of occupational segregation (the norm of thinking of certain jobs as "men's jobs" or "women's jobs"). A recent GAO report, for example, found that while women represent 49 percent of the overall workforce, they comprise 59 percent of the low-wage workforce.[12]

If Romney won't support small steps to address pay inequity, why would he support any of the larger and more structural changes that are long overdue and necessary to promote women's workplace equality? The fact that he never mentioned pay equity – directly or indirectly – when answering a direct question on the subject does nothing to alleviate this concern. And the fact that his answer to a question about a long-standing, structural problem that plagues working women through the country focused on nothing other than the hiring of his personal staff – and even then, he didn't talk about pay – is dismissive and insulting at best, and a decision to deliberately cover up his positions in this area, at worst.

## "IF YOU'RE GOING TO HAVE WOMEN IN THE WORKFORCE..."

While viewers were still stunned by the "binders full of women" remark, Romney plowed ahead to expand on his views of women in the workforce:

> I recognized that if you're going to have women in the workforce, that sometimes they need to be more flexible. My chief of staff, for instance, had two kids that were still in school. She said, I can't be here until 7:00 or 8:00 at night. I need to be able to get home at 5:00 so I can be there for – making dinner for my kids and being with them when they get home from school. So we said, fine, let's have a flexible schedule.[13]

If? *If?* Why does Romney preface "having women in the workforce" with "if"? Working women are here to stay. Indeed, recent data show that women comprise 48 percent of the workforce and are poised to overtake men within a few years. Romney's characterization of the issues, and the anecdotes he offered by way of illustration, would have been apt in the 1960s, or maybe even as late as the 1970s. But in 2012, getting hired is the least of women's problems. Antidiscrimination laws like Title VII and the PDA, which have been on the books for thirty-five and forty-eight years, respectively, caused a sea change that opened workplace doors to women.

Today, the real problems of gender inequality arise in the types of jobs women hold and how they are treated once they are employed. Unequal pay, sexual harassment, pregnancy discrimination, and the glass ceiling are just some of the most prevalent problems women in the workplace face. Work-family conflicts are also an important issue, one that Romney alluded to with his tale of flexibility in his desperation to find a qualified woman for his cabinet. But Romney brought up the issue only to suggest that work-family conflicts concern *only* women, and that such conflicts must lead to women who work only part of the day.

It should not be acceptable in this day and age for a presidential candidate to assume, as Romney did, that having women in the workforce means that the workday for them must end before the school bus arrives, or that only women need to worry about taking care of children or making dinner. Wouldn't a more flexible workplace help men, too?

## "I'M GOING TO HELP WOMEN IN AMERICA GET – GET GOOD WORK BY GETTING A STRONGER ECONOMY"

The entirety of Romney's plan to address women's issues is to usher in a "new economy," one in which employers will be so "anxious to get good workers they're going to be anxious to hire women." The logic is bizarre: prosperity will breed desperation; desperation will breed gender equality? Romney cites the loss during the current economic downturn of 580,000 jobs held by women as support for the idea that a stronger economy will help women. A stronger economy will help women – and men. But it will not help women relative to men.

In fact, while men and women have generally experienced similar levels of unemployment since the 1970s, men's unemployment rises more sharply than women's during periods of recession, and in the most recent such period, even more so. The simple explanation for this is workplace inequality itself: because men are paid more and are more likely to work in high-wage jobs, full-time jobs, and jobs with benefits, they are more expensive to employ. Thus, when employers have to cut back, laying off men does more for the employer's bottom line than does laying off women. And the occupational segregation that reserves most manufacturing jobs for men meant that it was men who were particularly hard hit by reductions in that sector. These are two reasons that men have been on the receiving end of more layoffs since 2008 than women have experienced.

Because the recession is not the cause of workplace inequality for women, a return to a more robust economy will not cure that inequality. Instead, workplace equality requires an understanding of the complexities of the problem and a will to address it. Romney made clear in this debate that he has neither that understanding nor that will.

## "EVERY WOMAN IN AMERICA SHOULD HAVE ACCESS TO CONTRACEPTIVES"

After each candidate had two minutes to opine on the issue of pay inequity (only one, Obama, seized that opportunity), another audience member was called on to ask a question. This voter asked Romney to distinguish himself from George W. Bush, with whom she had been disappointed.

Before answering her question, however, Romney insisted on going back to the pay equity question – or, more specifically, Obama's answer to it, in which he said that his health care law's mandate that employer-based insurance provide no-cost contraceptive coverage is an "economic issue for women." Obama pointed out that Romney has opposed this provision (as well as the rest of the health care law) and has supported other measures that would undermine women's access to contraception. The contraceptive mandate was necessary because employers, when left to their own devices, routinely excluded prescription contraceptives (used only by women) from otherwise comprehensive health insurance plans. And courts were loath to understand this sex-based exclusion as a form of unlawful sex discrimination under Title VII. (This issue is explained in Chapter 40.)

In his late rebuttal, Romney stated unequivocally: "I don't believe that bureaucrats in Washington should tell someone whether they can use contraceptives or not, and

I don't believe employers should tell someone whether they could have contraceptive care or not. Every woman in America should have access to contraceptives." What can this possibly mean? Surely Romney does not believe that permission to "use contraceptives" is a live issue. After all, the Supreme Court decided in the 1960s that the right of access to contraceptives is constitutionally protected by the Fourteenth Amendment. And employers don't dictate whether someone "could have contraceptive care." But they do decide whether to offer insurance policies that include coverage for prescriptions.

The issue when it comes to access to effective birth control is cost. Based on that finding, and the research showing the importance of family planning to women's health, the Institute of Medicine included no-cost contraception as one of the essential health services that all employer-based health plans must cover under the Affordable Care Act. (There is a narrow, yet hotly contested exception to contraception coverage for certain religious employers.) Obama's Department of Health and Human Services issued corresponding regulations to make this happen.

Romney, on the other hand, has opposed all efforts to maintain or increase women's access to contraception. He has promised to overrule health care reform if elected; he has promised to withdraw federal funding from Planned Parenthood, which provides low-cost contraception to millions of women; and he has supported "personhood" measures that would make some forms of birth control arguably illegal. In Romney's world, "access" to contraception simply means not being arrested for using it; in the real world, "access" is only guaranteed by ensuring that it is affordable and available. Perhaps he assumes that women can borrow money from their parents for contraception, on top of the money they are borrowing to attend college. Or maybe his promised reduction in the capital gains tax, which he offered as a means to help the overburdened "middle class," will free up some much-needed cash. Although one wonders how much overlap there is between women burdened by the tax rate on dividends and capital gains and those who cannot afford reliable birth control.

A version of this chapter appeared on October 18, 2012, at verdict.justia.com.

*Update: Barack Obama defeated Mitt Romney in the November 2012 presidential election. Deciding to forgo a third run for president in 2016, Romney has been making the rounds to meet with many of the Republican-party candidates. The issue of access to contraception under the Affordable Care Act continues to be hotly contested, as discussed in Chapter 40.*

# Conclusion

When I began writing the column on which this book is based, I was at the beginning of my career in legal education and also a new mother. I didn't see then how these three roles – legal commentator, professor, mom – would intersect in such interesting ways and, together, shape my thinking about gender and discrimination.

My first pregnancy coincided with my first year teaching at Hofstra Law School. As I bid good-bye to my students to begin my maternity leave, a male student yelled out from the back row: "What are you having?" I explained that my husband and I had decided not to find out the gender of the baby to preserve an element of surprise, to torture those people in our lives who felt they had some inherent right to know, and, perhaps most important, to avoid the stereotyped baby gifts – the frilly pink onesies for a girl; Yankees' uniforms for a boy. (This was New York, after all.)

"But how will you know what color to paint the nursery?" the student called out. I had to laugh, but I couldn't muster any response other than an off-the-cuff, "See, it doesn't matter – get it?" But I was secretly humbled by the daunting task before me – to raise a child, boy or girl, who would develop in the shadow of the gender-role expectations society so strongly imposes. Luke arrived two weeks later, a healthy, full-term baby boy who looked instantly at home in his bright yellow room. And his brother, Ben, arrived little more than two years later. He began life in a blue room, but only because it had been painted that way before he arrived. And they were joined – three years later – by another brother, Milo.

In the many iterations of my sex discrimination class, I taught the usual issues – sexual harassment, work-family conflicts, pay inequity – and helped my students learn the law and policy covered in the pages of this book. And at home, with my three sons, I stuck with the tenets of preschool feminism: do not use or reinforce gender-based stereotypes and do not partake in sexist traditions. But even those simple tenets can be hard to follow because gender is everywhere, like the mother who gives my son a bat as a party favor, while giving the girls a baton to twirl; or the parents who object to dress-up day at daycare, especially if it means their sons will don pink dresses with white rosettes. Or the many calls I got from the town of Huntington's vital statistics office trying to "verify" the suspicious information I had provided on Luke's birth certificate – that we had given him his (married) mother's last name was incomprehensible. (I got to repeat this process fifteen years later, as I enrolled him in the local public high school but could not accede to the demand for a "household surname," because there is no one name to which we all answer. The school's response was to switch his father's designation to "stepfather" on his official registration record, the only way the registrar could make sense of our names.)

I don't think I ever mastered – in class or as a mother – how to deal with stereotypes that remain largely true. When Luke would peer out the car window and say, "Hey, look at those guys fixing the power line," my instinct was to say, "You mean men and women, Luke?" But I drove past these workers a hundred times and had never, in fact, seen a woman in the truck. (And the women on the road-paving crews *always* seem to be holding the signs.) I can't quite bring myself to lie – to suggest to him that the men he is looking directly at are women – but I can't risk the possibility that he will go away thinking *only* men could or should do this work. So I respond with a subtle correction, noting that, yes, "the workers are fixing the power line."

Early on, Luke earned notches on his feminist belt. Upon discovering me sweeping up shards of broken glass, he tried to stop me, insisting that "only mens use brooms," which he deduced from living in a house where the only woman is not a natural housekeeper. He grappled mightily with Humpty Dumpty's gender identity ("guy ? girl ? guy? girl?") and did not hesitate in telling someone at my office that a picture of two girls in a bed of flowers was probably drawn by a boy. His early life plan: he and Ben would live in a beach house together, raise boy children, drive a race car with rainbow stripes, and use the vacuum and broom. (They would be law professors during the week and astronomers on the weekend, he told us, but both have long since dropped any aspiration for a legal career.) And as Luke's younger brothers reached their own verbal and critical thinking stages, they joined the conversation. Long-haired Ben shifts seamlessly between running Bessie's Diner, a makeshift restaurant he operates out of my kitchen with his best friend (and my surrogate daughter), Tess, and racking up dozens of goals on the soccer field. Milo's idea of a quick question on the way home from soccer practice, when he was all of seven, was, "Which came first, racism or sexism?"

By the time Luke was just three, I was ready to declare myself a success at raising a young feminist, who did not see the world in terms of pink-and-blue expectations. But in the car one day, Luke began peppering me with his usual barrage of questions: "Why don't Venus and Mercury have moons?" "Why was there no space before the Big Bang?" "What's a daughter?" With the last question, I almost crashed my car into the highway divider. I looked back for his telltale grin, to let on that he was only pretending not to know the answer to his own question. But I saw only his genuinely inquisitive face, waiting earnestly for a reply. "A daughter is a girl child," I explain, trying to keep my surprise at bay. "Do you have any daughters?" he asked with puzzlement in his voice, despite his certain knowledge that he and Ben, at the time, were my only children.

It was then that I realized that the project of raising open-minded, feminist sons was still in its early stages, as was my project of teaching generations of students about gender law – and establishing myself as a gender law scholar. Gender is complicated, and it is everywhere. And it cannot just be ignored. Gender is part of a nuanced and continuing conversation. Part of the equality project is gaining an appreciation of the differences between men and women – biological and social, and distinguishing between the two – and figuring out how individuals, institutions, and the law ought to deal with them. These Internet columns have allowed me to do a lot of this work. It is where I report on my more traditional academic research and analyze cases as they come down the pike, but also where I try out new ideas on a diverse audience of readers – and get valuable comments and e-mails with feedback from judges, lawyers, and even the litigants themselves, but also from general readers with little or no legal knowledge. It is my easy access to a convenient platform for ideas that enabled me to turn a postgame conversation with my son Ben, about the sexist comments of his soccer trainer (which he only shared, in the driveway, with one hand on the car door, ready to bolt to freedom rather than stay for my reaction), into a column about the role of masculinity in sport (Chapter 56).

What I have learned over these fifteen years of writing, teaching, and mothering is that the path to gender equality requires that we all think critically about the world around us and keep asking questions. It was thus music to my ears to be awakened to the sweet voice of my now-nine-year-old son Milo with this urgent question: "I feel sexist for even asking, but is it even possible for a woman to propose marriage to a man?"

*"That's an excellent suggestion, Miss Triggs. Perhaps one of*
*the men here would like to make it."*

ART 5 © Riana Duncan/Punch Limited. Used by permission.

# Notes

## INTRODUCTION

1  *We Did It!: The Rich World's Quiet Revolution: Women Are Gradually Taking Over the Workplace*, The Economist, Dec. 2009.

2  Courtney Connley, *27 Countries That Trump the U.S. When It Comes to Gender Equality*, blackenterprise.com, Nov. 25, 2015, http://www.blackenterprise.com/news/the-27-countries-that-trump-the-u-s-when-it-comes-to-gender-equality/.

3  World Economic Forum, The Global Gender Gap Report 2015; *see also* Gail Collins, *What Happened to Working Women?*, N.Y. Times, Oct. 16, 2015, at A23.

4  Gretchen Livingston, *Among 38 Nations, U.S. Is the Outlier When It Comes to Paid Parental Leave*, pewresearch.org, Dec. 12, 2013, http://www.pewresearch.org/fact-tank/2013/12/12/among-38-nations-u-s-is-the-holdout-when-it-comes-to-offering-paid-parental-leave/; *see also* Bryce Covert, *U.S. Paid Family Leave Versus the Rest of the World, in 2 Disturbing Charts*, thinkprogress.org, July 30, 2014, http://thinkprogress.org/economy/2014/07/30/3465922/paid-family-leave/; Rebecca J. Rosen, *A Map of Maternity Leave Policies Around the World*, The Atlantic, June 20, 2014.

5  *See, e.g.*, Claire Cain Miller, *Men Do More at Home, but Not as Much as They Think*, N.Y. Times, Nov. 12, 2015.

6  Eric Morath, *The Gender Pay Gap Widens as Men's Earnings Grow Twice as Fast as Women's*, Wall St. J., Oct. 20, 2015.

7  Nadya Agrawal, *21 Harrowing Stories of Sexual Harassment on the Job*, Huffington Post, Dec. 17, 2015, http://www.huffingtonpost.com/entry/21-harrowing-stories-of-sexual-harassment-on-the-job_566f39b1e4b0fccee16f84d8?utm_hp_ref=business&ir=Business&section=business.

8  Steve Kolowich, *Mustaches Outnumber Women Among Medical-School Leaders*, Chron. Higher Ed., Dec. 17, 2015, http://chronicle.com/article/Mustaches-Outnumber-Women/234645?cid=trend_right; Joan Williams & Jessica Lee, *It's Illegal, Yet it Happens All the Time*, Chron. Higher Ed., Sept. 28, 2015 (reporting on female graduate students who have been hounded out of STEM programs).

9  Emily Crockett, *Americans Believe in Women's Equality, But Don't Understand It*, RH Reality Check, Aug. 25, 2015, http://rhrealitycheck.org/article/2015/08/25/poll-americans-believe-womens-equality-dont-understand/.

10 Catalyst, *Women CEOs of the S&P 500*, Apr. 3, 2015, http://www.catalyst.org/ knowledge/women-ceos-sp-500.

11 A complete archive of my FindLaw columns can be found at http://writ.news.find law.com/grossman/, and a complete archive of the Justia columns can be found at https://verdict.justia.com/author/grossman.

## PART I. WHAT IS SEX DISCRIMINATION?

1 Gillespie v. J.C.B.C., Inc., No. PD12SB-02554, http://www.state.nj.us/lps/dcr/ downloads/orders/gillespie_order.pdf.

2 David R. Gillespie, CRT 257, 2004 WL 1476932 (N.J. Adm. June 10, 2004).

3 *See, e.g.*, Laura Masnerus, *McGreevey Steps Down after Disclosing a Gay Affair*, N.Y. TIMES, Aug. 13, 2004, at A1.

4 *"Ladies Night" Nixed in NJ*, USA TODAY, June 4, 2004, http://usatoday30.usatoday .com/news/nation/2004-06-03-ladies-night_x.htm.

5 CNN Live at Daybreak, June 3, 2004 (quoting Carol Costello), http://www.cnn.com/ TRANSCRIPTS/0406/03/lad.02.html.

6 Troy Graham & Jennifer Moroz, *Ladies' Night on Hold at Bar*, philly.com (June 3, 2004), http://articles.philly.com/2004-06-03/news/25370212_1_free-drinks-bar-owner-massage.

7 N.J. STAT. ANN. §10:5–1 (West 2013).

8 *See, e.g.*, L.W. v. Tom's River Reg'l Sch. Bd. of Educ., 189 N.J. 381, 402 (N.J. 2007) (addressing harassment is an aspect of accommodation).

9 635 P.2d at 684.

10 This principle is aptly demonstrated in *International Union, UAW v. Johnson Controls, Inc.*, 499 U.S. 187 (1991), in which the Supreme Court held that a policy excluding fertile women from jobs with lead exposure, designed to protect future offspring from birth defects, violated Title VII.

11 *Gillespie*, at *13.

12 *See* Graham & Moroz, *supra* note 6.

13 Courts in California, Iowa, Florida, and Pennsylvania have held sex-specific discounts unlawful. *See* Koire v. Metro Car Wash, 40 Cal. 3d 24 (1985); Ladd v. Iowa West Racing Ass'n, 438 N.W.2d 600 (Iowa 1989) (holding that sex-based discounts at a racetrack for food and beverages violated the state's Civil Rights Act); City of Clearwater v. Studebaker's Dance Club, 516 So. 2d 1106 (Fla. Dist. Ct. App. 1987) (finding that the state's antidiscrimination act prohibited sex-based promotional discounts); Pennsylvania Liquor Control Bd. v. Dobrinoff, 471 A.2d 941 (Pa. Commonwealth Ct. 1984) (finding sex discrimination where a club waived a one-dollar admission fee for women but not men). But others – in Illinois and Washington, for example – have accepted the legality of sex-specific discounts. *See* The Dock Club, Inc. v. Illinois Liquor Control Comm'n, 428 N.E.2d 735 (Ill. App. Ct. 1981) (upholding discounted drink prices for women on ladies' night because men were asked to pay only a regular (not inflated) price and "not a price established for the purpose of discouraging their patronage"); MacLean v. First Northwest Indus. of Am., 635 P.2d 683 (Wash. 1981) (reasoning that the "ladies' night" discount had a legitimate commercial goal).

14 42 U.S.C. § 2000e-2 (2012).

15 42 U.S.C. § 2000e(k) (2012).

16 Price Waterhouse v. Hopkins, 490 U.S. 228 (1989).

## CHAPTER 1. SEXUAL JEALOUSY

1  293 A.D.2d 255, 256 (N.Y. App. Div. 2003), *rev'd,* 100 N.Y.2d 326 (N.Y. 2003).
2  *Id.* at 255.
3  *Id.* at 256.
4  N.Y. Executive Law 21 § 296 (1)(a) (2003).
5  42 U.S.C. § 2000e (2012); Forrest v. Jewish Guild for the Blind, 3 N.Y.3d 295, 399 (N.Y. 2004).
6  100 N.Y.2d 326 at 330.
7  *Id.* at 256.
8  *Id.*
9  *Id.*
10 *See, e.g.,* Mauro v. Orville, 259 A.D.2d 89, 90 (N.Y. App. Div. 1999) (finding no discrimination where the employer and employee engaged in a consensual, intimate relationship for more than a year); Kahn v. Objective Solutions, Intl., 86 F.Supp.2d 377, 379–80 (S.D.N.Y. 2000) (holding that a voluntary romantic relationship cannot be the basis for a gender discrimination suit).
11 86 F.Supp.2d 377 (S.D.N.Y. 2000).
12 For a discussion of the equal opportunity harasser, see Chapter 17.
13 *See* 42 U.S.C. § 2000e-2(a) (2006) (employer discrimination must be *"because of* such individual's race, color, religion, *sex,* or national origin") (emphasis added).
14 Mittl v. New York State Div. of Human Rights, 794 N.E.2d 660 (N.Y. 2003).

## CHAPTER 2. TOO HOT TO BE A DENTAL HYGIENIST?

1  763 N.W.2d 862, 906 (Iowa 2009).
2  Goodridge v. Dep't of Pub. Health, 798 N.E.2d 941 (Mass. 2003) (licenses issued beginning May 2004).
3  *See* A. G. Sulzberger, *Ouster of Iowa Judges Sends Signal to Bench,* N.Y. TIMES, Nov. 3, 2010, at A1.
4  *See, e.g., Iowa: Court Upholds Firing of Woman Whose Boss Found Her Attractive,* N.Y. TIMES, Dec. 21, 2012, at A17.
5  2012 WL 6652747.
6  *Id.* at *1.
7  *Id.*
8  *Id.*
9  *Id.* at *2.
10 *Id.*
11 *See, e.g.,* Deboom v. Raining Rose, Inc., 722 N.W.2d 1, 7 (Iowa 2009).
12 *See* 42 U.S.C. § 2000e-2(a) (2006); IOWA CODE § 216.6(1)(a) (2009) ("It shall be an unfair or discriminatory practice for any person to . . . discriminate in employment . . . because of . . . sex").
13 Texas Dep't of Cmty. Affairs v. Burdine, 450 U.S. 248, 252–54 (1981); *see also* McDonnell Douglas Corp. v. Green, 411 U.S. 792, 802 (1973).
14 *Nelson,* 2012 WL 6652747, at *3.
15 *Id.* at 3.
16 *Id.* at 68. Sexual favoritism law is discussed at length in Chapter 12.
17 EEOC Policy Statement No. N–915–048, *available at* http://www.eeoc.gov/policy/docs/sexualfavor.html.

18 Miller v. Dep't of Corrections, 36 Cal. 4th 446, 451 (2005) (holding that a chief deputy prison warden's affairs with female employees at the prison were sufficient evidence of widespread sexual favoritism, creating an actionable hostile work environment).

19 *Nelson*, 2012 WL 6652747 at *5.

20 *See, e.g.*, Mallinson-Montague v. Pocrnick, 224 F.3d 1224, 1232 (10th Cir. 2000).

21 Phillips v. Martin Marietta, 400 U.S. 542 (1971) (holding that employer policy prohibiting the hiring of women, but not men, with preschool age children violated Title VII); *see generally* Tracy Bateman Farrell, *Sex-Plus Discrimination Claims under Title VII of Civil Rights Act of 1964 (42 U.S.C. §§ 2000e et seq.)*, 51 A.L.R. Fed. 2d 341 (2010).

22 *See, e.g.*, Corne v. Bausch & Lomb, Inc., 562 F.2d 55 (9th Cir. 1977); Tomkins v. Public Serv. Elec. & Gas Co., 568 F.2d 1044 (3d. Cir. 1977). These cases are discussed at length in the introductory note to Part III.

23 Nelson v. Knight, 834 N.W.2d 64 (Iowa 2013).

24 Dana Ford, *Iowa Supreme Court: OK to Fire "Irresistible" Worker*, CNN.COM (December 22, 2012, http://www.cnn.com/2012/12/21/justice/iowa-irresistible-worker/.

## CHAPTER 3. A TWIST ON THE PROBLEM OF SEX INEQUALITY IN COACHING

1 Medcalf v. Tr. of Univ. of Pa, 71 Fed.App'x 924 (3d Cir. 2003).

2 *A Row over "Reverse Discrimination,"* PENN. GAZETTE (March 1998).

3 42 U.S.C. § 2000e-2(a),(e) (2012).

4 *See generally* Johnson v. Transp. Agency, Santa Clara Cnty., Cal., 480 U.S. 616, 634 (1987) (holding that an employer did not violate Title VII when it chose to hire a female rather than a male on the basis of an affirmative action plan requiring sex or race be taken into account to remedy underrepresentation).

5 *See* Katie Manley, *The BFOQ Defense: Title VII's Concession to Gender Discrimination*, 16 DUKE J. GENDER L. & POL'Y 169, 177–78 (2009).

6 *Johnson*, 480 U.S. at 628–30.

7 Linda Jean Carpenter & R. Vivian Acosta, *Women in Intercollegiate Sport: A Longitudinal, National Study – Thirty-Five Year Update 1977–2012*, at 17–18 (2012), http://acostacarpenter.org/AcostaCarpenter2012.pdf; see also NCAA, Gender-Equity Report 2004–2010.

8 *Id.*

9 20 U.S.C. § 1681 (2000).

10 42 U.S.C § 2000e-2 (2000).

11 29 U.S.C. § 206(d)(1) (2000).

12 United States Equal Employment Opportunity Comm'n, EEOC Notice No. 915.002: Enforcement Guidance on Sex Discrimination in the Compensation of Sports Coaches in Educational Institutions, EEOC Compliance Manual, Oct. 29, 1997, at I, http://www.eeoc.gov/policy/docs/coaches.html.

13 *See competitiveedgesports.co.uk/?page_id=2.*

## CHAPTER 4. MIXED MOTIVES

1 539 U.S. 90 (2003).

2 42 U.S.C. § 2000e-2 (2012).

3 411 U.S. 792 (1973).

4  490 U.S. 228 (1989); *see* Chapters 5 and 6.
5  Pub. L. 102-166, § 1071, 105 Stat. 1071, 1075 (codified as amended 42 U.S.C. § 2000e-5 (2012)).
6  42 U.S.C.A § 2000e-2(m).
7  Desert Palace, Inc. v. Costa, 539 U.S. 90 (2003).
8  *Price Waterhouse*, 490 U.S. at 230 (O'Connor, J., concurring) (emphasis added).
9  Joseph J. Ward, *A Call for Price Waterhouse II: The Legacy of Justice O'Connor's Direct Evidence Requirement for Mixed-Motive Employment Discrimination Claims*, 61 *Alb. L. Rev.* 627, 649 (1997) (discussing the differing interpretations of the direct evidence rule by each circuit).
10  *Id.* at 651–53.
11  *Id.* at 655–56.
12  *Desert Palace*, 539 U.S. at 2149.
13  *Id.* at 2150 (quoting 42 U.S.C. § 2000e-2(m)).
14  557 U.S. 167 (2009).
15  *Id.* at 180 (Stevens, J., dissenting); *see also* Joanna L. Grossman, *The Supreme Court Curtails Federal Protection Against Age Discrimination*, FindLaw's Writ, June 25, 2009, http://writ.news.findlaw.com/grossman/20090625.html.

CHAPTER 5. SEX STEREOTYPING AND DRESS CODES

1  490 U.S. 228 (1989).
2  Jennifer L. Levi, *Some Modest Proposals for Challenging Established Dress Code Jurisprudence*, 14 Duke J. Gender L. & Pol'y 243 (2007).
3  444 F.3d 1104 (9th Cir. 2006) (en banc).
4  *Id.* at 1107.
5  *Id.* at 1107, 1114.
6  *See* Rene v. MGM Grand Hotel, Inc., 305 F.3d 1061 (9th Cir. 2002) (holding that a man harassed by his coworkers because he was gay could maintain an action for sexual harassment under Title VII); Nichols v. Azteca Rest. Enter., Inc., 256 F.3d 864 (9th Cir. 2001) (concluding that verbal harassment reflecting hostility toward the victim because he was too feminine constituted illegal sex stereotyping).
7  *Jespersen*, 444 F.3d at 1112.
8  No. 3:06-CV-465RM, 2009 WL 35237 (N.D. Ind. Jan. 5, 2009).
9  *Id.* at *2.
10  *Id.*
11  *Id.* at *4.
12  *Id.* at *5.
13  *Id.* (citing Doe v. City of Belleville, Ill., 119 F.3d 563, 580 (7th Cir.1997), *vacated and remanded on other grounds*, City of Belleville v. Doe, 523 U.S. 1001 (1998)).

CHAPTER 6. A VICTORY FOR TRANSGENDER EMPLOYEES

1  When this chapter was first written, it used the term "transsexual," the most common term at the time, rather than "transgender," which is the current preferred term. The language has been updated to reflect this evolution in the self-identification of the transgender population.
2  577 F. Supp. 2d 293 (D.D.C. 2008).

3   *Id.* at 296.
4   *Id.* at 299.
5   *See* Amanda S. Eno, *The Misconception of "Sex" in Title VII: Federal Courts Reeval-
    uate Transsexual Employment Discrimination Claims*, 43 Tulsa L. Rev. 765, 768
    (2008) ("approximately thirty-seven percent of the United States population lives in
    a state that has laws prohibiting transgender discrimination").
6   *Id.* at 767.
7   *See* 42 U.S.C. § 2000e-2 (2012).
8   Eno, *supra* note 5, at 773–75.
9   742 F.2d 1081 (7th Cir. 1984) (finding that Congress never considered Title VII to
    apply to anything other than the traditional concept of sex).
10  On efforts to amend Title VII to prohibit sexual orientation and gender identity
    discrimination, see Chapters 5 and 19; *see also* Employment Non-Discrimination
    Act of 2013, S. 815, 113th Cong. (2013), https://www.govtrack.us/congress/bills/113/
    s815/text/is; Jerome Hunt, *A History of the Employment Discrimination Act: It is
    Past Time to Pass This Law*, Center for American Progress (July 19, 2011),
    http://www.americanprogress.org/issues/lgbt/news/2011/07/19/10006/a-history-of-the-
    employment-non-discrimination-act/.
11  490 U.S. 228 (1989).
12  Eno, *supra* note 5, at 775–76.
13  *Id.* at 775.
14  378 F.3d 566 (6th Cir. 2004).
15  *Schroer*, 577 F. Supp. 2d at 303–5.
16  *Id.*
17  *Id.* at 306–8.
18  *Id.* at 306–7.
19  *See* EEOC Appeal No. 0120120821, 2012 WL 1435995, at *1 (EEOC Apr. 20, 2012).
    The case is discussed in Joanna L. Grossman, *The EEOC Rules That Trans-
    gender Discrimination is Sex Discrimination: The Reasoning Behind the Decision*,
    Justia's Verdict, May 1, 2012, https://verdict.justia.com/2012/05/01/the-eeoc-rules-
    that-transgender-discrimination-is-sex-discrimination.

CHAPTER 7. HOW FAST MUST FEMALE TRANSIT OFFICERS RUN?

1   308 F.3d 286 (3d Cir. 2002).
2   42 U.S.C. § 2000e et seq. (2012).
3   *Lanning II*, 308 F.3d at 302.
4   401 U.S. 424 (1971).
5   *Id.* at 431.
6   *See* Civil Rights Act of 1991, Pub. L. No. 102–66, §2, 105 Stat. 1071.
7   Rosemary Alito, *Disparate Impact Discrimination under the 1991 Civil Rights Act*, 45
    Rutgers L. Rev. 1011, 1014–19 (1993).
8   Lanning v. Se. Pa. Transp. Auth. (SEPTA), 181 F.3d 478 (3d Cir. 1999).
9   *Id.* at 494.
10  *Id.* at 489.
11  Lanning v. Se. Pa. Transp. Auth. (SEPTA), 308 F.3d 286 (3d Cir. 2002).
12  *Id.* at 291.
13  *Id.* at 293 (McKee, J., dissenting).

14  *Id.* at 296 n. 4 (McKee, J., dissenting).
15  On barriers to women in policing, see MARILYN CORSIANOS, POLICING AND GEN-
    DERED JUSTICE: EXAMINING THE POSSIBILITIES (2009).

### CHAPTER 8. WHO IS PROTECTED BY ANTIDISCRIMINATION LAWS?

1  315 F.3d 696 (7th Cir. 2002).
2  EEOC v. Sidley Austin Brown & Wood, No. 01 C 9635, 2002 WL 206485 (N.D. Ill.
   Feb. 11, 2002), *vacated*, 315 F.3d 696 (7th Cir. 2002).
3  *Id.*
4  *Id.* at *4.
5  EEOC v. Sidley Austin Brown & Wood, 315 F.3d 696, 699 (7th Cir. 2002).
6  467 U.S. 69 (1984).
7  *Id.* at 79 (Powell, J., concurring).
8  Kristin N. Johnson, *Resolving the Title VII Partner-Employee Debate*, 101 MICH. L.
   REV. 1067 (2003) (discussing the tests used by different circuits to determine whether
   Title VII covers partners alleging to be victims of discrimination).
9  EEOC v. Sidley Austin Brown & Wood, 315 F.3d 696, 703 (7th Cir. 2002).
10  *Id.* at 706.
11  *Id.* at 707.
12  *Id.* at 708 (Easterbrook, J., concurring).
13  534 U.S. 279 (2002).
14  EEOC v. Sidley Austin, LLP, 406 F. Supp. 991 (N.D. Ill. 2005); EEOC v. Sidley
    Austin, LLP, 437 F.3d 695 (7th Cir. 2006).
15  EEOC, Press Release, *$27.5 Million Consent Decree Resolves EEOC Age Bias
    Suit Against Sidley Austin*, Oct. 5, 2007, www.eeoc.gov/eeoc/cfmnewsroom/release/
    10-5-07.

### CHAPTER 9. PUNISHING THE COACH WHO STOOD UP FOR
### HIS FEMALE ATHLETES

1  *See generally* Deborah L. Brake & Joanna L. Grossman, *The Failure of Title VII as
   a Rights-Claiming System*, 86 N.C. L. REV. 859 (2008).
2  544 U.S. 167 (2005).
3  *Id.* at 171.
4  *Id.* at 172.
5  *Id.*
6  Jackson v. Birmingham Bd. of Educ., No. CV-01-TMP-1866-S, 2002 WL 32668124
   (N.D. Ala. Feb. 25, 2002), *aff'd*, 309 F.3d 1333 (11th Cir. 2002), *rev'd and remanded*,
   544 U.S. 167 (2005).
7  42 U.S.C. § 2000d – 2000d-7 (2012).
8  *See* Cannon v. University of Chicago, 441 U.S. 677 (1979) (implying private right
   of action under Title IX); Bossier Parish Sch. Bd. v. Lemon, 370 F.2d 847 (5th
   Cir. 1967) (implying private right of action under Title VI; cited with approval by
   Supreme Court in *Cannon*).
9  Lowrey v. Texas A&M Univ. Sys., 117 F.3d 242, 252 (5th Cir. 1997); Preston v. Virginia,
   31 F.3d 203, 206 (4th Cir. 1994).

10 *See* Gebser v. Lago Vista Indep. Sch. Dist., 524 U.S. 274 (1998); Davis v. Monroe Cnty. Bd. of Educ., 526 U.S. 629 (1999).
11 *Jackson*, 544 U.S. at 184.
12 *Id.* at 196 n.2.
13 327 F.3d 307 (4th Cir. 2003).
14 136 F.3d 276 (2nd Cir. 1998).
15 224 F.3d 701 (7th Cir. 2000).

### CHAPTER 10. BROADER PROTECTION AGAINST WORKPLACE RETALIATION

1 548 U.S. 53 (2006).
2 *Id.* at 58.
3 *Id.* at 53 (defining an adverse employment action as a "materially adverse change in the terms and conditions").
4 See Mattern v. Eastman Kodak Co., 104 F.3d 702, 707 (5th Cir. 1997); see Manning v. Metropolitan Life Ins. Co., 127 F.3d 686, 692 (8th Cir. 1997).
5 *See, e.g.*, Rochon v. Gonzales, 438 F.3d 1211, 1219 (D.C. Cir. 2006).
6 *Burlington*, 548 U.S. at 67.
7 *Id.* at 67.
8 *Id.* at 68 (emphasis added).
9 *Id.* at 54.
10 *Id.* at 68.
11 *Id.* at 73 (Alito, J., concurring).
12 *Id.* at 75.
13 This number has increased further – to 41.1 percent in 2013. *See* EEOC, Charge Statistics, http://www.eeoc.gov/eeoc/statistics/enforcement/charges.cfm.
14 *See* Deborah L. Brake & Joanna L. Grossman, *The Failure of Title VII as a Rights-Claiming System*, 86 N.C. L. REV. 902–4 (2008) (collecting studies).
15 *Burlington*, 548 U.S at 68.
16 *See* Brake & Grossman, *supra* note 14, at 903–4 & n. 237.
17 See *id.*
18 *See generally* Joanna L. Grossman, *The Culture of Compliance: The Final Triumph of Form over Substance in Sexual Harassment Law*, 26 HARV. WOMEN'S L.J. 3 (2003).
19 481 F.3d 578, 590 (2007).
20 *Id.* at 591.
21 For a fuller explication of this point, see Brake & Grossman, *supra* note 14, at 859.

### CHAPTER 11. THE SUPREME COURT PROTECTS RETALIATION VICTIMS BUT STILL LEAVES GAPS IN THE LAW

1 555 U.S. 271 (2009).
2 Although this case involved sexual harassment, the legal issue before the Supreme Court involved only retaliation for her complaint. Sexual harassment law is taken up in Chapters 12 to 30.
3 42 U.S.C. § 2000e-3 (2012).
4 *Id.*
5 *Crawford*, 555 U.S. at 275.
6 EEOC Compliance Manual, §§8-II-B(1).

7  *Crawford*, 555 U.S. at 276.
8  *Id.* at 282 (Alito, J., concurring).
9  *Id.* at 283.
10  *Id.* at 277-78.
11  *Id.* at 279.
12  *Id.* at 279.
13  562 U.S. 170 (2011). On the complete body of retaliation cases, see Deborah L. Brake, *Retaliation in an EEO World*, 89 IND. L.J. 115 (2014).
14  135 S. Ct. 2517 (2013); *see also* Joanna L. Grossman & Deborah L. Brake, *Revenge: The Supreme Court Narrows Protection Against Retaliation in University of Texas Southwestern Medical Center v. Nassar*, JUSTIA'S VERDICT, July 9, 2013, https://verdict .justia.com/2013/07/09/revenge-the-supreme-court-narrows-protection-against-work place-retaliation-in-university-of-texas-southwestern-medical-center-v-nassar.

PART II. SEXUAL HARASSMENT

1  Corne v. Bausch & Lomb, Inc., 390 F. Supp. 161 (D. Ariz. 1975).
2  Tomkins v. Pub. Serv. Elec. & Gas. Co., 422 F. Supp. 553, 556 (D. N.J. 1976).
3  27 F.2d 983 (D.C. Cir. 1977).
4  *Id.* at 989–90.
5  *Id.* at 990.
6  *See* EEOC, Guidelines on Discrimination Because of Sex, 45 FED. REG. 74,676, 74,677 (Nov. 10, 1980) (codified at 29 C.F.R. § 1604.11(c) (1980)). This section of the guidelines was rescinded in 1999 and replaced with new guidelines after the Supreme Court decided several cases affecting the standards for employer liability.
7  Claire Safran, *What Men Do to Women on the Job*, REDBOOK, Nov. 1976, at 217.
8  *See* U.S. MERIT SYSTEMS PROTECTION BOARD, SEXUAL HARASSMENT IN THE FEDERAL WORKPLACE: IS IT A PROBLEM? 20 (1981).
9  *See, e.g.*, CARROLL M. BRODSKY, THE HARASSED WORKER 27–28 (1976); LIN FARLEY, SEXUAL SHAKEDOWN: THE SEXUAL HARASSMENT OF WOMEN ON THE JOB 18–21 (1978) (discussing studies and surveys finding widespread sexual harassment); U.S. MERIT SYSTEMS PROTECTION BOARD, SEXUAL HARASSMENT IN THE FEDERAL WORKPLACE: AN UPDATE (1988); Douglas D. Baker et al., *The Influence of Individual Characteristics and Severity of Harassing Behavior on Reactions to Sexual Harassment*, 22 SEX ROLES 305, 305–6 (1990) ("Research findings over the past fifteen years indicate that sexual harassment is both a pervasive and serious problem"); Susan R. Meredith, *Using Fact Finders to Probe Workplace Claims of Sexual Harassment*, 47 ARB. J. 61, 61 (1992) (citing studies which estimate that 50 to 80 percent of female workers have been sexually harassed); Beth E. Schneider, *Consciousness About Sexual Harassment Among Heterosexual and Lesbian Women Workers*, 38 J. SOC. ISSUES 75, 83–85 (1982) (discussing a study showing that "significant proportions of each sexual identity group experienced [sexual harassment] incidents in the year prior to the study"). For narrative descriptions of this history, see Vicki Schultz, *The Sanitized Workplace*, 112 YALE L.J. 2061, 2074–82 (2003) (discussing the American women's movement); Vicki Schultz, *Reconceptualizing Sexual Harassment*, 107 YALE L.J. 1683 (1998) (discussing the current sexual desire-dominance paradigm).
10  EEOC, Guidelines on Discrimination Because of Sex, 45 FED. REG. 74,676, 74,677 (Nov. 10, 1980) (codified at 29 C.F.R. § 1604.11(c) (1980)).
11  *Id.*

12  477 U.S. 57, 64 (1986).
13  510 U.S. 17, 21 (1993).
14  523 U.S. 75, 79–80 (1998).
15  *Id.* at 72.
16  Faragher v. City of Boca Raton, 425 U.S. 775 (1998); Burlington Indus. v. Ellerth, 524 U.S. 742 (1998).

### CHAPTER 12. WORKPLACE AFFAIRS AND SEXUAL FAVORITISM

1  36 Cal. 4th 446, 451 (2005).
2  *See* 42 U.S.C. § 2000e-2(a) (2006).
3  *See, e.g.*, Miller v. Aluminum Co. of America, 679 F. Supp. 495, 500–01 (W.D. Penn. 1988), *aff'd*, 856 F.2d 184 (3d Cir. 1998); DeCintio v. Westchester Cnty. Med. Cent., 807 F.2d 304, 308 (2d Cir. 1986).
4  EEOC Guidance No. 915.048 at *3 (1990).
5  Cal. Gov. Code § 12940 (2014).
6  *See* State Dep't of Health Servs. v. Superior Court, 31 Cal. 4th 1026, 1040–42 (2003).
7  Murillo v. Rite Stuff Foods, 77 Cal. Rptr.2d 12, 17 (Cal. App. 1998).
8  42 U.S.C. § 1981a(b)(3)(D) (2012).
9  *Miller*, 36 Cal. 4th at 451.
10  *Id.* at 467.
11  Martha Chamallas, *Consent, Equality, and the Legal Control of Sexual Conduct*, 61 S. Cal. L. Rev. 777, 858 (1988).

### CHAPTER 13. LOLITA AT THE OFFICE

1  Doe v. Oberweis Dairy, 456 F.3d 704, 713 (7th Cir. 2006).
2  *See, e.g.*, Lissau v. Southern Food Serv., 159 F.3d 177, 178 (4th Cir. 1998).
3  Charles A. Phipps, *Misdirected Reform: On Regulating Consensual Sexual Activity Between Teenagers*, 12 Cornell J.L. & Pub. Pol'y 373, 428–29 (2003).
4  720 ILCS 5/11-1.50 (2014).
5  477 U.S. 57, 66 (1986).
6  Meritor Savings Bank v. Vinson, 477 U.S. 57, 67 (1986).
7  *Oberweis Dairy*, 456 F.3d at 713.
8  As explained in Chapter 28, the Supreme Court narrowed the definition of "supervisor" for harassment liability purposes in *Vance v. Ball State Univ.*, 133 S. Ct. 2434, 2439 (2013).
9  Jennifer Ann Drobac, Sex and the Workplace: "Consenting" Adolescents and a *Conflict of Laws*, 79 Wash. L. Rev. 471, 477–81 (2004).

### CHAPTER 14. SEX TALK IN THE WRITERS' ROOM

1  132 P.3d 211, 215 (Cal. 2006).
2  *See, e.g.*, Carr v. Barnabey's Hotel Corp., 28 Cal. Rptr. 2d 127, 129 (Cal. Ct. App. 1994).
3  *See, e.g.*, United States Steel Corp. v. United States, 385 F. Supp. 346, 347–48 (W.D. Penn. 1974).

4  523 U.S. 75, 81 (1998).
5  *Id.* at 81–82.
6  53 F.3d 1531, 1535 (10th Cir. 1995).
7  *Id.* at 1537.
8  *See, e.g.,* Williams v. Gen. Motors Corp., 187 F.3d 553, 564 (6th Cir. 1999) (finding the Tenth Circuit's reasoning in *Gross* "illogical").
9  Rabidue v. Osceola Refining Co., 584 F. Supp. 419, 430 (E.D. Mich. 1984).
10  *See, e.g.,* O'Rourke v. City of Providence, 235 F.3d 713 (1st Cir. 2001).
11  *Lyle,* 12 Cal. Rptr. 3d at 518.
12  *See id.* at 520 ("Thus, to the extent defendants can establish [their behavior] was within "the scope of necessary job performance" . . . defendants may be able to show their conduct should not be viewed as harassment.").
13  *Id.*
14  *Id.* at 215.
15  Christopher Noxon, *Television Without Pity,* N.Y. TIMES, Oct. 17, 2004.
16  *Id.*
17  CAL. GOV'T CODE § 12920 (West 2006); 42 U.S.C. § 2000e-2(a) (2006).
18  *See, e.g.,* Harris v. Forklift Systems, Inc., 510 U.S. 17, 21 (1993).
19  *See Harris,* 510 U.S. at 21–22.
20  *Lyle,* 132 P.3d at 223–24.
21  *Id.* at 226.
22  *Id.* at 227.
23  *Id.* at 228.
24  Deborah Zalesne, *Sexual Harassment Law: Has it Gone Too Far, or Has the Media?,* 8 TEMP. POL. & CIV. RTS L. REV. 351, 353–54 (1999).

### CHAPTER 15. SEX BEHIND BARS

1  36 Cal. 4th 446 (2005).
2  759 F.3d 768 (7th Cir. 2014).
3  *Id.* at 771.
4  *Id.*
5  *Id.*
6  *Id.* at 770.
7  *Id.*
8  *Id.*
9  *Id.*

### CHAPTER 16. WHEN THE SUPERVISOR BULLIES ONLY WOMEN

1  EEOC v. Nat'l Educ. Ass'n, 422 F.3d 840, 842–44 (9th Cir. 2005).
2  *See, e.g.,* Margaret Hart Edwards, *Men's Temper Tantrums That Bother Women May Be Sex Discrimination (9th Circuit Strikes Again),* FREE REPUBLIC (Sept. 23, 2005), http://www.freerepublic.com/focus/f-news/1490177/posts.
3  42 U.S.C. § 2000e-2(a) (2012).
4  *See, e.g.,* Corne v. Bausch & Lomb, 562 F.2d 55 (9th Cir. 1977); Tomkins v. Pub. Serv. Elec. & Gas Co., 422 F. Supp. 553 (D. N.J. 1976), *rev'd,* 568 F.2d 1044 (1977).

5 *See, e.g.,* Doe v. City of Belleville, 119 F.3d 563, 580 (7th Cir. 1997) (ruling that the male plaintiff was subjected to sex discrimination even though there was likely no sexual desire for the plaintiff), *vacated on other grounds,* 523 U.S. 1001 (1998).

6 *See, e.g.,* Giddens v. Shell Oil Co., No. 92-8533, 1993 WL 529956, at *1 (5th Cir. 1993) ("Harassment by a male supervisor against a male subordinate does not state a claim under Title VII even though the harassment has sexual overtones. Title VII addresses gender discrimination.")

7 *See, e.g.,* Reynolds v. Atlantic City Convention Ctr., Civ. A. No. 88-4232, 1990 WL 267417, at *15, *19 (D.N.J. 1990) (using the EEOC's definition of "sexual harassment" as "conduct of a sexual nature" to find that the refusal of male coworkers to work with the female plaintiff "because she was a woman" did not qualify as sex discrimination).

8 *See, e.g.,* Hicks v. Gates Rubber Co., 833 F.2d 1406, 1415 (10th Cir. 1987) ("[A]ny harassment... that would not occur but for the sex of the employee... may, if sufficiently patterned or pervasive, comprise an illegal condition of employment under Title VII") (quoting McKinney v. Dole, 765 F.2d 1129, 1138 (D.C. Cir. 1985), *aff'd after remand,* 928 F.2d 966, 971 (10th Cir. 1991)).

9 Vicki Schultz, *Reconceptualizing Sexual Harassment,* 107 YALE. L.J. 1683, 1737 (1998).

10 Kortan v. Cal. Youth Auth., 217 F.3d 1104, 1109 (9th Cir. 2000).

11 523 U.S. 75, 79–81 (1998).

12 510 U.S. 17, 25 (1993) (Ginsburg, J., concurring).

13 EEOC, 422 F.3d at 845.

14 *See, e.g.,* Jeremy A. Blumenthal, *The Reasonable Woman Standard: A Meta-Analytic Review of Gender Differences in Perceptions of Sexual Harassment,* 22 LAW & HUM. BEHAV. 33, 35 (1998) ("[M]en and women often, but not invariably, perceive social-sexual behavior, especially in the workplace, in different ways") (citations omitted).

15 EEOC, 422 F.3d at 845.

16 *See* Harris v. Forklift Systems, Inc., 510 U.S. 17, 21 (1993).

17 David C. Yamada, *The Phenomenon of "Workplace Bullying" and the Need for Status-Blind Hostile Work Environment Protection,* 88 GEO. L.J. 475, 515 (federal law is only violated when the bullying is on account of the bullied employee's membership in a group protected by Title VII).

18 HEALTHY WORKPLACE BILL, http://www.healthyworkplacebill.org (since 2003, twenty-five states have introduced a "healthy workplace bill" to prohibit workplace bullying, but no states have yet enacted such a law).

19 *See* Raess v. Doescher, 883 N.E.2d 790, 793 (Ind. 2008) (affirming the jury verdict).

## CHAPTER 17. THE EQUAL OPPORTUNITY HARASSER

1 *See* Kellie A. Wagner, *Connecticut Fire Chief Charged with Lewd Behavior, Creating Hostile Workplace,* CT LAW TRIBUNE, Mar. 20, 2001, http://www.law.com/jsp/article.jsp?id=900005527859.

2 Oncale v. Sundowner Offshore Services, 523 U.S. 75, 79–80 (1998).

3 *See, e.g.,* Robin Applebaum, *The "Undifferentiating Libido": A Need for Federal Legislation to Prohibit Sexual Harassment by a Bisexual Sexual Harasser,* 14 HOFSTRA LAB. L.J. 601, 616 (1997).

4 Brief for Lambda Legal Defense and Education Fund et al. as Amici Curiae Supporting Petitioner at 22, *Oncale,* 523 U.S. 75 (No. 96-568).

5 Holman v. Indiana, 211 F.3d 399, 401 (7th Cir. 2000).

6  *See* Dobrich v. Gen. Dynamics Corp., 106 F. Supp. 2d 386, 391 (D. Conn. 2000) (finding for the defendant because, although the defendant's conduct was aimed at the female plaintiff as well as several of her male and female coworkers, no male coworkers objected to the defendant's conduct).

7  Carpenter v. City of Torrington, 100 F. App'x 858, at *1 (2d Cir. 2004).

### CHAPTER 18. PERIODONTAL PERILS

1  Mota v. Univ. of Tex. Houston Health Sci. Ctr., 261 F.3d 512 (5th Cir. 2001).

2  Oncale v. Sundowner Offshore Servs., 523 U.S. 75 (1998).

3  *Id.*

4  42 U.S.C. § 2000e et seq. (2012).

5  20 U.S.C. §1681 et seq. (2012).

6  *See* Lissau v. S. Food Serv., Inc., 159 F.3d 177, 180 (4th Cir. 1998); Haynes v. Williams, 88 F.3d 898, 899 (10th Cir. 1996); Williams v. Banning, 72 F.3d 552, 555 (7th Cir. 1995); Tomka v. Seiler Corp., 66 F.3d 1295, 1313–17 (2d Cir. 1995); Greenlaw v. Garrett, 59 F.3d 994, 1001 (9th Cir. 1995); Cross v. Alabama, 49 F.3d 1490, 1504 (11th Cir. 1995).

7  *Oncale*, 523 U.S. at 78.

### CHAPTER 19. PUNISHING EFFEMINACY

1  Rene v. MGM Grand Hotel, Inc., 305 F.3d 1061 (9th Cir. 2002).

2  42 U.S.C. § 2000e et seq. (2012).

3  Sam Stein, *John Boehner Opposes ENDA: Dealing Blow to Bill's Chances*, HuffPost Politics (Nov. 4, 2013), http://www.huffingtonpost.com/2013/11/04/john-boehner-enda_n_4212250.html.

4  *See, e.g.*, Bibby v. Phila. Coca Cola Bottling Co., 260 F.3d 257, 261 (3d Cir. 2001) ("It is clear . . . that Title VII does not prohibit discrimination based on sexual orientation").

5  Jerome Hunt, *A History of the Employment Discrimination Act: It's Past Time to Pass This Law*, Center for American Progress (July 19, 2011), http://www.american progress.org/issues/lgbt/news/2011/07/19/10006/a-history-of-the-employment-non-discrimination-act/.

6  *Id.*

7  Employment Non-Discrimination Act of 2013, S. 815, 113th Cong. (2013), https://www .govtrack.us/congress/bills/113/s815/text/is.

8  Exec. Order No. 13087, 63 Fed. Reg. 30097 (May 28, 1998) (amending to Executive Order 11478).

9  ACLU, *Non-Discrimination Laws: State by State Information – Map* (visited June 15, 2015), https://www.aclu.org/maps/non-discrimination-laws-state-state-information-map.

10  523 U.S. 75 (1998).

11  Price Waterhouse v. Hopkins, 490 U.S. 228 (1989).

12  *Rene*, 305 F.3d at 1066.

13  *Id.* at 1068 (Pregerson, J., concurring).

14  Price Waterhouse v. Hopkins, 490 U.S. 228 (1989). *See* Chapters 4, 5 and 6.

15  Nichols v. Azteca Rest. Enters., 256 F.3d 864 (9th Cir. 2001).

16  *Rene*, 305 F. 3d at 1071.

17  Martin v. N.Y. State Dep't of Corr. Servs., 224 F. Supp. 2d 434 (N.D.N.Y 2002).

18  Loving v. Virginia, 388 U.S. 1 (1967).
19  *Id.* at 10.
20  *See, e.g.*, Zachary A. Kramer, *The Ultimate Gender Stereotype: Equalizing Gender-Conforming and Gender-Nonconforming Homosexuals under Title VII*, U. Ill. L. Rev. 465 (2004).
21  Videckis v. Pepperdine Univ., 2015 WL 8916764 (C.D. Cal. 2015).

## CHAPTER 20. LATE-NIGHT AFFAIRS WITH DAVID LETTERMAN

1  *David Letterman's Shocking Confession*, Access Hollywood (Oct. 1, 2009), http://watch.accesshollywood.com/video/david-lettermans-shocking-confession-october-1-2009/1311486575001?utm_source=accesshollywood.com&utm_medium=referral.
2  Karen Freifeld, *Letterman Extortion Case Dismissal Denied by Judge*, Bloomberg (Jan. 19, 2010, 2:53 PM), http://www.bloomberg.com/apps/news?pid=newsarchive&sid=ampEjHetC4xo.
3  *North Country* (Warner Bros. 2005).
4  Meritor Sav. Bank, FSB v. Vinson, 477 U.S. 57 (1986).
5  Public Statement, National Organization for Women President Terry O'Neill, *The Latest Letterman Controversy Raises Workplace Issues for Women* (Oct. 6, 2009), http://www.now.org/press/10-09/10-06.html.
6  Nat'l R.R. Passenger Corp. (AMTRAK) v. Morgan, 536 U.S. 101, 107 (2002).
7  Nell Scovell, *Letterman and Me*, Vanity Fair, Oct. 31, 2009.
8  *See* Kathy Jesse, *David Letterman, Even Retired, Keeps on Interviewing*, N.Y. Times, Dec. 2, 2015, at C1.

## CHAPTER 21. WHY HERMAN CAIN HAS NOT BEEN ABLE TO TALK HIS WAY OUT OF HIS EXPLODING SEXUAL HARASSMENT SCANDAL

1  Jonathan Martin et al., *Herman Cain Accused by Two Women of Inappropriate Behavior*, Politico (Oct. 31, 2011), http://www.politico.com/news/stories/1011/67194.html.
2  John Dean, *Thoughts on the Politics of the Sexual Harassment Charges against Herman Cain*, Justia's Verdict, Nov. 4, 2011, http://verdict.justia.com/2011/11/04/thoughts-on-the-politics-of-the-sexual-harassment-charges-against-herman-cain.
3  Emily Schultheis, *Under Cain, NRA Launched Sex Harassment Fight*, Politico, Nov. 5, 2011, http://www.politico.com/story/2011/11/under-cain-nra-launched-sex-harassment-fight-067669.
4  Civil Rights Act of 1991, Pub. L. No. 102-166, 105 Stat. 1071 (1991).
5  Claire Safran, *What Men Do to Women on the Job: A Shocking Look at Sexual Harassment*, Redbook, Nov. 1976, 148–49.
6  U.S. Merit Systems Protection Board, *Leadership for Change: Human Resource Development in the Federal Government*, Washington, DC, July 1995, 20.
7  Steve Holland, *Herman Cain: Woman's Statement About Sexual Harassment May be Released Today*, Christian Sci. Monitor, Nov. 4, 2011, http://www.csmonitor.com/USA/Elections/From-the-Wires/2011/1104/Herman-Cain-Woman-s-statement-about-sexual-harassment-may-be-released-today.
8  Burlington Indus. v. Ellerth, 524 U.S. 742, 761 (1998).

9   *See, e.g.,* Patterson v. County of Oneida, NY, 375 F.3d 206 (2d Cir. 2004).
10  *Herman Cain on Sexual Harassment Settlement: Not Recalling Signing It, Doesn't Mean I Didn't Sign It,* HUFFINGTON POST, Nov. 1, 2011, http://www.huffingtonpost .com/2011/11/01/herman-cain-sexual-harassment-settlement_n_1068719.html.
11  *Id.*
12  *See* Jeremy A. Blumenthal, *The Reasonable Woman Standard: A Meta-Analytic Review of Gender Differences in Perceptions of Sexual Harassment,* 22 LAW & HUM. BEHAV. 33, 35 (1998).
13  Harris v. Forklift Sys., 510 U.S. 17, 21–22 (1993).
14  See Phoebe A. Morgan, *Risking Relationships: Understanding the Litigation Choices of Sexually Harassed Women,* 33 LAW & SOC'Y REV. 67, 68 (1999).
15  *Id.* (one study found that between 42 percent and 44 percent of working women experience behaviors regarded as legally actionable, but only 7 percent file formal charges with their employers); *see also* James E. Gruber, *How Women Handle Sexual Harassment: A Literature Review,* 74 SOCIOLOGY & SOCIAL RESEARCH 3–4 (1989).
16  *See* Holland, *supra* note 7.
17  *See* Nicholas G. Hahn III, *The Devil and Herman Cain,* realclearreligion.org, Oct. 23, 2013, http://www.realclearreligion.org/articles/2013/10/23/the_devil_and_herman_ cain.html.

### CHAPTER 22. WHY HOSTILE ENVIRONMENT HARASSMENT IS A "CONTINUING VIOLATION"

1   536 U.S. 101, 104–05 (2002).
2   42 U.S.C. § 2000e-5(e)(1); Nat'l R.R. Passenger Corp. (AMTRAK) v. Morgan, 232 F.3d 1008, 1014 (9th Cir. 2000).
3   *Id.* at 1016.
4   *See* 42 U.S.C. § 2000e-2(a) (2012); 42 U.S.C. § 2000e-5(b) (2012).
5   *See* 42 U.S.C. § 2000e-5(f)(1) (2012); 42 U.S.C. § 2000e-6(a) (2012).
6   *Morgan,* 232 F.3d at 1014.
7   PHILIP J. PFEIFFER, EMPLOYMENT DISCRIMINATION LAW 770 (3d Ed. Supp. 2000).
8   BARBARA LINDEMANN & PAUL GROSSMAN, EMPLOYMENT DISCRIMINATION LAW 1351 (3d ed. 1996).
9   *See, e.g.,* Courtney v. La Salle Univ., 124 F.3d 499, 505 (3d Cir. 1997).
10  *See, e.g.,* Richard Lacayo, *Strange Justice: A Book on Clarence Thomas,* TIME (Nov. 14, 1994), http://www.time.com/time/magazine/article/0,9171,981809,00.html.
11  *Morgan,* 536 U.S. at 105.
12  *Id.* at 125.
13  *Id.* at 125–26.
14  524 U.S. 775, 807 (1998).
15  524 U.S. 742, 765 (1998).
16  *See, e.g.,* Guerra v. Editorial Televisa-USA, Inc., No. 97-3670-CIV-UNGARO-BENAGES, 1999 U.S. Dist. LEXIS 10082, at *12, *32, *36 (S.D. Fla. June 2, 1999) (finding one-week delay unreasonable).

### CHAPTER 23. WHEN SEXUAL EXTORTION IS SUCCESSFUL

1   310 F.3d 84, 89 (2d Cir. 2002).
2   *Id.* at 87.

3  14 F.3d 773, 779 (2d Cir. 1994).
4  *See, e.g.,* Lutkewitte v. Gonzales, 436 F.3d 248 (D.C. Cir. 2006).
5  *Ellerth,* 524 U.S. at 746.
6  *Id.* at 761.
7  Guidelines on Discrimination Because of Sex, 29 C.F.R. § 1604.11 (2016).
8  *Jin*, 310 F.3d at 94.
9  Catharine A. MacKinnon, Feminism Unmodified: Discourses on Life and Law 110 (1987).

### CHAPTER 24. THE CONSEQUENCES OF FAILING TO COMPLAIN ABOUT HARASSMENT

1  Hawk v. Americold Logistics, L.L.C., No. 02 Civ. 3528, 2003 U.S. Dist. LEXIS 3445 (E.D. Pa. Mar. 6, 2003).
2  Burlington Indus. v. Ellerth, 524 U.S. 742, 765 (1998); Faragher v. City of Boca Raton, 524 U.S. 775, 807 (1998).
3  *See, e.g.,* McIntyre v. Advance Auto Parts, No.1:04 Civ. 1857, U.S. Dist. LEXIS 1944 (N.D. Ohio Jan. 10, 2007); Conatzer v. Medical Prof'l Bldg. Servs., 255 F. Supp. 2d 1259, 1269–70 (N.D. Okla. 2003).
4  Madray v. Publix Super Mkts., Inc., 30 F. Supp. 2d 1371, 1375 (S.D. Fla. 1998), *aff'd* 208 F.3d 1290 (11th Cir. 2000); Barrett v. Applied Radiant Energy Corp., 240 F.3d 262, 267–268 (4th Cir. 2001); Shaw v. AutoZone, Inc., 180 F.3d 806, 813 (1999); Hylton v. Norrell Health Care of New York, 53 F. Supp. 2d 613, 618 (7th Cir. 1999); Jones v. USA Petroleum Corp., 20 F. Supp. 2d 1379, 1386 (S.D. Ga. 1998).
5  *See, e.g.,* Martha R. Mahoney, *Exit: Power and the Idea of Leaving in Love, Work and the Confirmation Hearings,* 65 S. Cal. L. Rev. 1283, 1289 (1992).
6  U.S. Merit Sys. Prot. Bd., Sexual Harassment in the Federal Workplace: Trends, Progress, and Continuing Challenges 13, 30 (1995).
7  *See, e.g.,* James E. Gruber & Lars Bjorn, *Women's Responses to Sexual Harassment: An Analysis of Sociocultural, Organizational, and Personal Resource Models,* 67 Social Sci. Q. 814 (1986).
8  *See* Lin Farley, Sexual Shakedown: The Sexual Harassment of Women on the Job 23 (1978).
9  *See, e.g.,* Douglas D. Baker et al., *The Influence of Individual Characteristics and Severity of Harassing Behavior on Reactions to Sexual Harassment,* 22 Sex Roles 305, 305–6 (1990); James E. Gruber & Michael D. Smith, *Women's Responses to Sexual Harassment: A Multivariate Analysis,* 17 Basic & Applied Social Psychology 543, 546 (1995); M. Sullivan & Deborah I. Bybee, *Female Students and Sexual Harassment: What Factors Predict Reporting Behavior?,* 50(2) J. Nat'l Ass'n Women Deans and Couns. 11 (1987).
10  *See* Gruber & Smith, *supra* note 9, at 548.
11  Joanna L. Grossman, *The First Bite Is Free: Employer Liability for Sexual Harassment,* 61 U. Pitt. L. Rev. 671, 726 (2000).
12  L. Camille Hebert, *Why Don't "Reasonable Women" Complain about Sexual Harassment?,* 82 Ind. L.J. 711, 740 (2007).
13  Gruber & Smith, *supra* note 9, at 553.
14  *Id.*
15  *Hawk,* 2003 U.S. Dist. LEXIS 3445, at *29.

CHAPTER 25. WHO IS RESPONSIBLE FOR SUDDEN, SEVERE HARASSMENT?

1  Walton v. Johnson & Johnson Servs., 347 F.3d 1272, 1293 (11th Cir. 2003).
2  Burlington Indus. v. Ellerth, 524 U.S. 742, 765 (1998); Faragher v. City of Boca Raton, 524 U.S. 775, 807 (1998).
3  Indest v. Freeman Decorating, Inc., 168 F.3d 795, 804 (5th Cir. 1999).
4  *Walton*, 347 F.3d at 1287.
5  542 U.S. 129 (2004). For a discussion of the opinion, see Joanna L. Grossman, *The Supreme Court's Ruling on Harassment that Results in Constructive Discharge: Why It is a Disappointment*, FINDLAW'S WRIT, June 22, 2004, http://writ.news.findlaw .com/grossman/20040622.html.
6  133 S. Ct. 2434, 2439 (2013).


CHAPTER 26. CHINKS IN THE HARASSMENT LAW ARMOR

1  480 F.3d 1287 (11th Cir. 2007).
2  *See, e.g.*, Martha R. Mahoney, *Exit: Power and the Idea of Leaving in Love, Work and the Confirmation Hearings*, 65 S. CAL. L. REV. 1283, 1289 (1992).
3  *See, e.g.*, Guerra v. Editorial Televisa-USA, Inc., 1999 U.S. Dist. LEXIS 10082, at *12, *32, *36 (S.D. Fla. June 2, 1999) (finding one-week delay unreasonable).
4  Baldwin v. Blue Cross/Blue Shield, 254 Fed. Appx. 800 (11th Cir. 2007); Baldwin v. Blue Cross/Blue Shield, 552 U.S. 991 (2007).


CHAPTER 27. DO EMPLOYER EFFORTS PREVENT HARASSMENT
OR JUST PREVENT LIABILITY?

1  Peter Aronson, *Mitsubishi Comes Back from Disaster of 1998*; EEOC, *Plaintiff's Side Hail Company for Actions on Sexual Harassment*, NAT'L L.J., April 29, 2002, at 1.
2  *See* Burlington Indus. v. Ellerth, 524 U.S. 742, 765 (1998); Faragher v. City of Boca Raton, 524 U.S. 775, 807 (1998).
3  For a full explication of this point, see Joanna L. Grossman, *The Culture of Compliance: The Final Triumph of Form Over Substance in Sexual Harassment Law*, 26 HARV. WOMEN'S L.J. 3, 41 (2003).
4  U.S. MERIT SYS. PROT. BD., SEXUAL HARASSMENT IN THE FEDERAL WORKPLACE: TRENDS, PROGRESS, AND CONTINUING CHALLENGES 41 (1995).
5  Robert Moyer & Anjan Nath, *Sexual Harassment Training Interventions*, 28 J. APPLIED SOC. PSYCHOL. 333, 343 (1998).
6  Aronson, *supra* note 1, at 2.


CHAPTER 28. WHO'S THE BOSS?

1  Vance v. Ball State Univ., 133 S. Ct. 2434, 2439 (2013).
2  Vance v. Ball State Univ., 646 F.3d 461, 472 (7th Cir. 2011).
3  Rogers v. EEOC, 454 F.2d 234, 238 (5th Cir. 1971).
4  *See* Baldwin v. Blue Cross/Blue Shield, 480 F.3d 1287 (11th Cir. 2007) (see Chapter 26); Hawk v. Americold Logistics, L.L.C., No. 02 Civ. 3528, U.S. Dist. LEXIS 3445 (E.D. Pa. Mar. 6, 2003) (see Chapter 24).

5  EEOC Policy Guidance on Vicarious Employer Liability for Unlawful Harassment by Supervisors, EEOC Notice No. 915.002 (June 18, 1999), http://www.eeoc.gov/policy/docs/harassment.html.
6  Ledbetter v. Goodyear Tire & Rubber Co., 550 U.S. 618 (2007).
7  Lilly Ledbetter Fair Pay Act of 2009, Pub. L. No. 111-2, 123 Stat. 5. *See* Chapters 47–50.
8  *Vance*, 133 S. Ct. at 2455 (Ginsburg, J., dissenting).
9  *Id.* at 2456.
10  *Id.* at 2464.

### CHAPTER 29. COSTLY MISTAKES

1  Letter from Sheldon Silver, Speaker of the Assembly, to Vito Lopez, Assemblyman (August 24, 2012), http://jcope.ny.gov/enforcement/2013/lopez/Tab%20N4.pdf.
2  May v. Chrysler Group, LLC, 692 F.3d 734 (7th Cir. 2012).
3  Letter from Sheldon Silver to Vito Lopez, *supra* note 1.
4  527 U.S. 526 (1999).
5  *May*, 692 F.3d at 746.
6  *See* Jesse McKinley, *Harassment Suit Is Settled against Former Assemblyman Vito Lopez and Sheldon Silver Is Settled*, N.Y. TIMES, Feb. 5, 2015, at A20.
7  See William K. Rashbaum, *Sheldon Silver, Former Assembly Speaker, Is Indicted*, N.Y. TIMES, Feb. 19, 2015, at A20.
8  *See* Mike Vilensky, *Former New York Assemblyman Vito Lopez Dies at 74*, WALL ST. J., Nov. 10, 2015; Benjamin Weiser & Susanne Craig, *Sheldon Silver, Ex-New York Assembly Speaker, Is Found Guilty on All Counts*, N.Y. TIMES, Nov. 30, 2015, at A1.

### CHAPTER 30. HANDS OFF THE MERCHANDISE

1  Urban Dictionary, http://www.urbandictionary.com/define.php?term=hands%20off.
2  EEOC v. KarenKim, Inc., 698 F.3d 92 (2d Cir. 2012).

### PART III. PREGNANT WOMEN AND MOTHERS AT WORK

1  505 U.S. 833, 856 (1992).
2  LEGAL MOMENTUM, *Pregnancy and Family: Issues*, http://www.legalmomentum.org/our-work/women-at-work/pregnancy-and-family-issues.html.
3  U.S. CENSUS BUREAU, MATERNITY LEAVE AND EMPLOYMENT PATTERNS OF FIRST-TIME MOTHERS: 1961–2008 (Oct. 2011), http://www.census.gov/prod/2011pubs/p70-128.pdf.
4  AT&T Corp. v. Hulteen, 556 U.S. 701, 724 (2009) (Ginsburg, J., dissenting).
5  *See* Deborah A. Widiss, *Gilbert Redux: The Interaction of the Pregnancy Discrimination Act and the Amended Americans with Disabilities Act*, 46 U.C. DAVIS L. REV. 961, 986–89 (2013). On the general development and implementation of pregnancy discrimination law, see Joanna L. Grossman, *Pregnancy and the False Promise of Equal Citizenship*, 98 GEORGETOWN L.J. 567 (2010); Joanna L. Grossman & Gillian Thomas, *Making Pregnancy Work: Overcoming the PDA's Capacity-Based Model*, 21 YALE J. L. & FEMINISM 15 (2009).

6 417 U.S. 484, 487–89 (1974).

7 *See* Reed v. Reed, 404 U.S. 71 (1971); Frontiero v. Richardson, 411 U.S. 677 (1973).

8 *Geduldig,* 417 U.S. at 496–97, n. 20.

9 *Id.* at 497 n. 20.

10 Sylvia A. Law, *Rethinking Sex and the Constitution,* 132 U. PA. L. REV. 955, 983 (1984).

11 Coleman v. Ct. of Appeals, 132 S. Ct. 1327, 1347 n. 6 (2012) (Ginsburg, J., dissenting).

12 429 U.S. 125, 128 (1976).

13 *Id.* at 148 (Brennan, J., dissenting).

14 *Id.* at 140–46.

15 Deborah Dinner, *The Costs of Reproduction: History and the Legal Construction of Sex Equality,* 46 HARV. C.R.-C.O. L. REV. 415, 444–45 (2011).

16 Act of Oct. 31, 1978, Pub. L. No. 95-555, 92 Stat. 2076; *see also* 123 Cong. Rec. 29635, 29640–65 (1977); 124 Cong. Rec. H6862–70; 124 Cong. Rec. H6878, 124 Cong. Rec. 21421 (1978).

17 *See* 42 U.S.C. § 2000e(k) (2012).

18 414 U.S. 632, 644 (1974).

19 *Id.* at 645–46; *see also* Turner v. Department of Employment Security, 423 U.S. 44 (1975) (invalidating Utah law prohibiting a pregnant woman from collecting unemployment benefits from twelve weeks prior to her due date until six weeks after she gave birth based on a conclusive resumption that she would be unable to work during that period).

20 *Id.* at 640 n. 9.

21 *Id.* at 646–47.

22 *See* 42 U.S.C. § 2000e(k) ("The terms 'because of sex' or 'on the basis of sex' include . . . because of or on the basis of pregnancy").

23 *See id.* ("[W]omen affected by pregnancy . . . shall be treated the same for all employment-related purposes . . . as other persons not so affected but similar in their ability or inability to work").

24 *See* Kristin Smith et al., *Maternity Leave and Employment Patterns: 1961–1995,* CURRENT POPULATION REPORTS 70–79 (2001).

25 20 F.3d 734, 735–36 (7th Cir. 1994).

26 *Id.* at 738.

27 *See id.* at 739 ("Troupe would be halfway home if she could find one nonpregnant employee of Lord & Taylor who had not been fired when about to begin a leave similar in length to hers") (emphasis in original).

28 *Id.* at 738.

29 *See* 42 U.S.C. § 2000e(k).

30 479 U.S. 272 (1987).

31 *See, e.g.,* Wendy W. Williams, *The Equality Crisis: Some Reflections on Culture, Courts, and Feminism,* 7 WOMEN'S RTS. L. REP. 175 (1982) (in favor of the "equal treatment" approach).

32 *See, e.g.,* Herma Hill Kay, *Equality and Difference: The Case of Pregnancy,* 1 BERKELEY WOMEN'S L.J. 1 (1985) (in favor of the "special treatment" approach).

33 *Guerra,* 479 U.S. at 285.

34 *See* Rebecca U. Cho, *Baby Love: Firms Let Dads Indulge,* L.A. DAILY JOURNAL (Mar. 6, 2008), http://www.lw.com/upload/pubContent/_pdf/pub2148_1.6.08.pdf (describing decision by large firms to extend eighteen weeks of maternity leave to their employees).

35 *See* 29 U.S.C. § 2611(4)(A)(i) (defining "employer" as anyone with fifty or more employees); 29 U.S.C. § 2612(a)(1) (guaranteeing twelve weeks of unpaid leave in order to care for newborn). For a broader view of the FMLA's protections, see Joanna L. Grossman, *Job Security Without Equality: The Family and Medical Leave Act of 1993*, 15 WASH. U. J.L. &POL'Y 17 (2004).

### CHAPTER 31. PREGNANT TRUCKERS AND THE PROBLEM OF LIGHT-DUTY ASSIGNMENTS

1  Reeves v. Swift Transp. Co., 446 F.3d 637, 638 (6th Cir. 2006).
2  *Id.* at 638–39.
3  *Id.* at 638.
4  *See* Urbano v. Cont'l Airlines, Inc., 138 F.3d 204, 205 (5th Cir. 1998) (employer policy of granting light-duty assignments only to employees who suffered occupational injuries does not violate the PDA); Spivey v. Beverly Enters., 196 F.3d 1309, 1313 (11th Cir. 1999) (same).
5  *See* 42 U.S.C. § 2000e(k) (2006); *see also* Cal. Fed. Sav. & Loan Ass'n v. Guerra, 479 U.S. 272 (1987).
6  29 U.S.C. § 2612(a)(1).
7  *Id.*
8  29 U.S.C. § 2611(2)(A)(ii) (2006).
9  Reeves v. Swift Transp. Co., 446 F.3d 637, 641 (6th Cir. 2006).
10  *Id.*
11  *See id.* ("The district court correctly noted that Reeves' view of the law demands preferential, not equal treatment, and therefore finds no support in the [Pregnancy Discrimination] Act.").
12  *Id.* at 642.
13  *See* United States Census Bureau, *Census Bureau Reports "Delayer Boom" as More Educated Women Have Children Later*, May 9, 2011, http://www.census.gov/newsroom/releases/archives/fertility/cb11-83.html.
14  Amy Joyce, *Verizon Bias Suit Deal Sets Record*, WASHINGTON POST, June 6, 2006.

### CHAPTER 32. A BIG WIN FOR PREGNANT POLICE OFFICERS

1  Verdict, Agreement and Settlement, Lochren v. County of Suffolk, No. 01CV03925, 2006 WL 6850118 (E.D.N.Y. June 14, 2006).
2  *Id.*
3  Complaint at 21–22, Lochren v. County of Suffolk, http://www.nyclu.org/node/828.
4  *Id.* at 29, 33.
5  *Id.* at 34.
6  *Id.* at 53–54.
7  *Id.* at 66.
8  *Id.* at 76–81.
9  *Id.* at 52.
10  *See id.* at 7 (arguing that the police department violated Title VII of the Civil Rights Act of 1964 as well as New York's Human Rights Law).
11  *See* 42 U.S.C. § 2000e(k) (2006).

12　*See, e.g.,* Elaine W. Shoben, *Disparate Impact Theory in Employment Discrimination: What's Griggs Still Good For? What Not?*, 42 BRANDEIS L.J. 597, 600–601 (2004).

13　*Id.*

14　*Lochren v. County of Suffolk (Challenging discriminatory policy affecting pregnant police officers),* NYCLU, http://www.nyclu.org/node/1085.

15　*See* Verdict, Agreement and Settlement, *Lochren,* 2006 WL 6850118.

16　*Id.*

17　*See* Complaint at 15–17, *supra* note 3.

18　*See, e.g.,* Ruth Colker, *Rank-Order Physical Abilities Selection Devices for Traditionally Male Occupations as Gender-Based Employment Discrimination,* 19 U.C. DAVIS L. REV. 761 (1986) (discussing the ways in which police and fire departments have attempted to maintain their exclusion of women by implementing physical ability exams).

19　*See* Shoben, *supra* note 12, at 603–6.

20　*See id.* at 606.

21　*See* MARTHA CHAMALLAS, INTRODUCTION TO FEMINIST LEGAL THEORY 372 (2d ed. 2003) (citing census data showing that only 18 percent of women will not have given birth by their forty-fourth birthday); JEANETTE N. CLEVELAND ET AL., WOMEN AND MEN IN ORGANIZATIONS: SEX AND GENDER ISSUES AT WORK 208 (2000) (estimating that 75 percent of working women are likely to give birth at least once while working).

22　CAL. GOV. CODE § 12945(a)(3)(C) (West 2012).

23　*See* CAL. UNEMP. INS. CODE § 3301(a)(1) (West 2004) ("Family temporary disability insurance shall provide up to six weeks of wage replacement benefits to workers who take time off work to . . . bond with a minor child within one year of the birth").

24　*See* A.B. 9245, 230th Ann. Leg. Sess. (N.Y. 2007) (allowing up to twelve weeks paid disability leave to care for a newborn).

25　*See* S.B. 7547, 235th Leg. Sess. (N.Y. 2011).

26　*See* An Act to Amend the Executive Law, in Relation to Reasonable Accommodation, N.Y. A.B. 4272 (eff. Jan. 30, 2015), codified as N.Y. Exec. L. § 296 (McKinney's 2015).

27　For a summary of these laws, see National Partnership for Women & Families, *Reasonable Accommodations for Pregnant Workers: State and Local Laws,* http://www.nationalpartnership.org/research-library/workplace-fairness/pregnancy-discrimination/reasonable-accommodations-for-pregnant-workers-state-laws.pdf; Amanda D. Haverstick, *Proliferating State & Local Pregnancy Accommodation Laws Make Modifying ADA/FMLA Procedures a Must for Most Employers,* FORBES, June 17, 2014, http://www.forbes.com/sites/theemploymentbeat/2014/06/17/proliferating-state-local-pregnancy-accommodation-laws-make-modifying-adafmla-procedures-a-must-for-most-employers/.

## CHAPTER 33. UNDUE BURDEN

1　Affidavit at 3–15, Thompson v. City of New York (filed with EEOC Mar. 17, 2014) (on file with author).

2　*Id.* at 21–24.

3　*Id.* at Exhibits A–F. Needless to say, DCAS may deny these allegations or argue for a different interpretation of them as the case proceeds through the EEOC process.

4　*Id.* at 4–5, 7–9.

5　*Id.* at 6, 9–12.

6　*Id.* at 13.

7   *Id.* at 14.

8   *Id.* at 15.

9   *Id.* at 16–17.

10   NYC Human Rights Law §8–107(22) (2015).

11   *Id.* § 8–102(16)(a) (McKinney 2015). The Pregnant Workers Fairness Act was an amendment to the New York City Human Rights Law that became effective on January 30, 2014. David Wirtz, *New York City Law Provides Reasonable Accommodation for Pregnancy, Childbirth and Related Conditions*, LITTLER (December 23, 2013), https://www.littler.com/new-york-city-law-provides-reasonable-accommodation-pregnancy-childbirth-and-related-conditions.

12   Wirtz, *supra* note 2.

13   *Id.*

14   Affidavit, *supra* note 1, at 20–24.

15   Robert Bernstein et al., *New York City Extends Human Rights Law to Pregnant Women with "Pregnant Workers Fairness Act,"* NATIONAL LAW REVIEW (Oct. 11, 2013), http://www.natlawreview.com/article/new-york-city-extends-human-rights-law-to-pregnant-women-pregnant-workers-fairness-a.

16   *See City of New York Dep't of Citywide Admin. Serv. General Examination Reg.*, CITYWIDE ADMIN. SERV. (2015), http://www.nyc.gov/html/dcas/downloads/pdf/misc/pdf_a_dcas_general_exam_regs.pdf.

17   135 S. Ct. 1338 (2015).

18   *City of New York Dep't of Citywide Admin. Serv. General Examination Reg.*, *supra* note 16, at E.11.4.

19   Young v. United Parcel Service, Inc., 135 S. Ct. 1338, 1355 (2015).

20   *See* Rachel L. Swarns, *Pregnant Officer Denied Chance to Take Sergeant's Exam Fights Back*, N.Y. TIMES, Aug. 9, 2015, at A13.

### CHAPTER 34. HARD LABOR: NEW PREGNANCY DISCRIMINATION GUIDANCE FROM THE EEOC

1   *See* National Partnership for Women & Families, *The Pregnancy Discrimination Act: Where We Stand 30 Years Later* (Oct. 2008), http://qualitycarenow.nationalpartnership.org/site/DocServer/%20Pregnancy_Discrimination_Act_-_Where_We_Stand_30_Years_L.pdf?docID=4281.

2   *See* Paul Igaski, *Is Complaining Worth the Risk?*, IMDiversity.com (Sept. 8, 2004), http://o2e1137.netsolhost.com/Villages/Careers/articles/igasaki_retaliation_for_eeo_complaints_0904.asp. On low reporting rates of harassment, see Chapter 24.

3   *See* U.S. Equal Emp't Opportunity Comm'n, Pregnancy Discrimination Charges EEOC & FEPAs Combined: FY 1997–FY 2011, http://www.eeoc.gov/eeoc/statistics/enforcement/pregnancy.cfm.

4   *See* Sue Shellenbarger, *More Women Pursue Claims of Pregnancy Discrimination*, WALL ST. J., MAR. 27, 2008, at D1.

5   EEOC Enforcement Guidance on Pregnancy Discrimination and Related Issues, July 14, 2014, www.eeoc.gov/laws/guidance/pregnancy_guidance.cfm.

6   707 F.3d 437 (4th Cir. 2013).

7   The Court issued an opinion in *Young v. UPS* a few months after this chapter was originally published. The ruling is explained in Chapter 35.

8   42 U.S.C. § 2000(e)(k).

9   *Id.*

CHAPTER 35. FORCEPS DELIVERY: THE SUPREME COURT NARROWLY
SAVES THE PREGNANCY DISCRIMINATION ACT IN YOUNG VS. UPS

1  Young v. United Parcel Service, Inc., 135 S. Ct. 1338, 1343, 1361 (2015).
2  *Id.* at 1344–47.
3  *Id.*
4  *Young*, 135 S. Ct. at 1342–48.
5  *Id.* at 1349.
6  *Id.*
7  *Id.* at 1350, 1352–53, 1362.
8  *Id.* at 1353.
9  McDonnell Douglass Corp. v. Green, 411 U.S. 1817 (1973).
10  *Id.* at 1353–54.
11  *Id.* at 1347.
12  *Id.* at 1354.
13  *Id.*
14  *Id.*
15  *Id.*
16  *Id.* at 1354–55.
17  *Young*, 135 S. Ct. at 1354–55.
18  *Id.* at 1344.
19  *Id.* at 1355.
20  *Id.*
21  *Id.* at 1354–55.
22  *Id.* at 1354.
23  *Id.* at 1365 (Scalia, J., dissenting).
24  *Id.* at 1367 (Kennedy, J., dissenting).
25  *Id.* at 1351–52.
26  *Id.* at 1352.
27  *Id.* at 1351.
28  *Id.*
29  *Id.*
30  *Id.* (citing E.E.O.C.C.M. § 626-I(A)(5), p. 626:0009 (July 2014)).
31  *Id.* at 1352.
32  100 F.3d. 1220 (6th Cir. 1996).
33  Some of the open questions are sketched out in Joanna L. Grossman & Deborah L. Brake, *Afterbirth: The Supreme Court's Ruling in* Young v. UPS *Leaves Many Questions Unanswered*, JUSTIA'S VERDICT, April 20, 2015, https://verdict.justia .com/2015/04/20/afterbirth-the-supreme-courts-ruling-in-young-v-ups-leaves-many-questions-unanswered.

CHAPTER 36. THE PREGNANCY DISCRIMINATION ACT
REACHES ADVANCED MATERNAL AGE

1  *Legislation to Prohibit Sex Discrimination on the Basis of Pregnancy: Hearings on H.R. 5055 and H.R. 6075 Before the Subcommittee on Employment Opportunities of the House Committee on education and Labor*, 95th Cong., Sess. 1 (1977) (testimony of Odessa Komer, vice president, United Auto Workers).

2  *See, e.g.*, Linda Bosniak, *Citizenship Denationalized*, 7 IND. J. GLOBAL LEGAL STUD. 447, 452 (2000) (recognizing that citizenship can be addressed "as a legal status, as a system of rights, as a form of political activity, or as a form of identity and solidarity").

3  Vicki Schultz, *Life's Work*, 100 COLUM. L. REV. 1881, 1886–92 (2000).

4  *See* U.S. CENSUS BUREAU, MATERNITY LEAVE AND EMPLOYMENT PATTERNS OF FIRST-TIME MOTHERS: 1961–2003 15–18 (Feb. 2008), http://www.census.gov/prod/2008pubs/ p70-113.pdf (showing that more pregnant women work through their pregnancies and return to work following childbirth than ever before).

5  *See* Reeves v. Swift Transp. Co., 446 F.3d 637, 638 (6th Cir. 2006) (upholding employer policy that granted light-duty work assignments to employees injured on the job, but not to pregnant employees).

6  *See* Troupe v. May Dep't Stores, 20 F.3d 734, 737–38 (7th Cir. 1994) (employer did not commit pregnancy discrimination when it fired a pregnant employee for excessive tardiness caused by morning sickness).

7  United States v. Virginia, 518 U.S. 515, 532 (1996).

### CHAPTER 37. THE PREGNANT WORKERS' FAIRNESS ACT: A TIME FOR CHANGE?

1  H.R. 5647, 112th Cong. (2012).

2  *See* 42 U.S.C. § 2000e(k) (2006).

3  *See id.*

4  *See* 29 U.S.C. § 2612(a)(1) (twelve weeks of unpaid leave); 29 U.S.C. § 2611(4)(A)(i) (defining employer as anyone with fifty or more employees); 29 U.S.C. § 2611(2)(A)(ii) (employee only eligible if she worked for her employer for at least 1,250 hours in the prior year).

5  *See, e.g.*, W. Gregory Rhodes, *Note, Watson v. Fort Worth Bank and Trust: A Plurality Proposal to Alter the Evidentiary Burdens in Title VII Disparate Impact Cases*, 67 N.C. L. REV. 725 (1989) (discussing the difficulty of proving disparate impact in employment discrimination cases).

6  42 U.S.C. § 2000e(k) (2012).

7  499 U.S. 187, 204 (1991).

8  No. H-11-2442, 2012 WL 739494, at *1 (S.D. Tex. Feb. 2, 2012).

9  *See, e.g.*, In re Union Pac. R.R. Emp't Practices Litig., 479 F.3d 936, 942 (8th Cir. 2007) (contraception); Saks v. Franklin Covey Co., 316 F.3d 337, 346 (2d Cir. 2003) (infertility).

10  20 F.3d 734, 735–36 (7th Cir. 1994).

11  *Id.* at 737.

12  *See id.* at 739 (holding that Troupe's failure to "find one nonpregnant employee of Lord & Taylor who had not been fired when about to begin a leave similar in length to hers... doomed her case") (emphasis in original).

13  *See, e.g.*, Reeves v. Swift Transp. Co., 446 F.3d 637, 640 (6th Cir. 2006) (employer policy of granting light-duty assignments only to employees injured on the job was "pregnancy-blind" and thus did not violate the PDA).

14  *See id.* at 641 (rejecting the pregnancy discrimination claim because the plaintiff could not show that her employer's policy masked an intent to discriminate, or that her employer fired her with an intent to discriminate against her on the basis of her pregnancy).

15 *See* 42 U.S.C. § 12112(b)(5)A) (2006). The ADA defines "disability" as "(A) a physical or mental impairment that substantially limits one or more of the major life activities of such individual; (B) a record of such an impairment; or (C) being regarded as having such an impairment." 42 U.S.C. § 12102(1).

16 *See, e.g.,* Gudenkauf v. Stauffer Communications, Inc., 922 F. Supp. 465, 473 (D. Kan. 1996). ("Pregnancy is a physiological condition, but it is not a disorder. Being the natural consequence of a properly functioning reproductive system, pregnancy cannot be called an impairment.")

17 *See* ADA Amendments Act of 2008, 42 U.S.C.A. § 12102 (2012); 29 C.F.R. pt. 1630 app. (2012) ("[S]omeone with an impairment resulting in a 20-pound lifting restriction that lasts or is expected to last for several months is substantially limited in the major life activity of lifting, and need not also show that he is unable to perform activities of daily living that require lifting in order to be considered substantially limited in lifting").

18 *See id.* ("Other conditions, such as pregnancy, that are not the result of a physiological disorder are also not impairments").

19 H.R. 5647, 112th Cong. (2012).

20 *Id.*

21 *See* 42 U.S.C. § 2000e(b) (for purposes of Title VII, an employer is anyone with at least fifteen employees).

22 S. 942, 113th Cong. (2013); H.R. 1975, 113th Cong. (2013).

## CHAPTER 38. THE SUPREME COURT DEALS A BLOW TO ONCE-PREGNANT RETIREES

1 AT&T Corp. v. Hulteen, 556 U.S. 701, 704 (2009).

2 Hulteen v. AT&T Corp., 498 F.3d 1001, 1003 (9th Cir. 2007).

3 *Hulteen,* 556 U.S. at 704–05.

4 *See* 42 U.S.C. § 2000e(k) (2006).

5 417 U.S. 484, 497 (1974).

6 42 U.S.C. § 2000e(k) (2006).

7 *Hulteen,* 556 U.S. at 705.

8 *Id.* at 705–6.

9 *Id.* at 706.

10 *Id.*

11 *Id.* at 706–7.

12 *Id.* at 707.

13 *Id.* at 709.

14 42 U.S.C. § 2000e-2(a)(1) (2006).

15 42 U.S.C. § 2000e-16(c) (2006).

16 *Hulteen,* 556 U.S. at 708; 42 U.S.C. § 2000e-2(h) (2006).

17 *See Hulteen,* 556 U.S. at 711.

18 *Id.* at 710–12.

19 *Id.* at 709–12; Teamsters v. United States, 431 U.S. 324, 352–53 (1977).

20 *Teamsters,* 431 U.S. at 352–53.

21 *Hulteen,* 556 U.S. at 707–8.

22 42 U.S.C. § 2000e-2(h) (2006).

23 *Hulteen,* 556 U.S. at 712.

24  *Id.* at 708.
25  *See id.* at 709 ("Benefit differentials produced by a bona fide seniority-based pension plan are permitted unless they are 'the result of an intention to discriminate'").
26  *See id.* at 720 (Ginsburg, J., dissenting) ("The plaintiffs . . . will receive, *for the rest of their lives,* lower pension benefits than colleagues who worked for AT&T no longer than they did") (emphasis added).
27  *Id.* at 719.
28  *Id.* at 720.
29  *Id.*
30  *Id.* at 717–18.
31  *Id.* at 719.
32  *See, e.g.,* Cleveland Bd. of Educ. v. LaFleur, 414 U.S. 632, 644 (1974) (invalidating school board rule forcing pregnant teachers to take unpaid maternity leave because it "amount[ed] to a conclusive presumption that every pregnant teacher who reaches the fifth or sixth month of pregnancy is physically incapable of continuing").
33  *Hulteen,* 556 U.S. at 724 (Ginsburg, J., dissenting).

## CHAPTER 39. IF SHE DOES NOT WIN IT IS A SHAME

1  Complaint at 1, Castergine v. Sterling Mets Front Office, LLC, No. 1:14-cv-05296 (E.D.N.Y 2014).
2  *Id.* at 5.
3  *Id.* at 6.
4  *Id.*
5  *Id.*
6  *Id.* at 7.
7  *Id.* at 8.
8  *Id.* at 7.
9  *Id.* at 8.
10  *Id.* at 10.
11  42 U.S.C. § 2000e(k) (2012).
12  *See* N.Y. Exec. Law § 296 (McKinney).
13  *See* Michelle R. Hebl et al., *Hostile and Benevolent Reactions toward Pregnant Women: Complementary Interpersonal Punishments and Rewards that Maintain Traditional Roles,* 92 J. Applied Psychol.1499 (2007).
14  *Id.* at 1508–9.
15  *See* Deborah L. Brake & Joanna L. Grossman, *Unprotected Sex: The Pregnancy Discrimination Act at 35,* 21 Duke J. Gender L. & Pol'y 67, 103–5 (2013) (reviewing studies).
16  *Id.* at 105.
17  Wiseman v. Wal-Mart Stores No. 08-1244-EFM, 2009 WL 1617669 (D. Kan. June 9, 2009).
18  Arizanovska v. Wal-Mart Stores, Inc., 682 F.3d 698 (7th Cir. 2012).
19  Brake & Grossman, *Unprotected Sex, supra* note 15, at 112.
20  Pregnancy Discrimination Act of 1978, 42 U.S.C. § 2000e(k) (2012).
21  *See* Joanna L. Grossman, *Pregnancy, Work, and the Promise of Equal Citizenship,* 98 Georgetown L.J. 567, 577 (2010) (collecting and describing studies).
22  *See* Joan C. Williams et al., *A Sip of Cool Water: Pregnancy Accommodation after the ADA Amendments Act,* 32 Yale L. & Pol'y Rev. 97, 103–4 (2013) (citing studies).

23 *See* Richard Sandomir, *Mets Resolve Suit with Executive They Fired When She Was Pregnant and Unmarried*, N.Y. TIMES, Mar. 13, 2015, at D3.

## CHAPTER 40. MUST EMPLOYERS WHO COVER PRESCRIPTIONS COVER CONTRACEPTION?

1 Standridge v. Union Pac. R.R. Co., 479 F.3d 936 (8th Cir. 2007).
2 EEOC Decision on Coverage of Contraception, September 19, 2001, http://www.eeoc.gov/policy/docs/decision-contraception.html.
3 Sylvia A. Law, *Sex Discrimination and Insurance for Contraception*, 73 WASH. L. REV. 363 (1998).
4 *Id.*
5 Pregnancy Discrimination Act of 1978, 42 U.S.C. §2000(e)-k (2012).
6 Cal. Fed. Sav. & Loan Ass'n v. Guerra, 479 U.S. 272 (1987).
7 UAW v. Johnson Controls, Inc., 499 U.S. 187 (1991).
8 EEOC Decision on Coverage of Contraception, *supra* note 2.
9 *Id.*
10 *Id.*
11 Erickson v. Bartell Drug Co., 141 F. Supp. 2d 1266 (W.D. Wash. 2001).
12 *Id.* at 1277.
13 Reports of such successes are detailed on the National Women's Law Center's website. *See* Contraceptive Equity Laws in Your State: Know Your Rights (Aug. 27, 2012), http://www.nwlc.org/resource/contraceptive-equity-laws-your-state-know-your-rights-use-your-rights-consumer-guide-0.
14 *See, e.g., Union Pac. R.R.*, 378 F. Supp. 2d at 1139; Mauldin v. Wal-Mart Stores, 89 Fair Empl. Prac. Cas. (BNA) 1600 (N.D. Ga. 2002); Glaubach v. Regence Blueshield, 149 Wn.2d 827 (Wash. 2003); Alexander v. Am. Airlines, Inc., 2002 U.S. Dist. LEXIS 7089 (N.D. Tex. Apr. 22, 2002).
15 In re Union Pac. R.R. Empl. Practices Litig., 378 F. Supp. 2d 1139 (D. Neb. 2005).
16 *Id.*
17 *Id.* at 1149.
18 Krauel v. Iowa Methodist Medical Ctr., 95 F.3d 674 (8th Cir. 1996).
19 *Standridge*, 479 F.3d at 941.
20 *Id.* at 942.
21 *Id.* at 943.
22 *Id.* at 946.
23 For up-to-date information, see National Conf. of State Legislatures, *Insurance Coverage for Contraception Laws*, http://www.ncsl.org/research/health/insurance-coverage-for-contraception-state-laws.aspx.
24 Treasury and General Government Appropriation Act, S. 2312, 105th Cong. (1998).
25 Employment Retirement Income Security Act, 29 U.S.C. §1144(127) (2012).
26 Equity in Prescription Insurance and Contraceptive Coverage Act, H.R. 2412, 110th Cong. (2007).
27 *See* Patient Protection and Affordable Care Act, Public Law 111–148 (Mar. 23, 2010); 45 C.F.R. Part 147 (2011); DHHS Press Release, Jan. 20, 2012, http://www.hhs.gov/news/press/2012pres/01/20120120a.html.
28 134 S. Ct. 2751 (2014).
29 *See* Little Sisters of the Poor Home for the Aged v. Burwell, 794 F.3d 1151 (10th Cir.), *cert. granted*, 136 S. Ct. 446 (2015).

## CHAPTER 41. FERTILE GROUND FOR DISCRIMINATION

1   Saks v. Franklin Covey Co., 316 F.3d 337 (2d Cir. 2003)
2   *Id.* at 341.
3   *Id.* at 342.
4   *Id.* at 341.
5   University of Minnesota Reproductive Medical Center, *Infertility Evaluation* (July 27, 2011), http://www.umphysicians.org/Clinics/ReproductiveMedicineCenter/ InfertilityEvaluation/.
6   American Society of Reproductive Medicine, *Infertility: An Overview*, http://www .reproductivefacts.org/Booklet_Infertility_An_Overview/.
7   William M. Mercer, Inc., Infertility as a Covered Benefit, May 31, 2006, http:// familybuilding.resolve.org/site/DocServer/Mercer_-_Resolve_Final_Report.pdf? docID=4361&JServSessionIda004=wp81gwj7l1.app212d.
8   2009 N.Y. Laws 54.
9   Employment Retirement Income Security Act, 29 U.S.C. §1114(127) (2012).
10  *Id.*
11  Pregnancy Discrimination Act of 1978, 42 U.S.C. §2000(e)-k (2006).
12  *Saks*, 316 F.3d at 346.
13  499 U.S. 187 (1991).
14  *Saks*, 316 F.3d at 346–7.
15  *Id.* at 341.
16  *Id.* at 347.

## CHAPTER 42. CAN A WOMAN BE FIRED FOR ABSENTEEISM RELATED TO FERTILITY TREATMENTS?

1   Hall v. Nalco Co., 534 F.3d 644 (7th Cir. 2008).
2   *Id.* at 646.
3   *Id.*
4   *Id.*
5   UAW v. Johnson Controls, Inc., 499 U.S. 187 (1991).
6   *Id.* at 197.
7   *Hall*, 534 F.3d at 649.
8   Saks v. Franklin Covey Co., 316 F.3d 337(2d Cir. 2003).
9   Pacourek v. Inland Steel Co., 858 F. Supp. 1393 (N.D. 1994).

## CHAPTER 43. IS LACTATION RELATED TO PREGNANCY?

1   Interview by Andrea Mitchell of Foster Friess (Feb. 16, 2012), http://video.msnbc.msn .com/andrea-mitchell/46417914#52092027.
2   *Id.*
3   Patient Protection and Affordable Care Act, Pub. L. No. 111–148, 124 Stat. 119 (2010).
4   Institute of Medicine, *Clinical Preventive Services for Women: Closing the Gaps* (July 19, 2011), http://www.iom.edu/Reports/2011/Clinical-Preventive-Services-for-Women-Closing-the-Gaps.aspx.

5 Grp. Health Plans and Health Ins. Issuers Relating to Coverage of Preventive Services under Patient Protection and Affordable Care Act, 45 C.F.R. §147 (2012).

6 2012 WL 739494.

7 Family and Medical Leave Act, 29 U.S.C. 2601 (1993).

8 EEOC v. Houston Funding II, Ltd., 2012 U.S. Dist. LEXIS 13644 (S.D. Tex.).

9 *Id.* at *3.

10 *Id.* at *4.

11 *Id.*

12 *Id.*

13 EEOC v. Houston Funding II, Ltd., 2012 U.S. Dist. LEXIS 13644 (S.D. Tex. 2012).

14 *Id.* at *3.

15 See Chapters 32–36.

16 EEOC v. Houston Funding II, Ltd., 717 F.3d 425 (5th Cir. 2013).

17 *Id.* at 430 (Jones, J., dissenting).

18 *See* 29 U.S.C. § 207(r) (2012).

## CHAPTER 44. A VICTORY FOR FAMILIES, BUT HARDLY A PANACEA

1 Nev. Dep't of Human Res. v. Hibbs, 538 U.S. 721 (2003).

2 *Id.*

3 Hibbs v. HDM Dep't of Human Res., 273 F.3d 844 (9th Cir. 2001).

4 *Id.*

5 Kazmier v. Widmann, 225 F.3d 519 (5th Cir. 2000).

6 Family and Medical Leave Act, 29 U.S.C. § 2601 (1993).

7 U.S. CONST. amend. XI.

8 *Hibbs*, 538 U.S. at 741.

9 U.S. CONST. amend. XIV, §5.

10 Seminole Tribe v. Fla., 517 U.S. 44 (1996).

11 City of Boerne v. Flores, 521 U.S. 507, 520 (1997).

12 *Hibbs*, 538 U.S. at 731.

13 Bradwell v. Illinois, 83 U.S. 130 (1872).

14 Goesaert v. Cleary, 335 U.S. 464 (1948).

15 Muller v. State of Oregon, 208 U.S. 412 (1908).

16 Hoyt v. Florida, 364 U.S. 930 (1961).

17 Craig v. Boren, 429 U.S. 190 (1976).

18 *Hibbs*, 538 U.S. at 737.

19 *Id.* at 737–38.

20 132 S. Ct. 1327 (2012).

21 *Id. at* 1345 (quoting *Hibbs*) (Ginsburg, J., dissenting).

22 *See* Bryce Covert, *The Politics of Paid Time Off to Have a Baby*, N.Y. TIMES, Nov. 23, 2015.

## CHAPTER 45. A SMALL STEP IN THE RIGHT DIRECTION: THE FAMILY AND MEDICAL LEAVE ACT AT TWENTY

1 Family and Medical Leave Act of 1993, Pub. L. No. 103–03, 107 Stat. 6 (codified as amended at 29 U.S.C. §§2612-2654 (2000)).

2   Joanna L. Grossman, *Job Security without Equality: The Family and Medical Leave Act of 1993*, 15 WASH. U. J.L. & POL'Y 17, 17–18 (2004)

3   *See* DAVID CANTOR ET AL., DEP'T OF LABOR, BALANCING THE NEEDS OF FAMILIES AND EMPLOYERS: FAMILY AND MEDICAL LEAVE SURVEYS 2000 UPDATE 2–16 (2000) (finding 77.6 percent of leave-needers listed "ability to afford" as one of the reasons for not taking leave).

4   Grossman, *supra* note 2, at 58.

5   *See* 29 U.S.C. §2612(a)(1), (c) (2000); 29 C.F.R. §825.100(a) (2003).

6   *See* 29 U.S.C. §2611(2)(A)(ii) (2000) (defining "eligible employee"); 29 C.F.R. §825.110(a)(2) (2003). Only 61.7 percent of employees are both eligible and in the employ of a covered establishment. *See* DAVID CANTOR ET AL., DEP'T OF LABOR, BALANCING THE NEEDS OF FAMILIES AND EMPLOYERS: FAMILY AND MEDICAL LEAVE SURVEYS 2000 UPDATE A-2-21 tbl.A2-3.1 (2000).

7   *See* 29 U.S.C. §2611(4)(A)(i) (2000) (defining "employer"); *see also id.* §2611(2)(B)(ii) (2000) (defining those employees excluded from coverage); 29 C.F.R. §825.110(a)(3) (2003).

8   *See* 29 U.S.C. §§2611(2)(B)(iii),2614(a)(1)(A) (2000); 29 C.F.R. §825.214(a) (2003).

9   *See* 29 U.S.C. §§2614(a)(2), 2614(c)(1) (2000); 29 C.F.R. §825.209 (2003).

10   *See* 29 U.S.C. §2615(a)(1) (2000) (making it "unlawful for any employer to interfere with, restrain, or deny the exercise of or the attempt to exercise, any right provided"); §2615(a)(2) (making it "unlawful for any employer to discharge or in any other manner discriminate against any individual for opposing any practice made unlawful by this subchapter").

11   538 U.S. 721 (2003).

12   132 S. Ct. 1327 (2012).

13   Grossman, *supra* note 2, at 18.

14   *Id.* at 33.

15   *See* Donna Lenhoff & Claudia Withers, *Implementation of the Family and Medical Leave Act: Toward the Family-Friendly Workplace*, 3 AM. U. J. GENDER & L. 39, 40 (1994) (noting the record speed with which President Clinton signed the bill after taking office, in contrast to "a carefully worded campaign promise by George Bush" and "two Bush vetoes" in the preceding years).

16   29 U.S.C. §2601(a)(1) (2000).

17   Grossman, *supra* note 2, at 46.

18   *Parental and Disability Leave: Joint Hearing on H.R. 2020 before the Subcomm. on Civil Serv. and the Subcomm. on Comp. and Employee Benefits of the House Comm. on Post Office and Civil Serv. and the Subcomm. on Labor Mgmt. Relations and the Subcomm. on Labor Standards of the House Comm. on Educ. and Labor*, 99th Cong. 16 (1985) (statement of Sen. Hatch).

19   139 CONG. REC. 2020 (1993).

20   *Id.*

21   *See* Nina J. Easton, *"I'm Not a Feminist But . . . "; Can the Women's Movement March Into the Mainstream?*, L.A. TIMES MAG., Feb. 2, 1992, at 12 (describing the emergence of "family-friendly" feminism and its role in the push for leave legislation).

22   *See* Ellen Galinsky & James T. Bond, *Work and Family: The Experience of Mothers and Fathers in the Labor Force, in* WHERE WE STAND: WOMEN AND WORK 79, 94 (Cynthia Costello & Barbara Kivimae Krimgold, eds., 1996).

23   *See* JAMES T. BOND ET AL., FAMILIES AND WORK INSTITUTE, BEYOND THE PARENTAL LEAVE DEBATE: THE IMPACT OF LAWS IN FOUR STATES (1991) (studying parental leave laws in Minnesota, Oregon, Rhode Island, and Wisconsin).

24 *See id.* at 29.
25 *See id.* at 41.
26 *Id.* at 77–78.
27 *See* Catalyst, Report on a National Study of Parental Leaves 37 (1986); *see, e.g.*, Michael Selmi, *Family Leave and the Gender Wage Gap*, 78 N.C. L. Rev. 707, 755–56 (2000).
28 139 Cong. Rec. 1730 (1993) (GAO Report).
29 *See, e.g.*, Michael Selmi, *The Work-Family Conflict: An Essay on Employers, Men and Responsibility*, 4 U. St. Thomas L.J. 573 (2007).
30 Comm'n on Family & Med. Leave, A Workable Balance: Report to Congress on Family and Medical Leave Policies 66–67 (1996).
31 *See* Cantor, *supra* note 3, at 2–1 to 2–2.
32 *Id.* at 2–13 to 2–14.
33 *See id.* at 2–5.
34 *Id.*
35 *See id.* at 2–3.
36 Pub. L. No. 95-555, 92 Stat. 2076 (1978).
37 Ronald D. Elving, Conflict and Compromise: How Congress Makes the Law 11–13 (1995) (describing the bill signing ceremony for the FMLA).
38 *Id.* (describing in detail the legislative history of the FMLA).
39 *See, e.g.*, Family and Medical Leave Act of 1989, H.R. 770, 101st Cong., §§103(a)(1), 104(a)(1) (1989).
40 *See* Family and Medical Leave Act of 1989, H.R. 770, 101st Cong., §101(5)(a) (1989) (applying, for the first three years, to employers with at least fifty employees within a seventy-five-mile radius, and then to employers with at least thirty-five employees within that same distance).
41 *See* Cantor, *supra* note 3, at 2–3.
42 *See id.*
43 *See, e.g.*, Valentina Zarya, *Inspired by Its Swedish Roots, Spotify Gives Moms and Dads 6 Months Leave*, Fortune, Nov. 19, 2015; *Netflix Offers New Parents One Year of Paid Leave*, Wall St. J., Aug. 5, 2015; Bryce Covert, *The Ripple Effects of Mark Zuckerberg's Two-Month Paternity Leave*, thinkprogress.org, Nov. 23, 2015, http://thinkprogress.org/economy/2015/11/23/3724990/mark-zuckerberg-paternity-leave/.

chapter 46. "best practices" to promote work-family balance

1 EEOC, Employer Best Practices for Workers with Caregiving Responsibilities (last modified Jan. 19, 2011), http://www.eeoc.gov/policy/docs/caregiver-best-practices .html.
2 Press Release, Stuart J. Ishimaru, EEOC Issues Employer Best Practices Document on Work/Family Balance (Apr. 22, 2009).
3 Best Practices for Workers with Caregiving Responsibilities.
4 *See* Catalyst, Statistical Overview of Women in the Workplace (2014), http://www.catalyst.org/knowledge/statistical-overview-women-workplace#footnoteref8_ fwxpxnq.
5 EEOC, Enforcement Guidance: Unlawful Disparate Treatment of Workers with Caregiving Responsibilities (May 23, 2007), http://www.eeoc.gov/policy/docs/ caregiving.html.
6 *Id.*

7 Congress passed the PDA to override the Supreme Court's refusal in a 1976 case to see pregnancy discrimination as a form of sex discrimination under Title VII Discrimination Act of 1978. The act amends the definition section of Title VII by adding a new provision: "The terms 'because of sex' or 'on the basis of sex' [in Title VII] include, but are not limited to, because of or on the basis of pregnancy, childbirth, or related medical conditions; and women affected by pregnancy, childbirth, or related medical conditions shall be treated the same for all employment-related purposes . . . as other persons not so affected but similar in their ability or inability to work." 42 U.S.C. § 2000e(k) (2014).

8 42 U.S.C. § 12112(b)(4) (2006).

9 Burlington N. & Santa Fe Ry. Co. v. White, 548 U.S. 53, 69 (2006).

10 BEST PRACTICES FOR WORKERS WITH CAREGIVING RESPONSIBILITIES.

11 *Id.*

## PART IV. FEMALE BREADWINNERS AND THE GLASS CEILING

1 *See* Michael Selmi, *Family Leave and the Gender Wage Gap*, 78 N.C. L. REV. 707, 715 (2000); Jessica Arons, *Lifetime Losses: The Career Wage Gap*, Center for American Progress, December 2008, http://www.americanprogressaction.org/issues/ 2008/pdf/equal_pay.pdf (finding, in 2007, that women earn seventy-eight cents on a dollar for every dollar a man earns in a year); *see also* Bureau of Labor Statistics, U.S. Dep't of Labor, *Highlights of Women's Earnings in 2003*, at 29 tbl. 12, 31 tbl. 14 (Sept. 2004) (reporting that women's median weekly earnings were 79.5 percent of men's in 2003, but only 73.6 percent for college graduates); Daniel H. Weinberg, U.S. Dep't of Commerce, Census 2000 Special Reports, *Evidence from Census 2000 about Earnings by Detailed Occupation for Men and Women* 7, 12 tbl. 5 (May 2004).

2 *See, e.g.*, Bureau of Labor Statistics, *supra* note 1, at 11 tbl. 1 (finding, based on data from the Current Population Survey, that women ages forty-five to fifty-four earn 73 percent of what men earn, while women ages twenty-five to thirty-four earn 87 percent of what men earn); FRANCINE D. BLAU ET AL., THE ECONOMICS OF WOMEN, MEN, AND WORK 150 (5th ed. 2006) ("women earn less than men in all age categories," and the ratio of women's earnings to men's decreases as they age).

3 *See* STEPHEN J. ROSE & HEIDI I. HARTMANN, INST. FOR WOMEN'S POL'Y RES., STILL A MAN'S LABOR MARKET: THE LONG-TERM EARNINGS GAP 9 (2004).

4 *See* Selmi, *supra* note 1, at 719–43 (reviewing data).

5 *See* ROSE & HARTMANN, *supra* note 3, at 10.

6 *See* Bureau of Labor Statistics, *supra* note 1, at 2, 25 tbl. 9, 26 tbl. 10, 35–36 tbl. 15, 37–36 tbl. 16 (reporting that among hourly workers, the median hourly wage for women is 85 percent of the median hourly wage for men).

7 Weinberg, *supra* note 1, at 14, 15 tbl. 9.

8 *See, e.g.*, U.S. Gen. Acct. Office, *Women's Earnings: Work Patterns Partially Explain Difference between Men's and Women's Earnings*, GAO-04-35 at 2 (Oct. 2003) (examining nationally representative longitudinal data set and concluding that women in 2000 earned only 80 percent of what men earned even after accounting for differing work patterns and other "key factors"); Weinberg, *supra* note 1, at 21 ("There is a substantial gap in median earnings between men and women that is unexplained, even after controlling for work experience . . . education, and occupation"); COUNCIL OF ECON. ADVISERS, EXPLAINING TRENDS IN THE GENDER WAGE GAP 11 (1998) (concluding that women do not earn equal pay even when controlling for

occupation, age, experience, and education); Michelle J. Budig, *Male Advantage and the Gender Composition of Jobs: Who Rides the Glass Escalator*, 49 Soc. Prob. 258, 269–70 (2002) (explaining that men are advantaged, net of control factors, in both pay levels and wage growth regardless of the gender composition of jobs).

9  Linda Babcock & Sara Laschever, Women Don't Ask: Negotiation and the Gender Divide 1, 5 (2003).

10  On this history, see Karen S. Boyd, *Glass Ceiling*, Encyclopedia of Race, Ethnicity, and Society, https://edge.sagepub.com/system/files/15_GlassCeiling.pdf.

11  *Id.*

12  *See* U.S. Dep't of Labor, Report on the Glass Ceiling Initiative (1991).

13  Christine Jolls, *Is There a Glass Ceiling?*, 25 Harv. Women's L.J. 1, 18 (2002).

## CHAPTER 47. THE SUPREME COURT SLAMS THE DOOR ON PAY DISCRIMINATION CLAIMS

1  550 U.S. 618 (2007).

2  42 U.S.C. 2000e-5(e) (2012).

3  Ledbetter v. Goodyear Tire & Rubber Co., 421 F.3d 1169 (11th 2005).

4  536 U.S. 101 (2002).

5  *See* EEOC Compliance Manual § 2-IV.C (July 27, 2000) (stating that each discriminatory paycheck constitutes "a wrong actionable under Title VII").

6  *See, e.g.*, Wedow v. City of Kansas City, 442 F.3d 661, 671 (8th Cir. 2006); Forsyth v. Federation Employment & Guidance Serv., 409 F.3d 565, 573 (2nd Cir. 2005) ("[E]very paycheck stemming from a discriminatory pay scale is an actionable discrete discriminatory act."); Shea v. Rice, 409 F.3d 448, 452 (D.C. Cir. 2005) ("[An] employer commit[s] a separate unlawful employment practice each time he pa[ys] one employee less than another for a discriminatory reason.").

7  *Ledbetter*, 550 U.S. at 628.

8  431 U.S. 553 (1977).

9  449 U.S. 250 (1980).

10  478 U.S. 385, 395 (1986).

11  *Ledbetter*, 550 U.S. at 644 (Ginsburg, J., dissenting).

12  *See, e.g.*, James M. Olson & Carolyn L. Hafer, *Tolerance of Personal Deprivation, in* The Psychology of Legitimacy: Emerging Perspectives on Ideology, Justice, and Intergroup Relations 157, 166–167 (John T. Jost & Brenda Major, eds., 2001).

13  *See* John T. Jost, *Negative Illusions: Conceptual Clarification and Psychological Evidence Concerning False Consciousness*, 16 Pol. Psychol. 397, 404 (1995).

14  *See* Faye Crosby, *The Denial of Personal Discrimination*, 27 Am. Behav. Sci. 371, 377–78 (1984).

15  532 U.S. 268, 271 (2001).

16  29 U.S.C. 206(d) (2000).

## CHAPTER 48. A CALL FOR CONGRESSIONAL ACTION TO REMEDY PAY INEQUALITY

1  550 U.S. 618 (2007).

2  *Ledbetter*, 550 U.S. at 628.

3  920 F.2d 446 (7th Cir. 1990).

4  *Ledbetter,* 550 U.S. at 661 (Ginsburg, J., dissenting); *see also* Civil Rights Act of 1991, Pub. L. No. 102-166, 105 Stat. 1071 (1991) (codified as amended at 42 U.S.C. §§ 1981, 2000e *et seq.*).
5  490 U.S. 900 (1989).
6  *See* 137 Cong. Rec. S15483, S15485 (daily ed. Oct. 30, 1991) (interpretive memorandum of Sen. Danforth) ("This legislation should be interpreted as disapproving the extension of this decision rule [in *Lorance*] to contexts outside of seniority systems").
7  *Ledbetter,* 550 U.S. at 653–54 (Ginsburg, J., dissenting).
8  42 U.S.C. § 2000e-2(a)(1) (2012).
9  Pub. L. No. 88-352, § 706(d), 78 Stat. 241, 260 (1964).
10  Pub L. No. 92-261, sec. 4(a), § 706(e), 86 Stat. 103, 105 (1972).
11  H.R. Rep. No. 101-644(I), at 25–26, 45–46 (1990).
12  H.R. Rep. No. 102-40(I), at 63–64 (1991), as reprinted in 1991 U.S.C.C.A.N. 549, 601–02.
13  *See* 137 Cong. Rec. H3922-05, H3922 (1991) (statement of Rep. Stenholm).
14  42 U.S.C. § 1981a(b)(3) (2012).
15  *Id.* at § 1981a(b)(2).

#### CHAPTER 49. THE LILLY LEDBETTER FAIR PAY ACT OF 2009

1  Pub. L. No. 111–2, 123 Stat. 5 (2009).
2  *See* George W. Bush, Statement of Administration Policy: H.R. 2831 – Lilly Ledbetter Fair Pay Act of 2007 (Apr. 22, 2008), http://www.presidency.ucsb.edu/ws/?pid=76981.
3  Sheryl Gay Stolberg, *Obama Signs Equal-Pay Legislation,* N.Y. Times, Jan. 29, 2009.
4  In addition to being a sought-after speaker, Ledbetter published a book about her experience. *See* Lilly Ledbetter, Grace and Grit: My Fight for Equal Pay and Fairness at Goodyear and Beyond (2013).
5  Ledbetter v. Goodyear Tire & Rubber Co., 550 U.S. 618, 661(2007) (Ginsburg, J., dissenting).
6  S. 181 (111th Cong.) (2009).
7  Pub. L. No. 111-2, 123 Stat. 5 § 2 (2009) (codified at 42 U.S.C. § 20003-5(3)(A)).
8  *Id.* at § 3.

#### CHAPTER 50. TAKING STOCK: IS THE LEDBETTER ACT WORKING?

1  42 U.S.C. § 2000e-5(3)(A) (2012).
2  583 F.3d 181 (3d Cir. 2009).
3  Mikula v. Allegheny Cty., 2007 WL 2811637 (W.D. Pa. 2007).
4  583 F.3d at 186.
5  Pub. L. No. 111-2 at § 3.
6  *Id.* at § 3b.

#### CHAPTER 51. THE LADY IN RED

1  *See* National Committee on Pay Equity, http://www.pay-equity.org/.
2  Carmen DeNavas-Walt et al., U.S. Census Bureau, Income, Poverty, and Health Insurance Coverage in the United States: 2012 at 11 (2013).

3   2011 Wisconsin Act 219 (formerly Senate Bill 202).

4   *See* DeNavas-Walt, *supra* note 2 at 8, Tbl. 1.

5   Myrle Croasdale, *The 63% Question: Why Are Female Physicians Lagging Behind?*, Am. Med. News (Sept. 13, 2004).

6   *See* Inst. for Women's Pol'y Res. Stephen J. Rose and Heidi I. Hartmann, Still a Man's Labor Market: The Long-Term Earnings Gap 9 (2004).

7   *See* The White House Council on Women and Girls, Keeping America's Women Moving Forward 4 (2012).

8   Noah Kristula-Green, *How Badly Have Republicans Alienated Women?*, The Daily Beast (Apr. 20, 2012).

9   Rose & Hartmann, *supra* note x, at 10.

10  *See* Daniel H. Weinberg, U.S. Dep't of Commerce, Census 2000 Special Reports, *Evidence from Census 2000 about Earnings by Detailed Occupation for Men and Women* 13 tbl. 6 (May 2004) (citing example of "teacher assistants," a lower-paid occupation, where the female median, $15,000, is 75 percent of the male median of $20,000).

11  *Id.* at 14, 15 tbl. 9.

12  *See* Michael Selmi, *Family Leave and the Gender Wage Gap*, 78 N.C. L. Rev. 707, 745–50 (2000); *see also* Nevada Dep't of Human Res. v. Hibbs, 538 U.S. 721, 730 (2003).

13  *See* EEOC, Equal Pay Act Charges, http://www.eeoc.gov/eeoc/statistics/enforcement/epa.cfm.

14  Usetheforce7980, *1960's Batgirl PSA Equal Pay*, YouTube (Jan. 5, 2011), http://www.youtube.com/watch?v=Mtq9RHRDWuA.

15  29 U.S.C. 206(d) (2012).

16  *Id.*

17  *See, e.g.*, Timmer v. Mich. Dept. of Commerce, 104 F.3d 833, 843 (6th Cir. 1997).

18  Deborah L. Brake & Joanna L. Grossman, *Title VII's Protection Against Pay Discrimination: The Impact of* Ledbetter v. Goodyear Tire & Rubber Co., Regional Lab. Rev. (Fall 2007).

19  *See* Nat'l Partnership for Women & Families, *What's the Wage Gap in the States and Top 50 Metropolitan Areas?*, http://www.nationalpartnership.org/issues/fairness/wage-gap-map.html (a state-by-state analysis of the relative severity of the wage gap).

20  42 U.S.C. § 2000e-2(a) (2012).

21  *See* Combating Punitive Pay Secrecy Policies, National Women's Law Center, http://www.nwlc.org/sites/default/files/pdfs/paysecrecyfactsheet.pdf (2012) (fact sheet about the problem of pay secrecy).

22  United States Government Accountability Office, Gender Pay Differences: Progress Made, but Women Remain Overrepresented among Low-Wage Workers, http://www.gao.gov/new.items/d1210.pdf (2011).

23  Katie Rogers, *Yvonne Craig, Actress Who Played Batgirl, Is Dead at 78*, N.Y. Times, Aug. 19, 2015.

24  On the California law, see Joanna L. Grossman, *For the Love of Batgirl: California Passes Much-Needed Equal Pay Law*, Justia's Verdict, Oct. 13, 2015, https://verdict.justia.com/2015/10/13/for-the-love-of-batgirl-california-passes-much-needed-fair-pay-law. On the New York law, see Joanna L. Grossman, *Enactment of the Women's Equality Agenda: A Fitting Bicentennial Birthday Gift for Elizabeth Cady Stanton*, Justia's Verdict, Nov. 10, 2015, http://verdict.justia.com/2015/11/10/enactment-of-the-womens-equality-agenda.

CHAPTER 52. UNFINISHED BUSINESS

1 *Awaiting America's Decision,* The Situation Room (aired Nov. 4, 2008) (transcript available on CNN.com).
2 Susan Faludi, *Second-Place Citizens,* N.Y. Times, Aug. 26, 2008, at A19.
3 *See* Emma Margolin, *Did Sarah Palin Just Compare Herself to Margaret Thatcher?,* MSNBC (Apr. 4, 2013).
4 *See* Kathleen Parker, *Feminist Template Obliterated,* USA Today (Sept. 11, 2008); *see also* Julia Baird, *From Seneca Falls to . . . Sarah Palin?,* Newsweek (Sept. 13, 2008).
5 *See* Kate Zernike, *Can You Cross Out "Hillary" and Write "Sarah"?,* N.Y. Times, Aug. 30, 2008.
6 *See* Elisabeth Crum, Institute for Women's Pol'y Res., Women's Vote Clinches Election Victory: 8 Million More Women than Men Voted for Obama (Nov. 6, 2008).
7 Ricardo Hausmann, Laura D. Tyson, & Saadia Zahidi, World Economic Forum, The Global Gender Gap Report 4 (2009).
8 Elena Kagan, the fourth woman, was confirmed to the Supreme Court in 2010, after this essay was originally written.
9 Sonia Sotomayor, *A Latina Judge's Voice,* Judge Mario G. Olmos Memorial Lecture (2001).
10 Emily Bazelon, *The Place of Women on the Court,* N.Y. Times, July 7, 2009, at MM22.
11 *Id.*
12 *See, e.g.,* David W. Allen & Diane E. Wall, *Role Orientations and Women State Supreme Court Justices,* 77 Judicature 156, 159–65 (1993); Gerard S. Gryski et al., *Models of State High Court Decision Making in Sex Discrimination Cases,* 48 J. Pol. 143, 146–53 (1986).
13 Bazelon, *supra* note 10.
14 AT&T Corp. v. Hulteen, 556 U.S. 701 (2009) (Ginsburg, J., dissenting).
15 *Id.* (quoting Wetzel v. Liberty Mut. Ins. Co., 372 F. Supp. 1146, 1157 (W.D. Pa. 1974)).
16 *Sotomayor Treads Lightly on Gun Issue,* CBS News (July 14, 2009).
17 Calderon v. Thompson, 523 U.S. 538, 571 (1998) (Souter, J., dissenting).
18 *See* Gender Equality: Dimensions of Women's Equal Citizenship (Linda C. McClain & Joanna L. Grossman, eds., 2009).
19 President Obama Announces White House Council on Women and Girls, White House Release (Mar. 11, 2009).
20 *Id.*

CHAPTER 53. WILL ABA'S PROPOSED SOLUTIONS FOR
GENDER INEQUITY WORK?

1 ABA Comm'n on Women in the Profession, The Unfinished Agenda: Women and the Legal Profession 14 (2001) (hereinafter The Unfinished Agenda).
2 *Id.* at 13.
3 *Id.* at 15.
4 *Id.* at 33.
5 *Id.*

6　*Id.* at 6.
7　*Id.* at 34.
8　*See* 42 U.S.C. § 2000e-2(a) (2012).
9　The Unfinished Agenda, *supra* note 1, at 20.
10　*Id.* at 24.

### CHAPTER 54. EQUALITY STILL ELUSIVE FOR WOMEN IN THE FEDERAL WORKFORCE

1　Nine to Five (IPC Films 1980).
2　U.S. Equal Employment Opportunity Comm'n, EEOC Women's Work Group Report (2014), http://www.eeoc.gov/federal/reports/women_workgroup_report.cfm.
3　*Id.*
4　*Id.*
5　*See* Federal Employment Reports, *Historical Federal Workforce Tables*, http://www.opm.gov/policy-data-oversight/data-analysis-documentation/federal-employment-reports/historical-tables/total-government-employment-since-1962/.
6　Alexander E. M. Hess, *The 10 Largest Employers in America*, 24/7 Wall St. (Aug. 21, 2013).
7　Women's Work Group Report, *supra* note 2; *see also* U.S. Government Accountability Office, *Women's Earnings: Work Patterns Partially Explain Difference between Men's and Women's Earnings* (Oct. 31, 2003).
8　Women's Work Group Report, *supra* note 2.
9　EEOC Guidance No. 915.048 (1990); *see supra* Chapter 46.
10　Women's Work Group Report, *supra* note 2.
11　*Women CEOs of the Fortune 1000*, Catalyst (Jan. 15, 2014).
12　Women's Work Group Report, *supra* note 2.
13　*Id.*
14　The "costly mistakes" problem is explored in Chapter 29.

### CHAPTER 55. "GIRLIE MEN"

1　Associated Press, *Calif. Gov. Not Sorry for "Girlie Men" Remark*, nbcnews.com (July 19, 2004), http://www.nbcnews.com/id/5460326/ns/politics/t/calif-gov-not-sorry-girlie-men-remark/#.U6nsrhZGhuY.
2　*Schwarzenegger Stands by "Girlie Men" Comment*, Wash. Times, July 19, 2004, http://www.washingtontimes.com/news/2004/jul/19/20040719-112726-3335r/?page=all.
3　Maureen Dowd, *Westerns and Easterns*, N.Y. Times, Sept. 12, 2004.
4　Patrick McGreevy, *Governor Targets 9 Assembly Democrats for Defeat*, L.A. Times, Aug. 23, 2004.
5　John F. Harris, *Cheney Calls Kerry Unfit*, Wash. Post, Sept. 2, 2004.
6　*Id.*
7　Peter Nicholas, *Gov. Criticizes Legislators as "Girlie Men,"* L.A. Times, July 18, 2004.
8　*Remarks by California Gov Schwarzenegger to the National Republican Convention*, Wash. Post Politics (Aug. 31, 2004), http://www.washingtonpost.com/wp-dyn/articles/A50470-2004Aug31.html.

### CHAPTER 56. PLAYING "TOO WOMANY" AND THE PROBLEM OF MASCULINITY IN SPORT

1  20 U.S.C. § 1681 (2014).
2  MASCULINITIES AND THE LAW: A MULTIDIMENSIONAL APPROACH 207 (Frank Rudy Cooper & Ann C. McGinley, eds., 2012).
3  For a comprehensive analysis of equity in athletics, see DEBORAH L. BRAKE, GETTING IN THE GAME: TITLE IX AND THE WOMEN'S SPORTS REVOLUTION (2010).
4  500 F.3d 1170 (10th Cir. 2007).
5  Williams v. Bd. of Regents of Univ. Sys. of Georgia, 477 F.3d 1282 (11th Cir. 2007).
6  84 F.3d 1226 (10th Cir. 1996).
7  *See, e.g.,* Doe v. Brimfield Grade Sch., 552 F. Supp. 2d 816 (C.D. Ill. 2008) (finding that allegations of male students harassing another male student by repeatedly hitting him in the testicles were sufficient to survive a motion to dismiss). This case was similar to *Seamons*, in which a coach reprimanded a student for complaining about harassment and told him to "stick up for himself." *Id.* at 820.
8  *See* UNIV. MINN., THE DECLINE OF WOMEN COACHES IN COLLEGIATE ATHLETICS (2012–13).

### CHAPTER 57. BINDERS FOR WOMEN, BLINDERS FOR ROMNEY

1  Amy Gardner, *Debate's Questioners Highlight Everyday Americans' Economic Anxieties*, WASH. POST, Oct. 17, 2012.
2  550 U.S. 618 (2007).
3  Amanda Marcotte, *Binders Full of Women Aren't Enough to Solve Pay Inequality*, N.Y. TIMES, Oct. 17, 2012.
4  *Id.*
5  BINDERS FULL OF WOMEN, http://bindersfullofwomen.tumblr.com/.
6  See http://bindersfullofwomen.com/?_sm_au_=iVVH1R61L2S4SNRq.
7  Christina Wilkie, *Mitt Romney on Women at Bain: They Don't Want to Work There*, HUFFINGTON POST BUSINESS (Oct. 18, 2012), http://www.huffingtonpost.com/2012/10/17/mitt-romney-women-bain_n_1974837.html.
8  Carol Hardy-Fanta and Kacie Kelly, "*Women of Talent: Gender and Government Appointments in Massachusetts, 2002–2007*" (2007), *Center for Women in Politics and Public Policy Publications*, Paper 1, http://scholarworks.umb.edu/cwppp_pubs/1.
9  A chart compiled by NCPE shows how slow the progress has been in reducing the wage gap; see http://www.gao.gov/new.items/d1210.pdf?_sm_au_=iVVH1R61L2S4SNRq.
10  29 U.S.C. § 206(d) (2012).
11  42 U.S.C. § 2000e-5(e) (2012).
12  *Id.*
13  Christina Wilkie, *Mitt Romney on Women at Bain: They Don't Want to Work There*, HUFFINGTON POST BUSINESS (Oct. 18, 2012), http://www.huffingtonpost.com/2012/10/17/mitt-romney-women-bain_n_1974837.html.

# Index